Kant's Transcendental Psychology

Kant's Transcendental Psychology

Patricia Kitcher

OXFORD UNIVERSITY PRESS
New York   Oxford

Oxford University Press

Oxford   New York   Toronto
Delhi   Bombay   Calcutta   Madras   Karachi
Kuala Lumpur   Singapore   Hong Kong   Tokyo
Nairobi   Dar es Salaam   Cape Town
Melbourne   Auckland   Madrid

and associated companies in
Berlin   Ibadan

Copyright © 1990 by Patricia Kitcher

Published by Oxford University Press, Inc.
200 Madison Avenue, New York, New York 10016

First issued as an Oxford University Press paperback, 1993.

Oxford is a registered trademark of Oxford University Press

Library of Congress Cataloging-in-Publication Data
Kitcher, Patricia.
Kant's transcendental psychology
by Patricia Kitcher.
p. cm.
ISBN 0-19-505967-0
ISBN 0-19-508563-9 (pbk)
1. Cognition.
2. Kant, Immanuel, 1724–1804—Contributions in psychology.
3. Kant, Immanuel, 1724–1804 Kritik der reinen Vernunft.
I. Title.   BF311.K57 1990   128'.092—dc20
89-78463

2   4   6   8   9   7   5   3   1

Printed in the United States of America

on acid-free paper

For P.S.K.

Preface

Many people have helped me in the course of my study of Kant and in writing this book. At Wellesley, Ingrid Stadler spent hours taking me through the three *Critiques*, more hours, I fear, than I have spent teaching any undergraduate. I also benefited from Richard Rorty's Kant seminar at Princeton. Over the years my correspondence with Gary Hatfield has been a source of inspiration and support. Hatfield's own work and his responses to mine have encouraged me to believe that it is not crazy to take Kant's psychology seriously and to try to understand it in its own context.

Three people have been kind enough to read the entire manuscript and to offer their criticisms: Henry Allison, Philip Kitcher, and Jonathan Vogel. It was particularly kind of Professor Vogel to send detailed criticisms, since we only met once. Henry Allison read drafts of each of the chapters, which we then discussed at length. Anyone writing on Kant would be extraordinarily fortunate to have such a critic and I hope that I have used his expertise wisely. Philip Kitcher read more drafts of these chapters than either he or I care to remember. I am also grateful for Jill Buroker's comments on Chapters 2 and 3, many of which led me to make substantial revisions. While we were colleagues at Minnesota, John Earman and I had several conversations about Leibniz. More recently, I have been able to discuss Kant's predecessors with Nicholas Jolley. Although I have learned from both, neither of these fine scholars should be blamed for any mistakes in my interpretations of Leibniz or Hume. I would also like to thank four research assistants, Randy Wojtowicz, Warren Dow, and Valerie and Gary Hardcastle, for their careful and prompt help, and the Committee on Research at the University of California, San Diego, for funding them. I am particularly grateful to the Hardcastles for organizing the bibliography and the indices.

A book project incurs personal debts as well. I am grateful to my father for spending many lunch hours in Sterling Memorial Library at Yale hunting for obscure German books, and to both my parents for supporting my work long before it was fashionable to have working daughters. In the last two years of intensive work on the book, my sons, Andrew and Charles, have never complained about my not being able to do things for them; they only expressed the wish that I did not have to work so hard. This book could not have been written without the enormous patience and loving support of my husband, Philip Kitcher. For a year he met the children virtually every day after school so that I could have enough time to complete it.

Finally I would like to thank the editors of the *Philosophical Review* for permitting me to use materials from several articles. Although I rewrote the chapters completely, many of the ideas and arguments from "Discovering the Forms of Intuition" (*Philosophical Review* XCVI, 1987: 205–248) and "Kant's Paralogisms" (*Philosophical Review* XCI, 1982: 515–547) recur in Chapters 2 and 7. The basic idea for Chapter 4, and indeed for the book, was presented in "Kant on Self-Identity" (*Philosophical Review* XCI, 1982: 41–70), although I have changed many of the arguments as my ideas have changed. I am also grateful to J.-C. Smith and to D. Reidel for permission to use material from section III of "Kant's Dedicated Cognitivist System" (in J.-C. Smith, ed., *Historical Foundations of Cognitive Science*, Dordrecht, Holland: D. Reidel, 1989, pp. 189–209).

A Note on References: In the notes I give the reference for citations, other than those from the *Critique of Pure Reason*, in the Akademie Edition (*Kant's gesammelte Schriften*, edited by the *Koniglichen Preussischen Akademie der Wissenschaften*, 29 vols., Berlin: Walter de Gruyter and predecessors, 1902–), by citing the volume number and pages after "AA," as well as the standard English source. For the *Critique*, I use the standard "A" and "B" citations from Kemp Smith (Norman Kemp Smith, trans., *Immanuel Kant's Critique of Pure Reason*, New York: St. Martin's, 1968) in the text.

La Jolla, California   P.W.K.
February 1990

Contents

1. What Is Transcendental Psychology?, 3
   The "Dark Side" of the Critique, *3*
   Countercurrents: Reinhold to Austin, 5
   Kant Against "Psychology," 11
   Transcendental Psychology, 14
   In Defense of Transcendental Psychology, 21

2. The Science of Sensibility, 30
   What the Transcendental Aesthetic Is About, 30
   Early Modern Theories of Spatial Perception, 32
   Kant's Analysis of Spatial Perception, 35
      Intuition, Matter, and Form, 35
      Pure Forms (and Nativism), 37
      The Method of Isolation, 39
      Distance, Extent, and Shape, 40
      Touch: Leibniz Versus Berkeley, 41
      Kant's Empirical Assumptions, 43
      The Isolation Argument, 44
   Two Arguments of the Metaphysical Exposition, 45
      The Standard View, 45
      The First Argument, 46
      The Second Argument, 48
   The Transcendental Exposition, 49
      The Role of Geometry, 49
      Geometry and the Space of Perception, 50
      Parsons's Interpretation, 53
      Kant's Results, 54
   The Forms of Intuition and Contemporary Evidence, 55
      Depth Perception, 55
      Is the Space of Perception Euclidean?, 56

The Assumption of a Common "Outer Sense," 57
Is Spatial Perception Determinate?, 58
Discovering the Forms of Intuition, 59

3. Transcendental Psychology in the Transcendental
   Deduction, 61
   What (If Anything) Happens in the Deduction Chapter?, 61
   Representing Objects, 65
   The Problem, 65
   The Views of Leibniz and Christian Wolff, 67
   Empiricism and Sensationism, 67
   Associationism, 69
   A Priori *Necessary Synthesis, 70*
   What Is an Object of Representations?, 70
   Unity and Synthesis, 73
   What Is Synthesis?, 74
   The Law of Association, 77
   Associationism and Apriority, 79
   Representations and Concepts, 80
   Kant's Defensible Results, 81
   Synthesis and the Productive Imagination, 81
   Robert Paul Wolff on Rules of Synthesis, 82
   The "Problem" of Early Cognition, 83
   Constructing Representations of Objects and the "Binding" Problem, 84
   Making Judgments About Objects, 86
   The Problem of Judgment, 86
   The Synthesis of Intuitions, 88
   The "One-Step" Deduction, 89
   Constructing Judgments, 89
   The Objective and Subjective Sides of the Deduction, 90

4. Replying to Hume's Heap, 91
   Troubles with Apperception, 91
   Avoiding the Subjective Deduction, 91
   Apperception as the *Cogito*, 91
   Strawson and the Self-Ascription Reading, 92
   The "Logical" Reading of Apperception, 94
   Two Mistaken Assumptions, 95
   Hume, 95
   Hume's Problem, 97

Hume's Absence, 97
Kant's Knowledge of Hume's Position, 98
The Denial of Real Connection, 100

Synthesis and Apperception, 102

Connecting Cognitive States by Synthesis, 102
Transcendental Synthesis, 103
Apperception and Transcendental Synthesis, 104
Apperception, 105

Arguing for the Synthetic Unity of Apperception, 108

Apperception and Representation, 108
Judgments, 110
Kant's Functionalism, 111
Intuitions, 113
The Reply to Hume, 114

5. A Cognitive Criterion of Mental Unity, 117

Unity of Apperception as Mental Unity, 117

Synthetic Connection, 117
Connection and Connectibility, 118
The Plan of the Chapter, 120
Refining the Account of Synthetic Connection, 121
Is the Self the Combiner?, 122

Locke and Leibniz on Personal Identity, 123

The Issue, 123
Leibniz Versus Locke, 123
Moral Responsibility, 125
The Problem of Self-Consciousness, 126

Modern Mentalism, Wiggins, and Parfit, 128

Modern Mentalism, 128
Wiggins's Argument Against Mentalism, 130
Parfit's Denial of Personal Identity, 131

Objections Considered, 133

Is the Cognitive Criterion Too Weak?, 133
Is It Too Strong?, 134
Is It Too *A Priori*?, 135
Modularity, 137
Summary of the Account, 138

Apperception and Kant's System, 139

Too Many Selves, 139
The Ideality of Time, 140

6. Perceiving Times and Spaces: The Cognitive Capacity
   at the Center of the Deduction, 142

   *Cognitive Tasks, Apperception, and the Deduction of the
   Categories, 142*

   Perception: The Eighteenth-Century Background, 147

      The Standard View, 147
      Intellectual Theories of Perception, 148

   The Synthesis of Apprehension in A, 148

      A99, 148
      A119–20, 149
      Examples from the Pölitz Lectures, 150
      The Case for the Synthesis of Apprehension, 151
      A99 Revisited, 152

   A Role for Concepts in Perception in A, 153

      The Need for Nonreproductive Synthesis, 153
      Perceptual Recognition, 153
      Concept Application, 153

   ¶ *26 in the B Deduction, 155*

      The Centrality of ¶ 26, 155
      Perception as "Scanning an Image," 156
      Perceiving Times and Spaces, 157
      Differences Between the Editions, 158
      P-Functions as Spatial and Temporal C-Functions, 160
      Perceiving Objects by Perceiving Spatial and Temporal Arrays, 161

   Kant's Long Argument, 162

      Additional Considerations, 162
      The Basic Argument, 162
      Universal Applicability and Objective Validity, 163
      The Argument from Apperception, 166
      How the Argument Fails, 167

   Defending the Long Argument Interpretation, 169

      Some Advantages, 169
      Henrich's Antipsychological Reading, 170
      Allison's Apsychological Reading, 171
      The Loss of Generality, 173
      ¶ 26 as Completing the Argument of the Metaphysical Deduction, 173
      How Serious Is the Loss of Generality?, 174

   Transcendental Psychology in the Second Analogy, 174

      Guyer's Interpretation, 174
      Guyer's Objection to a Psychological Reading, 177

Versus Guyer's Antipsychologism, 177
What Kant Has Shown, 178

7. The Limits of Transcendental Psychology, 181
   Kant's Paralogisms, 181
   Puzzles of the First Paralogism, 183
   Understanding the First Paralogism, 187
   Identity Through Time, 195
   Leibniz and the Simplicity of the Soul, 198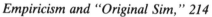

8. Cognitive Constraints on Empirical Concepts, 205
   Kant and Cognitive Science, 205
   Do We Employ Necessary and Sufficient Conditions?, 207
      Difficulties with the Classical View, 207
      Kant on Concepts and Concept Application, 209
      Empirical Warrant and the Open-Ended Character of Experience, 210
      When Should We Codify Our Concepts?, 211
      Implications for Necessary and Sufficient Conditions, 212
      Further Implications, 213
   Empiricism and "Original Sim," 214
      Quinean Empiricism, 214
      Current Directions, 216
   Concepts and Reasoning, 217
      The Task of Inference, 217
      Analytic and Synthetic Approaches to Concepts, 217
      How to Carve Nature at the Joints, 219
      The Structure of Concepts, 221
      Examples of Dependency Relations, 222
   Implementing the Demand of Reason, 225
   Theoretical and Experimental Implications, 227
   Conclusion, 230

Notes, 231
Bibliography, 273
Index of Cited Passages, 283
General Index, 289

Kant's Transcendental Psychology

1

What Is Transcendental Psychology?

The "Dark Side" of the *Critique*

But it [the deduction of the categories] is also an essay in the imaginary subject of transcendental psychology. . . . The theory . . . , like any essay in transcendental psychology, is exposed to the *ad hominem* objection that we can gain no empirical knowledge of its truth. . . .

Yet there is no doubt that this doctrine [about our cognitive faculties] is incoherent in itself and masks, rather than explains, the real character of [Kant's] inquiry. . . . [1]

P. F. Strawson opens his important essay on Kant's *Critique of Pure Reason* with these brief denunciations of transcendental psychology in order to justify a particular interpretive strategy. Although he is forthright that "[t]he idiom of the work is throughout a psychological idiom," [2] he will not read the book psychologically, but as an analytical argument. He describes this strategy as one of "disentangling" [3] the psychological and the analytical sides of the *Critique*. In the discussions of the Aesthetic, Analytic, and Dialectic that follow, however, there is little disentangling. Psychological topics are raised only to be dismissed. His treatment of synthesis is typical: The hope is to "bypass" this doctrine "altogether." [4] In practice, the *Bounds of Sense* either ignores Kant's frequent appeals to psychological processes and faculties or administers a quick scolding about alleged lapses from philosophical sanity. The many studies spawned by this deservedly influential book follow its interpretive model. Such widespread acceptance disguises the radical character of Strawson's approach to the *Critique*. Even a superficial reading of the text, particularly the central deduction of the categories, reveals that, if interpreters do excise or ignore all the discussions of cognitive processes and powers, then they will have very little left to read.

Among twentieth-century scholars, Strawson's attitude toward transcendental psychology is distinguished only by its explicitness and eloquence. Contempt for this aspect of the *Critique* has been almost universal.[5] In *Kant's Analytic*, whose simultaneous appearance with the *Bounds of Sense* produced a revival of interest in Kant, Jonathan Bennett also recoils from hints of "psychologism." So he "flatters" Kant by crediting him with a Wittgensteinean, rather than a psychological, view of concepts and of synthesis.[6] Two recent books, which stand to inherit the mantle of Bennett and Strawson as dominant influences on Anglo-American Kant studies, continue the pattern. Although Henry Allison and Paul Guyer offer dramatically opposed interpretations and evaluations of the *Critique*, they are united on this point. Guyer refers to Kant's "bouts of transcendental psychology"; and Allison labors to de-psychologize central doctrines.[7] Taking Dieter Henrich and Gerold Prauss as representative, transcendental psychology has the same unenviable place in German scholarship that it has in the English-speaking academy.[8] Avoid it!

Norman Kemp Smith complained in 1918 that some scholars were ignoring Kant's psychological doctrines: "No interpretation which ignores or under-estimates this psychological or subjective aspect of [Kant's] teaching can be admitted as adequate."[9] Unfortunately, his account of transcendental psychology made the doctrine so unattractive that he undoubtedly lost rather than gained converts to its importance. On his reading, Kant took the processes that contributed to cognition to be unconscious and hypothetical, not attributable to the empirical self but not rightly attributed to the noumenal self either. These were his results after promising the reader that he would try, to the best of his ability, to make sense of transcendental psychology, despite the delicacy and difficulty of the task.[10] Others must have been daunted by this interpretive fiasco, but H. J. Paton took up his familiar role of defending Kant against Kemp Smith's interpretations. The activities described by transcendental psychology are not mysterious, but conscious; further, we may slip between the horns of the empirical–noumenal dilemma by characterizing these activities not as psychological, but as logical.[11] Although Paton may be closer to a solution than Kemp Smith, as W. H. Walsh points out, there is still a large problem:

How can something be part of an actual process and yet be merely logical?[12]

Since I propose to examine transcendental psychology, I need to dispel the initial reaction that the topic is just not worthy. Scholars do not avert their eyes from this side of the *Critique* merely because Strawson has a wonderful way of characterizing positions he opposes or because Kemp Smith and Paton failed to make much sense of Kant's doctrine. (They left other work for later interpreters.) Powerful currents within and without Kant scholarship have combined to keep transcendental psychology out of the mainstream, beyond the pale of serious philosophical discussion. The first task of this chapter is to chart those currents. From the metacritical efforts of the late eighteenth century to contemporary behaviorism, I will argue that, although certain intellectual trends have been influential in relegating transcendental psychology to a lowly status, none of them actually furnishes cogent objections to it. Rebutting objections is hardly sufficient to reopen this area of inquiry, however. I will also provide a positive account that reveals transcendental psychology as a sane and even illuminating approach to philosophy.

Countercurrents: Reinhold to Austin

From the beginning, readers recognized the psychological side of the *Critique*. And, from the beginning, they were puzzled over the status of its psychological claims. Karl Leonhard Reinhold (1758–1823), whose *Briefe über die kantische Philosophie* had been instrumental in popularizing Kant's views, concluded that the *Critique* was insufficiently critical in its use of key psychological concepts.[13] He proposed to remedy this defect by providing a critical foundation for the critical philosophy, a metacritique.[14] Anchoring Kant's assumed but insufficiently examined psychological concepts, particularly the ubiquitous "representation" (*Vorstellung*),[15] required finding a self-evident first principle from which they could be deduced. Since this principle could not be a formula, a concept, or a definition, Reinhold inferred that it could only be a description of a self-revealing fact, yet one general enough to permit the deduction of all the psychological machinery of the *Critique*. Descartes supplied the fact: Only the fact of consciousness can survive skeptical doubt. To make this starting place truly presuppositionless, no psychological or metaphysical theories can be assumed. This leaves only a description, or phenomenology, of what appears in consciousness to be the first fact of philosophy.[16]

Reinhold convinced his student, Jakob Friedrich Fries (1773–1843), that the *Critique* could not stand on its own. Fries's rescue effort proceeded in a somewhat different direction, however. He took the key to lie in a proper understanding of the methodology of the *Critique*, which, unfortunately, its author did not posses. What the *Critique* actually presents are regressive arguments from empirical facts of consciousness to various forms as their preconditions. Its arguments are *a posteriori*, even though its conclusions are about *a priori* faculties. The faculties are there all along, but we only learn about them through self-observation, hence experience. Thus, Kant's protestations to the contrary, his philosophy rests on psychology. Worse still, it rests on casual psychology. Fries's new critique would correct this defect by beginning with a careful self-observation of mental processes.[17]

Reinhold's and Fries's efforts to vindicate Kant's psychology only succeed in making the issue seem intractable. They raise what appear to be very serious problems: What justifies introducing particular faculties? Mustn't arguments to the preconditions of experience presuppose empirical facts and thus be *a posteriori*? But their metacritical solutions are un-Kantian and profoundly unsatisfactory. Reinhold insists on a Cartesian starting point, while Fries opts for premises based on self-observation. To anyone who has appreciated Kant's insights into the errors of Cartesianism, however, these suggestions are hopeless. Kant never tires of repeating the point that we have no special access to our minds that could furnish an invulnerable starting point for philosophy.[18] In the *Anthropology*, he criticizes introspection as unreliable, unstable, unnatural, and a potential route to lunacy![19] Reinhold and Fries offer fairly direct psychological readings of Kant. However, both maintain that the integrity of Kant's psychology must be underwritten by some type of introspection. As the foibles of introspection were demonstrated again and again during the nineteenth and twentieth centuries, this approach would become less and less attractive. I shall argue that the legitimacy of appealing to certain faculties and of using factual premises can be defended by less dubious means.

Despite these troubles, psychological readings of the *Critique* were prevalent for the first 100 years of its existence.[20] Reviewing the literature on Kant's psychology in 1870, Jürgen Bona Meyer set the stage by quoting Kuno Fischer: "The question of whether the critique of reason is supposed to be metaphysical or anthropological is a real problem, unavoidable in the history of the development of German philosophy since Kant."[21] Later, Bona Meyer staked out a familiar (but untenable) position. Clearly, Kant deliberately used psychological foundations, so he must agree that the *a priori* can be known through direct self-observation.[22]

At this point two works appeared that enabled later interpreters to avoid Kuno Fischer's fundamental question, by eliminating the psychological [anthropological] alternative. As with Reinhold and Fries, the blows were delivered by men who described themselves as committed Kantians. A few years before Bona Meyer's study, Hermann von Helmholtz completed his massive *Physiological Optics* (1856–1866). Its third and final volume contained a sustained discussion of Kant. Like most psychologists, Helmholtz took Kant to be a nativist about spatial perception.[23] Although he did not believe that there was decisive evidence in favor of the empiricist position, he criticized nativism as unnecessarily complex and nonexplanatory. He also objected to Kant's theories of space and geometry, citing Riemann's work in geometry and Eugenio Beltrami's descriptions of what it would be like to walk through a non-Euclidean space.[24] With these attacks, the best known of Kant's psychological doctrines, the theory that Euclidean space is the form of outer perception, was subjected to systematic and seemingly devastating criticisms by one of the major scientists of the latter half of the nineteenth century. The revolutionary developments in physics that followed apparently sealed the case.

Kant's *metaphysical* claims about the forms of intuition and the overall importance of the doctrine were certainly undercut by the discovery that physical space is not Euclidean. Nevertheless, the psychological aspect of Kant's position could still be true, as others have noted.[25] He could be right that Euclidean space is the form of human perception. As Helmholtz candidly admitted, he could not make a conclusive case against Kant's position. I return to the question of spatial perception in Chapter 2. Further, whatever their associative links, Kant's *other* psychological doctrines are relatively independent of the physics of space and time.

Gottlob Frege administered the decisive blow to Kant's psychology. In the *Foundations of Arithmetic*, Frege was explicit about the principles to be used in conducting his [or this] work. His well-known first principle is "always to separate sharply the psychological from the logical, the subjective from the objective...."[26] Even more bluntly, he declared that "psychology should not imagine that it can contribute anything whatever to the foundations of arithmetic."[27] Early readers had accused Kant of psychologism. Reinhold complained that the entire epistemological tradition had confused the strictly logical question about the conditions of knowledge with the metaphysical question about the subject of knowledge.[28] Johann Friedrich Herbart, who was at Jena with Fries, took Kant's great failing to be the attempt to found philosophy on psychology: "logic as a whole is *an ethics of thought, but not a natural history of the understanding.*"[29] It was Frege, however, who made the sin of psychologism unforgivable in a serious philosopher.

Others have demonstrated the dominant influence that Frege's conception of philosophical investigations has exercised on the subsequent development of philosophy.[30] I only repeat the highlights, and then consider two episodes that appear to be of particular relevance to Kant scholarship. Before the twentieth century, most epistemology was psychologistic. As Alvin Goldman notes, the historical literature is "replete with descriptions and classifications of mental faculties and endowments, processes and contents, acts and operations."[31] Frege attacked psychologism directly only in philosophy of mathematics and in logic. He made these areas central to philosophy, however, through his influence on Russell, Wittgenstein, and Carnap. The three founders of analytic philosophy established logic, philosophy of mathematics—and Fregean philosophy of language—as paradigms of the philosophical enterprise.[32] This model has been so dominant that even recent philosophy of mind has been largely antipsychologistic![33]

Frege's influence on the course of Kant scholarship extends beyond the general direction that he provided for analytic philosophy. In 1894 he wrote a stinging review of Edmund Husserl's recently published *Philosophie der Arithmetik*: "When reading this book I came to recognize the devastations which have been brought about by the incursion of psychology into logic. . . . "[34] Duly chastised, Husserl turned from psychologism with a vengeance. The *Logical Investigations* devotes several chapters to cataloging its evils. Beyond the familiar criticism of confusing the normative with the empirical, psychologism would make the laws of logic merely probable and contingent, rather than necessary.[35] Like Strawson, Husserl sees two sides to Kant's philosophy, one of which must be dismissed: "For even a transcendental psychology also is a psychology."[36] Thus, Frege's influence also appears to be responsible for the strong antipsychologistic stance of phenomenology,[37] which has been a major force in the development of Continental philosophy. Kant scholars trained in this tradition would be just as wary of psychologism as their analytic counterparts—and equally aware that Kant had transgressed the proper bounds of philosophy. I end this brief account of Frege's role in the fall of Kant's psychology with a footnote. J. L. Austin was a towering figure in British philosophy. When his translation of *Die Grundlagen der Arithmetik* appeared in 1950, it produced an important revival of interest in Frege among the next generation of philosophers.[38] One prominent member of that group was Strawson.

What is psychologism? I have postponed this essential question, because the answer is complex. "Psychologism" is a blanket condemnation for importantly different types of arguments. In its central usage, "psychologism" refers to the fallacy of trying to base normative principles on factual premises. As in the citation from Herbart, it is often presented by analogy with ethics (and later with the "naturalistic fallacy" in ethics). At one extreme, there is what might be called "strong" psychologism in logic: the attempt to establish the validity of logical principles by appeal to facts of human psychology. Although such a move is clearly fallacious, I find no evidence of this kind of psychologism in Kant. The principles defended by appeal to transcendental psychology—most famously, "All alterations take place in conformity with the law of the connection of cause and effect"—are not logical, but metaphysical.[39]

Reinhold's critique amounts to a different charge of psychologism. Kant tries to extract conclusions that are necessary and certain from psychological premises. As I argue later, however, although he frequently describes his results as "certain," he really means that the reasoning is certain, and so are the conclusions—given the presumption of experience for creatures with our mental capacities.[40] Others have noted that Kantian necessity is also relativized to worlds that could be experienced by creatures with our mental capacities.[41] Thus, although the arguments invoke psychological factors, the conclusions contain implicit psychological qualifications, so there is no fallacy. Later, I argue a related point for the crucial notion of apriority.

Frege denied any relevance of psychology to philosophy of mathematics or to logic. "Weak psychologism" is the view that psychological facts may be important to philosophical or normative claims, even though they cannot establish such claims. In logic, even weak psychologism seems inappropriate. Given Frege's influence, however, weak psychologism was also banished from the rest of philosophy. This move now appears extreme. For how can we hope to understand the nature of thought or the limits of knowledge—or to prescribe methods for improving our reasoning practices—without having some understanding of the capacities that make cognition possible?

Kant's epistemology is clearly weakly psychologistic. It does not, for that reason, rest on a fallacy of confusing the normative with the factual. Goldman observes that it is only against the background of philosophy's recent past that it is even surprising to hold that epistemologists should be concerned with the strengths and weaknesses of the cognitive processes that underlie our capacity for knowledge.[42] Since Kant's project was to determine our ability to have certain types of knowledge, he naturally began by considering the mental equipment that we standardly have. Despite the venerable and almost reflexive character of the psychologism charge against transcendental psychology, Kant is only guilty of weak psychologism. And that is not automatically a sin. In later discussions of specific topics, I argue for the relevance of claims of transcendental psychology to philosophical issues.

Finally, the ideology of twentieth-century psychology has had highly negative implications for the status of transcendental psychology. Assuming that introspection was the only way to study mental processes, J. B. Watson and other behaviorists convinced their colleagues that they could write a psychology and "never use the terms consciousness, mental state, mind, content, . . . imagery, and the like."[43] If the self-conscious methodology of behaviorism is granted, then Kant erred even in trying to talk about cognitive processes. Further, his claims were often cast in terms of "faculties," and faculty psychology has long been regarded as bogus by psychologists. Given the views of their colleagues in psychology, most Kant scholars concluded that transcendental psychology had no value for philosophers, or for anybody else. W. H. Walsh is a refreshing exception. Refusing to join the chorus of detractors, he made the sensible observation that a "faculty" is simply a short way of referring to a set of powers or capacities, and hence perfectly legitimate.[44] Faculties are still officially banned from psychology, but the journals contain constant references to short-term memory systems, phonemic processors, face recognition modules, and the like. The rise in the fortunes of cognitive psychology (and more recently cognitive science) has been even more dramatic. Psychologists have realized that they cannot even explain behavior without appealing to the cognitive processes that lie behind it—and that such processes can be studied without resorting to introspection.

Transcendental psychology runs counter to the empiricism, behaviorism, and most importantly, antipsychologism that have permeated recent philosophy. As a result, it has been accused of resting on introspection, being refuted by empiricist psychology, committing the fallacy of psychologism, and, generally, depending on a methodology that fails to meet the standards of either philosophy or psychology. In this intellectual climate it is no wonder that Kant scholars believe that their contributions to philosophy and its history will be greater, the less that they say about this doctrine. Individually, however, none of these charges stands up, so their collective weight should not continue to block serious discussion of transcendental psychology—as it has for the last 100 years.

As historians became convinced of the errors of transcendental psychology, they tried to divorce the Critical philosophy from it. Granted that there were many references to psychological faculties and processes; there were also negative comments about the value of psychology. These have been given prominence in order to plead the case that Kant saw, at least dimly, that psychology could not play the role that he appeared to give it in his own system. Before embarking on a study of transcendental psychology, I will consider a final objection: Given Kant's own reservations about psychology, this material should be dismissed.

Kant Against "Psychology"

In a sense, Kant's attitude toward psychology is clear. He claims that Empirical Psychology is unable to contribute to *a priori* knowledge (B152) and ought to be banished from metaphysics (A848/B876). He devotes an entire chapter to deflating the pretensions of Rational Psychology. In a well-known passage in the *Metaphysical Foundations of Natural Science*, he argues that Empirical Psychology can never be a proper (*eigentlich*) natural science, because it is not quantitative.[45] He continues by noting additional defects. Psychology cannot really be a good experimental science either, because it is not possible to isolate different thoughts. Further, observation through inner sense or introspection alters the state of the object observed.[46] (In the *Anthropology*, he recommends external behavior as a better source of evidence for anthropology.[47])

Besides attacking psychology in general, Kant appears to undercut his own psychological claims. In a frequently cited passage from the first preface, he confesses that the subjective side of the deduction, which is concerned with cognitive faculties of the understanding, is "somewhat hypothetical in character" and inessential to his chief purpose (Aviii).[48] Since references to faculties are muted in the second edition, these hedges are often thought to indicate a recognition that he had erred in casting his arguments in psychological form. He also makes several remarks that seem to anticipate the antipsychologism of later philosophy. Thus, he reminds logicians to observe the rule that "pure logic . . . does not, as has sometimes been supposed, borrow anything from [empirical] psychology . . . [!]" (A54/B78). In explaining the novel aims and procedures of a transcendental deduction, he draws a contrast with Locke's efforts to discover the psychological origins of various concepts (A86/B118–19). He characterizes the field of his study as "transcendental logic."

Together these pieces seem to create a convincing picture of disillusionment with transcendental psychology. That picture is badly out of focus, however. We cannot understand any of Kant's comments on psychology until we know how he saw the contrasting fields of psychology and logic. The *Anthropology* offers a clear, but to modern readers, shocking, answer to this question.

> The lower cognitive power is characterized by the passivity of the inner sense of sensations; the higher by the *spontaneity* of apperception—that is, of pure consciousness of the activity that constitutes thinking—and belongs to *logic* (a system of the rules of the understanding), just as the former belongs to *psychology* (to a sum-total of all inner perceptions under laws of nature) and establishes inner experience.[49]

Taking psychology first, its job is to seek laws governing perceptions observed through introspection. Kant's usage closely follows the definition given by Christian Wolff in the prolegomena to *Psychologia empirica*: "we experience that of which we are aware (*cognoscimus*) by attending to our perceptions. Hence *we come to know the subjects dealt with in empirical psychology by attending to those occurences in our souls of which we are conscious.*"[50] Given Empirical Psychology's calling, to search for regularities among items revealed to introspection, we can appreciate Kant's dismal and prescient appraisal of the enterprise.

Wolff also championed the demonstrative science of Rational Psychology. Rational Psychology begins with the principles of Empirical Psychology, and then "gives the reason for whatever actually occurs in the soul or can occur in it." Alternatively, through analysis and demonstration, Rational Psychology deduces the essential properties of the soul that contain the sufficient reason for what occurs in it.[51] Although Rational Psychology can fall into error—by giving a spurious reason—Wolff did not think that this raised any practical difficulties. The demonstration of why something occurs in the soul would be false, but the fact of its occurrence would still be attested to by Empirical Psychology.[52] Kant's opposition to Rational Psychology is well known and well argued.[53] Although he offers specific criticisms of associationist psychology (see Chapter 3[54]), his general denunciations of psychology are aimed at the two disciplines just presented.

If psychologists would be surprised by the strange and cramped pursuits that Kant places under their banner, logicians would be equally dismayed by his *largesse* about logic. The Anthropology's account of logic as a system of the rules of the understanding is no slip of the pen. He begins his logic lectures by explaining that "the understanding . . . is bound in its acts to rules we can investigate."[55] The topics in these lectures are even more revealing: presentations, consciousness, empirical concepts as springing from the senses, comparison, and abstraction.[56] As Hatfield observes, seventeenth- and eighteenth-century authors do not discuss these matters to provide psychological backing for principles of formal logic. They take the intellect or understanding to be the logical or epistemic power, and their goal is to study that power itself.[57]

Kant's work is plainly within this tradition. At the beginning, he explains that he is not offering a "critique of books and systems, but of the faculty of reason in general, in respect of all knowledge after which it may strive *independently of all experience*" (Axii). He begins the Transcendental Logic by noting the two fundamental sources of knowledge in our minds (A50/B74). He contrasts transcendental logic with general logic: the former "also would go to the origin of cognitions of objects, in so far as that origin cannot be attributed to objects" (A55–56/B80, amended translation). Although his conclusions encompass many issues, the central argumentative project of the *Critique* is the examination of cognitive faculties—sensibility, understanding, imagination, and reason—to determine which aspects of our knowledge derive from them, rather than from objects. None of his remarks about what he called "psychology" disturbs that fundamental interpretive anchor.

What of Kant's prefatory retreat from the subjective side of the deduction? The passage is quite ambivalent:

> [It is not essential, for] . . . the chief question is simply . . . what and how much can the understanding and reason know apart from all experience? not:—how is the faculty of thought itself possible? The latter is, as it were, the search for the cause of a give effect, and to that extent is somewhat hypothetical in character (though, as I shall show elsewhere, it is not really so) . . . [Axvii].

Later I argue that transcendental psychology analyzes cognitive tasks to determine the general specifications for a mind capable of performing those tasks. That is how Kant is going to show that certain aspects of our knowledge are grounded in our faculties: by showing that any faculty that can perform the task at all must meet certain specifications and that the knowledge produced by a faculty with those specifications will always include certain elements. Thus, highly abstract descriptions of faculties are essential to his project.

His ambivalence has two sources. First, he is concerned that in his efforts to provide abstract descriptions of features that minds must have to be capable of knowledge, he may have fallen into giving explanations of how the mind has those features. Faculty terminology makes confusion between these importantly different projects quite easy. For a faculty name could refer to the actual cause of certain mental processes (*The* Memory), or it could just indicate the type of process required (a memory, which might be produced by ten separate mechanisms). His second worry is more provincial. Rational Psychology tried to find the sufficient reason for various aspects of mental life, and Kant does not want his project to be confused with what he regards as a disreputable enterprise.[58] His subsequent reference to offering *opinions*, where other opinions are equally possible (Axvii), is probably an oblique criticism of the Wolffians.[59]

Kant's reservations about the subjective deduction do not show that he came to doubt transcendental psychology. His problem is how to express his novel ideas without seeming to be offering hypothetical causes. In the second edition the arguments are presented in a different form, with fewer references to distinct faculties, and greater emphasis on the types of processes required. And there is no apology.

Transcendental Psychology

Kant introduces a new, transcendental method into philosophy. He explains:

> I call all knowledge *transcendental* which is not concerned so much with objects, but with our manner of knowing objects, insofar as that should be possible *a priori* [A11–12/B25, amended translation].

***

> what can alone be entitled transcendental is the knowledge that these representations are not of empirical origin . . . [A56/B80–81].

***

> Such [transcendental] proof does not show that the given concept . . . leads *directly* to another concept. . . . The proof proceeds by showing that ex-

perience itself, and therefore the object of experience, would be impossible without a connection of this kind [A783/B811].

Putting these together, transcendental knowledge concerns how we know objects. Its specific province comprises those features of cognition that can be traced to *a priori* origins. Transcendental knowledge is established by transcendental proofs, which show that experience would be impossible but for the *a priori* origins of certain features of our cognition.

The focus on *a priori* origins is clear in the text. Nevertheless it is often missed. Besides a general antipathy to any hint of psychology, scholars are thrown off by Kant's insistence that accounts of the *empirical* origins of concepts or beliefs are without philosophical interest (A86/B118–19). They infer that the general question of origins must also be irrelevant. Even in the crucial passage where he contrasts his method with Locke's empirical method, and a transcendental deduction with a *questio facti*, however, he ties his project to origins. A *deduction* must provide a "certificate of birth quite other than that of descent from experiences" (A86–87/B119). Many other passages and an entire appendix, The Amphiboly, stress the importance of origins to transcendental philosophy (e.g., A44/B61–62).

If empirical origins are irrelevant to philosophy, why are *a priori* origins a central concern? Kant is explicit about the overarching goal of his book. He wants to show that we can have knowledge of synthetic *a priori* propositions. *A priori* origins are critical, because of their role in the justification of *a priori* knowledge. At this point, we must come to grips with the varying uses of "*a priori*" in the *Critique*.

"*A priori*" has three primary senses for Kant. A claim or judgment is "*a priori*$_L$" if it has a particular logical form: It is universal and necessary. Kant presents these as mere marks of apriority (B3–4), but it is simpler to take this to be one sense of the term. It is this sense of "*a priori*$_L$" that is used in setting up the problem. He wants to defend our claims to know propositions that are universal and necessary.

The second sense connects with Kant's interest in origins: A proposition or concept is *a priori*$_O$ if it includes elements that do not derive from sensations (B1). This may seem a needlessly convoluted way of saying that these items are innate. Even this sense of "*a priori*$_O$" should not be confused with "innate," however. Kant clarifies his position in the polemic against Eberhard:

> The *Critique* admits absolutely no divinely implanted or innate *representations* . . . There must, however, be a ground in the subject which makes

it possible for these representations to originate in this and no other manner. . . . This ground is at least innate. . . .[60]

Theorists err in moving from evidence about nonempirical elements to claims that beliefs, or concepts, or mechanisms[61] are innate. For these are disguised and unjustified hypotheses about the *causes* of nonempirical elements in cognition. The expression "*a priori*$_O$" enables Kant to state only what is known: The element does not derive from the senses. Kant's third and most complex sense of "*a priori*" is epistemological. He provides an explicit definition. "In what follows . . . we shall understand by *a priori*$_K$ knowledge, not knowledge independent of this or that experience, but knowledge absolutely independent of all experience." (B2–3). This definition raises two immediate problems. The memorable opening sentence of the Introduction proclaims that all our knowledge begins with experience. If so, then how can any knowledge be *completely* independent of experience? Further, there appear to be just two types of knowledge for Kant: *a priori*$_K$ and empirical. The critical philosophy is clearly not in the business of producing merely empirical knowledge. Its results are intended to be *a priori*$_K$ (e.g., Axv). As we have just seen, however, transcendental proofs begin with experience, or with the possibility of experience.

Many have tried to resolve these conflicts by suggesting that Kant is only ruling out particular experiences as a basis for *a priori*$_K$ knowledge; it need not be independent of experience in general. This seems correct, but excessively vague. What is experience in general? There is a further problem about the central notion of "experience." This term is used in different senses in different arguments. At points, Kant construes having experience as involving making judgments and bringing items under concepts (e.g., A124–25). At other times, experiencing seems to require nothing more than perceiving (e.g., B164–65). As many have noted, the multiple ambiguity of "experience" raises the likelihood that some arguments will be trivial or question begging. If the richer sense of "experience" is assumed, it would hardly be news that experience requires that items can be brought under concepts.

Both difficulties with "experience" can be resolved by employing a more technical term. Kant's quarry is *cognitive* experience. Different passages study the necessary conditions for the possibility of experience in different senses of "experience," because there are many aspects to cognitive experience that need to be considered. Or, expressing the multiplicity more plainly, there are many types of *cognitive task* that make up the totality of cognitive experience. "Experience in general" refers to the repertoire of cognitive tasks that we can perform. This is the range of our experiences, independently of particular content. *A priori*$_K$ knowledge is knowledge that is established independently of particular experiences, but it is tied to our cognitive capacities. Kant's initial characterization of *a priori*$_K$ knowledge is purely negative: It is established independently of experience. Much later, he provides positive accounts. *A priori*$_K$ knowledge of synthetic claims can be produced in two quite different ways. Mathematical proofs can yield *a priori*$_K$ knowledge, because they are constructive (A713/B741). [62] The second mode of producing synthetic *a priori*$_K$ knowledge is via transcendental proofs (A783/B810). In the Introduction, Kant explained the problem with synthetic *a priori* claims. They assert that the predicate concept is universally and necessarily connected with a subject concept, even though the predicate concept is not contained in the subject concept. In the case of *a posteriori* claims, no problem arises. The subject and predicate concepts are connected by experience: an individual sees something that is a body and that has weight. Since experience cannot justify either universal or necessary claims, something else is needed as the basis of the connection in synthetic *a priori* claims. Kant's well-known answer is that the third thing that makes the connection is not any particular experiences, or even all experiences taken together, but the possibility of experience, that is, the possibility of our performing any cognitive tasks at all.

> The proof proceeds by showing that experience itself, and therefore the object of experience, would be impossible without a connection of this kind. Accordingly, the proof must also at the same time show the possibility of arriving synthetically and *a priori* at some knowledge of things which was not contained in the concepts of them [A783/B811].

How this works will be made clear.

With some understanding of the notions of "*a priori*" in play, we can consider the general problem of the synthetic *a priori*. A standard assumption is that if Kant intends to prove synthetic *a priori* propositions, then his premises must be synthetic *a priori* and his inferences must preserve these properties. Since "*a priori*" is used in different senses, this strategy would require us to determine whether all premises are "*a priori*" in the same sense. Fortunately, this daunting project need not be undertaken, because Kant does not conceive of himself as giving a *logical* proof. He believes pure logic to be incapable of delivering the results he seeks. [63] So the rationale for confirming that the premises have the same status as the conclusion misconstrues the nature of transcendental proof. Still, as we have seen, Kant does not take his arguments to be empirical in the normal way. They are supposed to produce *a priori*$_K$ knowledge, but not because they are logical proofs of *a priori*$_K$ claims.

Kant's general argumentative strategy can be framed in terms of these three senses of "*a priori*." He will justify our ability to know certain *a priori*$_L$ propositions, by showing through an *a priori*$_K$ argument, that these propositions contain elements that are *a priori*$_O$. The starting point is experience, that is, various tasks that make up cognitive experience. These tasks are analyzed in order to show that they require certain elements that cannot be supplied by the senses.

Since cognition is a joint product of our cognitive faculties and information supplied by the senses, these elements must have their source in our cognitive faculties themselves. They are *a priori*$_O$. Such elements include spatial properties of perceived objects and necessary connections among events as we know them. Since they are *a priori*$_O$, these elements will be invariant across all objects as we perceive them and all events as we know them. Thus, in the world of our perception and cognition, or our "experience," as Kant puts it, certain claims will hold universally, such as "all objects are side by side in space" and "all events have causes." Further, these claims will be necessary, in an unusual sense of "necessity." For Kant, something is necessary if it is true in all situations that we can experience, constituted as we are.[64] Because spatial properties are *a priori*$_O$, were any object to be perceived by us, it would be perceived as having a determinate position in space. Within the world of our experience, objects are necessarily spatial.[65]

This is Kant's broad argument. Through reflecting on the sources of various elements in cognition, we can see that we are justified in making universal and necessary claims within the world of our cognitive experience, because, having followed his transcendental proof, we can see that, within this realm, these claims are universal and necessary. Alternatively, by considering *a priori*$_O$ sources of elements of cognition in a transcendental proof, claims that were *merely a priori*$_L$ become *a priori*$_K$. His response to the *quid juris* on behalf of the *a priori*$_O$ concepts involved in such claims is, "We can do no other." Unless the *a priori*$_O$ elements in these concepts were supplied by our cognitive faculties themselves, we could not perform even simple cognitive tasks; these concepts are indispensably necessary for the possibility of any cognitive life for us at all. Further, since these elements are *a priori*$_O$, they will be invariant features of human cognition. Locke's accounts of the occasioning causes for empirical concepts have no sweeping implications for our cognitive lives.[66] By contrast, transcendental investigations of the sources of knowledge—transcendental psychology—disclose universal and necessary features of human cognition.

Kant's transcendental proofs appeal to psychological factors to justify *a priori*$_L$ claims, but there is no fallacy of psychologism. He does not argue from the *a priori*$_O$ origin of spatial elements to the claim that all objects are necessarily spatial, because he does not argue for the latter claim at all. As he insists, he shows only that the proposition that all things are side by side in space is valid, when limited to objects as perceived by us (A27/B43). Still many find the transcendental defense of the *a priori*$_L$ status of claims of mathematics and of various metaphysical principles profoundly unsatisfying.[67] Whether formally fallacious or not, this is just not the sort of proof that is required. Husserl's attitude is typical. Psychology is irrelevant, because we have insight into the truth of logical [and so mathematical] laws.[68] Although such alternatives seem no better than Kant's approach, these matters are beyond the scope of my study. Regardless of its appropriateness to mathematics or metaphysics, transcendental psychology seeks to determine the necessary and universal elements of human cognition, and so is of great interest to epistemology and to cognitive psychology as well, as I shall argue.

Having located transcendental psychology in the general context of the *Critique*—it is the new transcendental method—I will consider the analyses of cognitive tasks in more detail. So far, my account has not distinguished two importantly different types of arguments:

1. Arguments showing that we must have a certain type of faculty (i.e., something in the constitution of the mind that supplies *a priori*$_O$ elements) if knowledge, or a particular kind of knowledge, is to be possible; arguments showing that a particular set of faculties is sufficient for knowledge, or for a particular type of knowledge. (These analyses of the necessary or sufficient conditions for knowledge, or for a particular type of knowledge, may be called *epistemic analyses*.)

2. Arguments showing that, given an account of the cognitive tasks that we perform that would be accepted by all parties to the dispute, it follows that we possess one or several of the types of faculties noted in arguments of type 1. (Because they are concerned with capacities that we actually have, I call the second kind of study *analyses of empirical capacities*.)

For example, Kant considers how we can know empirical laws of nature. Part of the answer is that we must have a faculty of reason that is capable of systematizing particular judgments, a faculty that introduces a systematicity into our judgments not derived from experience. An analysis of an empirical capacity then establishes that we have such a faculty, thus showing that we have the ability to achieve such knowledge.[69] (Whether we succeed in discovering laws of nature or bungle it is a matter of the accidents of history.)

Discussions of Kantian epistemology focus on the first type of argument, or a depsychologized version of it, to the exclusion of the second. It is critical to realize, however, that had Kant only offered epistemic analyses, then his conclusions could only be conditional: We can have X knowledge, if . . . , or, only if . . . .[70] To take the most obvious example, he would be utterly unable to show that we have knowledge that the causal principle holds throughout the world of our experience.

Kant clarifies the importance of analyses of empirical capacities to his theoretical philosophy in a passage lamenting the less fortunate position of practical philosophy:

> But human insight is at an end as soon as we arrive at fundamental powers or faculties, for their possibility can in no way be understood and should not be just arbitrarily imagined or assumed. *Therefore, in the theoretical use of reason only experience could justify their assumption. Such empirical proof* . . . *is, however, denied to us with respect to the pure practical faculty of reason* [my emphasis].[71]

In the case of practical reasoning, it is question begging to assume that we make *bona fide* moral judgments in order to argue that certain conditions are necessary for this practice. For the skeptic's claim is that our apparent moral judgments are no such thing.

By contrast, the epistemological skeptic grants that we carry out certain cognitive tasks. For example, in stating his position, he acknowledges that we can have mental representations or that we can determine that one of our mental states follows another in time. Should one of Kant's opponents deny that we can perform a certain cognitive task—as Hume famously denies any ability to attribute self-identity—then the task cannot be used in arguments against him. Once a cognitive task is granted, Kant argues that some important feature[s] of it reflects the way we think, rather than the way the world is, by arguing that we cannot account for the presence of that feature as an acquisition from the world through our senses. In the phrase of his empiricist opponents, that feature was never "in the senses." Thus, there must be something in our mind, some faculty, that supplies it. A necessary or sufficient condition for some cognitive achievement is met.

In contemporary terminology both epistemic analyses and analyses of empirical capacities are "functional analyses."[72] They provide a functional specification of the kind of processing, or faculty, required for a given cognitive task; alternatively, they decompose a cognitive task into its basic subtasks and so reveal that it involves elements that cannot be supplied by the senses. There is a significant difference between the two types of analyses, however. Epistemic analyses have a normative dimension. To return to the earlier example, Kant wants to determine what is required for us to be *empirically justified* in raising a generalization to the status of an empirical law of nature. One requirement is that we have a systematizing faculty. Thus, normative and factual claims comingle in transcendental psychology, but there is no fallacy of psychologism. The normative claims are established by normative arguments; appeals to actual cognitive tasks only establish the *existence* of faculties, or other mental equipment, specified in the normative argument. Although Kant does not try to squeeze normative conclusions out of factual premises, these premises are nonetheless crucial to his epistemological project. To borrow a well-known epistemic analysis from Strawson, Kant does not wish to argue merely that we can reidentify particulars only *if* we can operate with spatial relations or some analog of them.[73] He wants to show that we *can* always assign perceived objects determinate spatial position.[74]

In Defense of Transcendental Psychology

Earlier I rebutted some general objections to an enterprise like transcendental psychology. Having described Kant's project in detail, I turn to objections to his particular version—and to my description of it. What is transcendental psychology the psychology of?[75] If we adhere to the letter of Kant's ontology, then there are only two possible answers to this question and both seem unacceptable. Transcendental psychology is a study of the phenomenal self, and hence empirical. It is the study of the unknowable noumenal self, and hence impossible. Following Kemp Smith, Strawson elects the second option and proceeds to reveal the incoherence of maintaining that a timeless unknown self is responsible for important elements in cognition.[76]

Some aspects of transcendental idealism raise additional problems that I consider much later, but the way out of this dilemma for transcendental psychology itself is clear. Many commentators have noted that the two official selves of the *Critique* are joined by a third self, who turns out to be its central character, the "I" of apperception, or the thinking self.[77] Transcendental psychology is the psychology of the thinking, or better, knowing, self.

If the phenomenal–noumenal distinction is exclusive and exhaustive, then transcendental psychology must be about the phenomenal self, and so empirical, for the straightforward reason that no positive doctrines can be noumenal. Although it provides only a highly abstract, functional description of a thinking self, the description is still positive. As we will see in Chapter 5, Kant resists placing the thinking self in the phenomenal realm for reasons having nothing to do with transcendental psychology.[78] Given his own doctrine of noumena, and an exhaustive dichotomy, however, the thinking self must be phenomenal. Hence, transcendental psychology must be empirical, in this sense, even though it is very different from what he regarded as "empirical psychology," and, as I shall argue, quite different from contemporary empirical studies.

Another common complaint, familiar from the discussion of Reinhold and Fries, centers on Kant's appeal to faculties. The plethora of faculty names suggests a less attractive argumentative structure than the one I present. Given a cognitive task, Kant invents or borrows a list of candidate faculties that might carry it out. He then deletes options until one remains, which he claims to be necessary for the task.

In fact, only two alternatives matter for transcendental psychology: All the salient features of a cognitive task derive from experience; some feature[s] must be traced to the constitution of the mind itself. Kant begins with widely shared assumptions about the range of cognitive tasks that we can perform: We can perceive, imagine, judge. But he eschews his contemporaries' mechanical and psychological speculations about *how* the tasks are done. His own analyses of particular empirical capacities justify the positing of a faculty. Since the task requires nonempirical elements, something, some faculty, must supply them. Different names appear, because as he investigates different cognitive tasks, he cannot attribute them to the same faculty without committing the fallacy of double definition. It is a matter for empirical discovery whether the same faculty enables us to represent objects and to judge them. He could label the faculties "X," "Y," "Z," and so forth. Instead, he enhances the familiarity and memorability of his doctrines by adapting standard terminology, where apt: "sensibility" for the faculty concerned with perception, "imagination" for the faculty that represents things that are no longer present, "understanding" for the faculty of concepts, "reason" for the faculty concerned with inference. In the first edition, he adds new terms of his own, "the synthesis of recognition in a concept," for example, to allow himself enough distinctions. *Pace* Reinhold and Fries, the danger in the method is not borrowing unexamined theories but failing to posit enough distinct faculties or trying to chart the relations among faculties encountered in different tasks.

I turn to the most likely objection to my account of Kant's psychology. The enterprise I present as *transcendental* psychology is too empirical. In the case of analyses of empirical capacities, experience contributes two essential elements. Most obviously, it establishes the existence of various cognitive activities, judging, representing objects, ordering events in time, or whatever. Experience makes another vital contribution to both types of analysis, however. For what besides experience can tell us what the senses can and cannot pick up from the environment? And, in the absence of such considerations, Kant is in no position to argue either that a faculty is necessary for a particular epistemic task or that the existence of a task establishes the existence of a faculty. On my reading, Kant has a reply to one of Strawson's opening charges against transcendental psychology—the charge there can be no empirical evidence for its truth. However, that may only reinforce the impression that I transform transcendental psychology into a glorified empirical psychology. I consider this objection in two parts. Is transcendental psychology, as I describe it, too empirical to be attributable to Kant? Is it too empirical to be philosophy?

The results of the Critical philosophy are supposed to be *a priori*$_K$, necessary, and certain (e.g., Axv). Can analyses of cognitive tasks lead to conclusions with these properties? For Kant, *a priori*$_K$ knowledge is absolutely independent of the content of all experiences but dependent on facts about cognitive capacities. What sort of facts? Does he presuppose only the existence of cognitive activities? Or can facts about those activities, such as the kind of information available through the senses, also be included? From our perspective, such information clearly belongs to empirical psychology. At this point, we must recall the very great differences between our conceptions of psychology and logic, and Kant's. He locates the study of cognitive faculties in the domain of logic. As already noted, the Transcendental Logic opens by observing that we have two faculties, one for receiving impressions and a second for knowing objects. Presumably, the starting assumption about receptivity includes widely held beliefs about the limitations of the senses. In that case, Kant would still regard his results as *a priori*$_K$, even though his analyses draw on both types of facts about cognitive capacities, because they *only* draw on facts about cognitive capacities.

Could Kant have regarded the results of such analyses as necessary? As already noted, he employs an unusual sense of "necessity." Something is necessary if it is true in all worlds that we can experience constituted as we are. Given this conception, if his account of the features of human cognition required for various cognitive tasks is true in the actual world, then it is necessarily true.

Kant's claims for certainty are considerably more problematic. Certain claims are immune from refutation. Beginning with assumptions about cognitive capacities, it may seem that he could not hope for certain results. As he explains in the Methodology, however, his notion of "certain" is also relativized:

> pure reason does, indeed, establish secure principles, not however directly from concepts alone, but always only indirectly through relation of these concepts to something altogether contingent, namely *possible experience* [the range of our cognitive tasks or capacities]. When such experience is ... presupposed these principles are indeed apodeictically certain... [A736–37/B764–65].

Granted that we have experience, that is, granted broadly shared assumptions about our cognitive capacities, Kant maintains that his conclusions about the necessary and universal features of cognition are certain.

Even allowing these substantial assumptions, however, certainty seems beyond his reach. The analyses themselves could be mistaken. In the case of analyses of empirical capacities, the danger may be less acute. These only look at the end points: What does a task involve? What do the senses contribute? So there may not be much room for error. Turning to epistemic analyses, the picture is even less comforting. How are their normative elements to be preserved from refutation? Enlightening as they are, can Kant's insights into the requirements of particular kinds of knowledge never be supplanted?

I do not see how this problem can be overcome. Like many philosophers before and since, Kant is overconfident about the accepted wisdom of his day and overconfident about his understanding of epistemology, so he claims certainty for his results. Although transcendental psychology, as I present it, cannot deliver certain results, this does not imply any misreading of his method. No method is infallible, so his claims for certainty will be wrong on any reading. As I argue below, however, more recent methods for guaranteeing certain results in philosophy fare no better.

Is transcendental psychology too empirical to be philosophy? If, like Reinhold, we insist on a Cartesian starting point, then this is not philosophy. However, many arguments—including Kant's in the Paralogisms—demonstrate the impossibility of a presuppositionless beginning to philosophical inquiry.[79] He makes assumptions, but so must we all. Transcendental psychology investigates the faculties required for the performance of basic cognitive tasks. Is this glorified empirical psychology? I adapt the notion of a cognitive task from Allen Newell and Herbert Simon's idea of a task analysis. In *Human Problem Solving* they muse on the question of whether their work is really psychology. Since task analyses tell us more about the nature of the task than about particular subjects who perform it, they acknowledge that the resistance to the "psychology" label has some justification.[80] The same is true for Kant's work. He is totally uninterested in the actual physical or psychological embodiments of particular mental processes; the only goal is to explore the requirements of various cognitive tasks. In this respect his work is centrally in epistemology and very different from empirical psychology.

Nevertheless, there is a relation between transcendental psychology and what we (but not Kant) call "empirical psychology." They are different modes of addressing a common subject matter. Kant explains the relation between transcendental studies and empirical studies for the case of space. From the Transcendental Aesthetic, we know that the spatial features of perceived objects derive from our own faculties. Thus, we have transcendental knowledge of the fact that all objects that we perceive are spatial. We can also learn empirically that various objects are spatial, however. "The distinction between the transcendental and the empirical belongs therefore only to the critique of knowledge; it does not concern the relation of that knowledge to its objects" (A56–57/B80–81). The relation would be the same between transcendental psychology and empirical psychology. We learn from transcendental psychology that we must have a productive imagination, because some cognitive tasks require *a priori*$_o$ contributions from such a faculty. However, we could also learn from simple observation that people see more than meets the eye.

Besides commonality of subject matter, there is a further relation between transcendental psychology and empirical psychology. In defense of applying the "psychology" label to their work, Newell and Simon argue that highly abstract, normative analyses of the requirements of knowledge are relevant to experimental work aimed at identifying psychological mechanisms. The same point applies to transcendental psychology. If we discover that certain cognitive tasks require the syn-

thesis of diverse representations, then we have an abstract description
of mechanisms that can be sought and further described through empirical investigations. Kant sees this relation clearly:

> What I call applied logic . . . is a representation of the understanding and
> of the rules of its necessary employment *in concreto*, that is, under the
> accidental subjective conditions which may hinder or help its employment.
> It treats of attention, and its impediments and consequences, of the source
> of error, of the state of doubt, hesitation, and conviction, *etc.* [A54–55/
> B78–79].

What he calls "applied logic" we call "empirical psychology." Transcendental psychology determines the general specifications for a mind
capable of performing various cognitive tasks. It therefore guides and
constrains empirical psychology in its attempt to determine the "subjective conditions" under which the mind actually performs those tasks
(A53/B77, A54–55/B78–79).[81]

Transcendental psychology is a kind of psychology and it has striking
affinities with empirical psychology: It makes empirical assumptions
about cognitive capacities; it has the same basic subject matter; it can
guide empirical research. On the other hand, in trying to determine
what the mind must contribute for various cognitive tasks to be possible,
its driving concerns are epistemological, and its abstract specifications
are far removed from paradigmatically empirical work. So it is also
epistemology and a branch of philosophy. We tend to place studies under
one discipline or another; but in reality they can belong to both. Nothing
of substance turns on whether Kant's new transcendental method is
called "transcendental psychology" or "transcendental logic." I use the
former label for two reasons. Given the contemporary meanings of
"psychology" and of "logic," it is somewhat less misleading. And in the
spirit of the Roundheads, this is the name under which his work has
been abused.

In pursuing Kant's transcendental psychology, I break with the dominant tradition of interpretation in Anglo-American philosophy. As a
final piece of defense, I will explain why. What I call "epistemic analyses" are often presented in a different guise. All agree that a central
project of the *Critique* is to investigate the conditions that are necessary
for the possibility of knowledge. This neutral description is then glossed
by suggesting that Kant is analyzing the *concept* of "objective knowledge," "experience," or "objective experience" or that he is investigating the "logic" of various sorts of knowledge claims. In the
eighteenth-century sense of "logic," the last description is accurate, but
that is not the intended sense.

These redescriptions bring the *Critique* into the mold of post-Fregean philosophy. There are however, four substantial reasons for preserving transcendental psychology and resisting analytic interpretations. I have already given one: The classic objections to transcendental psychology *(1)* can be turned aside. The second will be argued throughout the book: Transcendental psychology, as Kant conceives of it, has important con- *(2)* tributions to make to philosophy and psychology. A third reason comes from the work of W. V. Quine. In a series of papers, culminating in "Two Dogmas of Empiricism," Quine demonstrated two crucial theses about analytic philosophy. If philosophy takes formal logic as its model, then its results can attain the special status of logical theorems only by employing analytic definitions of any nonlogical vocabulary. But the required analytic definitions are impossible, because there is no such thing as analytic truth—because the only candidate for analytic truth is truth by convention, and nothing can be true "by convention."[82] If *(3)* Quine's position is granted (and it would be inappropriate for me to reargue it here), then we diminish the arguments of the *Critique* by casting them in analytic form.

Finally, these glosses run counter to Kant's own attitude toward an- *(4)* alyticity, which is surprisingly close to Quine's.[83] As commentators sometimes lament, his introductory account of analyticity makes it a boring psychological property: In analytic judgments, the predicate is "thought in" the subject (A6/B10ff). Further, he denies that empirical or *a priori* concepts can be defined[84]; only arbitrarily invented concepts can be defined. In his own lifetime Kant resisted Fichte's and Eberhard's attempts to replace his synthetic claims with analytic counterparts. His "Open Letter" to Fichte complains that such a strategy reduces the pure theory of science to logic, and no real object can be gotten out of pure logic.[85] The reply to Eberhard (written by Schultz, but approved by Kant) is even more Quinean:

> Let one place just so many marks in the concept of the subject that the predicate, which he wishes to prove of the subject, can be derived from its concept through the mere principle of contradiction. This trick does not help him at all. For the *Critique* grants to him without dispute this kind of analytic judgment. Then, however, . . . it asks: how did it come about that you have placed so many different marks in this concept?[86]

Kant's novel approach to philosophical questions has also been given an analytic interpretation. The new method of transcendental philosophy is supposed to be the "transcendental argument." Transcendental arguments are intended to refute skepticism of the potent Cartesian variety. They start by assuming only the experience of a self-identical being. Their special characteristic is that they ensnare skeptics in self-contradiction. Once a skeptic grants that he has experience, an analysis of the concept of a possible experience shows that it is is part of the meaning of "experience" that the proposition the skeptic doubts must also be true.[87]

Despite its popularity, this interpretation of Kant's transcendental method has serious weaknesses. The argument form itself has been subjected to devastating criticisms that have yet to be satisfactorily answered.[88] It is also far from clear that Cartesian skepticism is a primary target of the *Critique*.[89] Later, I argue that Kant does not and cannot *assume* a subject of experience who is identical through time.[90] The preceding discussion implies additional shortcomings. Transcendental arguments employ a notion of analytic truth that Kant rejects and Quine refutes.

It seems time for another approach. No one doubts that a central project of the *Critique* is to examine how the workings of our thought processes are reflected in the knowledge claims we make. An essential part of the complex doctrine of transcendental idealism is that what we know is partly a reflection of our ways of knowing. The questions concern the value of this study. So far I have only tried to dispel initial doubts. In what follows, I will argue that transcendental psychology has important contributions to make to contemporary discussions. Within philosophy its positive doctrines form the basis for an excellent account of mental unity (see Chapters 4 and 5); its negative teachings about the limits of transcendental approaches provide needed discipline for contemporary speculations (see Chapter 7).

If we look beyond the bounds of Kant scholarship and philosophy, the need to reconsider transcendental psychology is even clearer.[91] As already noted, the face of psychology has changed. Cognitive psychology and cognitive science are now areas of intense and exciting work. If transcendental psychology aims to determine what our faculties must bring to cognition, then any lasting results will be significant contributions to cognitive science. Kant was not an interdisciplinary cognitive scientist. He was totally uninterested in the embodiments of cognitive processing; he had only a raconteur's interest in the effects of culture on cognition; he specifically denied any interest in how children acquire knowledge; and he could have had no understanding of the twentieth-century discipline of computer science. His sole objective was to determine what our cognitive powers had to be like for them to be capable of producing knowledge. Contributions to interdisciplinary projects need not be interdisciplinary, however. Because he was not distracted by other issues, Kant was able to offer unusually rich analyses of the task environment of various aspects of cognition. I argue later that these analyses can provide insights and direction for contemporary research in cognitive science (see Chapters 3, 5, and especially 8).

In neglecting transcendental psychology, scholars lose the opportunity to contribute to current debates in philosophy, psychology, and cognitive science. They also harden the *Critique's* reputation as an intellectual tyrant. All must pay tribute to its greatness. Graduate students must master enough of its doctrines to pass comprehensives; a well-rounded intellectual must recognize its pervasive influence on Western thought. Behind the scenes, however, those who know admit that it is impossible to read and that its major sections are fatally flawed: The Aesthetic is outmoded; the celebrated transcendental deduction is impenetrable by finite understandings. Perhaps there are a few worthwhile negative lessons. If we attend to their psychological doctrines, however, the Aesthetic offers important insights about perception, the Analytic raises serious issues about representing and judging, and the transcendental deduction is a long but coherent argument. So I will argue in Chapters 2, 3, and 6. Not surprisingly, the book is also much easier to follow if you read all of it.

Although I do not make the mistake of ignoring transcendental psychology, I do not aspire to Kemp Smith's goal of an adequate treatment of Kant's teaching. Given the range of topics and the sophisticated level of the discussions, it is hard to see how any individual could offer a complete account. My aim is only to begin the rehabilitation of the dark, psychological side of Kant's work, so that it is available for contemporary research. Even my treatment of transcendental psychology is far from exhaustive, because I do not consider the Second and Third Critiques and other relevant texts at all. Nor do I deal with all the discussions in the First Critique. Many careful and illuminating studies of Kant's epistemic analyses shine through their analytic garb. Rather than duplicate efforts, I focus on the neglected analyses of empirical capacities. In a well-known passage Descartes extols the virtues of a single architect for a city. Although this may produce superficial elegance, surely the needs of inhabitants are better met when many contribute their expertise.

2

The Science of Sensibility

What the Transcendental Aesthetic Is About

"The science of all principles of sensibility *a priori*, I call *transcendental aesthetic*" (A21/B35, amended translation). This introduction leaves no doubt about the subject matter of the Transcendental Aesthetic. Its doctrines concern sensibility, one of the two fundamental faculties required for knowledge, just as the doctrines of the Transcendental Analytic concern understanding, the second fundamental faculty. Every beginning student of Kant is taught this fact, sometimes through appeal to the analogy of colored spectacles. After class, however, Kantians do not seem to accept the basic point about the Aesthetic that they dutifully impart to students. Few recent discussions make any but fleeting references to the Aesthetic's science of sensibility.

Scholars avoid this issue because they believe that Kant's theory of sensibility is both unphilosophical and obviously flawed. For reasons surveyed in Chapter 1, current opinion will reject any theory involving a psychological faculty as unphilosophical and false to Kant's own principles. The virtually universal consensus that the doctrine of the forms of intuition is, in any case, hopeless was probably created by Hans Vaihinger's lengthy summation of his predecessors' views,[1] which was made widely available to Anglo-American philosophers by Norman Kemp Smith. Here is the charge (in Kemp Smith's words):

> This distinction between matter and form is central in Kant's system (because it is essential to his solution to the problem of the synthetic *a priori*). . . .
> Kant proceeds to argue: (a) that the distinction is between two elements of fundamentally different nature and origin. The matter is given *a pos-*

teriori in sensation; the form . . . must lie ready *a priori* in the mind. (b) Kant also argues that form, because of its separate origin, is capable of being contemplated apart from all sensation. The above statements rest upon the unexpressed assumption that sensations have no spatial attributes of any kind. In themselves they have only intensive, not extensive, magnitude. Kant assumes this without question and without the least attempt at proof.[2]

For the parade case of space, the doctrine of the forms of intuition is not only about a psychological faculty; it rests on an unsupported and implausible psychological premise.

Although sensibility is the focal topic of the Aesthetic, it has been easy to discuss this part of the *Critique* and still avoid faculty psychology, by concentrating on other weighty matters: space, time, and mathematics. Jaakko Hintikka has offered an interpretation of "intuition" that even makes it possible to discuss this crucial concept of the Aesthetic without dealing with sensibility.[3] Although Hintikka's interpretation is not widely accepted,[4] the fact that it has a significant place in the literature is a measure of current eagerness to read the Aesthetic without touching on any doctrines of transcendental aesthetics.

In this chapter I try to reverse the long-standing negative appraisal of Kant's work on sensibility. Both Kant and his critics take the claim that space is the form of outer intuition to be the test case. That will also be my topic, partly because of precedent and partly because he has a much stronger argument about space than about time, and the resulting doctrine is less problematic.[5] Far from being an embarrassing failure, I will argue that the *Critique*'s first effort in transcendental psychology— the analysis of spatial perception—is largely successful and offers important insights into the phenomenon.

Spatial perception is a central issue in the development of Kant's philosophy for a variety of reasons. From his first published work, *Thoughts on the True Estimation of Living Forces*, he was fascinated with the problem of why space has three dimensions and why it is apparently impossible for us to imagine a space of more than three dimensions.[6] As many others have observed, he was vitally concerned with the Newton–Leibniz debate over the nature of space [and time]. From his earliest writings, he was also deeply perplexed about the status of mathematics.[7] Does mathematics apply to nature, and if so, how? Further, as I argue later, spatial perception was a prominent item on the philosophical agenda. In reflecting on contemporary puzzles about spatial perception, Kant realized that it must involve *a priori* elements.[8] This critical insight provided what he believed to be correct solutions to the problems of the nature of space and the status of mathematics. His analysis of the task of spatial perception thus became the prototype for transcendental philosophy. By determining the *a priori*$_0$ origins of our perceptual representation of space, he argues that certain features will be invariant throughout the world of our experience. My focus is almost exclusively on the neglected topic of the transcendental psychology of spatial perception. However, I believe that Kant adopted the position that space is a form of outer intuition, because it provided a single solution for pressing problems in all three areas: the metaphysical status of space and time, the epistemological status of mathematics, and contemporary debates about spatial perception. The ability of one theory to solve important problems in three previously unconnected areas is remarkably strong evidence for its truth. If we ignore the transcendental psychology of perception, then it is impossible to appreciate the strength of Kant's conviction that, whatever its peculiar consequences, his theory had to be right. Since sensibility is the topic of the Aesthetic, this practice also makes it extraordinarily difficult to follow the cryptic argumentation of major passages. I shall argue that abstracting from the context of perception also distorts our understanding of the theory of geometry.[9] The main reason for reconsidering Kant's analysis of spatial perception is the one already given, however. Despite more than 100 years of philosophical detractors, this account has been, and continues to be, a significant contribution to the subject. To appreciate the strengths of that analysis, we need to do something he does not do in the text: Consider the problem of spatial perception as it came to him.

Early Modern Theories of Spatial Perception

Kant's predecessors tried to explain a number of perceptual puzzles. An important *explanandum* was our ability to perceive the third dimension. William Molyneux, the Dr. Molyneux of Locke's *Essay*, gave the problem its classic formulation:

> For *distance* of itself, is not to be perceived; for 'tis a line (or a length) presented to our eye with its end toward us, which must therefore be only a *point*, and that is *invisible*.
>
> (*Dioptrika Nova*, 1692)[10]

Descartes had tried to solve Molyneux's puzzle in *La Dioptrique*, published 54 years earlier. The best-known feature of Descartes's account was the hypothesis of natural geometry. On this view, one way that we know about distance is by the relation of the eyes to each other in perception. Given the distance between the eyes and the angles between the line connecting the eyes and the lines of sight to the object, we may calculate the distance by a "sort of natural geometry" that enables us to determine the height of the triangle formed by the two eyes and the object.[11]

Descartes' hypothesis of natural geometry was widely influential. It was also the target of one of the most important works in eighteenth-century psychology, *An Essay Towards a New Theory of Vision*. Berkeley's attack on natural geometry was two-pronged. Negatively, he argued against the "receiv'd Opinion" on the grounds that we are not aware of the angles of the lines of sight, not to mention the interocular distance. Then there is the problem of children and others ignorant of geometry. Positively, he argued that there were various distance clues that we are aware of and able to use, because experience has taught us the regular correlation between these clues and tactile distance.

Berkeley vacillated about the ability of touch to inform us about distance. In the *Principles* and the *Three Dialogues*, he adopted the position that touch does not provide evidence for outness or outer objects. In *Alciphron* and *The Theory of Vision or Visual Language: Vindicated and Explained*, he returned to his more popular position that the objects of touch are without the mind. Nevertheless, this theory was widely accepted, perhaps because of the dramatic empirical support that he was able to cite in the latter work. In 1728 the *Philosophical Transactions of the Royal Society* published William Cheselden's report of the results of an operation that provided sight to a "young Gentleman" of 13 or 14. By Cheselden's account, the boy "when he first saw . . . was so far from making any Judgment about Distances, that he thought all Objects whatever touch'd his Eyes. . . ."[12] So much for the Rationalist theory that we perceive distance by means of an innate geometry. Besides Berkeley's own citation, the Cheselden case was widely reported on the Continent. Like Washoe's "baby in my drink" today, the Cheselden boy's testimony would have been known to most scientifically literate people in the last two thirds of the eighteenth century.

To what extent was Kant aware of the controversy over spatial perception? Ranged on one side of the debate we find Descartes, Barrow, Malebranche, and Molyneux. Leibniz also jumps into the fray in his critique of Locke's discussion of Molyneux's query about the cube and the sphere. Twenty-four years before Cheselden's dramatic report, Leibniz points out the need for care in questioning the newly sighted, for they will be "dazzled and confused by the strangeness," and what they "actually do on the spot" might be quite misleading.[13] Lining up behind Berkeley, more or less, are Voltaire, a converted Condillac, a host of other French philosophers, including D'Alembert, Diderot, and Buffon, Dr. Robert Smith, David Hartley, and Thomas Reid.[14] Given the number and influence of the protagonists, it is hard to see how Kant could have avoided at least a superficial acquaintance with the drama.

Turning to more specific points, Kant had a German translation of Berkeley's *Three Dialogues* in his library.[15] The publication date is 1781, making its influence on the first edition of the *Critique* doubtful. However, he may well have seen an earlier translation by Johann Christian Eschenbach, the first German translator of Berkeley. In the First Dialogue, Philonous raises Molyneux's difficulty about the perception of distance. It is uncertain whether Kant could have had access to the *Essay on Vision* itself. Jessop maintains that an edition of *Alciphron* with the *Essay* appended to it was translated into German around 1756, but later bibliographers have been unable to verify the claim.[16]

Eschenbach introduced Johann Nicolaus Tetens to British philosophy, and in turn, Tetens's work was closely studied by Kant.[17] Tetens addresses the problem of spatial perception in his *Philosophische Versuche über die menschliche Natur und ihre Entwickelung*, which appeared between the *Inaugural Dissertation* and the 1781 version of the *Critique*.[18] He accepts a Humean principle that ideas must be abstracted from experience.[19] The idea of space cannot be abstracted from particular alterations and impressions made by objects themselves, however. Rather, it is abstracted from the act of seeing or feeling.[20] When, for example, I see that a tower is further from me than a tree, I move my eyes, and that is felt as something present and absolute.[21] So we have an impression from which the idea may be abstracted. In essence, Tetens accepts Berkeley's criterion for a solution—if information about our eyes is to be used in computing distance, then it must be conscious—but then claims a richer deliverance from introspection. Oddly, he maintains that his introspective account of spatial perception is exactly the view offered in the *Inaugural Dissertation*.[22]

Vladimir Satura has collected all the published sources of Kant's reflections on psychology. Two sources have him referring explicitly to the Cheselden case, and arguing that we acquire our concept of bodily form from touch, because vision only presents us with flat images.[23] These references occur in Stärke's version of the lectures on anthropology, usually referred to as the *Menschenkunde*, and Kowaleski's edition of Graf Heinrich zu Dohna-Wundlacken's metaphysics lecture notes. Scholars have long debated the accuracy of these reports of Kant's lectures. Nevertheless, in the former case at least, it seems reasonable to believe that these issues were covered, because Stärke's account is compatible with the discussion in *Anthropology from a Pragmatic Point of View*. In his own version of the lectures, Kant claims that we can acquire the concept of bodily form only from touch. He also notes that someone whose sight is restored by an operation must learn to see.[24] The anthropological lectures were not published until 1798, but he began lecturing on these subjects in the fall of 1772.

Neither Descartes's theory of natural geometry nor Berkeley's famous account of vision is mentioned in the *Inaugural Dissertation*'s discussion of sensibility, in either version of the Transcendental Aesthetic, or in the corresponding portion of the *Prolegomena*. (Had Kant cited these theories, I would not have appealed to the lecture notes of a 14-year-old count.) It is important not to be misled by Kant's silence, however. He habitually fails to mention predecessors who defined the issues he takes up in the *Critique*. The first edition's discussion of dogmatic idealism does not refer to Berkeley either and Newton's name does not appear in any Critical discussion of space or time. (See Chapter 4 for further examples.[25]) Of course, there was no need to remind his contemporaries that this labyrinth arose from Newton's theories. I have not belabored the historical evidence just to prove that Kant was aware of the controversy over spatial perception. That is fairly obvious. What I have tried to show is that he could reasonably assume his readers' familiarity with the problem, and with the theories of Descartes, Berkeley, and Leibniz. Hence, he does not trouble to do what I have just done: Set the stage for his solution to the problem.

Kant's Analysis of Spatial Perception

Intuition, Matter, and Form

Both the *Inaugural Dissertation* and the *Critique* prepare the way for an account of spatial perception by analyzing the elements of perception in general. The *Dissertation* offers a three-part analysis of sensory perception: the sensory representation itself (which Kant fails to mention explicitly), its matter, and its form. Sensations caused by the sensible object are the matter of sensory representations. The form "arises according as the various things which affect the senses are coordinated by a certain natural law of the mind."[26]

Just as the sensation which constitutes the *matter* of a sensual representation is evidence at least for the presence of something sensible, but in
respect of its quality is dependent upon the nature of the subject to the
extent that the latter is capable of modification by the object in question,
so also the *form* of the same representation is undoubtedly evidence of a
certain respect of relation in the sensa [sense impressions]. But properly
speaking it is not some adumbration or schema of the object, but only a
certain law implanted in the mind by which it co-ordinates for itself the
sensa which arise from the presence of the object.[27]

This passage uses "form" ambiguously to refer to both a property of
sensory representations and a law of the mind that produces sensory
representations out of sensa. To avoid confusion I will refer to the
putative law of the mind as "process form" and to the putative property
of the representation as "product form." The thesis is that as sensations
depend on both the objects and the sensory organ, sensory representations depend on both properties of the sensa and the mind's mode of
producing representations out of sensa.

The *Critique* presents the same tripartite analysis of perception, although it uses four terms: "sensation," "intuition," "matter," and
"form." With the new terminology Kant is able to sharpen the contrast
between sense impressions and sensory representations.[28] He introduces
the name "intuition" for sensory representations, that is, subjectively
available representations of external or internal objects produced by
outer or inner sense.[29] Here the matter of sensory representations is not
sensations themselves, but something corresponding to sensations. Sensations are the effects of objects on the faculty of sensibility (the sensory
organs taken collectively) (A19–20/B33–34); the matter of intuitions
comprises those features of representations that derive from sensations,
for example, color (A20,21/B34,35). Kant offers a justification for why
there must also be form:

That in which alone sensations can be ordered and posited in a certain
form cannot itself be sensation; and therefore while the matter of all
appearance is given to us *a posteriori* only, its form must lie ready for the
sensations *a priori* in the mind . . . [A20/B34, amended translation].

This is a very difficult passage. One implicit claim is that because
sensations and sensory representations or intuitions are distinct, some
process must produce intuitions out of sensations (even if it only produces representations whose qualities all derive from sensations). Kant's
discussion is predicated on the recognition that we do not standardly
perceive sensations, or the effects of objects on our sensory organs.[30]

This point would have been familiar to his readers, partly because of its role in solving the problem of inverted retinal images. (The problem vanishes when we recognize that we do not perceive our retinal image; we perceive via the image.) Thus, the first and most straightforward claim in the passage:

(1) Given that sensations and intuitions are distinct, there must be some process that produces intuitions out of sensa, even though that process might yield intuitions with qualities that all derive from sensations.

Intermingled with it are three other separable points:

(2) There is a certain product form in [all] intuitions, namely a certain relation of the elements or parts.

(3) If there is a certain product form in intuitions, then there must also be a certain process form.

(4) Given that what assures the product form characteristic of intuitions is not a sensation, but a process form, then it must "lie in the mind *a priori*."

Plainly, (2), (3), and (4) require justification considerably beyond what I have provided for (1). Further, even if (2) can be established, that will not suffice to defend (3) or (4). In the succeeding paragraph, Kant introduces a concept of a "pure" form. This notion is crucial in demonstrating the connections among the preceding claims and in setting up the analysis of spatial perception.

Pure Forms (and Nativism)

A representation is "pure" just in case "nothing is met in it that is due to sensation [*zur Empfindung gehört*]" (A20/B34, amended translation). A part, aspect, or feature of a representation may also be "pure" (A20/B34). In the first edition Kant repeats the point that, *ipso facto*, a pure form includes "no sensation (nothing empirical) in itself" (A29a, amended translation). Thus, a feature or an entire representation is pure if it does not derive from sensation, if it cannot be traced back to sensations. He continues, "The pure form of sensible intuitions in general, in which all the manifold of intuition is intuited in certain relations, must be found in the mind *a priori*" (A20/B34). Since it has not yet been established that there are any pure forms, this claim should be viewed as a hypothetical: If there is a pure product form of all intuitions, then it must be traced to a process form that lies in the mind *a priori*. Chapter 1's discussion of Kant's multiple uses of "*a priori*" can clarify this claim. Since pure forms, if there be such, cannot be traced to sensations, they are *a priori*$_O$. That is, the pure product forms are *a priori*$_O$. Does this make pure process forms innate, even though they are described as *a priori*? Several pieces of evidence suggest that this must be so. In the *Inaugural Dissertation*, Kant had claimed that the form of sensory representations was determined by "stable and innate laws [of the mind]."[31] Further, in the polemic against Eberhard already cited in Chapter 1, he writes:

> The *Critique* admits absolutely no divinely implanted or innate *representations*. . . . There must, however, be a ground in the subject which makes it possible for these representations to originate in this and no other manner. . . . This ground is at least innate. . . . Only this first formal ground, e.g., the possibility of a representation of space, is innate, not the spatial representation itself [my underscoring].[32]

On the other hand, as noted earlier, Kant believes that in the case of vision at least, we learn to see (i.e., to have perceptual representations of objects in space). Further, he has no sympathy for lazy nativist hypotheses.[33]

The way out of this interpretive impasse is to recognize that a "ground" is not a "process." I believe that Kant's eschewing talk of stable and innate laws in the *Critique* reflects a more sophisticated analysis. Suppose that the pure product form of human intuition could be produced from sensa by any member of a set S of processes $\{P_1, P_2, P_3, \ldots\}$. Although we must have some innate initial process to produce our first intuitions, the course of those intuitions could affect the process form, by substituting a different member from S. Thus, the actual processes that produce the pure product form of adult human intuition might be neither stable nor innate, and Kant never claims either attribute in either version of the *Critique* or in the *Prolegomena*. He is trying to avoid unnecessary causal hypotheses. All he needs to argue is that if there is a pure product form in human intuition, then some member of S must be available to produce that form, although not necessarily the same member at all times. The *ground* of any pure product form would lie in our constitution, because perception is a conjoint product of the sensations we receive and our ways of dealing with them—and a pure form cannot be traced to sensations. However, that does not imply that the process (or processes) that actually enables us to have spatial representations is innate.

If we abstract from the differences among the members of S, then we can describe them all indifferently as "pure process forms" of intuition. And this is exactly how Kant's terminology works. In its fundamental meaning, the "pure form of intuition" refers to a feature of intuitions themselves. Kant uses "form" in this sense to provide a functional characterization of mental operations. In the latter contexts, "form" is elliptical for the "mental operation, whatever it is, if there is just one, or whatever they are, if there are many, that produce[s] the pure form in sensory representations" (see A20/B35, A22/B36, A26/B42, A27/B43, A29). Hence, the ambiguity noted earlier between "product form" and "process form" and "process form" is not vicious but principled. Kant's second use of "pure form" is extremely abstract, because it is of no concern to transcendental psychology which of many possibilities is realized in us. Thus, we should resist the temptation to read the claim that pure process forms lie in the mind *a priori* as a fancy way of saying that they are innate. Kant means only what he says: pure forms—product *and* process—are *a priori*$_O$.

Kant also uses "*a priori*" to describe the epistemological status of claims produced by his transcendental method.[34] Thus, fully explicated, his claim is: We know *a priori*$_K$ that if there is a pure or *a priori*$_O$ product form of intuitions, then there must be some pure or *a priori*$_O$ product form producer—a pure process form—that yields intuitions with that feature from sense impressions. In this heavy psychological passage, Kant is not indulging in speculation about psychological mechanisms for which he has no evidence. He is offering a simple analysis of the task of perception involving pure forms, and his analysis is correct. Further, this analysis fills in the gaps in the four claims from his preceding paragraph (see above). Claim (3)—that if there is a product form in sensory representations, then there must be a process form that accounts for the presence of that feature—makes sense on the assumption that the product form he has in mind is pure. Likewise, claim (4)—that this process form must be *a priori*$_{[O]}$—will follow, if the product form is pure. The earlier paragraph is somewhat confusing because he is drawing on common background assumptions about perception and anticipating his analysis of pure forms at the same time. As already noted, standard assumptions about the distinction between sense impressions and sensory representations support (1); the later analysis shows the connections among (2), (3), and (4). What remains to be supported is the crucial assertion (2), that sensory representations have pure product forms.

The Method of Isolation

Kant proceeds at once to explain how to discover pure or *a priori*$_O$ product forms. His famous method of isolation follows in part from the definition of a pure form. One discovers pure product forms of intuition by eliminating those elements of a representation that are conceptual and then by eliminating those elements that can be traced back to sense impressions. For the purposes of this chapter, it will be unnecessary to take up the vexed question of how to distinguish conceptual and sensory representations.[35] He explains the second isolation as follows: We take away "what is due to sensation, impenetrability, hardness, color, etc." (A20–21/B35, amended translation). In a reflection, he explains that we are to take away anything that strikes the senses.[36] The isolation yields positive results: Extent and form (*Ausdehnung* and *Gestalt*) are features of sensory representations that do not derive from sensations. The *Inaugural Dissertation* makes the related claim that "space itself cannot be gotten out of the senses."[37]

Current readers should be puzzled by these pronouncements. Nothing in the preceding discussions prepares us for the result and Kant offers no hint of an argument in either the Aesthetic or the *Dissertation* passages. Vaihinger, Kemp Smith, and many others try to fill out the enthymeme by assuming that Kant adopted the implausible claim that spatial relations (or perhaps all relations) are incapable of being sensed.[38] (Kemp Smith's version of this charge is cited at the beginning of the chapter.) There are three serious objections to this move. The view it imputes to Kant is inconsistent with the *Dissertation* claim that the form of the representation does reflect an aspect or relation of the sensa. Further, it makes the theory vulnerable to a fatal objection. If sensations can provide no relational information at all, then whether we perceive something to be square, triangular, round, or oval will be independent of our actual sensations.[39] As critics from Feder to Herbert to Vaihinger have pointed out, however, this consequence of the implausible enthymematic premise that they attribute to Kant is totally implausible. Finally, the logic of the passage standardly cited in support of this interpretative stratagem is the reverse of what is needed: "Since, however, . . . neither the intuition of space nor that of time is to be met with in [sensation], its magnitude is not extensive [i.e., measurable in units] but intensive [i.e., not measurable in units]"[40] (A166/B208). The argument is not that space is not encountered through sensation, because sensation conveys only intensive information, but that since space and time are not met with in sensation, it [sensation] conveys only intensive information.

Distance, Extent, and Shape

The contemporary debate over spatial perception enables us to make a much more plausible interpolation that reveals the logic of Kant's reasoning. All sides recognized that distance could not be registered in the visual system. As Molyneux observed, distance is a line straight out from the eye, and so cannot be seen. In the absence of distance information, however, it is impossible to determine the size of perceived objects, for objects of vastly different sizes will produce the same size images on the retina (or fundament, in eighteenth-century terminology), if they are at sufficiently different distances from the perceiver. Thus, without distance information, it is impossible to determine the extent of an object in any dimension (not merely the third). It is not even possible to determine relative dimensions (e.g., that an object is wider than it is tall, because if it is tilted toward or away from the viewer, its height will be foreshortened on the retina). If vision cannot supply information about any dimensions of perceived objects, however, then it can tell us nothing about their shapes. The same point can be made slightly more formally. Given the well-established fact that the organ of vision is a nearly planar retina[41] and the obvious geometrical fact that a two-dimensional configuration could be the planar projection of indefinitely many different three-dimensional objects, it follows that by itself the retinal array can provide no information about shape or size at all. Planar projections preserve some spatial properties of three-dimensional objects: left–right relations, up–down relations, and betweenness relations. But they lose precisely the information that Kant attributes to pure or *a priori*$_\mathrm{O}$ forms: extent (in any dimension) and form.[42]

Touch: Leibniz Versus Berkeley

Since the only serious candidates for sensing distance were vision and touch, the only remaining possibility is that distance is registered in tactile sensations. This option was, of course, the central tenet of Berkeley's *Theory of Vision*. It can be captured in three claims: (1) true visual images are flat; (2) our ideas of distance derive from the sensations of touch produced during motion; (3) we falsely believe that our visual images are three-dimensional because, through past association, flat visual images call up three-dimensional tactile images, which are then mistaken for three-dimensional visual images.[43]

Berkeley's view was widely accepted[44] and Kant undoubtedly had knowledge of it. So he could not simply dismiss tactile sensations as a source of distance information unless he was aware of compelling reasons for believing that, whatever its popularity, the touch and motion hypothesis had to be wrong. Further, he must have believed that his readers were sufficiently familiar with these objections to accept his assumptions.

The influential critic was Leibniz. In the *New Essays on Human Understanding*, he offered several reflections that tell against Berkeley's position. Although this discussion is directed at Locke's negative answer to Molyneux's question about the cube and the sphere (the *Theory of Vision* did not appear until 5 years after Leibniz wrote the *New Essays*), it makes two points that cut directly against Berkeley's claims for touch.[45]

First, Leibniz notes that people who are paralyzed could and must learn geometry through sight. Since Berkeley's claim that touch is necessary (and sufficient) for acquiring ideas of distance and magnitude ascribes a crucial role to motion, the actual or assumed case of a paralyzed individual learning geometry would be a counterexample. Second, Leibniz observes that geometry is usually learned by sight without employing touch. In opposition to Berkeley's general Empiricism, this discussion implies that our spatial ideas must have some source other than the senses. An individual who is paralyzed could not acquire such ideas from touch—nor, of course, could he acquire them from visual images, since the starting premise of the debate over spatial perception was that retinal images cannot supply three-dimensional spatial information.[46]

Leibniz's general position is that it is essential to distinguish *images* from *exact ideas*, which are composed of definitions. He uses the case at hand to illustrate his point: the *images* of sight and touch are disparate, but the individual who is blind and the individual who is paralyzed have the same *exact ideas* of geometry.[47] It is generally agreed that Kant read the *New Essays* about 1769.[48] One year later, in the *Dissertation*, he introduced the theory that space is the form of outer sense; 1769 was the year that "gave him great light."[49] Seemingly, Leibniz's unintended reply to Berkeley was a significant part of that illumination, for it provided the final piece of the problem of spatial perception that would be solved by the form of intuition doctrine. Although composed around 1704, the *New Essays* were not published until 1765. They would have been current in the minds of Kant's intended audiences in 1770, 1781, and 1787.

Leibniz offered persuasive reasons for doubting that perceptual information about distance derives from touch. Vision and touch were the only serious candidates for the sensory sources of information about distance, however. And, as I have already argued, in the absence of distance information, it is impossible to determine the *Ausdehnung* or *Gestalt* of perceived objects. Hence, Kant asserts that extent and form cannot be gotten out of the senses.[50] *Pace* Vaihinger, Kemp Smith, their sources and disciples, he had no need to help himself to an implausible premise about our inability to perceive spatial relations; his starting assumption is a reasonable summation of the results of the debate over spatial perception up to that point. Further, if the enthymematic premise is that distance cannot be sensed, then he can maintain that the size and shape of perceived objects are a pure product form of intuition, without being saddled with the unacceptable consequence that whether we perceive something to be a cube or a sphere is totally independent of our sensations. Even though a two-dimensional retinal array provides no depth or size or shape information, because it could be the planar projection of different three-dimensional objects, any putative three-dimensional interpretation of the two-dimensional array must be an interpretation of *that array*. Thus, as the *Inaugural Dissertation* explains, the sensory representation or intuition does reflect relations among the sensa.

Kant seems incredibly (even annoyingly) cryptic to us, but there was little need to remind his audience of the familiar points on which his discussion turns. The inability of vision to register depth was the common assumption that gave rise to the problem of spatial perception; the implausibility of the touch hypothesis had just been discussed in the recently published *New Essays*. What he is doing in this passage is drawing out the obvious, but in his view momentous, consequences of these well-known facts. Given these facts, and the fact that we are capable of perceiving objects in spatial arrays, it follows that the spatial properties of objects of perception are a pure, *a priori*$_0$ product form of intuition and that any possible theory of spatial perception must appeal to some pure, *a priori*$_0$ process form (or forms).

Kant's Empirical Assumptions

Having defended Kant against a venerable charge that he makes an unwarranted psychological assumption, I should note that he does begin his analysis of spatial perception with a different empirical assumption. In the *New Essays*, Leibniz had argued that however disparate their images might be, an individual who is blind and an individual who is paralyzed employ the same ideas of geometry. Kant assumes that all outer senses employ a common mode of spatial representation. This is his initial description of our empirical capacity of spatial perception:

> By means of outer sense, a property of our mind, we represent to ourselves objects as outside us, and all without exception in space. In space their shape, magnitude, and relation to one another are determined or determinable [A22/B37].

That is, spatial representations do not differ from one sensory mode to the next. All outer sensory systems enable us to locate objects in the same all-embracing spatial network. This is a contingent matter, however. It is possible (although remarkably inconvenient) for spatial locations assigned to objects in visual perception to be incommensurable with those assigned through tactile perception. In describing transcendental psychology, I noted that Kant needs to analyze actual empirical capacities if he is going to argue that we have any of the faculties required for objective knowledge, so it is not a fault of his argument that he starts with empirical assumptions, but a virtue. Leibniz offered a mathematical rationale for attributing the same spatial ideas to individuals who are blind and to individuals who are paralyzed. They must share the same geometry. Although Kant undoubtedly concurs that the spatial representations produced through touch cannot differ from those produced through vision, because geometry describes space and there is only one actual geometry (A165/B206), he has not yet raised any considerations about geometry by A22/B37 in the Aesthetic. Presumably, he feels justified in making this assumption on the basis of the sort of commonsense empirical observations and conjectures that Leibniz offers in the New Essays.[51] Further, even Berkeley, who argues for the opposite view, grants that, prima facie, the ideas of vision and of touch appear to be the same.[52] So Kant's starting assumption is, and would have seemed, quite plausible. Nevertheless, if he is mistaken about our empirical capacity for spatial perception, then his conclusion that there is one form of outer sense will be in error. At the end of the chapter I consider contemporary research that bears on the assumption that all outer intuitions represent objects in the same spatial framework. I will also try to assess the soundness of his second opening assumption (see A22/B37, cited earlier): Through outer space sense, we are able to assign all objects a definite position in space relative to other objects.

The Isolation Argument

I read the opening pages of the Transcendental Aesthetic as offering the following argument. In light of his own and his predecessors' reflections on spatial perception, Kant takes it as given that shape and size of perceived objects cannot be traced to vision or touch, and hence not to sensation at all. These properties therefore indicate a pure or a $priori_O$ product form of intuition, a feature of intuitions that does not derive from sense impressions. Since a pure product form requires a pure *a priori*$_O$ process form, it follows that we have some faculty that is necessary and sufficient for the production of full spatial intuitions out of two-dimensional sensa. Thus, the regularity we observe in our perceptions, that all perceived objects are located in space, derives from our faculty of perception itself. We now understand the origin of spatial perception, and so understand its nature. It is not a simple registering of information about objects beyond ourselves, but a reflection of our own ways of perceiving. Further, having followed Kant's analysis of the task, we know *a priori*$_K$ that, as long as we are able to perceive normally, all objects that we perceive will be locatable in one all-embracing spatial network. As we shall see in Chapter 6, this result of the Aesthetic provides an essential premise for the argument for the special status of the categories.

On my interpretation, the first few pages of the Aesthetic offer both the basic outline of Kant's theory that space is the form of intuition and the major *perceptual* arguments in favor of his position. This material is presented with shocking brevity, because other vital issues need to be addressed in the rest of the text: the resolution of the debate over the nature of space and the defense of the *a priori* status of geometry. Interwoven with discussions of these topics are further reflections on the transcendental psychology of spatial perception. I will look at the first two arguments of the Metaphysical Exposition[53] and at the Transcendental Exposition in order to fill out Kant's analysis of our capacity for spatial perception and to illuminate these notoriously difficult texts by considering them in relation to transcendental psychology.

Two Arguments of the Metaphysical Exposition

The Standard View

The usual approach to the Metaphysical Exposition takes the first two arguments to be aimed at establishing the apriority of our representation of space, the last two to be demonstrating its intuitive character. Although the logic of this interpretation is obvious, commentators have been hard pressed to find material in the first two arguments that can serve as reasonable premises for the intended conclusion. If we reflect on the controversy about spatial perception and on the solution offered in the opening discussion of pure forms, then we can look at these passages in a new way. Kant has already presented a major argument for the claim that we know *a priori*$_K$ that space is an *a priori*$_O$ form of sensible intuition. What I will argue is that these subsequent discussions draw on that result in disclosing unusual features of the representation of space.

The First Argument

Kant begins with the claim that the representation of space is not an empirical concept. This denial should be read in the same way as the denial that Ronald Reagan is a black woman. Both descriptions are to be rejected. The focus of his analysis is spatial perception. The exposition is hampered by a terminological problem, however. Leibniz had claimed that the space encountered in perception is not really in perception but is an intellectual abstraction from perception. Thus, Kant cannot straightforwardly focus on spatial perception, as opposed to the conception of space, without begging the question against Leibniz. The resulting discussion is somewhat contorted because he feels he must use the neutral expression, the "representation" of space.

Here is the argument:

> Space is not an empirical concept which has been derived from outer experiences. For in order that certain sensations be referred to something outside me (that is, to something in another region of space from that in which I find myself), and similarly in order that I may be able to represent them as outside and alongside one another, and accordingly as not only different but as in different places, the representation of space must be presupposed. The representation of space cannot, therefore, be empirically obtained from the relations of outer appearance. On the contrary, this outer experience is itself possible at all only through that representation [A23/B38].

The argument seems to be the following. The concept of space is not empirical, because I can abstract this notion from an experience only if I represent that experience as spatial; but representing the experience in spatial terms requires that I already have the representation of space. Despite appearances, this cannot be the intended argument. For this simple argument could be used, *mutatis mutandis*, to show that the concept "horse" is not empirical either. The concept "horse" is not empirical because I cannot extract this notion from any experience unless I represent the experience in equine terms, and this requires that I already have the representation "horse."

An obvious disanalogy with the "horse" example is the ubiquity of spatial representation. Kant's claim is that in order to represent anything at all as different from myself, I must represent it in a spatial location diverse from my own. Unlike more limited representations, I could have no experience of any external object, or no experience of any object as external, if I lacked a representation of space. Even if we grant this point about our representation of the external world, it is not clear that this line of argument can support the claim that space is a pure process form of intuition. As numerous critics have pointed out, the representation of space could be necessary for experience of external objects, and it could be acquired through our sensing of external objects.[54]

If we bear the preceding discussion in mind, then we can find a more plausible reconstruction of Kant's reasoning. The argument has the form of an implicit *reductio*. Suppose that we acquire the concept of space from outer experience. We can acquire the concept of space from outer experience only if our outer senses can register spatial properties of distance, size, and shape. As we have seen, however, everyone acknowledges that these properties are not registered by vision. Further, Berkeley's suggestion that touch provides perceptual information about distance appears to be contradicted by actual or *Gedanken* experiments. So the perceptual representation of spatial features must have some source other than the senses. The space of perception is not an empirical representation at all, because this representation was never in the senses.[55]

Kant makes it difficult for readers of the *Critique* by stopping the argument once he has gotten to the point of showing that an empirical derivation of the concept of space requires a prior representation of space. The parallel argument in the *Dissertation* is more explicit. He shows the dependence on the prior representation and then notes that things in space affect the senses, "[but] that the space itself cannot be gotten out of the senses."[56] Why is this crucial element left implicit in the later work? Kant has already reminded his readers that spatial properties cannot be traced back to the senses in the discussion of pure form, a discussion that has no equivalent in the *Dissertation*. The method of isolation serves to raise this point to a methodological principle in the construction of theories of mental functioning. Presumably, Kant did not feel his readers to be in need of further reminders.

Despite the abbreviated presentation and the terminological difficulty noted earlier, Kant's argument against an empirical account of the representation of space is fairly straightforward and quite reasonable. Given the well-established and well-known facts about spatial perception then current, it follows that our representations of the space of perception are not empirical in the sense required by the Empiricist *Credo*.

The Second Argument

The second argument is notorious because Kant appears to be resting his account of spatial perception on an experiment in imagination:

> Space is a necessary *a priori* representation, which underlies all outer intuitions. We can never represent to ourselves the absence of space, though we can quite well think it as empty of objects. It must therefore be [*Er wird also*] regarded as the condition of the possibility of appearances, and not as a determination dependent upon them [A24/B39].

Kemp Smith makes the imaginative exercise reading seem inevitable by the way he renders the beginning of the third sentence. He translates "*also*" as "therefore," which strongly suggests that the sentence is a conclusion that is supposed to follow from the preceding sentence. Further, he adds a gratuitous "must" that has no warrant in the German. In this context, however, "*also*" could well function as an adverb rather than as a conjunction, in which case, it should be translated as "so," "in this way," or "in this manner." Kant's sentence should be rendered something like: "It [space] is in this way regarded as the condition of the possibility of appearances, and not as a determination dependent upon them." Thus, I believe that the logical relations among Kant's claims are not what the Kemp Smith translation implies. First, Kant characterizes [the representation of] space as a necessary *a priori* representation that underlies all outer intuitions. Next, he notes that we can never represent the absence of space, though we can represent it as empty of objects. And, in the crucial third sentence, he points out that, in this way [i.e., as a necessary *a priori* representation, the paragraph's topic], space is regarded as a condition of the possibility of appearances, not as a determination dependent upon them.

Correct translation of this clause is essential for an understanding of the logic of Kant's argument. Now let us consider his target. The phrase "and not as a determination dependent upon them" is a decisive clue. In opposition to Newton's view of absolute space, Leibniz maintained that space was dependent upon objects. Further, although Leibniz's concerns about space were mainly metaphysical, he did offer an account of how we come to form the notion of space in the fifth letter to Clarke. Our representation of space (and perhaps space itself) is an abstraction from the relations among actual objects.[57] In this passage, and others, Kant appears to be criticizing this genetic account (see A25/B39 and A40/B57).

He cannot just deny that the perception of space depends on objects without begging the question against Leibniz, so we need to consider what argument he has available to support the conclusion. If we locate the argument in the preceding sentence, then we are back to argument from imagination. I suggest instead that the working premise is contained in the first sentence: "Space is a necessary, *a priori*$_{[O \text{ and } K]}$ representation that underlies all outer intuitions." Kant is making the straightforward point that the result he has just established in the isolation argument— that our representation of space requires a pure process form of intuition—shows that the Leibnizian doctrine that the representation of space is obtained by abstraction from the actual relations among objects cannot be maintained.[58]

Since the isolation argument establishes that space is an *a priori*$_O$ form of intuition, the first two arguments of the Metaphysical Exposition do not need to demonstrate that space is an *a priori*$_O$ representation. Rather, they are polemical explorations of the implications of this point. Specifically, in the first argument, Kant points out that an empirical derivation of the concept of space is not possible. In the second, he extracts the conclusion that Leibniz's theory that the representation of space derives from objects is also incompatible with the facts he has established. Thus, Kant argues that in light of his analysis of the task of spatial perception, the two influential rivals to the forms of intuition doctrine must be given up.

The Transcendental Exposition

The Role of Geometry

Kant elevates the discussion of geometry from one argument among five in the A edition to an independent section in B. In the *Prolegomena* the question of the status of mathematical propositions dominates the account of the forms of sensibility. Thus, it has seemed to many that Kant's interest in the status of Euclidean geometry (hereafter Geometry) was the spur for his theory of space and, *a fortiori*, for his theory of sensibility. In *Kant and the Claims of Knowledge*, Paul Guyer offers impressive evidence to show that the *a priori* status of Geometry was the driving force behind Transcendental Idealism itself.[59] This issue is extremely difficult. The applicability of Geometry to the empirical world was unquestionably a central concern. Nevertheless, I believe that its importance has been overestimated.

Even in the second edition, where Geometry is much more prominent, it enters the discussion only *after* Kant has argued that space is a form of intuition. The order suggests that the implications for Geometry confirm, rather than inspire, the theory of space. Further, Ted Humphrey has pointed out that Kant did not develop the Critical version of the analytic–synthetic distinction until some time after the completion of the *Dissertation*.[60] Without the distinction, he cannot formulate the problem about the synthetic *a priori* status of Geometry. The *Critique*'s theory that space is the form of intuition is, however, essentially unchanged from the doctrine originally presented in 1770. Again, this suggests that the case of Geometry is important confirmation of the theory of space rather than its *raison d'être*. Further, as already noted, Kant's unalterable faith in the forms of intuition is much more understandable on the assumption that he believed this one theory to solve several distinct and pressing problems.

Geometry has been assigned a preeminent role in the Aesthetic partly because twentieth-century commentators have deep interests in the status of mathematics and none in the theory of sensibility. Most discussions are only concerned with whether the type of psychological theory that Kant offers could support his claims about the *a priori*$_L$[61] status of Geometry. The reverse dependency is never considered. Once we recognize that the theory of geometry makes an essential contribution to the theory of spatial perception, it is easier to give credence to the idea that three separate issues are brought together in one theory.

Geometry and the Space of Perception

I focus on the lengthier, more self-conscious discussion about Geometry in the 1787 edition, which begins with an explicit statement of Kant's objectives:

I understand by a transcendental exposition the explanation of a concept, as a principle from which the possibility of other *a priori* synthetic knowledge can be understood. For this purpose it is required (1) that such knowledge does really flow from the given concept, (2) that this knowledge is possible only on the assumption of a given mode of explaining the concept [B40].

The Transcendental Exposition is to show that the theory of spatial perception—specifically, the doctrine that we know *a priori*$_K$ that space is the *a priori*$_O$ form of outer sense—provides insight into the synthetic *a priori*$_L$ status of Geometrical propositions, and that without that theory it would be impossible to understand how Geometry could enjoy this status.

Kant's well-known argument for the latter claim, that we could never understand how the propositions of Geometry could be synthetic *a priori*L unless we accept his theory of the perception of space, proceeds by elimination. If the truths of Geometry are synthetic, then they cannot be established by conceptual analysis. These propositions are supposed to be "*a priori*L" however; they are necessary and universal (B41, compare A24). How could we ever know that all the objects we encounter in perception invariably have certain spatial properties? There are only two possibilities. Either we have foreknowledge of the actual objects to be encountered or we know something about our perceptual capacities and limitations. Since the former option requires us to have powers we obviously lack, the only remaining possibility is that we have *a priori*K knowledge of *a priori*O elements of perception (A26–27/B42–44). Further, Kant has just shown that we do know *a priori*K that all the objects we perceive have spatial properties.

The usual and reasonable view of this argument is that it does nothing to establish the thesis of the forms of intuition. Even if it is clear that, if we accept the synthetic *a priori*L status of Geometry, then we must accept the theory of sensibility, that does not matter, because we do not accept the antecedent claim. The point I wish to make is that if, like Kant, we accept the antecedent, then this argument does not simply provide an independent proof of the thesis established earlier. To see this, we must first recognize that the thesis that we know *a priori*K, that space is a pure *a priori*O form of intuition, will not explain how the propositions of Geometry can be known to hold of all actual objects of perception. Our *a priori*K knowledge must be more specific. We must know *a priori*K that our perceptual system is so constituted that we always perceive objects in *Euclidean* space.

Where do we acquire this additional information? Standing behind this discussion is an assumption that connects the practice of Geometry and the space of perception. Kant begins with the uncontroversial assumption that we can prove theorems of Geometry. Then he assumes—for reasons finally spelled out in the Methodology—that geometrical proof requires the construction of figures in perceptual space. Although this theory strikes modern readers as bizarre, Michael Friedman has recently argued that the appeal to construction is an unsuccessful attempt to fill a genuine gap in the geometrical proofs of the day.[62] Given these two assumptions, we can trace a connection between geometrical proof and the space of perception. Although never made explicit, Kant's reasoning must be something like this:

1. We can prove theorems in Geometry.
2. Geometrical proof requires the construction of figures in perceptual space.
3. Therefore, Geometrical figures are constructible in the space of perception.
4. If Geometrical figures are constructible in the space of perception, then the properties of that space must be compatible with the properties described in the fundamental propositions of Geometry.
5. Any geometry whose fundamental principles are consistent with the fundamental principles of Euclid is Euclidean.
6. Therefore, Geometry provides a true description of the space of perception [3, 4, and 5].

Had Kant made these assumptions, then he would believe that Geometry correctly describes the space of perception. He has just shown, however, that we know *a priori*$_K$ that the space of perception derives from a pure, *a priori*$_O$ process form of intuition. It follows that Geometry is a true description of the pure form of intuition. Whether we can now be said also to know *a priori*$_K$ that the space of perception will always be Euclidean depends on whether something like the argument just sketched can provide *a priori*$_K$ knowledge. Kant seems committed to this view, because otherwise the claim that the forms of intuition—and only they—can justify the *a priori*$_L$ status of Geometry would break down.

I will not explore this issue about Geometry, because my concern is the doctrine of sensibility. The appeal to Geometry in the Transcendental Exposition enables Kant to elaborate his theory of spatial perception: Given the practice of geometrical proof, it follows that the space of perception is correctly described by the fundamental propositions of Geometry. Geometry bears exactly the same relation to the theory of spatial perception in the *Dissertation*. It describes the spatial relations that constitute the form of sensible intuition.[63] Thus, Geometry fills what would be a serious gap in Kant's account of spatial perception by telling us exactly what the spatial form of sensible intuition is. This point is not emphasized in 1787, because he is highlighting the recently formulated quandary about the status of mathematics. Nevertheless, we cannot understand why he believes that the theory of sensibility is the only possible explanation of the alleged synthetic *a priori* status of Geometry unless we recognize the role that Geometry plays in the theory of spatial perception.

Parson's Interpretation

Although this interpretation enjoys considerable textual support, it is inconsistent with prevailing views about the relation between sensibility and Geometry in Kant. In a well-known article, Charles Parsons maintains that the theory of intuition can explain the universal applicability of Geometry to objects of outer intuition only if we refrain from attributing anything to the form of intuition that "is not revealed in the way objects present themselves to us in perception." Parsons's reasonable assumption is that if Kant is going to vindicate the universal applicability of Geometry to objects of perception by appealing to a form of intuition, then that form must be manifest in the objects of perception.[64] This implies that we could determine the Euclidean or non-Euclidean features of perceived objects through perceptual inspection. As a number of critics have noted, however, we can do no such thing.[65] The difficulty can be illustrated using one of Kant's own examples. However carefully we peer at them, we cannot tell whether two putative straight lines through two points are in fact straight.

On my account, the connection between Geometry and the properties of perceived objects is not direct, but mediated by several independent assumptions. There is no suggestion that we come to understand that space is a form of intuition by discerning Euclidean properties in the objects we perceive. By the time we reach the Transcendental Exposition, Kant has already established that the spatial properties of objects imply that space is a form of intuition, with no appeal to Geometry. Further, as we have seen,[66] he assumes (following Newton and Leibniz [67]) that positions in space are perfectly determinate relative to one another. Alternatively, he assumes that the space of perception is a system of perfectly definite positions. Thus, before Geometry takes center stage, it is already clear that the space of perception has a determinate character that derives from a pure *a priori*$_o$ process form. Against this background, our ability to prove theorems of Geometry and the assumption about the role of construction in proof enable Kant to fill out the theory of sensible intuition. Since Geometry can be done (and if this practice requires construction), it follows that Geometrical figures are constructible in perceptual space, and hence that the fundamental propositions of Euclid are compatible with the properties of the spatial *representation* that is the form of intuition. Thus, it follows that Geometry provides a true description of the form of outer sense. (It also follows that figures that are not Geometrical will not be constructible in the space of perception.)

By recognizing the work that has already been done in investigating spatial perception, we can avoid Parsons's assumption about perceptual inspection. Further, this interpretation is flatly contradicted by Kant's discussion of the very objection (and example) Parsons raises:

> Empirical intuition is possible only by means of the pure intuition of space and of time. *What geometry asserts of pure intuition is therefore undeniably valid of empirical intuition.* The idle objections, that objects of the senses may not conform to such rules of construction in space as that of the infinite divisibility of lines or angles, must be given up [A165/B206, my emphasis].

This passage (from the Axioms of Intuition) makes it plain that the order of argumentation that I attribute to Kant is right. At least in the *Critique*,[68] he does not believe that we know the propositions of Geometry to be true on the basis of perceptually inspecting actual objects. Rather, he believes that perceived objects have certain properties, because certain propositions of Geometry are true.

Kant's Results

Although the argument I sketch connecting geometry and sensibility would allow Kant to carry out the projects of the Transcendental Exposition, it is unsound. Even if Friedman is right that the constructive view of proof is motivated, it is still false. Moreover, the description of constructive proof eventually offered in the Methodology is remarkably obscure. My point is not to defend all the theses of the Transcendental Aesthetic, but to show the reciprocal relations among them. The analysis of spatial perception tells us that outer intuition has a certain a priori$_o$ form. Kant answers a major question raised by that account—what exactly is this form?—by appealing to our ability to prove Geometrical theorems. Sensibility is not merely the handmaiden to Geometry; Geometry is part of the theory of sensibility. If these reciprocal influences are suppressed, then we cannot follow the reasoning of the Transcendental Exposition. Nor can we grasp the full significance of the forms of intuition.

Both Kant's defense of the synthetic a priori$_L$ status of Geometry and his elaboration of his analysis of spatial perception fail, because they depend on his unusual and erroneous view of geometrical proof. The implications of this failure for the status of mathematics have been widely studied. How does it affect the issue of spatial perception? It leaves him in an odd position. He has shown that a representation of space is the *a priori*$_0$ form of human intuition, but he has no way of further specifying what that representation is.[69] In a more positive light, he has uncovered an important research problem. What, exactly, is the spatial form of human perception?

The Forms of Intuition and Contemporary Evidence

Depth Perception

As noted in Chapter 1, subsequent developments in mathematics and physics have badly undercut Kant's metaphysical claims about space, time, and the forms of intuition. How should his transcendental psychology of spatial perception be judged in light of contemporary views in perceptual psychology? Without trying to offer a comprehensive review, I will consider two issues that appear to undermine his position. Then I will turn to recent work that bears on two of his empirical assumptions: (1) the assumption that there is one spatial representation common to the intuitions produced by all outer senses and (2) the assumption (borrowed from Newton and Leibniz) that the representation of space is a system of positions in which all objects can be located in definite positions relative to one another.

On my account, Kant theorized that the perceptual representation of space is a pure *a priori*$_0$ form of intuition in order to resolve a continuing puzzle about how we perceive the third dimension, and so the spatial properties of objects. A casual reading of the history of psychology might suggest that depth perception has now been explained, and that the explanation is totally different from what he imagined. In 1838 Charles Wheatstone discovered the importance of binocular disparity in the stereoscopic perception of depth.[70] It turns out that we use two slightly different two-dimensional retinal images in achieving a three-dimensional representation of the viewed scene.

Wheatstone's discovery adds an important new resource; however, it does not eliminate the mystery of depth perception, for two reasons. First, although we can assign depths to objects in some cases just by taking advantage of binocular disparity, the explanation of how we do this is far from complete. To get a sense of the outstanding problems, consider the fact that before our visual system can utilize binocular disparity, it must match items in the left and right retinal arrays. Information in the two arrays underdetermines correct matches, but somehow the system accomplishes this task and assigns depths.[71] Second, binocular disparity is useless at long distances, and we can perceive depth monocularly at short and long distances. One hundred and fifty years after Wheatstone wrote, both the character of our three-dimensional representation of space and the puzzle of how we use monocular and binocular information to achieve it are active areas in perceptual research.[72]

Is the Space of Perception Euclidean?

In the *Mathematical Analysis of Binocular Vision*, R. K. Luneberg offers experimental evidence for the view that visual space is not Euclidean, but Lobachevskian.[73] On the other side, R. B. Angell cites experiments that he interprets as showing that the geometry of two-dimensional visibles (visual appearances) is neither Euclidean nor Lobachevskian, but Riemannian. Angell explains the discrepancy between his findings and Luneberg's on the grounds that they are looking at different phenomena: Luneberg is interested in judgments about the relations among perceived objects: he is interested in visual appearances.[74] Finally, in a recent issue of *Science*, a trio of psychologists offers evidence for Kant's view. They report on experiments in which a very young blind or blindfolded child is taken by various routes to different items laid out in a room. The experimental question is whether the child can then find a new route between two previously visited items. Subjects can accomplish the task. Although this may show certain things about the way subjects represent space (see below), it is hard to see how it provides any support for the authors' claim that subjects probably use a Euclidean metric.[75]

As this very brief review suggests, the present status of Kant's hypothesis about the Euclidean nature of perceptual space is unclear. Luneberg's pioneering effort has sometimes been cited as a refutation, but more work needs to be done to determine the properties of our perceptual representation of space. Unless we reach the surprising result that our ability to do Euclidean geometry is a major clue to our representation of space, however, the final outcome of this work will not alter present evaluations of Kant's account. He believed that Geometry was the royal road to knowledge of perceptual space on the basis of an obscure theory of proof. Even if the space of perception turns out to be Euclidean, or mostly Euclidean, he had no evidence that it must be so. The burden of my argument has been that the interesting and well-argued part of Kant's analysis is the claim that *some* three-dimensional spatial representation is a pure form of human intuition.

The Assumption of a Common "Outer Sense"

I noted earlier that Kant's analysis of spatial perception rests on the empirical assumption that one system of spatial representation is common to all outer senses. For the project of transcendental psychology to succeed, he must analyze actual empirical capacities, so an empirical basis is appropriate. But the capacity must be real. Although the assumption of one spatial representation common to all outer senses agrees with common sense, it is nonetheless a substantial assumption. Notice that he is not claiming that we can use information from different senses to figure out what objects are where, say, by assigning a higher degree of reliability to touch. He is claiming that one type of spatial representation is the form of sensibility regardless of which outer sense supplies the sense impressions. As noted, he may have felt justified in adopting this assumption on the basis of Leibniz reflections in the *New Essays*. However, recent work offers some dramatic evidence that his assumption about our empirical capacity is correct.

Paul Bach-Y-Rita and his colleagues at the Pacific Medical Center have been trying to develop a device that will enable blind people to perceive their surroundings.[76] It consists of a 20 × 20 matrix of solenoid vibrators mounted on the back of a stationary dentist's chair, a camera that can be manipulated by the subject, and a movie screen. When an image is flashed on the screen, the camera transforms the video image into a tactile image of vibrating and nonvibrating "pixels." Subjects can use the hand-held camera to scan the image on the screen. With practice they can recognize such objects as coffee cups and telephones and they can recognize the arrangement of objects.

After quite a bit of training with the device, subjects were presented with looming images. When the tactile image was suddenly magnified by a quick turn of the zoom lever of the camera, subjects ducked their heads as if something were coming toward them. One of the subjects was a blind psychology professor, who had lectured for years on the relationship between the visual angle subtended by an object and its distance from the observer. He was genuinely amazed to experience this phenomenon for himself. The conditions of these experiments are obviously quite different from the standard conditions of tactile perception. Nevertheless this work clearly suggests that our sense of touch is capable of creating spatial representations strikingly similar to those achieved through vision. More work needs to be done in this area, but for now, Kant's assumption of a single perceptual representation of the spatial arrangement of objects for all outer senses seems well supported by the data.

Is Spatial Perception Determinate?

Kant makes a second, related assumption about our capacity for spatial perception. He assumes that through perception, the shape, size, and relative location of all objects are determined or determinable. Alternatively, he assumes that the spatial locations of all perceived objects are comparable. This assumption stands behind his belief that there is one form of outer sense. As we will see in Chapter 6, it is also critical for his defense of the categories.[77] I discuss the assumption in two stages. First, I look at the more general position that in assigning size and, particularly, location to one object, we are tacitly fixing the spatial parameters of virtually every other object. Then I consider the stronger claim that the spatial features of all objects are completely determinate relative to our perceptual system.

In *The Hippocampus as a Cognitive Map*, psychologists John O'Keefe and Lynn Nadel offer a defense of Kant's theory of spatial perception.[78] They distinguish between two types of spatial representations. The spatial position of an object can be represented in terms of a *ROUTE*. A route is a set of instructions that explains how to reach the location of the object by engaging in particular activities—turn left, go straight, and so forth—at a sequence of landmarks. By contrast, one can represent the spatial position of an object in terms of a *MAP*. A map is a set of places that are systematically related to one another by a group of spatial transformation rules.[79] When we locate something by assigning it a place on a map, we are implicitly locating it relative to all the other objects in the region covered by the map. This is not the case with routes. The Capitol and the Washington Monument could both be mentioned on a route guide through Washington that would provide no information about their relative location. Conversely, if both sites are located on a map, then their relation to one another is completely determinate.

O'Keefe and Nadel's distinction provides a clear formulation of Kant's assumption about our perceptual capacity: Our perceptual system represents the spatial location of objects in terms of maps. Our ability to construct maps does not have to be established by careful psychological experimentation. What O'Keefe and Nadel show is that many human and animal *perceptual* tasks involve the use of spatial maps. (This more limited conclusion is also supported by the experiments with blind toddlers cited earlier.) These experiments suggest that Kant was right in his basic assumption about the way in which spatial perception works. Our perceptual system appears to represent the spatial position of objects in a way that does locate objects relative to all others.

Even if our perceptual system represents spatial properties in maps, it does not follow that the spatial properties of objects are *perfectly* determinate with respect to our perceptual system. My point is a simple one. Suppose that perception involves locating objects in a general system that coordinates all positions. Still, we cannot assume that all the particular mechanisms subserving this function will operate optimally. Different mechanisms could operate under different conditions. There is no reason to believe that the operations of these systems are mutually exclusive or exhaustive. Thus, the spatial properties of a perceived object might be indeterminate or ambiguous. Some recent work suggests that this may be the case.[80] However, even if these results are confirmed, they will not necessarily undermine Kant's assumptions or claims. As he realized, transcendental psychology involves only very abstract descriptions of cognitive functioning. So long as the assumption that the perceived spatial properties of objects are determinate is a reasonable idealization, his claim for one form of outer sense will also be a reasonable idealization, even if the particular subjective conditions (i.e., the actual mechanisms) in which that form is realized fall somewhat short.

Discovering the Forms of Intuition

Kant's analysis of spatial perception has almost always been regarded as a major contribution by perceptual psychologists. In part, this is because he has been misread as a simple nativist. So his views were highly influential in the nineteenth-century battles between nativism and empiricism. Current research includes several programs that are Kantian in name or spirit. Some of these also rest on oversimplifications of what views really are. Despite these errors, however, psychologists have a much more realistic assessment of Kant's contributions to perception than philosophers. The most valuable and distinctive aspect of his work is precisely that most repugnant to his twentieth-century commentators: the thesis of transcendental psychology that there is a specific *a priori* form of human sensibility.

Although he resisted any specific nativist hypotheses, he recognized that the basic spatial form of perceived objects can come only from the human perceptual system itself. Spatial perception seems so familiar that we tend not to think of it as a phenomenon at all. His analysis shows that it is not diaphanous, but has distinctive properties of its own. On the basis of the practice of Euclidean geometry, he believed that he knew what the essential properties of spatial perception were. That belief was ill founded. It is a difficult experimental problem to determine the properties of our spatial representations of objects. Kant did not discover the *a priori*$_O$ form of outer sense, as he thought; he discovered the problem of the *a priori*$_O$ form of outer sense. If psychologists can specify the inherent properties of human spatial perception, then they will discover the *a priori*$_O$ form of outer intuition.

Since this project should be carried out by psychologists, there may be a temptation to think that it no longer has any philosophical significance. As he originally conceived of it, Kant's doctrine of the forms of intuition had implications for philosophy of mathematics, the metaphysics of space and time, metaphysics generally, and epistemology. It is doubtful that the consequences of more accurate accounts will be as numerous or as momentous. Nevertheless, they will inform us about the limitations and propensities of our perceptual access to important aspects of reality. Such theories are standardly believed to have important epistemological implications. So, for example, Thomas Kuhn's claims about the limitations of perception provided half of the support for his revolution in philosophy of science (incommensurability of language was the other half).[81] We cannot hope to determine the philosophical implications in advance of results and without substantive philosophical theories of the role of perception in various epistemological enterprises. Since the results will concern the bounds of sense, however, they should have important implications about the nature and limits of our knowledge.

3

Transcendental Psychology in the Transcendental Deduction

What (If Anything) Happens in the Deduction Chapter?

Rumor has it that when a well-known Harvard Professor taught the *Critique* for the first time, he reached the second chapter of the Analytic of Concepts—"The Deduction of the Pure Concepts of Understanding"—and postponed classes for two weeks while trying to figure out something to say. This chapter evokes the same incoherent mixture of reverence and disdain among Kant scholars that the Critical philosophy as a whole evokes among nonspecialists. It is widely regarded as (1) the philosophical heart of the book; (2) difficult to the point of being unintelligible; and (3) utterly barren of plausible or interesting philosophical positions or arguments. Not surprisingly, commitments to (2) and (3) have led more tough-minded Kantians to doubt the viability of (1).

Over the years, the value of this chapter has repeatedly been questioned, at least by Anglo-American scholars.[1] Kemp Smith promulgated Erich Adickes's and Hans Vaihinger's incredible explanation for its alleged failings: the chapter was quickly pieced together from notes that included doctrines that Kant had already [sic] abandoned, as well as newly worked out positions.[2] In attempting to defend against the "patchwork" charge, Paton famously compared the difficulty of following its reasoning to crossing the Great Arabian desert by foot. (To avoid confusion, I will capitalize "Deduction" when referring to this chapter, and use the lowercase to refer to the deduction as a whole.) Jonathan Bennett cut through the exegetical niceties of the patchwork debate: "The Deduction is not a patchwork, but a botch."[3] As noted in Chapter 1,

Strawson recommended that we skip the doctrine of synthesis, which is a central topic of the chapter. His analysis of the deduction focused instead on the Refutation of Idealism and on the Analogies, where he saw anticipations of the antiskeptical "transcendental" arguments of the 1950s. Most recently, Guyer has dismissed the arguments of the Deduction chapter, again finding solid argumentation only after reaching the Principles chapter.[4] Even as sympathetic an interpretor as Allison concedes that the Deduction "fails to demonstrate how the categories make experience possible, [and so seems to lose] . . . much, if not all, of its philosophical significance."[5]

The suspicion that nothing of serious philosophical interest transpires in the Deduction chapter is the result of two independent factors. First, Kant's organization leads to mistaken expectations. In the "Clue to the Discovery of All Pure Concepts of the Understanding," widely referred to as the "Metaphysical Deduction," he introduces the list of categories. At the beginning of the Deduction, he explains that the categories require a "deduction," or a proof of their legitimacy. Readers expect that they are about to be given such proofs, but no proofs appear. Most of the categories are not even mentioned, much less argued for, in the chapter. Specific arguments about individual categories can be found only in the Metaphysical Deduction and in the Principles. This suggests that the Deduction plays only a supporting role in the main enterprise. It must complete some unspecified, unfinished business from the Metaphysical Deduction, or provide preliminaries for the arguments of the Principles.

The Deduction chapter performs both these functions, as I argue in Chapter 6.[6] That is not its only significance, however, despite the misleading implications of the sequence of Kant's discussion. His remarks in the preface to the First Edition provide a more accurate picture of its importance: This chapter cost him the greatest labor and is of unrivaled importance as an exploration of the faculty of understanding (Axii). As the Transcendental Aesthetic examined sensibility to discover $a \; priori_O$ elements in cognition, the central purpose of the Deduction is to reveal the $a \; priori_O$ contributions of the understanding. It does this by analyzing very basic empirical capacities (e.g., representing objects and making judgments about objects) in order to determine what faculties we must possess and what processes we must carry out, given that we are able to perform these tasks. Only when these broad analyses are complete is Kant in a position to argue that certain concepts are indispensable to, and invariant features of, our cognitive lives.

The second reason for the low status of the Deduction chapter is that scholars avoid these analyses. Nowhere has the antipsychologistic approach to Kant had more damaging effects than on interpretations of this chapter. Chapter 2 argued that we cannot appreciate the strength of the Transcendental Aesthetic unless we consider the analysis of spatial perception. Even in the absence of this material, however, scholars could evaluate the theories of space, time, and mathematics. With the Deduction chapter, there is nothing but transcendental psychology. Since it is off limits, commentators can only sift through what remains to find other threads either to recast as analytical arguments[7] or to tie to some argument about the categories in the Metaphysical Deduction or in the Principles. As a result, there is little interpretive consensus and the chapter appears confused and disjointed, a paradigm of futile Teutonic obscurity.

Kant's early readers also had difficulty with the Deduction, but that is hardly surprising, given the novelty and abstractness of the arguments and, in some cases, a lack of desire to understand.[8] There are also substantive problems. In analyzing specific tasks, the neat dichotomy between sensibility and understanding breaks down. Further, analyses of several different tasks are used to establish the mind's contributions to knowledge. Nevertheless, in this and the next three chapters, I will argue that Kant has coherent lines of argument in both editions, arguments that begin with insightful analyses of cognitive tasks and end with claims to justify a special status for the categories. In the end (in Chapter 6), it will turn out that even the best argument for the categories fails, in part, because it contains a mistake in transcendental psychology. That does not vitiate all that comes before, however. I will argue that Kant's analyses of the tasks of representing objects and of judging them demonstrate the necessity of various synthesizing activities of the mind. They thus provide important evidence for the general thesis of transcendental idealism that what we know is partly a function of our ways of knowing. That is why Kant labored over this material and why the chapter is the heart of the book. These analyses and the resulting doctrine of synthesis also enable him to provide an account of mental unity that is both an effective reply to Hume's skepticism and, as I will argue, significantly better than more recent accounts.

In this chapter I focus on two task analyses that are the centerpieces of the objective side of the Deduction in the two editions: How are we able to represent objects? How are we able to make judgments about objects? Chapter 4 follows the central task analysis of the subjective side of the Deduction: What must a subject be like to have representational states? This analysis and the earlier ones result in an account of mental unity that I explore and develop in Chapter 5. Finally, Chapter 6 brings these analyses and a new task analysis (How are we able to perceive spatial and temporal arrays of objects?) together in one long argument for a special status for the categories. Almost all my discussions of the transcendental deduction deal with material from the Deduction chapter. For reasons already given, interpretations of the deduction often race lightly through this chapter and then concentrate on the more compact arguments of the Principles, chiefly the argument of the Second Analogy. My interpretation does the opposite. The deduction is not completed until the Principles, so I offer a brief account of the Second Analogy at the end of Chapter 6. However, this is presented only as a coda to an interpretation that is firmly centered on the Deduction chapter.

If we allow ourselves to consider Kant's psychological analyses, then we can follow the argumentation of this chapter. Further, we can make a more realistic assessment of its worth. When this material is ignored and the chapter is seen only as an obscure lemma for a proof of the categories in the Metaphysical Deduction or in the Principles, then a mixed verdict is precluded. Either the proof (of the other section) works or it does not. By attending to the details of Kant's analyses, we can determine whether his laborious exploration of the faculty of understanding yielded any positive results. To what extent, if any, can he justify his revolutionary claim that the mind itself is responsible for important elements of cognition? Do his analyses provide insights of enduring value into different aspects of cognition? Although this is the best reason for reconsidering transcendental psychology, I will just add that this approach also permits quick resolution of three classic interpretive puzzles associated with the chapter: Is the argument "regressive," because it merely analyzes the necessary conditions for knowledge,[9] in a strong sense of "knowledge," or "progressive" in arguing from weak premises to a strong conclusion? What are the relative merits of the first and second versions of the Deduction chapter? What is the relation between the "subjective" and "objective" sides of the chapter, and is the former really necessary?

Kant analyzes a variety of cognitive tasks. Sometimes he makes strong assumptions about our capacities; other times, quite minimal assumptions. So the movement of argument is neither consistently progressive nor consistently regressive. This approach also provides a systematic account of the differences between the first and second versions of the Deduction chapter, in terms of the different cognitive tasks that they analyze and the comparative successes of the analyses.

Kant's prefatory admission that only the objective Deduction is essential to his purpose (Axvi) is often cited as a means of throwing out transcendental psychology with the subjective Deduction, as I note in Chapter 1. As I argue there, however, his ambivalence toward the subjective Deduction rests on an understandable confusion between providing a highly abstract description of capacities a mind must have to carry out various cognitive tasks and speculating about the psychological mechanisms that realize those capacities.[10] Even if the subjective Deduction were eliminated, however, transcendental psychology would remain. The objective Deduction aims to establish the legitimacy of the categories by showing that we must employ these concepts if we are going to be capable of having very basic cognitive relations to objects. This project leads Kant to explore the prerequisites of cognition, which inevitably involves discussion of the processes of cognition, whether or not he assigns them to particular faculties. Thus, the objective and subjective Deductions are two sides of one enterprise. On the objective side, we start with different forms of object cognition and try to decompose these tasks into their essential subtasks. The subjective Deduction examines the same problem from the point of view of the subject: What capacities must a subject have to enjoy various cognitive relations to objects?

Representing Objects

The Problem

The objective side of the Deduction examines how in general (Kant's ubiquitous *"überhaupt"*) objective knowledge, or knowledge of objects, is possible for creatures with our basic cognitive constitution. Some discussions offer epistemic analyses of the conditions required for valid, intersubjective knowledge claims.[11] Since these have been widely discussed, my efforts are directed toward the more obviously psychological analyses of empirical capacities. Among these, I focus on the most basic and most central task analysis of each of the two editions. These analyses start with very minimal—and actual—capacities and are fairly sound. So they offer the best defense of the claim that the mind influences knowledge and the strongest foundation for an argument that certain concepts are and must be invariant features of cognition.

We can know an object only if we can represent it and the first edition highlights this most basic subtask: How is an object of representations possible (A104ff)? To understand Kant's analysis, we must begin by anchoring his fluid terminology. In German philosophy of this time, the most general term for a mental state was "*Vorstellung*," which is usually translated as "representation." However, Kant does not believe that all *Vorstellungen* (representations) represent (see A320/B376). Although this is no more inconsistent that the contemporary claim that atoms can be split, it can be confusing. So I use "cognitive state" as the generic term.[12] There is an important complication, however. "*Vorstellung*" can be used to indicate the *contents* of cognitive states. It exhibits the same ambiguity as the English terms "representation" and "idea" (which is one reason that, from a strictly translational perspective, "representation" is a very good rendering of "*Vorstellung*"). When the "content" sense is indicated, I will translate "*Vorstellung*" as "the contents of a cognitive state," and where the term is ambiguous, I will use "cognitive state or its content." Although these renderings are inelegant, I believe that they will permit a clearer discussion of substantive issues. They also have the advantage of keeping the essential duality of "*Vorstellung*" constantly before us.

In the *Logic*, Kant claims that there are two types of cognitive states that "consciously refer to objects": intuitions and concepts. He gives these referring states the common name "*Erkenntnisse*,"[13] which might be translated as "cognitions" (but which Kemp Smith barbarously translates as "modes of knowledge"). Because it is more perspicuous, I will describe these representational cognitive states as "representations." And, again, where the context indicates, I will sometimes use "the contents of representations." Where "*Erkenntnis*" is used as a mass noun, I will render it as "cognition" or "knowledge." In this terminology, one project of the first edition Deduction is to consider what is required for a cognitive state to be a representation.[14] In Brentano's well-known terminology, Kant is trying to understand how a mental state could be "intentional."

Like most topics Kant discusses, this issue arose in the context of contemporary debates. As we saw in Chapter 2, however, he rarely gives any space to presenting previous positions, even when they are essential to an appreciation of his views. (We will see an even worse example of this expositional shortcoming in Chapter 4.) Kant's analysis of the task of representing objects is clearer when viewed against the contemporary options that he rejects and (apparently) accepts. So before turning to that analysis, I will consider where his predecessors and contemporaries stood on the issue.

The Views of Leibniz and Christian Wolff

Leibniz made "perception" a central notion in his metaphysics. Monads are the basic constituents of reality and they alter by having different perceptions. Monads teem with perceptions, including *petite perceptions* of which they are unaware. Through these masses of perceptions, each monad mirrors the entire universe. Although Leibniz is explicit about the distinction between *petites perceptions* and conscious perceptions, he says very little about the nature of perceptions.[15] Four points seem clear, however. First, Leibniz believes that mental states are in active causal community with each other. Indeed, all previous mental states have some effect on subsequent states.[16] Second, given the mirroring analogy, Leibniz must regard perceptions as representations. They mirror or represent the universe. Tetens believed that the Leibniz–Wolff concept of representation implied that every modification of the soul is a representation.[17] However (third), since monads do not causally interact (they are "windowless"), perceptions must represent states of the universe without being in causal contact with what they represent. Finally, perception involves unity. For the multifarious contents of a perception are represented together in a simple substance.[18]

Christian Wolff offered a systematic presentation of Leibniz's widely scattered philosophical writings. On the topic of representation, Wolff's account was particularly neat. He distinguished the "powers" of the soul from its various capacities. The soul's fundamental power is the *vis representiva*, the power of representation. Allegedly, the unity of the soul and the commonalities across its various expressions prove the uniformity of this power. The task that remains is to show how each mental capacity could be reduced to the *vis representiva*.[19] Alternatively, the task was to show how each capacity could be deduced from the definition of the essence of the soul, the *vis representiva*.

For reasons that will be explored in detail in Chapters 7 and 8, Kant could not accept this kind of account. The operations of actual capacities could not be explained by appealing to definitions, even definitions purporting to capture essences. From Kant's perspective, Leibniz and Wolff make the question of representation fundamental, but they fail to provide an adequate solution to it.

Empiricism and Sensationism

Turning from the Leibnizeans to the Lockeans, we find a diametrically opposed account of representation. Mental states represent the objects that cause them. Objects cause impressions in the mind that resemble the objects themselves, so the question of how they represent is answered in the causal story. They represent objects by resembling them. By Kant's time, this seemingly more plausible account had been badly shaken. According to Locke himself, there was no resemblance between property and idea in the case of secondary qualities. As we saw in the discussion of Berkeley in Chapter 2, however, it was not clear to Locke's successors that we directly perceive primary properties, like shape and distance. Rather, we seem to perceive objects by perceiving their sensible, that is to say, secondary qualities, which do not resemble anything in the object itself. So how do our mental states represent objects?

In an illuminating article, Rolf George makes a persuasive case that sensationism formed part of the background to Kant's epistemological discussions.[20] Sensationism is the position that the sensations produced by objects impinging on the senses are nonreferential. George credits Malebranche as the original discoverer of this position but suggests that it may have come to Kant via Condillac. Kant must have been somewhat familiar with Condillac's views, because Tetens discusses them.[21] Further, the distinction between nonreferential sensations and referential perceptions was central to Reid's philosophy, which was quite influential in Germany at the time Kant was writing.[22] In describing sensations as the ways we are affected by objects (A19–20/B34) and in denying that sensations are objective representations, Kant seems to adopt the sensationist position.

Given the sensationist premise, the problem of how cognitive states represent becomes pressing, since mere causal interaction is insufficient. Reid did not really offer a solution to the problem. His primary concern was to make philosophers recognize the "commonsense" distinction between sensation and perception, in order to blunt the force of skepticism.[23] George suggests that Kant's own approach may have been influenced by Condillac's view that reference to objects is achieved by various sensations being pulled together in a judgment.[24] I believe that something like Condillac's position that perception involves judgments, or Reid's position that perception involves concepts, does shape the discussion in the A Deduction. It also undermines the analysis, however. As I argue below, the problem is that these assumptions were highly controversial, so Kant had no right to make them in analyzing the task of representing objects. Despite this miscue, however, many aspects of his analysis depend only on well-established and much less controversial assumptions, and these can be preserved.

Associationism

Finally, let's consider Hume. In the *Inquiry Concerning Human Understanding* (which Kant owned in German translation[25]), Hume examines our belief in objects. Although he casts the issue in terms of belief, not reference, the discussion covers the relevant territory. How do we come to believe that an object is present?

> Whenever any object is presented to the memory or senses, it immediately, by the force of custom, carries the imagination to conceive that object which is usually conjoined to it; and this conception is attended with a feeling or sentiment [namely] . . . a more vivid, lively, forcible, firm, steady conception of an object than what the imagination alone is ever able to attain.[26]

For example:

> I hear at present a person's voice with whom I am acquainted. . . . This impression of my senses immediately conveys my thought to the person, together with all the surrounding objects. I paint them out to myself as existing at present, with the same qualities and relations of which I formerly knew them possessed.[27]

Although resemblance enters into Hume's account, the crucial role is played by the law of association. How, on the basis of sensation, can we achieve reference to an object? Objects have multiple properties. Each property causes a resembling impression in the mind. Since these impressions are experienced together, the ideas produced by them are bound together by the law of association. Again through the operation of the law of association, when a fresh instance of one of these impressions is in the senses, it brings these ideas to mind and conveys its own inherent liveliness to them. So when we hear the voice of an acquaintance, we immediately have a lively conception of the person's face, build, manner, and so forth. That is all there is to belief in an object.[28] Hume expresses satisfaction with his account: "Here, then, is a kind of pre-established harmony between the course of nature and the succession of our ideas."[29] In nature, various properties and objects are linked together. Thanks to the operations of custom, these properties and objects are also connected in our thoughts.

But Hume knows that this simple story does not work. In his earlier and more extended treatment in the *Treatise*, he recognized that the law of association is inadequate to explain our beliefs in objects.[30] The properties of objects are constantly, if subtly, changing. Further, our impressions are in constant flux. How do such irregular impressions produce stable clusters of ideas to be called up by a present impression? Kant notes the same weakness in the law of association: "If . . . cognitive states reproduced one another in any order, just as they happen to come together, this would not lead to any determinate connection of them, but only to accidental heaps . . . " (A121, my underscoring, amended translation). To make up for this defect in the operation of association, Hume assumes that the imagination (through various propensities) produces more uniformity in the connections among ideas than exists in the connections among impressions.[31] Here he is considerably less sanguine about his account of belief in objects and commends carelessness and inattention as good alternatives to delving into these perplexities.[32]

Representation was a central issue for the Leibnizeans and the Lockeans, and for the lesser-known school of sensationism. By the time Kant was writing, two classic solutions to the problem, the Empiricists' resemblance assumption and Wolff's *via representiva*, were no longer viable options. On the issue of causation, Leibniz's successors took the reference of cognitive states to objects to involve a causal relation.[33] This view was shared by Kant from his earliest writings and spelled out clearly in a passage in the *Reflexionen*:

> Leibniz takes all sensations (deriving from) certain objects for representations of them. But beings who are not the cause of the object through their cognitive states [or their contents] must in the first instance be affected in a certain way so that they can arrive at a representation of the object's presence. Hence sensation must be the condition of outer cognitive states [representations?] but not identical with it. . . . Hence representation is objective, sensation subjective.[34]

So causal connection is necessary for representation, but not all cognitive states caused by objects represent.

A Priori Necessary Synthesis

What Is an Object of Representations?

Kant introduces his analysis of the task of representing objects by asking what it means to talk about an "object of representations" (A104). Although this task is, in some respects, very minimal, he does assume that we are able to represent objects. So this part of the Deduction is not intended to address highly skeptical opponents. His conclusions should only be accepted by those who grant our capacity to represent objects. Besides this essential empirical assumption, his analysis rests on two widely shared background assumptions (and, as noted, on a controversial assumption to be discussed further below). First, the problem of representing an object should be cast as the problem of how various cognitive states can yield a representation of an object. This assumption derives support from his theory of perception, which I discuss in Chapter 6. However, the underlying rationale rests on contemporary scientific views that were accepted by both the Leibnizean and the Lockean traditions. Vision is the paradigm sense and our retinas receive a constant and varied stream of stimulation.[35] Hence, Hume describes the mind as an inner theater that witnesses constant flux,[36] and Leibniz refers to a myriad of *petites perceptions*. So the problem of representing objects is really the problem of how we can represent objects on the basis of a varied and fluctuating stream of cognitive states.

The second, related, well-entrenched background assumption is that the *simulacra theory*—the view that we perceive objects by their giving off *simulacra* of themselves which (somehow) migrate into our minds— is false.[37] Kant refers to this empirical fact explicitly in the *Prolegomena*:

> For I can only know what is contained in the object in itself if it is present and given to me. It is indeed even then inconceivable how the intuition of a present thing should make me know this thing as it is in itself, as its properties cannot migrate into my faculty of representation.[38]

Our senses do not take in whole objects or their properties through some type of migration. Rather, we can derive information about objects only by the effects of their various sensible properties on our various sensory organs.

Kant begins his analysis with an apparently simple point. To represent an object, a set of cognitive states must be consistent and coherent:

> Since the contents of representations [*Erkenntnisse*] are to relate to an object, they also agree and relate to one another in a necessary way, that is, they must have that unity which makes up the concept of an object [A104–5, my translation].

If one of my representations represents the desk before me as black and another represents it as brown, then they cannot both be (accurate) representations of the same object (at the same time). However, this is merely a superficial reflection of a deeper point, as becomes clear in the next paragraph. To yield a representation of an object, cognitive states must be united in an overarching representation.

Kant continues by noting that although unity is necessary for representing objects, we cannot derive it from objects. Objects are nothing to us, because they correspond to cognitive states, and so should be distinguished from them (A105). "It is clear that . . . we have only to do with the diverse elements [*Mannigfaltigen*] of our cognitive states [*Vorstellungen*] . . ." (A105, amended translation). A similar point is given prominent notice in B: "Combination . . . cannot be borrowed from . . . [objects], and so, through perception, first taken up into the understanding" (B134). To represent an object, we must unify information from multiple cognitive states from various sensory modalities. Since the goal is to explain how we achieve a unified representation (in our heads or minds), it is unavailing to appeal to objects outside us.

Although this point may seem painfully obvious, it is worth dwelling on for a moment, since it is so often missed. So, for example, the contemporary "ecological" school of perception founded by J. J. Gibson makes exactly this error. Gibson was concerned to show that the environment is a richer source of information than many perceptual psychologists had realized. In particular, he argued that the environment contains a variety of high-level invariants, such as ratios and proportions, that do not alter under local changes in optical stimulation. The recognition of higher-level environmental properties has been important in recent work on perception. However, Gibson drew the wrong conclusion from his discoveries:

> the function of the brain when looped with its perceptual organs is not
> to decode signals, nor to interpret messages, nor to accept images. These
> old analogies no longer apply. The function of the brain is not even to
> *organize* the sensory input or to *process* the data, in modern terminology.
> The perceptual systems, including the nerve centers at various levels up
> to the brain, are ways of seeking and extracting information about the
> environment from the flowing array of ambient energy.[39]

That is, Gibson inferred that once we have discovered invariances in the environment, we have an account of our perception (and so, representation) of them. But the fact that the environment contains invariances does not (by itself) explain how we are able to represent them, any more than the fact that various qualities are united in objects explains how we are able to produce representations in which these qualities are united. Gibson's critics echo Kant: He has failed to explain how we perceive invariances, because he has not explained how (by what processes, by what means of decoding) we derive representations of invariances from fleeting sensory information, which is all that we receive.[40]

Unity and Synthesis

Since the object cannot impart its unity to cognitive states or their contents, something else must unify them in a representation of an object. Kant claims that the required unity can be created only if the intuition (representation) "can be produced by such a function of synthesis in accordance with a rule that makes possible the necessary *a priori* reproduction of those diverse elements, and their union in a concept" (A105, my translation). Far too much is packed into this sentence and this doctrine. To begin to appreciate the strengths and weaknesses of Kant's analysis, it is necessary to separate his points. This claim contains four distinct subclaims:

1. The unity of intuitions requires a function of synthesis.
2. This function must be carried out in accordance with a rule.
3. This rule makes possible the necessary *a priori* reproduction of various contents. [YET can -FORMING]
4. Finally, this rule makes it possible for various contents to be united in a concept.

Although none of these claims is exactly limpid, the third seems especially problematic. Why "necessary" and "*a priori*"? Unless Kant is being clumsily redundant, he cannot mean "*a priori*" in the sense in which it is equivalent to "universal" and "necessary." If we look back to his introductory remarks, and forward to his summation of his position on representing objects, then it seems that the sense of "*a priori*" he has in mind must be what I distinguish as "*a priori*$_O$" in Chapter 1. We are looking for "*a priori*$_O$" conditions, which remain even "when everything empirical is abstracted from experience" (A96). He concludes that representing objects requires a "pure," "nonempirical" concept of a transcendental object (A109). This concept cannot contain anything definite but refers only to the necessary unity of an object representation, which is "nothing but the necessary unity of consciousness, and therefore also of the synthesis of the diverse elements, through a common function of the mind, which combines it in one representation" (A109, amended translation). That is, the unity of representations is not empirical, but derives from the mind. Alternatively, the function of the mind that produces unity cannot be traced back to sensations. Reading this later explication back into A105, I think Kant's third claim is itself complex:

(3a) this rule makes possible the necessary reproduction of various contents.

(3b) [although not itself *a priori*$_o$], the rule must involve *a priori*$_o$ elements, or relate to *a priori*$_o$ elements, that enable it to produce unity.

What Is Synthesis?

Before we can make any progress with this complex analysis of representing objects, we need to understand the key technical term "synthesis." Synthesis is an absolutely central notion of the Deduction. It is mentioned more than 60 times in the A edition, and reappears in the less overtly psychological B Deduction, both under its own name and as "combination." As will be evident, it is not possible to depsychologize this notion as it occurs in Kant's text. Thus, it is rarely the subject of extended discussion, despite its great prominence.[41] Much of this and the next two chapters will deal with various aspects of the synthesis doctrine. A fundamental difficulty in following the text of the Deduction chapter is that this doctrine is quite complex, and Kant's discussions are highly compressed. The complexities need to be explored *seriatim*. However, I will try to give some sense of the whole by beginning with a summary presentation of a large chunk of the doctrine, even though some claims will only receive needed detail and defense later.

Kant introduces the term "synthesis" with an explicit definition:

By *synthesis*, in its most general sense, I understand the act of adding different cognitive states [or their contents] [*Vorstellungen*] to each other, and of comprehending their diverse [elements] in a single representation [*Erkenntniss*] [A77/B103, amended translation].

Again, the synthesis is "what gathers the elements of representation together and unites them in a definite content" (A77/B103). As at A105, Kant sometimes speaks of "functions of synthesis." His definition of "function" suggests that the two notions are closely related: "By 'function' I mean the unity of the act of bringing various cognitive states [or their contents] under one common one" (A68/B93, amended translation). This is why the depsychologizing project is futile. In these introductory passages, common to both Deductions, Kant defines "synthesis" as an act performed on cognitive states.

A synthesis is an act, or to be more neutral, a process that produces a representation, by adding or combining diverse elements contained in different cognitive states in a further state that contains elements from these states. The easiest way to think about syntheses may be to regard them as processes that realize (mathematical) functions. Given a set of input states, a synthesis produces a certain output state. Thus, Kant's talk of *rules* of synthesis, or *functions* of synthesis, is, as it often seems in the text, pleonastic. The domain of syntheses comprises cognitive states (including representations); their range, cognitive states and representations. Kant provides no account of the intrinsic nature of cognitive states, representations, or syntheses. These matters are beyond the interest and capabilities of transcendental psychology.[42] Syntheses might be processes that produce physical states from sets of physical states, that produce immaterial states from sets of immaterial states, or that produce symbols from symbolic inputs.

Kant regards representations as comprehending, or containing, the diverse elements (Kemp Smith's "manifolds") of other cognitive states and as possessing unity, precisely because they are produced from those states by syntheses. That is, as I will argue in Chapter 4, he believes that a representation represents something, in part because it was produced by sensory states that were themselves caused by the sensible properties of the object striking the sense organs (and in part because it can lead to further representations). In contemporary terminology, Kant holds a "functionalist" theory of the content of representations.

What about the unity of representations? For Kant, as for Leibniz, unity is a central feature of representations. As is clear in the Paralogisms, however, he does not believe that the unity of representations derives from their inherence in a simple substance. At one level, Kant's position on unity is clear enough. A representation produced by synthesis has unity, because the contents of various states are united in it. This explanation is merely verbal, however. How are these contents united? In what sense are they united? Kant's answer is, "Through synthesis." The representation has unity, and the contents are united, because the representation was produced through synthesis; it is, as he says so often, a "synthetic unity."

One way to grasp Kant's point about the relation between unity and synthesis is to consider the now familiar example of a Necker cube (see Figure 3.1). What happens when we perceive figure (a)? We scan the lines and vertices, and the relations among them, and on the basis of that information, we interpret the figure as (b) or (c). What is peculiar about this figure is that we are able to perform two processes, which realize two different functions and so yield different outputs, on the basis of the same stimulus values. Now consider the vertices that I have marked 1 and 2. We can interpret these vertices as both lying on the front plane of the solid figure, as in (b), or as both lying on the back plane, as in (c). What cannot happen is that we interpret vertex 1 as forward and vertex 2 as to the back. We cannot do this in the following

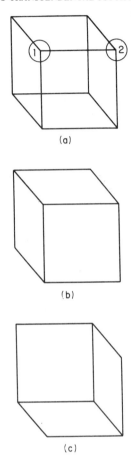

Figure 3.1 The Necker Cube (a) can be perceived as (b) or (c). (Drawn by Philip Kitcher.)

sense: Such an interpretation will not produce a stable visual representation of a three-dimensional cube. When Kant describes the diverse elements of different states as being united in a representation, or that representation as possessing unity, what he means is that there is some process that realizes a function that yields that representation as a stable output,[43] given the right cognitive states as inputs. (I use a visual image only to illustrate the point. Kant takes it to apply to all states produced by synthesis.) Representations produced through synthesis inevitably involve unity. For if they lacked it, they would not exist (A105, B132).

With some understanding of the doctrine of synthesis, we can make considerable sense of the first two subclaims of A105. Neither objects nor their properties can migrate into our minds. We take in information about objects through their effects on different senses at different times. Because objects are outside the mind, we cannot explain how this information is united in a representation by appealing to objects. The only alternative is that some process within the mind—synthesis—carries out the unification. So subclaim 1 is justified. Because a synthesis is a process that takes some cognitive states as inputs, and yields others as outputs, it can be described as a function, or as a rule (make R1 from inputs CS1, CS2 and CS3). So subclaim 2 is also justified. For reasons that will be clear later, I skip to subclaim 3b: Although not itself *a priori*$_O$, the rule of synthesis that is required to reproduce multiple contents from cognitive states must involve or relate to *a priori*$_O$ elements.

To see the significance of this aspect of Kant's analysis, it is helpful to take stock of what has already been shown. Has he already demonstrated that our capacity for representing objects can only be explained by reference to *a priori*$_O$ elements? In a sense, he has. Representation requires that the diverse elements of cognitive states be combined. Since this combination takes place on items in the mind, it must be carried out by an activity of the mind. So the mind itself supplies this precondition for cognition. Still, this is not very exciting. One could argue that the ability to be affected by sensible properties is also in the mind and so demonstrates the mind's necessary contribution to cognition. A clearer way to cast the issue is in terms of Kant's technical notion of *a priority*$_O$: Can combination be traced back to the senses? Was the combination or synthetic unity required for representing objects ever in the senses?

The Law of Association

Empiricists thought it was. This was clear in the preceding discussion of Hume. Different ideas become united through the law of association *when they are sensed together, or nearly together*. At A105 Kant takes a cryptic and backhanded, but nonetheless deliberate, slap at this position. The law of association does not explain how we represent objects; the law is itself explained by the rules of synthesis that make reference to objects possible: "[the synthesis must be governed by] . . . a rule [that] . . . makes possible the necessary *a priori* reproduction of the diverse elements" (A105, my translation).[44] This allegedly fundamental law of the mind is derivative.

The groundwork for this claim was laid in the discussion of the "Synthesis of Reproduction in Imagination." Kant accepts the law of association:

> cognitive states which have often followed or accompanied one another finally become associated, and so are set in a relation whereby, even in the absence of the object, one of these cognitive states can, in accordance with a fixed rule, bring about a transition of the mind to the other [A100, amended translation].

However, he notes that this law "presupposes that appearances are themselves actually subject to such a rule, and that in the diverse elements of these cognitive states a coexistence or sequence takes place in conformity with certain rules" (A100, amended translation).

He illustrates the point by a series of examples, beginning with the oft-quoted case of cinnabar: "If cinnabar were sometimes red, sometimes black . . . " (A100). What he means is, "If we *represented* cinnabar sometimes as red, sometimes as black . . . "[45] This discussion has some major problems, but the point Kant is making is a sound one. The law of association can get a foothold only if, whenever we are in sensory contact with cinnabar, for example, we construct a representation of it as red from our various sensory states. For, as he observes, this law presupposes that the contents of our representations display certain patterns. The gentle force of association cannot connect representations of "red" and "cinnabar" unless these representations occur together. The crucial point, which is badly obscured by the use of "*Vorstellung*" instead of "*Erkenntnis*," is that this law operates on representations of objects or properties. When ideas with *particular contents* have regularly been experienced together, they will tend to be associated. Without the assumption that ideas have determinate, repeatable contents, the law makes no sense. In that case, however, the law presupposes and cannot explain our ability to construct representations of objects and properties.

There is a second difficulty with Kant's argument. Even if the law of association operates on representations, Empiricists could reply that something like this law explains how various cognitive states are united in representations. When cognitive states occur together, they tend to become associated, and through this association produce representations of objects and properties.

This account of the prerequisites of association occurs in Kant's preliminary review of the topics of the Deduction. Fortunately, both the terminological and the substantive difficulty are removed in the formal presentation of his position. The problem with association is the one I noted in discussing Hume:

If cognitive states [*Vorstellungen*] reproduced one another in any order, just as they happen to come together, this would not lead to any determinate connection of them, but only to accidental heaps, and consequently would not give rise to any representation [*Erkenntnis*] [A121, amended translation].

The stream of cognitive states is too fluctuating and too varied to yield representations by the simple mechanism of spatiotemporal contiguity. Another way to see the difficulty is to recognize that the law of association is but one principle. It links cognitive states related by spatiotemporal contiguity. So, for example, it would connect cognitive states produced by observations of striking matches and flames, and cognitive states produced by observations of different parts of telephones. Only in the second case, however, do we unite those cognitive states in the representation of an object. The law of association operates in the same way in all cases, however, and so could not explain how we achieve different types of representations. Kant concludes that we need a rule that connects a cognitive state with another particular cognitive state in preference to others (A121). Spatiotemporal contiguity is too promiscuous.

Associationism and Apriority

This argument, which is somewhat mishandled at A100 and then presented more clearly at A121, is the basis of Kant's claim at A105 that the rule for producing representations of objects must involve or relate to a priori$_O$ elements and of his later claim that object representation requires a pure, nonempirical concept of an object. But has he really demonstrated the need for an a priori$_O$ contribution? His case for the inadequacy of association seems perfectly sound. Spatiotemporal contiguity is in the senses, so if it were an adequate foundation for our representations of objects, then this matter would be purely empirical. However, the fact that *this* sense-based aspect of mental life is inadequate does not show the impossibility of some other, more subtle pattern of sensory stimulation being the basis of object representation. The law of association had a preeminent place in post-Humean Empiricism.[46] Against this background it is not surprising that Kant sometimes concludes that a capacity requires a priori$_O$ elements, on a basis of an argument showing that it cannot be explained by the law of association.

Suppose, however, that there are many, more subtle, sensory patterns, whose presence leads our minds to form particular types of representations. Does this show that these aspects of cognition derive from the seney require a substantial contribution from the mind itself? If patterns are quite remote from the eventual representation, at deal of processing is required to construct the representation, then we might be tempted to say the representation is a reflection of the mind itself. Even in this case, however, there is a more obvious answer. The exasperation of many scholars over nineteenth-century debates that pitted nativism *against* empiricism was often justified. For, in the kind of case just described, the obvious answer is "both." To understand how we are able to construct representations of objects, for example, we need to look at both the patterns of our sensory stimulations and the ways the mind uses those patterns to construct representations.

Because Kant's argument for a priori$_O$ elements is really an argument against the law of association, it is not totally successful. He does not rule out the possibility just described, so he cannot legitimately claim that our representations of objects do not derive from the senses. On the other hand, by arguing against association, he shows the need to consider how the mind constructs representations on the basis of more subtle sensory patterns. Our capacity for object representation is not data driven in any simple or obvious way. So any explanation must appeal to more elaborate mental construction than mere association, and this may reveal that the resulting representations are underdetermined by the sensory data. They may include elements that were never in the senses.

The discussion of subclaim 3b enables us to deal quickly with claim 3a: This [a priori$_O$] rule makes possible the necessary reproduction of various contents. To produce a representation, we must connect the multiple contents of cognitive states that occur at different times in one representation. So those contents must be available, in some sense, for them to be connected. Kant describes this situation as requiring the "reproduction" of the contents. Again, what he has actually shown is that some rule for reproducing and connecting the diverse elements of cognitive states other than the law of association is necessary for representing objects. He has not shown that this rule is a necessary and universal feature of human cognition, because it derives from a priori$_O$ sources.

Representations and Concepts

I turn to the last piece of the analysis, subclaim 4: The [necessary and a priori$_O$ rule of synthesis that yields a representation] makes it possible to unite the diverse elements in a concept. Kant supports this claim with a simple assertion: "All representation [*Erkenntnis*] demands a concept" (A106). Here is the controversial premise noted earlier. The task of representing an object requires the use of concepts. George... be right that Kant gets this idea from Condillac. The problem... has no right to make the assumption. If Tetens is a reliable witness, ... then whether or not cognitive states could enable us to represent objects in the absence of concepts was a disputed question.

Nevertheless the major issue in the dispute over the existence of mere cognitive states is not yet decided. . . . *Are there cognitive states in us that are regarded as images and signs, sufficiently articulate, and sharply enough separated from others in the imagination, so that they themselves and through them, their objects, can be differentiated from others? . . . Are they and can they be fully prepared and apperceptible without being actually apperceived at the same time? Or must they perhaps receive that material clarity only first, through the same act through which they are actually perceived and are actually used as pictures and signs? through the act in which they are informed with consciousness, and become ideas [my emphasis]?* That is, it is an open question whether cognitive states can indicate objects before they have been brought under intellectual representations. Since analyses of empirical capacities can only presuppose well-established facts, this part of Kant's analysis rests on a mistake, even if the claim turns out to be correct.[48]

Kant's Defensible Results

Synthesis and the Productive Imagination

The core of Kant's analysis is that we cannot represent objects at all unless there is some process that can construct unified representations on the basis of the multiple contents of cognitive states occurring at different times through the mediation of different senses. Any possible explanation of object cognition must include an account of this process of connection or synthesis. Further, this process cannot be governed by the unaided law of association. Synthesis must be carried out inside the mind, so it requires some mental faculty that has the power of synthesizing. Kant labels this faculty "imagination" (A120). More precisely, because he believes that we have an empirical "reproductive" faculty of imagination (that is governed by the empirical law of association), he claims that we have a second, "productive" imagination, which is a "transcendental," "*a priori*$_o$," and "pure" faculty. "Productive" is used to make a contrast with a faculty that (only) follows the law of association, so the first epithet is justified. So is the characterization of the productive imagination as "transcendental," if that indicates only that this faculty is necessary for knowledge. If it means that this faculty makes any a priori$_0$ contribution to cognition, then this claim, like those for apriority$_0$ and purity, has not been adequately supported.

Kant posits a mental faculty, but this is hardly wild psychological speculation. His analysis invokes two unwarranted assumptions: Representations must be able to be brought under concepts, and there is but one rule for connecting the contents of cognitive states in a representation, that associated with the concept of an object in general (the transcendental object = x) (A109). Perhaps the latter assumption is not what it appears. He may intend "the rule" associated with the concept of a transcendental object only as a metarule that stands indifferently for a variety of rules. He offers no argument that there must be a single rule for representing objects. Still, the presentation is misleading and the "transcendental object = x" appropriately disappears from the second edition, even though he maintains his general position on the synthetic unity required for representing objects (B137, B139). These assumptions should not be granted. Even if they are rejected, however, the central portion of the analysis remains intact. We can represent objects only if the imagination has rules of synthesis for combining the multiple contents of cognitive states in a unified representation. Why has this reasonably clear, well-argued, and modest proposal been denigrated so consistently? The main reason is the nearly universal resistance to any appearance of psychological material in philosophy. However, Kant's discussions of synthesis have also raised two specific objections that need to be addressed. One arises because his arguments for *rules* of synthesis sometimes involve a confusion of levels. The effects of this confusion can be seen clearly in the most extensive discussion of the theory of rule-governed synthesis available in English, Robert Paul Wolff's unfashionably psychological commentary.[49]

Robert Paul Wolff on Rules of Synthesis

Wolff regards rule-governed synthesis as the centerpiece of Kant's work, because it promises to solve the problem of unity among diversity. If an activity is governed by a rule, then it has a coherence and completeness (and hence a unity), despite the diversity of its parts. I do not agree that Kant is trying to explain the unity of an activity (synthesis). As I note earlier, the *explanandum* is the unity of a representation; the *explanans* is that it was produced from diverse states by a rule-governed synthesis. Wolff goes on to characterize a number of features of rule-directed activities. He then observes, however, that synthesis must be "preconscious."[50] The problem is that it is very hard to see how rule-directed activities, as he describes them, could be preconscious (or unconscious). Wolff tackles these matters explicitly, but I suspect that many readers have engaged in similar reflections. The upshot is that Kant's position seems incoherent.

Although textual infelicities (which I note later) makes these interpretive problems understandable, Kant's basic position on rule-governed synthesis is clear. The syntheses that produce representations are not conscious processes. He attributes them to the imagination, which is explicitly characterized as a "*blind*, but indispensable function of the soul" (A78/B103, my emphasis). Further, Kant has as clear an understanding as anyone of the distinction between conscious and unconscious rules. He presents this very distinction in the *Groundwork*: "Everything in nature works according to laws. Only a rational being has the capacity of acting according to the conception of laws."[51] Wolff's description of rule-governed activities strongly suggests that rule followers act according to their conception of the rules. But rules govern syntheses only as the law of gravity governs the movements of the planets: Theorists can appeal to these rules to describe what is happening. Kant's text is confusing, because he makes unwitting shifts between the perspective of the individual who is engaging in various mental activities and that of the theorist who is describing those activities.[52] So, for example, he suggests that individuals can only represent a number if they are conscious of its production from the synthesis of units (A103). Wolff relies heavily on this passage, and does not take account of the fact that in the very next paragraph, Kant doubts that we [as individuals] are aware of any such thing, even though we [as theorists] must assume that it takes place.[53]

The "Problem" of Early Cognition

The second problem about synthesis arises because it seems to many that accounts of early cognition must be, like their subject, inarticulate. So in trying to describe the prerequisites of various cognitive tasks, including full conceptual thought, Kant and his heirs must lapse into babble. Onora O'Neill addresses this worry in her unusually sympathetic article on transcendental psychology.[54] She offers a strategy for avoiding the difficulty. Instead of trying to describe what life would be like without indispensable concepts, Kantians can shift the burden to opponents. As the opponents try to describe a situation where these concepts are lacking, Kantians could point out that *they* have fallen into incoherence.[55] Although this tactic might be useful in some cases, I believe that it misrepresents the thrust of Kant's psychological analyses. In analyzing cognitive tasks, he looks at the ability, then looks at the known resources, and then argues that we can only explain the ability by assuming some additional resources (typically a faculty and/or *a priori*$_O$ elements). His criticism of opponents would not be that they are incoherent but that they cannot explain the cognitive abilities that we have. Once we see the form of these analyses, however, the reply to the charge of inevitable inarticulateness is straightforward. Since Kant appeals to known resources, his accounts of the early stages of cognition are no more problematic than those of his peers; in particular, there is nothing in his method that requires him to try to describe these "from the inside."

Kant's many appeals to rules and his efforts to describe the early stages of cognition raise suspicions about the soundness of the doctrine of synthesis. As I have just argued, however, neither of these issues provides any justification for dismissing the account. Kant's confusions about rules are only text deep. When he is being careful, he presents these rules as unconscious; it is only when trying to explain cognition that we must be cognizant of rules of synthesis.

Constructing Representations of Objects and the "Binding" Problem

In Chapter 6 I consider how the analysis of the task of representing objects contributes to an argument for a special status for the categories. Since that demonstration is unsuccessful, if ingenious, any enduring value of the analysis must be intrinsic. Kant's analysis is both partial and preliminary, but it advances the subject. The Lockeans realized that cognitive states can inform us about objects only if they are derived from sensory contact with objects, but they saw little need for elaborate mental processing. Connections among mental states could be explained by appealing to the law of association. Leibniz and his followers appreciated that representation involved the unity of diverse contents in a single state. At one level, the doctrine of synthesis is a classic Kantian "synthesis" of the insights of his predecessors. By appealing to synthesis, he can explain how representations can have unity and yet be anchored in sensory contact with objects. Although this point will be more fully developed in the next chapter, synthesis also provides the basis for Kant's plausible functionalist account of how cognitive states can rep-

resent at all. This is possible because representations are produced fi ___
sensory states that are directly caused by objects themselves and because
they can interact with other representations to produce further representations.

At another level, however, Kant's account is no mere synthesis of
previous views. In revealing the dependence of a simple task like representing objects on synthesis, he gives a forceful demonstration of the
need to consider the constructive powers of the mind. His contemporaries accepted the facts on which his analysis rests. We have unified
representations of objects; we receive a constantly varied stream of
sensory stimulation from diverse senses. But they did not fully realize
the startling implications of those facts. If conscious life is a series of
unified representations, and sensory stimulation offers a diverse and
ever-changing flow of information, then the mind must constantly be
engaged in synthesizing. Hence, the Deduction's constant references to
synthesis.

With the renaissance of interest in cognition, this issue has reemerged,
sometimes under the name of the "binding" problem. Anne Treisman
discusses aspects of it in a recent article in *Scientific American*.[56] How,
for example, can the color, shape, and luminance of an object all be
brought together in a representation of one object with those various
properties? Treisman's work has offered dramatic experimental confirmation of the theoretical argument for the existence of processes of
connection. We must engage in combining, because sometimes we do
it erroneously. By requiring subjects to take in a variety of items at a
glance, she and her colleagues induced them to perceive "illusory conjunctions."[57] When rapidly presented with a display of a purple E, an
orange S, and a green V in a row, for example, some subjects will claim
that they have seen an orange V. The illusion is so strong that subjects
often resist the suggestion that they have erred.

Like synthesis, the binding problem has a ubiquitous quality. For as
Patricia Churchland has observed, if we can figure out how the nervous
system integrates information from various sources, then it is not clear
that there would be anything interesting left to know about it.[58] Current
work has focused on how information from different sensory modalities
can be combined and on how different features within a modality can
be combined. Kant emphasized the problem created by the temporal
dimension of cognition:

> all our representations are subject to time ... and in it they must be or-
> dered, connected, and brought into a relation. This is a general obser-

vation which must be understood as fundamental throughout what follows [A99, amended translation].

Although there may be as many different binding problems as there are features to be combined, the temporal issue seems fundamental. For it is hard to see how any binding problem can be completely solved without solving a problem of temporal integration; and if there is any uniform solution to binding problems, then it seems plausible to believe that it would involve temporal integration. Thus, in insisting that the temporal character of cognitive life requires synthesis, and in ruling out the simple solution of spatiotemporal contiguity, Kant offers an abstract analysis of the task of representing objects that is still useful in conceptualizing the problem to be solved.

Finally, although the analysis of representing objects does not demonstrate the necessity of a priori$_O$ elements, it makes this a serious possibility. Even basic representations of objects need to be constructed. Thus, the constitution of our minds may influence our knowledge in very basic ways. Although this is a far weaker result than Kant wanted, even a plausibility argument for the thesis that what we know reflects our ways of knowing is an important result. What is hard to understand about the recent history of philosophy is how this result could ever have been regarded as irrelevant to epistemology and the philosophy of mind.

Making Judgments About Objects

The Problem of Judgment

The objective Deduction takes a very different form in the second edition. In a well-known footnote to the preface of *The Metaphysical Foundations of Natural Science* (1786), Kant estimates that the deduction of the categories could be carried out "almost by a single conclusion" from an exact definition [or analysis] of the act of judgment.[59] Accordingly, the second edition Deduction focuses on the task of making judgments about objects, although there are still important references to the requirements of representing objects (e.g., B137). By "judgment" Kant does not mean an expressed judgment; he uses the term ambiguously between silent or expressed judgments and the representational cognitive states that produce them. Like the analysis of representing objects, this analysis is not directed against skeptical opponents. Paragraph 19, where the discussion is centered, presupposes that we can make judgments about objects.

Kant opens the discussion with an explicit criticism of previous accounts. Logicians characterize judgment as "a relation between two concepts" (B141).[60] Of what this relation consists, however, they do not inform us. To appreciate Kant's analysis of this capacity it is again helpful to consider some contemporary alternatives. By Tetens's account, most teachers of reasoning regard judgments as "nothing more than the comparison and recognition of identity and differences [between ideas]."[61] This view was shared by Leibnizeans and Lockeans. Locke was explicit that in judging we presume agreement or disagreement between ideas, even if we do not see it clearly.[62] The principle of sufficient reason entails that the predicate of a judgment be related to the subject by difference or by partial identity. Condillac concurs: "[In judging] . . . we compare our ideas, the consciousness we have of them is the cause of our knowing that they are the same . . . or else is the cause of our knowing that they are not the same. . . ."[63] Tetens points out that this widespread assumption cannot be correct.

> Since not every relation [between ideas or concepts in a judgment] consists in identity or difference [or containment or lack of containment], the act of judging cannot always be comparison. . . . There must be many more judgments of different forms. . . .[64]

Besides comparison, the other obvious option for connecting ideas in a judgment was the law of association. This alternative is very much on Kant's mind. He sets up the problem by announcing that he will try to explain how judgment—as opposed to mere association of ideas—is possible (B141). Later, he observes that, in a judgment, we claim that properties occur together in an object (e.g., "Bodies are heavy"). The law of association only connects ideas through their co-occurrence in the subject: "When I have the impression of a body, I also have the impression of heaviness" (B142). Presumably, the problem with association is the one encountered before. It is too promiscuous. The contents of representations may be connected by association, even when the properties represented are not connected in objects.

Kant's analysis of the task of making judgments includes several negative theses. We make judgments about objects. Assume provisionally that judgments involve a connection of concepts. This connection cannot be a matter of conceptual connection (one concept being identical with or contained in the other), for in judging that objects are heavy, "I certainly do not say that the [contents of] these cognitive states belong *necessarily to each other* . . . " (B142, my translation, original emphasis). On the other hand, the connection of concepts in a judgment about objects cannot be explained by invoking the law of association, because association is too promiscuous. Although Kant does not recur to this point in analyzing judgment, I might add that because objects themselves are outside our minds, there is no point in appealing to them to explain how we connect concepts in a judgment. If connections established by the law of association are too liberal and conceptual connections are too strong, then how can concepts be connected in a judgment that represents the properties they signify as connected in an object?

The Synthesis of Intuitions

It is easier to follow Kant's positive analysis if we recall the parallel problem about representing objects. Since objects themselves could not furnish the requisite unity for representations, we needed a surrogate: a rule of synthesis for connecting the multiple contents of cognitive states. The reasoning underlying the account of judgment is the same. The connection of concepts in a judgment can only be explained by positing some (nonassociative) rules of synthesis that do the connecting.

Looking back to Kant's earlier analysis of representing objects, we can see that judgment actually requires two levels of synthesis. One level is needed to produce representations from the fluctuating stream of cognitive states. In the present discussion, he investigates how the contents of given representations [*Erkenntnisse*] can be related in a judgment.[65] He poses the problem in terms reflecting the standard view: How are two *concepts* related in a judgment? However, having shown the difficulty in appealing to conceptual connections, he casts his solution in terms of representations and intuitions and their contents. If the contents represented in a judgment are going to relate to an object, then they must be related to each other by a synthesis of intuitions (B142). That is, the relation between contents that are represented in a judgment can be grounded in sensory data only if there are rules of synthesis that enable us to connect the contents of representations that are themselves fairly directly related to objects (see also A69/B94). Thus, judgments require a synthesis of intuitions [*Erkenntnisse*] (B142).

Kant's analysis of making judgments is hard to follow, because it is intertwined with considerations about the requirements of apperception. If those elements are teased out, then the analysis is quite straightforward. The representations in judgments are not related by identity, difference, containment, or mere association; rather, they belong to one another by virtue of a synthesis of intuitions. In a sense, there is one relation between representations in a judgment: They are related by a synthesis of intuitions. In another sense, however, the relation varies, because it is produced by sensory data (by rules for synthesizing that data into representations) and by rules for synthesizing representations into judgments. That is why logicians cannot tell us of what these relations consist.

The "One-Step" Deduction

In paragraph 20 Kant moves quickly from this analysis to an argument for a special status for the categories. He has shown that judgments must be constructed by rules or functions of synthesis. The Metaphysical Deduction claimed that there are twelve forms of judgment and that the categories are associated with those forms. Kant now asserts that the categories are (or are associated with) the rules or functions that produce judgments (B143). With these additions, the analysis of judgment is able to provide a direct argument for the universal applicability of the categories: Anything that we can know, or at least anything that we can judge, must be amenable to synthesizing by functions associated with the categories.[66]

Although almost the one-step deduction that Kant promised, the argument is too quick. As many have noted, he does not adequately defend the table of judgments or the alleged connections between these forms and the categories.[67] Further, nothing in the analysis of making judgments establishes that the rules of synthesis are even *a priori*. Again, he has only shown that the law of association cannot serve as such a rule.

Constructing Judgments

Although I accept the usual verdict that this analysis cannot serve as the basis for a sound argument for the categories, I believe that it has intrinsic merits. Most important, Kant reveals the inadequacy of popular alternatives. Judgments about objects cannot merely be a matter of relations between concepts or terms. This would include relations of containment, and also syntactic relations among expressions (see B128–29).[68] A purely formal approach to judgment can never explain our capacity for making judgments about objects. On the other hand, the obvious failings of the law of association suggest that judgments cannot be explained by appealing to simple patterns of sensory stimulation either. So, like the analysis of representing objects, Kant's constructive account of judgment requires us to consider more seriously how the mind might construct judgments on the basis of more subtle sensory patterns. Like the previous account, it also opens up the possibility that our mental apparatus affects cognition in very fundamental ways. It even raises the *possibility* that the mind has a limited set of rules for constructing judgments, so that there are, in fact, forms of judgment. Thus, the analysis of making judgments about objects offers a plausibility argument for some of Kant's key doctrines.

The Objective and Subjective Sides of the Deduction

Kant's discussions of synthesis and representing and judging objects are far too cryptic, because they are overshadowed by a particular consequence of his analyses. Once this discovery is announced, other issues are not fully explored but are pushed to one side. In the second edition the analysis of judgment does not occur until five sections into the chapter, and is largely cast in terms of this other issue. I have not discussed this result, partly to permit an exploration of other points, and partly because I will be devoting Chapters 4 and 5 to an extended study of it.

Both the analysis of representing objects and the analysis of judgment demonstrate the need for synthesis. This is Kant's constant theme in the Deduction chapter, presented in several variations in both editions. For knowledge to be possible, we must synthesize cognitive states in representations, representations in judgments, and combine judgments with further judgments through reasoning (A303/B359ff). More generally, "Cognition [*Erkenntnis*] is a whole in which the contents of cognitive states are compared and connected" (A97, my translation). It is a theme with two parts. At all levels, the constructive syntheses required for basic cognitive tasks reveal possibilities for mental structures to influence cognition; and, at all levels, they place a requirement on the subject. Any subject capable of performing these tasks must have cognitive states related by synthesis. This is why the objective and subjective Deductions are inseparable and can be distinguished only in terms of focus. In this chapter, I have looked at cognitive tasks from the objective side. Given that we can represent and judge objects, how in general is this possible? The next two chapters explore the subjective side. What must a subject be like simply by virtue of being able to have mental representations?

4

Replying to Hume's Heap

Troubles with Apperception

Avoiding the Subjective Deduction

When Kant focuses on the demands that cognitive tasks put on the subject, he proclaims the existence of a "transcendental unity of apperception". "Why not call it the transcendental *diversity* of apperception?", Richard Rorty once inquired.[1] Rorty's irony reflects a common reaction among less sympathetic readers of the *Critique*. With this doctrine Kant's tendency to sesquipedality becomes intolerable. The troubles that contemporary readers have with apperception go far deeper than matters of terminological style, however. This doctrine is Kant's principal teaching about the necessary attributes of a being capable of cognitive experience. As such, it is the centerpiece of the subjective Deduction. For reasons now familiar, recent interpreters have sought to downplay the subjective side of this chapter and to cleanse its central claims of any taint of psychology. The doctrine of apperception presents a formidable challenge to this strategy. Its centrality is beyond question and its topic is a necessary attribute of a thinker. Seemingly, the only way to protect Kant against the charge of psychologism is to maintain that it is a nonpsychological, or innocuously psychological, claim about thinkers. Three versions of this strategy are well represented in the literature. As I will argue, all have serious weaknesses.

Apperception as the Cogito

The simplest strategy interprets *die transzendentale Einheit* (unity) *der Apperception* as a German variation of Descartes' *cogito*.[2] On this reading, the doctrine of apperception is the starting premise of the deduction of the categories. Presumably, this interpretation is suggested by the precise wording of the best-known statement of the doctrine: "It must be possible for the I think to accompany all my cognitive states" (B131, amended translation). It may also be favored, because the *cogito* is perceived as the correct starting place for a philosophical argument.[3] If the doctrine of apperception asserted nothing more than the *cogito*, then it would be a certain, even if psychological, premise. Despite these advantages, there is an overwhelming objection to this assimilation. Kant criticizes the *cogito* explicitly and at length in the Paralogisms chapter.[4]

Strawson and the Self-Ascription Reading

Strawson introduced a second reading that distances apperception from unwonted psychological connotations. Apperception is the doctrine that subjects must be able to ascribe mental states to themselves.[5] In Strawson's words:

> Unity of consciousness to which a series of experiences belong implies, then, the *possibility* of self-ascription . . . [that is] the *possibility* of consciousness, on the part of the subject, of the numerical identity of that to which those different experiences are by him ascribed.[6]

The idea that self-ascription is the core of the apperception thesis is echoed by more recent British commentators:

> *T. E. Wilkerson*: "Self-consciousness is more happily described as the ability to identify one's own experiences as one's own."[7]

> *Ralph C. S. Walker*: "an experience cannot be mine unless I am at least potentially aware of it as such."[8]

> *Roger Scruton*: "It [the unity of apperception] consists in my immediate awareness that simultaneous experiences belong to me."[9]

The perceived virtue of this reading is that it allows an appealing reconstruction of the deduction of the categories, in terms of the "logic" of self-ascription. Again, apperception is the first premise and it asserts that subjects must be able to self-ascribe mental states. In the Refutation of Idealism and the Second Analogy, the argument can then be made that self-ascription of mental states requires that we can make certain kinds of judgments about objects.[10] As Strawson puts it:

The more fundamental point of the Kantian provisions is that the experiences of such a subject [one who can self-ascribe] must themselves be so conceptualized as to determine a distinction between the subjective route of his experiences and the objective world through which it is a route.[11]

Although this reconstruction does not purport to vindicate the categories per se, it is regarded as a good argument for a position quite like Kant's. The argument is supposed to be good, because it has the form of a transcendental argument.

In Chapter 1 I noted the intrinsic problems of transcendental arguments and argued that there are systematic reasons for not casting Kant's reasoning in this mold.[12] Since the Strawsonian reconstruction of the argument from apperception has enjoyed widespread acceptance, I add three further objections to this key example. All are directed against the reconstruction as an interpretation.[13]

First, a textual point. In Kemp Smith's translation, apperception is presented in terms of *ascribing* experiences only once, at A122. "For it is only because I ascribe all perceptions to one consciousness (original apperception) that I can say of all perceptions that I am conscious of them." "Ascribe" is Kemp Smith's translation of "*zählen zu.*" However, it would be at least as reasonable to render the phrase: "For it is only because I classify all perceptions with one consciousness . . . ," or, "For it is only because I take all perceptions to belong to one consciousness. . . ." When Kant presents the relation between cognitive states and a single consciousness, he standardly uses *gehören* ("belong") and its derivatives,[14] so the last rendering of A122 seems best. Without this one piece of explicit textual support, the self-ascription reading must rely on highly contentious texts, such as B132 and A116.

On this reconstruction, the Refutation of Idealism assumes a central role, because that is the only place where Kant talks about cognitive relations to objects being necessary to consciousness of one's own existence. Should the Refutation have such prominence? Since it was added in the second edition, the first edition cannot be interpreted along these lines. Further, there is no indication either in the prefatory footnote about the Refutation, in the second edition Deduction, or in the Refutation itself that this section is needed to complete the deduction of the categories. The more obvious hypothesis is that Kant was stung by the comparison of his position to Berkeley's, and added this section and a couple of other remarks to reinforce the explicit contrast that he had drawn in the *Prolegomena.*[15] Berkeley denied the existence of the material world; while discussing the category of actuality, Kant interrupts himself to offer a reply. The location itself suggests that the Refutation is not an integral part of the deduction, but only an aside, a reply to critics. Nathan Rostenreich raises a substantive objection to linking the Refutation and the doctrine of apperception.[16] The Refutation is concerned with the empirical consciousness of one's own existence—the recognition of one's particular mental history (Bx1). Kant explicitly contrasts apperception with the empirical unity of consciousness, however (B139–40). In Chapter 5 I return to the issue of self-ascription and argue that the ability of subjects to identify cognitive states as their own is only a small and bungled part of the doctrine of apperception.[17]

The "Logical" Reading of Apperception

The most direct strategy for depsychologizing the doctrine of apperception is to present it as a logical, as opposed to psychological, thesis. Wilkerson combines this strategy with the self-ascription reading: "The unity of self-consciousness is . . . a formal unity consisting simply of the formal fact that experiences are mine."[18] Allison claims that the act of becoming aware of the identical self is "the form of the act of reflection . . . it is nothing more than the 'logical act' . . . [original scare-quotes]."[19] This approach seems to be supported by numerous texts (e.g., the I think is a *logical* subject of thought [A350], or a *formal* subject of thought [A105]. It is not always clear what is meant by "logical" or "formal" in these readings. No one believes that it is a fact of formal logic that mental states belong to a subject of thought.[20] The force of "formal" is carried by the implicit contrast with "psychological."[21] Thus, this approach makes sense only on the presupposition of a sharp contrast between what Kant meant by "logical" and what we mean by "psychological." As Chapter 1 made clear, however, this presupposition is false. Kant believes that logic investigates the rules governing the understanding. Transcendental logic "concerns itself with the laws of understanding and reason solely insofar as they relate *a priori* to objects" (A57/B82).

   In criticizing these well-known approaches to apperception, I do not suggest that commentators have not been ingenious or that they have not provided useful insights into Kant's position. My point is that they have tied themselves to an interpretive strategy that is bound to be inadequate. The doctrine of apperception is about the primary attribute of thinkers that is necessary for cognition. As such, it is a thesis in transcendental psychology and can only be understood in these terms.

Besides this central difficulty, two other widespread mistakes have hampered interpretations of apperception, one interpretive and one historical.

Two Mistaken Assumptions

As noted, apperception is often regarded as the unargued first premise of the transcendental deduction.[22] This interpretation makes some sense, if Kant's doctrine is assimilated to the *cogito*. Even then, however, it is not very plausible. Could Kant have expected his readers simply to grant a thesis that presupposed the soundness of his own highly technical vocabulary? In any case, this assimilation is highly questionable in light of Kant's later criticisms of the *cogito*.

The historical mistake supports the interpretive one. Historians have taken Kant to be ignorant of Hume's attack on certain metaphysicians [Descartes], who claim to espy a simply and continuing self in themselves. Later, I will present conclusive evidence that he was aware of this critique. Thus, a fairly standard assumption about apperception, that Kant adopted Descartes's starting point for philosophy without benefit of Hume's insights, is exactly backward.

Hume

Given that Kant was aware of Hume's famous denial of mental unity, he could not simply assert that mental life involves unity. He had too much respect for Hume to ignore his criticisms. To maintain the unity of a thinker, he had to demonstrate it. If we reconsider the task analyses of the last chapter in this light, however, then they offer something close to the needed demonstration. The analyses of representing and judging objects establish two important facts about thinkers. Most obviously, any thinker who shares our basic constitution, and so takes in information through a stream of sensory impressions, must have a productive imagination. They also demonstrate a slightly less obvious fact. To represent objects, for example, the productive imagination must combine information from diverse cognitive states in a unified representation. Some cognitive states must, therefore, depend on the existence of others.[23] The syntheses that result in judgments create further dependency relations. Thus, *pace* Hume, there must be real connections among some cognitive states.

To represent objects and to judge them, a thinker must synthesize the contents of diverse cognitive states, thereby creating a "synthetic unity"—a unity produced by synthesis—among the states, as well as a synthetic unity in the contents of the resulting state. This synthetic unity is required for tasks that make up cognitive experience. Further, Kant thinks that the rules guiding the syntheses are *a priori*$_o$. This synthetic unity should, therefore, be characterized as "transcendental," within his system. From these analyses, Kant can extract an argument for a "transcendental [or "synthetic"] unity of apperception," with a clear anti-Humean import. (And although the labels may strike us as pretentiously technical, they have a point.)

Conceivably, this outcome of his analyses is a happy coincidence. It seems far more reasonable, however, to assume that it was intended. In which case, Kant's analyses of cognitive tasks have two objectives: Reveal the influence of the mind's own constitution on cognition and demonstrate the existence of real connections among the cognitive states of a single thinker, thus replying to the most skeptical of Hume's positions. I will argue later that we can make a great deal of sense of specific aspects of the apperception doctrine, if we take the Deduction chapter to have both goals.

Although the analyses of representing and judging objects yield the desired conclusion, they cannot provide direct arguments against Hume. They begin by assuming that we can represent and judge objects "outside" us, and Hume denied this in "Of skepticism with regard to the senses."[24] To succeed in his antiskeptical argument, Kant must show that the unity of a thinker is a necessary condition for some cognitive task that even Hume will not deny. This leads him to consider another cognitive capacity. How can thinkers have cognitive states that at least represent some content *to them*? It is this analysis that leads Kant to hold that the transcendental unity of apperception is an absolutely fundamental fact about any cognitive being.

Although the argument *from* apperception for the categories is unsound, the breach occurs at a later stage.[25] In this chapter I argue that the case for apperception is solid and constitutes an effective reply to Hume. This result is nearly as significant for philosophy as a demonstration of the categories. For in establishing the necessary unity of apperception, Kant defends a cognitive account of mental unity that is superior both to contemporary rivals and to present-day accounts. When the doctrine of apperception is approached as it must be—as a conclusion established by transcendental psychology—it emerges as a powerful solution to the problem of mental unity.

In the next section, I document Kant's knowledge of Hume's position and give a precise statement of it. With that available I shall argue that synthesis creates exactly the relation among cognitive states that Hume denied. Finally, I present Kant's arguments for the claim that merely being able to have cognitive states that represent something to us requires that our states be connected by synthesis. This is Kant's reply to Hume's skepticism about personal identity. In Chapter 5 I elaborate and defend the resulting account of mental unity, thus supporting my contention that this is a major, if largely unappreciated, contribution of the Deduction chapter.

Hume's Problem

Hume's Absence

My interpretation of the subjective Deduction depends on the historical claim that the doctrine of apperception is, in part, a reply to Hume's skepticism about personal identity. Having criticized others, it is only fair to point out that my own interpretation faces an obvious, seemingly insurmountable, objection. Hume's name does not appear in any of the passages where I claim that Kant is trying to refute the bundle theory of the self. His account of personal identity is not mentioned even once in the *Critique*!

Although this evidence may seem conclusive, the picture changes dramatically if we consider Kant's references to opponents systematically. He regularly fails to mention the protagonists in his discussions by name: Leibniz is not mentioned in the Paralogisms chapter or in the Aesthetic's discussion of space and time[26]; none of Kant's discussions of space or time in the *Critique* refers to Newton; the Second Analogy contains no reference to Hume; and, most surprisingly, in the first edition, Kant's interest in causation is not linked to Hume at all until the Discipline of Pure Reason, 550 pages after his celebrated reply in the Second Analogy. As I noted in Chapter 2, some of Kant's reticence about his targets is probably due to the fact that they were obvious to his readers. Whatever the reason, the habit of not placing his discussions in their historical context has enormous potential for misleading later scholars. Imagine trying to understand the Aesthetic's metaphysical claims about space and time outside the context of the Newton–Leibniz debate! In the case of Hume and apperception, that potential has been fully realized.

Kant's omission has been compounded by an error of Norman Kemp Smith's. One of Kemp Smith's most important contributions was the discovery that Kant would have been familiar with Hume's extensive discussion of causation in the *Treatise*, through generous citations in the German translation of James Beattie's *Essay on the Nature and Immutability of Truth*.[27] When discussing a passage from the Deduction, however, he writes, "Kant teaches, in agreement with Hume, *though, as we may believe, independently of his direct influence*, that there is no single empirical state of the self which is constant throughout experience" (my emphasis).[28] He supports this opinion with a footnote reminding his readers that personal identity is not discussed in the *Inquiry* and claiming that it is not mentioned by Beattie. This is simply false, however. As we will see, Beattie allows Hume to speak for himself in laying out the theory of the self that he intends to ridicule. Robert Paul Wolff has suggested that Kemp Smith makes this error because he checked the sixth edition of Beattie's book, whereas the German translation was made from the first.[29] This is not right either. In the sixth edition, Beattie simply leaves out Hume's name, referring to him instead, for example, as "our author," but still provides generous citations on personal identity.[30] However it came about, Kemp Smith's testimony that Kant had no direct knowledge of Hume's position has led subsequent scholars away from the obvious hypothesis that the Deduction's many references to the necessary unity of mental life were directed against his predecessor's denial of unity.

Kant's Knowledge of Hume's Position

Kant knew about Hume's attack on the self and so did his readers. Besides Beattie's long and popular (if silly) discussion, Hume's theory was also referred to by J. C. Lossius (who probably knew it through Beattie).[31] Tetens attempted a reply of his own in his *Philosophische Versuche*.[32] His presentation suggests that his audience was familiar both with Hume's denial of personal identity and with the criticisms of Reid and Beattie. In Tetens's estimation the replies of Reid and Beattie are "not incorrect, but unphilosophical." Unfortunately, his own solution is both: There is an additional feeling that accompanies mental states that Hume "overlooked."

At the time Kant was writing the *Critique*, Hume's views on personal identity were known in Germany and were considered obviously false, as they had been in his native Scotland. Still, the "refutations" of this scandalous position were far from satisfactory. Did Kant believe that it was important to discover the real error of Hume's ways? He clearly

appreciated the insights behind Hume's skeptical positions and t
that he could learn from them. Further, the denial of the self presents
an enormous intellectual challenge, because it is both obviously false
and very difficult to refute. Given these provocations, had Kant *not*
responded to Hume's challenge, scholars would need to consider why
he felt no obligation to do so.

Beattie's *Essay on Truth* provided Kant with the following excerpts
from Hume's attack:

> The question concerning the substance of the soul is unintelligible...
> What we call a *mind* is nothing but a heap or collection of different
> perceptions (or objects) united together by certain relations and supposed,
> though falsely, to be endowed with perfect simplicity and identity... If
> anyone, upon serious and unprejudiced reflection, thinks he has a different
> notion of himself, I must confess I can reason with him no longer. All I
> can allow him is, that he may be in the right as well as I, and that we are
> essentially different in this particular. He may perhaps perceive something
> simple and continued, which he calls *himself*; though I am certain there
> is no such principle in me. But setting aside some metaphysicians of this
> kind, I may venture to affirm of the rest of mankind, that they are nothing
> but a bundle or collection of different perceptions, which succeed each
> other with inconceivable rapidity, and are in a perpetual flux and move-
> ment.... There is properly no simplicity in the mind at one time, nor
> identity in different (times), whatever natural propension we may have
> to imagine that simplicity and identity.... They are successive perceptions
> only that constitute the mind....[33]

Beattie omits some parts of Hume's position on the self. He fails to
mention the causal theory and Hume's despair in the appendix. [34] Still,
the excerpts contain three central and distinctive theses about the self,
two in opposition to the Cartesian view. As Hume notes, there is no
reason to believe that there is an entity in one that thinks; *a fortiori*,
there is no reason to believe that there is a simple, thinking self.

Like Kant, Hume accepts Locke's analogy between sensory perception and a faculty of "inner sense" through which we "perceive" the
contents of our minds. Although Locke's characterization of our ability
to monitor and report mental states is misleading, Hume was not misled
by it on this point. Whatever he expected inner sense to divulge, he
realized that it did not enable him to perceive a thinking self. His conces-
sion that another may perhaps perceive such a self is an obvious bit of
mockery. Since inner sense does not show us a self at all, it cannot
disclose the existence of a simple self. Kant agrees with Hume's reasons

for denying the Cartesian account. In the Deduction, he points out, in terms strikingly reminiscent of Hume's discussions, that inner sense does not reveal a self:

> The consciousness of the self, according to the determinations of our state in inner perception, is merely empirical, and always changing. There can be no permanent and continuing self in this flux of inner appearances... [A107, my translation].

***

> For the empirical consciousness, which accompanies different representations, is in itself diverse and without relation to the identity of the subject.... [If inner sense were the only means of cognizing a self], I should have as many-colored and diverse a self as I have representations of which I am conscious to myself [B133–34].

Kant repeats this point in the Paralogisms chapter, twice in the first edition and once in the second (A350, A381, B413). These passages fairly shout allusions to Hume. A107 is the text that led Kemp Smith to consider and reject any direct influence. In specifying the absence of *direct* influence, he was presumably conceding indirect influence, although this subtlety may have been lost on later scholars.

Hume's third claim about the self presents his positive conception. A mind is a collection of different perceptions that are connected by certain relations that lead us to mistake a succession of different things for one enduring object. Although Beattie's citations do not say what those relations are, Kant would have no trouble figuring it out. In the *Inquiry*, Hume is explicit about the kinds of possible connections among mental states: resemblance, [spatiotemporal] contiguity, and causation.[35] Further, he would know what these relations signify for Hume. Although they might lead the mind to feel connections or identity across perceptions, they would not establish any real or necessary connections among them.

The Denial of Real Connection

Before considering Kant's reply to this position, it will be helpful to have a more precise characterization of it. The best place to find clarification is the famous passage in the appendix to the *Treatise*, where Hume admits that his account of personal identity is inconsistent. There are two principles that he can neither renounce nor render consistent: "that all our distinct perceptions are distinct existences, and that the mind never perceives any real connection among distinct existences."[36] As all readers quickly realize, these two principles are consistent, an issue to which I return later. For now I want to focus on the first principle, for that is the key to his positive view. In the discussion, he elaborates: "All perceptions are distinct. They are, therefore, distinguishable, and separable, and may be conceived as separately existent, and may exist separately, without any contradiction or absurdity."[37] In describing minds as made up of distinct perceptions only, Hume is denying any relations of existential dependence.[38] The mental states that constitute a single mind may exist separately without contradiction or absurdity; they do not depend upon each other for their existence or properties.

Why does Hume despair over his treatment of personal identity? In its more elaborate version, his second principle asserts: "If perceptions are distinct existences, they form a whole only by being connected together. But no connections among distinct existences are ever discoverable by human understanding. We only *feel* a connexion. . ."[39] He could achieve local consistency by maintaining that all perceptions are distinct and so have no real connections among them. He is obviously unwilling to accept this solution, however. Why? Consider his most famous explanation. We say that A's cause B's, because after A-perceptions and B-perceptions have been constantly conjoined, we expect a B-perception after experiencing an A-perception. Unfortunately, this statement of Hume's account ignores its hidden qualification. For if every time that *I* see an A, *someone else* sees a B, then there will be no expectation of a B, upon the presentation of an A. The qualification is that the perceptions belong to a single mind. Hume's account of causal thinking—like all his explanations of human thought—presuppose that the thoughts in question belong to a single mind. Individual minds are theoretical presuppositions of his own philosophy. Hence, it is not enough to provide an account (even an implausible one) of how the vulgar mistakenly come to believe in individual minds.[40] He must find some way of actually connecting diverse states in individual minds, but real connections among distinct existences cannot be found. The inconsistency Hume rightly fears is not within his account of personal identity, but between the demands of his general theory and the two principles he cannot renounce.[41]

Since Beattie does not quote from the appendix, Kant may not have had access to passages I have used to clarify Hume's position. Nevertheless, he knew enough about Hume's general views about causation and existential inferences to see the implication of the bundle theory. In the *Inquiry*, Hume is explicit that the existence of a cause without the existence of its effect is consistent and conceivable.[42] In his introduction to the Analogies, Kant is explicit that the principles that he will try to justify in reply to Hume concern relations of *"existence"* between objects (A179/B222). Thus, he would understand Hume's positive theory as implying that the different perceptions that we think of as belonging to one mind can exist in total separation from one another. The wonderful epithet "heap," which recurs in Kant's text,[43] itself confirms this reading. For Hume a person is a collection of intrinsically unrelated perceptions.

Hume failed to resolve the inconsistency within his system, because he believed that no connections could be discovered among distinct existences. At 107, where Kant virtually repeats Hume's description of the absence of a self in introspection, he also offers what appears to be a diagnosis of his predecessor's methodological error:

> The consciousness of the self, according to the determinations of our state in inner perception, is merely empirical and always changing. There can be no permanent and continuing self in this flux of inner appearances. What has *necessarily* to be represented as numerically identical cannot be thought as such through empirical data. To render such a transcendental presupposition valid, there must be a condition which precedes all experience, and which makes experience itself possible [A107].

As implicit criticism, this is inaccurate. Although Hume needed to establish actual connections among perceptions, he did not need *necessary* connections. Nevertheless, Kant's remarks provide a clear blueprint of his own strategy. He will try to establish the unity of a mind by arguing that we can explain how we perform various tasks that make up cognitive experience only by assuming such unity. He has a skeptical opponent, so insofar as his remarks are directed against Hume, he can only assume very minimal cognitive tasks.

Synthesis and Apperception

Connecting Cognitive States by Synthesis

Hume maintained that perceptions were distinct and unconnected. The Deduction chapter constantly refers to an act performed on cognitive states, "synthesis" in the first edition, "combination" [*Verbindung*] or "synthesis" in the second. Chapter 3 explored some aspects of the theory of synthesis. Synthesis is a process that realizes a function that yields representations as outputs from cognitive states or representations as inputs. Here I consider what this theory implies about the connections among cognitive states. For convenience I repeat Kant's original presentation of synthesis:

> By *synthesis*, in its most general sense, I understand the act of adding different cognitive states [or their contents] to each other and of comprehending their diverse [elements] in a single representation [A77/B103, my translation].

Synthesis is an act or process that leads to the diverse elements of different states being comprehended [*begreifen*] in a single representation. This is an odd turn of phrase. Kant's point seems to be that the elements of the earlier cognitive states are preserved or reflected in the resulting state. Without those cognitive states and their particular elements, syntheses would have nothing to combine and preserve. It follows that the later state exists and has a particular content, only because the earlier states existed. Synthetic processes thus lead to a relation of existential dependence among cognitive states. If Kant can demonstrate that syntheses, as just described, are required for cognitive tasks that Hume must acknowledge, then he will have established precisely the relation among cognitive states that his predecessor denied. Synthesis also induces a second, weaker relation among the earlier states. They are *connectible* by synthesis.

It might seem easier to note that "synthesis" appears to be a causal process for Kant, and thus that earlier and later cognitive states would be related as partial causes to effects. The problem with this terminology is that establishing a causal relation among cognitive states would not suffice to rebut Hume's denial of existential connection. For Kant has not yet argued against Hume's analysis of causation. Thus, in the Deduction he has to take a different tack. He needs to argue for a connection among cognitive states that is stronger than Hume's, without presupposing the Second Analogy's defense of a strong notion of causation.

Transcendental Synthesis

Although Kant discusses empirical syntheses, his real interest lies in transcendental syntheses. As we saw in Chapter 1, something is transcendental if it is a prerequisite for cognitive experience and involves *a priori*$_O$ elements.[44] In Chapter 3 I noted that Kant's arguments for *a priori*$_O$ elements in the syntheses required for representing and judging objects fall short. They establish only the necessity of syntheses guided by some rules other than the law of association. Insofar as the goal is only to demonstrate real connections among cognitive states, however, he only needs to establish the first condition for transcendental status. Syntheses are required for tasks that constitute cognitive experience.

Apperception and Transcendental Synthesis

Given what Kant means by "synthesis" and what he means by "transcendental," it would be shocking if he began the transcendental deduction by assuming the existence of transcendental syntheses. He virtually equates the doctrine of transcendental synthesis with the doctrine of apperception, however. At 118 he claims that a transcendental synthesis of imagination is prior to and necessary for apperception and at B134 that a priori synthesis is sufficient for it. "Synthetic unity of the diverse [elements] of intuitions, as produced [*hervorgebracht*] a priori, is thus the ground of the identity of apperception itself which precedes all my determinate thought" (amended translation). Finally, he identifies the two at B135:

> This amounts to saying, that I am conscious *a priori* of *a necessary synthesis of cognitive states, which is called the original synthetic unity of apperception*, under which all my given cognitive states must stand, but under which they must be brought through a synthesis [my translation, my emphasis].

Two synthetic unities are required for cognition. In the last chapter, we considered the synthetic unity of a representation that represents an object. Here Kant maintains that there must be a synthetic unity among cognitive states themselves. The unity of apperception, under which all my cognitive states must stand, is created through synthesis. Since the syntheses that create the unity of apperception are required for cognition, and since the unity itself is required for cognition, it is also a transcendental, or partly transcendental (see earlier), unity.

In proclaiming a transcendental unity of apperception, then, Kant asserts that a real connection among cognitive states, produced by *a priori*$_o$ syntheses, is a prerequisite for cognition. Clearly, this doctrine could not be assumed at the beginning of an argument. Equally clearly, it has nothing to do with the *cogito*.

So far, I have highlighted certain elements of this crucial passage—synthesis and synthetic unity—while ignoring others. What of the claim that I am "*a priori* conscious of a necessary synthesis of cognitive states," and what of the term "apperception" itself? "*A priori* conscious" suggests a special type of consciousness. It is hard to see what this could be, however. The only awareness that we have of our states is through inner sense. If Kant means to assert that we have another similar faculty, through which we are aware of a necessary synthesis of cognitive states, or a unity of apperception, then his position would be no better than Tetens's suggestion that Hume simply overlooked a feeling that accompanies perceptions. In Kant's version, Hume would overlook (or lack?) a special mode of self-awareness.

Henry Allison suggests that "*a priori* conscious" is just a "clumsy way of referring to . . . an awareness of something as necessarily the case."[45] This seems right, in light of Kant's multiple uses of "*a priori*." If the unity of apperception can be shown to be a necessary condition of cognitive experience, then our knowledge of the doctrine would be *a priori*$_K$. For the argument for apperception would not depend on particular experiences, but only on the possibility of cognitive experience. Further, what we know would have the logical form of *a priori*$_L$ claims.[46] In any world in which we can have cognitive experience, the unity of apperception would obtain. It is a necessary truth, in Kant's sense of "necessity." STOCKS

Apperception

I turn to "apperception" itself. On my account, the "unity of apperception" refers to the fact that cognitive states are connected to each other through syntheses required for cognition. "Apperception" does not indicate any awareness of a separate thing, a "self," or even that different cognitive states belong to a separate thing, a "self." Rather, they belong to the unity of apperception in being connected by syntheses to each other.

This account of apperception is not intended to be exhaustive. Certainly one important part of Kant's doctrine that I have not mentioned is the connection between apperception and the categories. He believes that the unity of apperception is brought about by syntheses that are guided by rules associated with the categories. I omit this aspect, because it does not bear on the soundness of the reply to Hume and because I do not believe that the arguments for categorically determined syntheses succeed.

Robert Pippin has objected that an earlier version of this account of apperception leaves out something else that is fundamental: the apparent reflexivity of apperception. He believes that it is an essential part of the Critical philosophy that "all human experience is ineliminably reflexive

... because, according to Kant, whenever I am conscious of anything, I also "apperceive" that it is *I* who am thusly conscious."[47]

One reason that it is difficult to give an adequate account of apperception is that this term, and its close relative "self-consciousness," were used by Kant's predecessors.[48] So questions arise about whether his usage implies any substantive agreements with earlier views. Certainly, Christian Wolff took human consciousness to be inherently reflexive, and he captured this claim in a doctrine of "apperception." According to Wolff, all cognition would be reflexive, because it involves both perception and "apperception," our ability to perceive our own perceptions, and so ourselves.[49] Despite the common terminology, Kant appears to reject this view completely when he complains that systems of psychology (presumably Wolff's) confuse inner sense and apperception (B153).

For textual reasons that I give later, I do not agree with Pippin's strong claims for reflexivity. Still, there are clearly elements in Kant's discussion that point in this direction. I suspect that these derive from some intriguing ideas of Leibniz. In two of his best-known works, the *Principles of Nature and of Grace* and the *Monadology*, Leibniz characterizes apperception as follows:

[Apperception is] ... consciousness or reflective knowledge of this inner state [of a monad] itself and which is not given to all souls, or to any soul all the time.

***

[A]nimals [who can reason] ... [have] souls [that] are capable of performing acts of reflection and of considering what is called 'I'.

***

29. [I]t is the knowledge of necessary and eternal truths which distinguishes us from simple animals, and gives us reason.

*** REFLECTION
AUTHORITY / ANIMALITY ?
30. It is also by the knowledge of necessary truths and by their abstractions that we rise to *reflective acts*, which enable us to think of what is called *I*. ...[50]

Leibniz's offers four intertwined theses. Apperception is a reflective consciousness of an inner state; it distinguishes rational animals from all others; it is required for reasoning; it is through the reflective acts involved in reasoning that we come to be aware of an I. The third claim seems pivotal. A reflective consciousness of inner states is required for reasoning. Although the terminology is Baroque, the point seems straightforward. Beyond whatever we do that is like animals, we also have the ability to engage in conscious reasoning. We can consider what our ideas imply and whether they are consistent, for example. This is possible only because we can recognize our inner states as such, as cognitive states that represent the world to be in various conditions. Although much of the time (Leibniz guesses three quarters), we do not consciously reason, and so are like beasts (and crude empiricists),[51] when we do, we must take note of our cognitive states as such and hence have a reflective awareness of ourselves as I's, as subjects of thoughts.

Given Kant's interest in the prerequisites of cognition, he should have been struck by this claim about reasoning. In the *Anthropology*, he echoes Leibniz's view that it is apperception, the ability to say "I," that separates us from the animals.[52] Further, the preliminary discussion of the topics of the A Deduction includes several claims about cognitive tasks requiring us to be conscious of something: our states, ourselves, our synthesizing (A103, A107, 108). On the other hand, the considered accounts of cognitive tasks, in Section 3 of the A Deduction, and in the B Deduction, explain cognition by reference to the synthesizing activities of the imagination, which he acknowledges to be a blind (i.e., unconscious) faculty. I think the problem may be that Kant recognizes that there is some truth in Leibniz's case for the necessity of reflective awareness, but he also recognizes with Hume that we are not, in fact, aware of anything that we could call a self. And he is uncertain about how to do justice to both points.

In any case, as Pippin acknowledges, in introducing apperception at B132, Kant affirms that all my cognitive states must be capable of belonging to the unity of apperception, *"even if I am not conscious of them as such."* Pippin suggests that this qualification indicates the sophistication of Kant's view. The claim is not that we are always conscious of cognitive states as our own but that the possibility of this awareness is "an inseparable component of *what it is* consciously to perceive, imagine, remember, etc."[53] But how does this happen? Various cognitive tasks may require conscious attention, or the possibility of conscious attention.[54] However, Kant is clear that such empirical consciousness can never lead to the unity of apperception. The decisive text is B134:

> For the empirical consciousness, which accompanies different cognitive states, is in itself diverse and without relation to the identity of the subject. That relation comes about, not simply through my accompanying each cognitive state with consciousness, but only in so far as I *conjoin* the contents of one cognitive state with those of another, and am conscious

of the synthesis of them. Only in so far, therefore, as I can unify a diversity of elements of given cognitive states in *one consciousness*, is it possible for me to represent to myself the identity of the consciousness across these cognitive states [amended translation, original emphasis; compare A117a].

No individual cognitive acts can reveal the unity of apperception. This unity only comes about through the syntheses that must be performed on cognitive states for cognition to be possible and that create a synthetic unity across the states. Further, we can only recognize that unity and represent it to ourselves by recognizing these syntheses. Although Kant may have been tempted to believe that certain cognitive activities require reflective awareness of our own states, he sees clearly that individual cognitive acts cannot lead us to justifiable claims about the unity of apperception. Thus, the heart of his account of apperception is that the unity of mental life is the outcome of synthesizing activities required for cognition and can only be understood as such.

Arguing for the Synthetic Unity of Apperception

Apperception and Representation

There can be no doubt that Kant maintains that mental life involves a certain unity, the unity of apperception. If he does not simply beg the question against Hume's denial of unity—because he certainly knew of it—then some of his many remarks about apperception must indicate where he thinks his predecessor erred. All of Kant's analyses of cognitive tasks establish the need to synthesize cognitive states. As noted, however, many also begin with nonskeptical assumptions. To answer Hume, he must appeal to some fact about mental life that his predecessor takes for granted.

Kant seems to offer just such an antiskeptical argument at the dramatic moment when he proclaims the doctrine of apperception. The message and the prominent treatment are the same in both editions. I begin with the A version:

We are conscious *a priori* of the complete identity of the self in respect of all cognitive states which can ever belong to our knowledge, as being a necessary condition of the possibility of all cognitive states. <u>For in me</u> <u>they can represent something only in so far as they belong with all others</u>

to one consciousness, and therefore must be at least capable of being so connected. [A116, amended translation, my underscoring].

Kant's fluid terminology raises a problem, since he claims that all cognitive states [*Vorstellungen*] must represent, although he does not always hold this.[55] The problem is merely terminological, I believe. Just prior to this passage he suggests that intuitions are nothing to us, unless they can participate "directly or indirectly" in consciousness. Kant acknowledges unconscious cognitive states, as well as intuitions and judgments.[56] I believe that his point is that any cognitive state, properly so called, must either represent something to a subject or contribute to such a representation (and so participate indirectly in it). This is a property that Hume could not deny. He clearly believes that both impressions and ideas represent some content or other to subjects. If Kant is right that any cognitive state can be representational only if it belongs to, or could be connected to, a synthetically produced unity of apperception, then Hume is wrong.

The B edition fastens on the same property, the ability of cognitive states to represent:

> It must be possible for the I think to accompany all my cognitive states; *for otherwise something would be represented in me which could not be thought at all, and that is equivalent to saying that the cognitive state would be impossible, or at least would be nothing to me* . . . The thought that the cognitive states given in intuition one and all belong to me, is therefore equivalent to the thought that I unite them in one self-consciousness, and [that] presupposes the possibility of . . . synthesis . . . (B132–34).

Here Kant's point emerges in two steps: If cognitive states did not belong to one consciousness, then they would not represent; cognitive states belong to one consciousness in that they are connected or are connectible by synthesis.

Obviously, these are not full-dress arguments, but only cryptic pointers about what is wrong with opting for disconnected heaps of cognitive states. Still, Kant must have believed that these remarks were supported by his various discussions of the need for synthesis, since it is not obvious that representation requires synthetic connection. For an argument against Hume, he would need to cover two cases, impressions and ideas. (I will use Kant's "intuitions" and "judgments," because Hume's terminology embodies the mistake that ideas are just like impressions, except fainter.) Putting the issue in terms of cognitive tasks, Kant would need to show that the capacity to have intuitions and judgments that at

least represent something to a subject require syntheses that connect
intuitions and judgments to other cognitive states.

Judgments

The clearest discussion of the issue concerns judgments and occurs as
Kant prepares the reader in the A Deduction:

> Without the consciousness that what we think is the same as what we
> thought a moment before, all reproduction in the series of cognitive states
> would be useless. *For it would in its present state be a new cognitive state
> which would not in any way belong to the act whereby it was gradually
> generated*, and the diverse elements would never form a whole, because
> the unity would be lacking that only consciousness can provide to it. If,
> in counting, I forget that the units, which now hover before me, have
> been added to one another in succession, I should never know that a total
> is being produced through this successive addition of unit to unit, and so
> would remain ignorant of the number [A103, amended translation, my
> emphasis].

Although this discussion runs several points together (which I disentangle later), it brings out a crucial consideration. A thought or judgment
can have a particular content only if it has been generated from particular
types of intuitions.

To see the problem Kant is addressing, consider what it is about a
cognitive state that would enable it to have the content "five things" or
"there are five things." As was clear in Chapter 3, resemblance is not
an option at this point. Not only do judgments not resemble intuitions,
but intuitions do not resemble objects. So a judgment cannot have the
content "there are five things" by somehow resembling five things. A
judgment achieves content in being generated from a particular set of
intuitions. But for its mode of generation, it would not have this content.
Kant's claim is not merely that intuitions are used to generate, produce,
or cause judgments, but that if particular intuitions were not involved
in the generation of a judgment, then it would not have its particular
content, and so would not be the judgment that it is. So the judgment
depends for its existence on the intuitions that are used to generate it.
I have noted that Kant's introductory account of synthesis suggests that
diverse elements of earlier states are "comprehended"—somehow preserved and united—in the resulting state, so that syntheses create relations of existential dependence. Here we get a less metaphorical
account of this process. It is not that syntheses gather up elements and
comprehend them as one might gather apples and place them together

in a basket. Rather, the diverse elements of earlier states are preserved in the later state, because the content of the later state is, in part, constituted by its generation from those particular types of intuitions. This point is very close to the first half of Kant's famous summation of his position: "Without sensibility no object would be given to us, without understanding no object would be thought. Thoughts without content are empty, intuitions without concepts are blind" (A51/B75). Since sensibility provides intuitions, Kant is asserting that thoughts would lack content without intuitions. Given his belief that thoughts are generated from intuitions, there is only a small step to the position that thoughts would lack content unless they were generated from intuitions.

The point is somewhat obscured in the passage, because Kant suggests that individual cognizers can complete the ascent to judgment only by recognizing how their states were generated! Although he retreats from the claim that we are conscious of the generation of a cognitive state in the very next paragraph, it complicates the discussion. As I note in Chapter 3, the vacillation in this passage[57] (first he claims we watch the synthesis, then that we are just aware of the outcome, and then that we must assume that we are aware of the generation) may be a result of confusing levels. Since, when theorizing about judgment, we can explain how judgments have particular contents only by reference to their mode of generation, Kant mistakenly assumes that in judging itself, we must take note of the generation of our state. Leibniz's idea that some types of cognition require a reflective awareness of our state may also contribute to the confusion.

Despite these complications, Kant's analysis of how judgments can represent makes a powerful case that they must be related by synthetic connections (and so stronger than Humean connections) to other cognitive states. Here he does not start with objects and ask how we represent them; he starts with judgments and asks how they can represent. This enables him to show that the representational character of judgments cannot simply be assumed. It must be explained, and the only viable explanation involves their mode of generation, hence syntheses and synthetic connection to other states.

Kant's Functionalism

In this crucial passage Kant suggests an account of the representational content of judgments that is like that defended by contemporary functionalists.[58] Functionalists take cognitive states to have particular contents in virtue of their causal relations to stimuli, responses, and other cognitive states. (One important disanalogy that I consider later concerns the importance of behavior to content.) Could Kant have held a view that is so close to contemporary wisdom? Besides the texts cited, three external pieces of evidence support this interpretation. The first was noted in Chapter 3. By the time Kant was writing, causal connection was widely held to be essential to representation, and he always supported this view.[59] However, he also believed that judgments are not in an immediate [causal] relation to objects but that they are only related through intuitions (A68/B93). Hence, it would be natural for him to believe that the representational character of judgments could only arise through their dependence on intuitions.

Second, Kant's position is not very different from the account that he had been reading in Tetens:

The reference of cognitive states to other preceding modifications [of the mind] is their essential characteristic. . . .

And everything that we call a representation [*Vorstellung*] of anything arises from such modifications of our being which refer to other preceding alterations. . . .

The analogy of representations [*Vorstellungen*] with alterations of the soul, of which they are what remains behind, makes them capable of being signs and images of them. They correspond to them. . . . The reference of representations to preceding modifications is the general analogy between cause and effect.[60]

Tetens seems to maintain a hybrid between a resemblance view and a causal view. Cognitive states can represent, because they are caused by modifications of the soul [which are themselves caused by objects], because there is a general analogy between causes and effects. Kant departs from this position by dropping the vestige of resemblance contained in the final clause.

Finally, a somewhat speculative consideration. Functionalism has been widely adopted, because philosophers have come to realize that "nothing is intrinsically a representation of anything," in Daniel Dennett's phrase.[61] Once this point is fully appreciated, some relational account of content seems inevitable. At the time Kant was writing, the hopelessness of theories of intrinsic representation was clearly in evidence. Representation by resemblance was thoroughly discredited, as was Wolff's idea of a *vis representiva*. Under these circumstances it would not be surprising for him to adopt a relational view.

Intuitions

What about intuitions? The crucial contention that cognitive states can represent only if they are connected by synthesis in a unity of apperception explicitly includes intuitions in the A edition (A116). Presumably, this is also the import of "intuitions without concepts are *blind*." Once we consider the problem of how judgments could have particular contents, the solution of their method of generation seems straightforward. With intuitions, it is hard to see what the problem is. Kant introduces the notion of "intuition" by claiming that it is the representation [*Erkenntniss*] through which we are in immediate relation to objects (A19/B33). This is not quite right, as the discussion of "objects of representation" in Chapter 3 shows.[62] Intuitions must themselves be constructed from cognitive states that are the result of immediate, but fleeting and ever-changing, sensory contact with objects. Still, the fluid terminology raises no substantive problems. Intuitions are in relatively immediate contact with objects compared to judgments. Given this fairly direct contact, it might seem that intuitions have a particular content, because they are regularly produced by the presence of particular objects. To see why this relation is insufficient to account for the representational quality of intuitions, consider a popular example from philosophy of psychology. The height of the mercury in a thermometer varies regularly with the temperature, but it does not represent the temperature—at least, it does not represent the temperature *to the thermometer*.

The question about intuitions is how they can be (or function as) representational for a subject. At B132 Kant asserts that a cognitive state that could not be connected with others in one consciousness would be impossible or at least would be "nothing to me." As noted earlier, the same locution is used at A116—intuitions are nothing to us unless they are at least capable of being connected in the unity of apperception. Kant is quite insistent on this point, and mentions it in several other passages (A117a, A120). These remarks are probably aimed at the Leibnizean doctrine of *petites perceptions*, which had received prominent treatment in the recently published *New Essays*. They also contribute to a case against Hume, however.

Leibniz offered some good reasons for believing in unconscious perceptions. For example, the argument about perceiving the roar of the sea. People standing on the shore hear the roar by hearing the noise of each wave, but these cannot be separately distinguished.[63] Kant defends unconscious ideas in the *Anthropology*, by repeating this reasoning for the example of seeing a man in a far-off meadow.[64] In these circumstances he says that we are not conscious of the ideas, but mediately conscious of them. We can know that we have them by inference. The roar of the ocean is, however, only the tip of the iceberg of Leibniz's doctrine of *petites perceptions*. By appealing to the fact the mind always thinks, the principle that nature never takes leaps, the identity of indiscernibles, and preestablished harmony, he argues that each individual's *petites perceptions* reflect the entire universe.[65]

This bloated metaphysical doctrine appears to be the subject of Kant's repeated denials. Unconscious, inert "perceptions" would represent nothing to their subjects, because they have no effects in cognitive life.[66] They would be no more to their subjects than levels of mercury are to thermometers. Despite the soundness of this basic point, Kant's specific claim is too strong. Intuitions can represent, can be something to us, only if they can be reported in conscious judgments or if they can have an indirect influence on other cognitive states. (The second clause also applies to unconscious cognitive states. These must contribute to states that do represent.) He overlooks, or perhaps rejects, a possible alternative, a perennial danger in transcendental psychology. If a cognitive state covaries with an external stimulus and produces appropriate behavior, then there is some (perhaps weak) sense in which it represents that object to its subject.

Kant considers this possibility explicitly in a well-known letter to Marcus Herz, written in 1789.

> [Unless the categorial condition for the unity of apperception is met] I would not even be able to know that I have sense data; consequently for me, as a knowing being, they would be absolutely nothing. They could still (I imagine myself to be an animal) carry on their play in an orderly fashion, as cognitive states connected according to empirical laws of association, and thus even have an influence on my feeling and desire, without my being aware of them. . . . This might be so without my knowing the slightest thing thereby, not even what my own condition is.[67]

Even if cognitive states did influence behavior, they would still make no contribution to cognition, unless they could be synthesized with other cognitive states. Although this is an interesting point, it does not show that intuitions could not represent at all, unless they are synthesized in judgments.

The Reply to Hume

If sound, the considerations Kant invokes to banish hordes of *petites perceptions* would also enable him to conclude that Humean impressions must belong to the synthetic unity of apperception. For if they did not, they could not be representational, or even contribute to representations, and so could not be cognitive states at all. Together with the analysis of judgments, this would establish his general claim that to represent something, or to contribute to a representation, cognitive states must belong to a synthetic unity of apperception. Although the reasoning is not up to the mark, it comes close enough. The case for judgments is sound and the reflections about intuitions show that totally unconnected Humean impressions could not be representational. Because they depend for their representational character either on behavior or on synthetic connection with judgments, they cannot exist separately. No cognitive state, properly so called, can exist separately and in isolation.

Through his analyses of how intuitions and judgments can represent at all, Kant is able to meet Hume's challenge about mental unity in a very satisfying way. Hume despaired because he had two principles (all perceptions are distinct, the mind never perceives any real connection among distinct existences) that he could not reconcile with his own psychological account, which presupposes a single mind. Rather than simply favor his own theory, he conceded defeat. Kant's reflections about the prerequisites of representation provide an ideal way out. Since the two principles are also in conflict with something that no one in this tradition can deny—cognitive states are representational, or contribute to representation—they must give way.

The considerations about representation are only part of Kant's overall demonstration of the unity of apperception. Every cognitive task that he analyzes yields the same result. Cognition requires syntheses and syntheses create a unity of apperception, in the sense of actual dependence relations among cognitive states. They also presuppose another kind of unity—the ability of cognitive states to be synthesized with each other. This is the central result of the subjective Deduction: All aspects of cognition require a synthetic unity of apperception. Hence, any philosopher who reflects on the necessary conditions for knowledge must recognize the unity of apperception. For students of cognition, if not for cognitive agents, every cognitive state must be apperceptive.

In the Deduction Kant insists over and over, and then over again, on the unity of apperception, because someone who mattered denied it. He also claims that many important results can be derived from the doctrine of the unity of apperception. This is a legitimate premise for further arguments, only because, at the very moment when he announces the unity of apperception, he explains how denying mental unity involves a serious mistake about the nature of cognitive states. In Chapter 6 I will return to the central argument of the Deduction and follow its development from the doctrine of apperception and the analyses of cognitive tasks. As promised, the next chapter develops and extends Kant's views about synthetic connection and the unity of apperception as a plausible account of the unity of a mind. As I will argue, his analyses of the prerequisites of cognition yield a deep understanding of the grounds of mental unity.

5

A Cognitive Criterion of Mental Unity

Unity of Apperception as Mental Unity

Synthetic Connection

Through his analyses of the prerequisites of cognition, Kant discovers a connection that links cognitive states. Even the most minimal cognitive task—the capacity to have cognitive states that represent something to the subject—demands a synthesis of states (or their diverse elements) in further states. But acts of synthesis both create and presuppose relations among cognitive states. Synthesis creates a relation of dependence. The resulting state depends for its content, and so for its existence as a particular cognitive state, on the existence of the earlier states. Synthesis also presupposes that the earlier states are synthesizable, that their diverse elements can be synthesized in a resulting state.

To make discussion clearer, I shall describe the state that results from synthesis as a "synthetic product" and the states that are used in the production of that state as "synthetic progenitors." We can then define a general relation of connection by synthesis between any two cognitive states: CS_1 and CS_2 are *connected by synthesis* just in case they are related as synthetic product and synthetic progenitor, or they are coprogenitors of some further state. Although this may seem cumbersome, Kant's basic idea is simple. Synthetic connection is a relation of contentual connection. Synthetic products are contentually dependent on synthetic progenitors. The elements of coprogenitors are combined in further states. Kant's way of putting this appears needlessly abstract:

117

Diverse elements [*Mannigfaltigen*] of progenitors are comprehended [*begreifen*] in the product state (A77/B103). Contemporary philosophers and cognitive scientists would say instead that *information* in states that are closer to the sensory periphery is *processed* and so transformed into useful perceptual or conceptual *information*. The superficial clarity of our term "information" is quite misleading, however, for it suggests both that lower-level states are, in fact, representational, and that there are no particular problems in understanding how they can be so. Even if "*Mannigfaltigen*" (particularly in Kemp Smith's rendering, "manifolds") is annoyingly elusive, it has the advantage of only implying what Kant knows, and what we know. Sensory contact with objects induces a vast and ever-changing array of changes in our internal states, which we can somehow use to create useful perceptual and conceptual representations, whose contents depend on those changes.

Connection and Connectibility

Both the A and B Deductions present the unity of apperception in terms of the connection and connectibility of cognitive states by synthesis. In A:

> All cognitive states which can ever belong to our knowledge... [must] belong with all others to one consciousness, and therefore must be at least capable of being connected in it....
> This synthetic unity [of apperception] presupposes or includes a synthesis.... [This] productive synthesis of the imagination can take place *a priori*[1];... [it is] prior to apperception and is the ground of the possibility of all knowledge [A116–18, amended translation].

Cognitive states belong to a unity of apperception, because they have been connected to each other by synthesis. However, Kant adds an important qualification: Cognitive states must be at least capable of being connected (with all others) in one consciousness. So *possible* connection seems sufficient.

This vacillation (does belonging to the unity of apperception require actual or possible synthetic connection?) results from the reciprocal relations between synthetic connection and apperception. The end of the cited passage is quite clear. Syntheses precede apperception, making it and knowledge possible. On the other hand, Kant introduced his topic as follows: to investigate "the inner ground of the connection of cognitive states... in one knowledge..., we must begin with apperception" (A116, amended translation). This suggests the reverse dependency.

Synthetic connection of cognitive states and knowledge depend on the unity of apperception.

This "chicken and egg" problem is not deeply worrying, however. It arises because, as noted, synthesis both creates one kind of connection among cognitive states, contentual connection, and presupposes another, the connectibility of progenitor states. To see Kant's solution, consider whether a set of states that were connectible by synthesis but that involved no actual connections would belong to a unity of apperception. Kant's answer is clearly no. The unity of apperception (and cognition) can only be generated by actual syntheses (A118; compare B134, B135). Once connections are established among cognitive states, once we have a functioning thinker, then other cognitive states that are connectible to those already connected would also belong to the same thinker. For a set of states to belong to one consciousness, each must at least be capable of being connected [by synthesis] "with all others" (A116).

In sum, cognitive states belong to one consciousness just in case they are connectible by synthesis with a set of states already connected by synthesis, and all such states are connectible with each other. The B version defends the same view:

As *my* cognitive states (even if I am not conscious of them as such) they must conform to the condition under which alone they *can* stand together in one universal self-consciousness, because otherwise they would not without exception belong to me. . . .

The thought that the cognitive states given in intuition one and all belong to me, says after all, no more than that I unite them in one self-consciousness, or at least can unite them in it; and although this thought is not itself the consciousness of the *synthesis* of the cognitive states, it presupposes the possibility of that synthesis. That is, only because I can comprehend their diverse elements in one consciousness do I call these one and all *my* cognitive states [B132–34, amended translation, original emphasis].

To belong to the unity of apperception cognitive states must be able to belong to one universal self-consciousness; that is, they must all be able to be synthesized with each other. At the end of the section, Kant reaffirms that cognitive states must be brought to the unity of apperception by means of a synthesis (B135). So again, a unity of apperception is created when cognitive states are connected through syntheses; a state belongs to a given consciousness if it can be synthesized with cognitive states already connected by synthesis.

The doctrine of apperception is plainly an abstract account of the unity of a mind. It is almost never considered in this light, however.[2] Two factors appear to be responsible for the neglect. One is the failure to realize that Kant's claims about a unity of apperception were made against the background of Hume's denial of mental unity. Second, Kant's account of mental unity highlights the operation of synthesis and "synthesis" is taken to be too psychological to be worth pursuing in philosophical discussions. When the Human background and the abstract psychological operation of synthesis are left out, however, there is little left to the doctrine. This may explain why it has been assimilated to the *cogito* or regarded as a rather empty analytic claim: All my states are mine.

The Plan of the Chapter

In this chapter I argue that we continue to ignore this account of mental unity to our own disadvantage. The question of the grounds of mental unity is pressing in both philosophy and the cognitive sciences. Philosophers have venerable moral and metaphysical interests in understanding the unity of a mind. More recently, psychologists and cognitive scientists have realized that the apparent unity of consciousness is something that needs to be explained, and that it is rather hard to do so. Kant's cognitive analyses offer a fresh and promising approach. Starting with the most basic fact about a mind—its capacity for knowledge—he argues that the states of any mind, like ours in achieving knowledge on the basis of a vast and fleeting array of sensory stimulations, must be connected or connectible by synthesis. Whatever other factors may or may not unite cognitive states in a mind, synthetic connection is fundamental and invariably present. Failing this relation, our minds would not be minds at all. Since it emerges from attempts to understand cognition, this is a cognitive, as opposed to a bodily, moral, or legal account of mental unity.

As with other results in transcendental psychology, the cognitive account of mental unity is highly abstract. In the remainder of this section, I will try to clarify Kant's position by making explicit an important point that he leaves implicit and by explaining why he cannot assert something he occasionally appears to assert. The resulting account is still very preliminary. Nevertheless, I will demonstrate its strengths in the next three sections: first, by comparing it to contemporary rivals, the theories of Locke and Leibniz; second, by comparing it to current theories of mental unity; and finally, by considering some probable objections.

Although this chapter is mainly laudatory, I conclude my examination of apperception by addressing an awkward question. What is the relation between this doctrine and Kant's other views about the self? One reason scholars have avoided Kant's ideas about the self is that he has too many of them. The self has so many roles to play in his system that the doctrine of apperception threatens to become entangled with other concerns about the self. I suggest a way of preserving this sensible account, but only at the expense of other views that he would not happily sacrifice. So the last section is deliberately revisionist.

Refining the Account of Synthetic Connection

Synthesis is, I have argued, Kant's solution to Hume's problem about how cognitive states are connected to each other, and so united in a mind. Synthesis involves relations of contentual connection: the elements of earlier states being combined in later states, the contents of later states depending on the elements of earlier states. If synthesis only involves contentual connection, however, then it may be too liberal as a criterion of mental unity. If Harry screams, "Smoke!", then I will have a cognitive state whose content depends on the content of one of Harry's states. We are never of one mind, however, except figuratively. Kant is unconcerned by this type of case, because his account of synthesis involves a restriction that is not obvious,[3] although it is an immediate consequence of his general view of the sources of knowledge. Harry's cognitive state can affect one of mine only by causing a sensation in me via outer sense. Kant's implicit restriction is that synthesis operates without benefit of transmission through outer sense. That is, two cognitive states, CS_1 and CS_2, can only be synthetic progenitors of a resulting state CSR, if the contents of CSR depend on the elements of CS_1 and CS_2, without the mediation of some additional state, CS_3 (an outer sensation). Either or both of CS_1 and CS_2 may be outer sensations. But if they are coprogenitors of some third state, then its content cannot depend on elements contained in CS_1 or CS_2 courtesy of some additional outer sensation. This (implicit) restriction is violated by the putative counterexample. If this restriction on connection by synthesis is borne in mind, then Kant's position is still that cognitive states belong to the same consciousness if they are connected or connectible by synthesis.

By viewing the doctrine of apperception in light of Hume's criticisms of simple selves, we can recognize a familiar pattern. Although Kant opposes the skeptical conclusion, his position preserves a number of the skeptic's insights.[4] Persons are not mere heaps of perceptions, but we are no more than contentually interconnected systems of cognitive states (at least as far as we can ever know). Selves are not substances, nor are they anything that cognitive states are connected to. These negative aspects of the apperception doctrine are not fully explored until the Paralogisms chapter (the subject of Chapter 7). Even in the Deduction, however, it is reasonably clear that cognitive states belong to the unity of apperception, not by virtue of belonging to something else, but because they stand, or can stand, in relations of synthetic connection with each other.

Is the Self the Combiner?

This point is repeated in a number of texts already cited (especially B133–34, A118). Nevertheless, significant counterindications in the Deduction need to be addressed. At B159 Kant declares, "I exist as an intelligence which is conscious solely of its power of combination. . . . " Further, in many discussions the I is presented as what does the combining: "I unite them," "I combine them." Taken at face value, these expressions imply that a thinker is not a contentually interconnected system of states, but that which connects cognitive states. This interpretation is given further support by the fact that Kant links spontaneity and apperception quite closely.[5] So it is tempting to interpret the self, or consciousness, or apperception as something like the power or source of spontaneity itself.

While tempting, this approach does not lead to a coherent position. The self cannot be identified with acts of spontaneity, since these are distinct events. It could only be the agent that performs these acts. But acts or processes of synthesis could not be performed by agents. They are unconscious activities within agents that enable them to have cognitive capacities required for agency. In Daniel Dennett's useful terminology, they are "subpersonal" processes, not acts performed by persons.[6]

As we saw in the preceding chapters, Kant is not always clear on this point. Nevertheless he is clear, and explicit, that we have no way of identifying the empirical consciousness that accompanies [or synthesizes] different cognitive states (B133). Further, were selves identified as powers or faculties of spontaneity, then self-identity would be a matter of faculty identity, and Kant would need an account of faculty identity, which he does not present. This omission is unsurprising, since it is hard to see how faculty identity could rest in anything but the identity of a substance, and he explicitly denies that self-identity requires the identity of a substance.[7] Thinking selves are not merely systems of cognitive states, because some faculty must always be present to synthesize states. These faculties are crucial in creating the unity of apperception. The identity of consciousness is, however, a matter of the connections that are or can be created; for the reasons just given, it cannot reside in the identity of what connects. When Kant says that cognitive states belong to a self only because I combine them, he is giving a synoptic version of a more complex doctrine: Cognitive states belong to the unity of apperception only because some faculty in whatever material or immaterial form in which those cognitive states are currently realized or preserved creates synthetic connections among them.

Locke and Leibniz on Personal Identity

The Issue

The topic of this chapter has several names: "mental unity," "self identity," and "personal identity." Although the last expression is the most common, I usually cast the discussion in terms of mental unity. As John Perry has argued, the term "identity" has been misleading.[8] For the question of personal identity is not about the identity of two things. There is no question of a gallant young officer being identical with an aging general; the two have different properties, and so fail to meet the uncontroversial criterion of the indiscernibility of identicals. The issue of personal identity is about individuation. What relation between the two different temporal stages of a person, the gallant young officer and the aging general, makes them stages of the same individual? This terminological confusion has produced substantive confusion. It led Bernard Williams to claim that the memory criterion for personal identity had to be rejected, because it could come into conflict with the logical principle of the transitivity of identity.[9] Since it avoids confusion and is more perspicuous, I follow Perry in describing the issue in terms of finding the "unity" relation for minds or persons. What relation unites diverse states in one mind? For reasons that will be apparent later, Kant's theory is more appropriately described as one of "mental" rather than "personal" unity.

Leibniz Versus Locke

Kant was familiar with Locke's well-known views on the unity of consciousness. In the Third Paralogism he echoes Locke's reason for concluding that continuity of the thinker does not require continuity of substance. For all we know, the contents of cognitive states can be transmitted from one thinking substance to another (A362–64a).[10] Although he follows Locke up to a point, he does not adopt the memory criterion, but offers the deeper relation of synthetic connection. As we have seen, Kant rarely engages in explicit critical discussions of competing views. I shall suggest later that he makes a glancing objection to Locke, in the course of laying out his own position. In this case it is clear why he had no need to belabor the shortcomings Locke's view. Leibniz provides extensive citations from Locke's discussion and a completely adequate criticism of the memory criterion in the *New Essays*.[11]

Leibniz reiterates the standard eighteenth-century objection: Memory does not *make* someone the same individual through time. His reasons are interesting, however, and shed considerable light on the background to Kant's reflections.

> within each substance there is a perfect bond between the future and the past, which is what creates the identity of the individual. Memory is not necessary for this, however, it is sometimes not even possible, *because of the multitude of past and present impressions which jointly contribute to our present thoughts; for I believe that each of a man's thoughts has some effect, if only a confused one, or leaves some trace which mingles with the thoughts which follow it*. One may forget many things, but one could also retrieve them, much later, if one were brought back to them in the right way [my emphasis].[12]

The memory criterion is too crude. As has often been noted, actual memory is too strong a requirement. Leibniz's more original point is that memory is also too crude in failing to appreciate mental dynamics. Like Hume, Locke pictures mental life as a sequence of separate states. Aside from some states containing memories of earlier states, there is no commerce among them. Leibniz observes that this is unfaithful to the phenomena. Earlier experiences affect later thoughts in many ways other than simply permitting recall of the experience itself. These interactions reveal continuity of mental life as much as memory does. Leibniz goes further and conjectures that since perceptions and thoughts must leave some trace in the mental apparatus to be recalled, each induces a permanent change that affects all subsequent activity.

Kant would accept many of Leibniz's points. Actual memory is an unrealistically strong criterion, and memory is, in any case, too superficial. Memory rests on synthesis, for the state to be remembered can represent some state of affairs only through the operations of synthesis. As Leibniz notes, there are many other influences of earlier states on later ones, and these also rest on synthesis. So, for example, an associative connection across states would depend on the existence of synthetic connections, as we saw in Chapter 3.[13] Memory is only one manifestation of the relations that are possible among cognitive states through the basic operation of synthesis.[14] In fixing on memory, Locke has failed to uncover the deeper ties that unite a mind, so Kant wisely rejects memory in favor of a cognitive criterion.

Although Kant would be sympathetic to Leibniz's criticisms, he could not agree with the positive doctrine. Nothing but metaphysical speculation supports the idea of a "perfect bond between the future and the past . . . which creates the identity of the individual." Kant replaces this metaphysical bond with an argument from transcendental psychology. We can account for the many relations among cognitive states and for the presence of very basic cognitive capacities only by assuming synthetic connections among cognitive states. Since it rests on argument by inference to the best (or better, only) explanation, rather than on metaphysical assumptions, Kant's account is clearly superior to Leibniz's.

Moral Responsibility

Although Kant's cognitive theory is deeper and better grounded than either of its contemporary rivals, there is another side to the story. For all its problems, memory would have an important virtue as the unity relation for persons. Locke casts his discussion in terms of this virtue, and Leibniz recognized it in the *Discourse on Metaphysics* (which antedates Locke's *Essay*).[15] "Person" is, as Locke puts it, a "forensic" term that is used in the assignment of moral and legal praise and blame. With the memory criterion, a person would be responsible only for those acts where his own conscience can accuse him. Further, moral responsibility requires that the agent be conscious of his actions. What Locke wants to claim is that continuity of consciousness—the very capacity that enables us to be responsible—is what makes the same person.[16] Even though consciousness of one's actions is essential to being a person, it does not follow that the continuity of a person depends on continuity of some power of consciousness. As we saw earlier, this approach leads to a substantival account—or lapses into obscurity. Locke does not see how we can assume that sameness of person requires sameness of substance in our present state of ignorance. He tries to avoid obscurity by assimilating sameness of consciousness to memory. But the two are not the same and memory is too strong a criterion. So none of this works, and the potential virtue of a memory criterion remains unrealized.

Still, the issue of finding a unity relation for persons that is adequate to their moral dimension exerts tremendous pressure on Kant's discussion. Both Locke and Leibniz (in the *Discourse*) try to force the capacity that is necessary to being a person, self-consciousness, into the role of the unity relation for persons. Kant's term "apperception" and his definition of "person" in terms of the capacity for self-consciousness in the Third Paralogism are clear indications of the influence of his predecessors. Thus, it is hardly surprising that he makes occasional references to "self-consciousness" in describing the synthetic connections that unite states in a self. The problem is that this solution is merely verbal. Even though he recognizes the importance of self-consciousness to personhood, he has no idea of how we are conscious of our experiences or our cognitive states as our own.

The Problem of Self-Consciousness

Kant's bewilderment is understandable if we reflect on his historical position. Descartes believed that we are directly aware of a continuing mental substance; Locke urged that the same consciousness accompanies all our mental states; in the *Discourse*, Leibniz claimed that we have a memory or consciousness of immediately past happenings that gives us knowledge of the I.[17] When pressed, however, these theories of self-consciousness and self-identity collapse. Besides begging the question in favor of the immateriality of the soul, Descartes gives no indications of how we tell that we are the same mental substance.[18] Locke's position becomes obscure, once the assimilation of consciousness to memory is seen to be erroneous. Leibniz recognized the shortcomings of memory and reduced its role in the *New Essays* to informing us (usually reliably) about our past; he now takes self-identity to be constituted by the metaphysical continuity of a substance.[19] Kant saw the failures of his predecessors. He criticizes Descartes at length in the Paralogisms. And he explicitly dismisses the "same consciousness " idea of Locke and the early Leibniz (without mentioning either by name) at B133: "the empirical consciousness that accompanies different cognitive states, is in itself diverse and without relation to the identity of the subject." This leaves him with a problem, because self-consciousness is essential to our status as persons, and he has no way of accounting for it. His half-hearted solution is that we recognize a cognitive state as our own, because we have introspected the synthesizing activity that produced it (A108) Kant is driven to this idea by the need to explain self-consciousness within his theory of mental unity—synthetic connections among cognitive states—and encouraged to think that it is true by Tetens' psychology.[20] Still, as we have seen, he cannot quite bring himself to accept this alleged help from introspection, and he denies synthesis watching almost as often as he puts it forward.[21] Still, it is unfortunate that he ever mentioned it, since synthesis watching has provided a perfect vehicle for ridiculing the psychology of the *Critique*.

Apperception is not primarily a theory about the *consciousness* of mental states as belonging to ourselves. As noted, at the end of B132, Kant declares that "all my cognitive states (even if I am not immediately [*gleich*] conscious of them as such) must conform to the conditions that are necessary for them to belong together in one universal self-consciousness . . . " (my translation, my underscoring). Those conditions are that they be able to be synthesized with *each other* (B133). Self-ascription has seemed central for two reasons. Commentators have recognized the Lockean–Leibnizean vocabulary, "apperception," "self-consciousness," without always appreciating how muddled Locke and Leibniz were about self-identity and self-consciousness, and *a fortiori* without recognizing that Kant saw these muddles and tried to avoid them. The second reason has been the tendency to read Kant in light of Descartes' agenda for philosophy.[22] Since Descartes assumed only the *cogito*, his successors must play by the same rules. So the deduction of the categories must proceed by assuming only that we can self-ascribe mental states. In Chapter 6 we shall see that the categories enter the account, because (Kant argues) cognitive states are connectible with each other only if they can also be subsumed under the categories. Synthetic connection and so the categories are crucial for the entire range of our cognitive capacities, however, and not just for our ability to ascribe states to ourselves. Further, the categories and synthetic connection are not sufficient for self-ascription. So there is no especially close connection between apperception, the categories, and self-ascription, despite the current popularity of understanding the deduction in relation to these issues. Kant has no serious views about how the distinctive abilities of persons relate to the continuity of a mind with certain capacities. These abilities are simply grafted onto his account of mental unity in terms of synthetic connection. For this reason his theory is more accurately described as one of "mental" rather than "personal" unity.

Although Kant fails to advance our understanding of self-ascription,[23] this is not a major objection to his theory of mental unity. As already noted, the fact that an ability is crucial to being a person does not imply that continuity of the faculty that underlies that ability is necessary for continuity of the person. This failing might also seem critical for a different reason. John Perry has argued that there is a persistent confusion in the personal identity literature between a metaphysical question ("What relation holds between two mental states when they *are* states of the same mind?") and epistemological questions ("How do we *tell* when two states belong to the same mind?" "How does the subject *tell* when past states are his?").[24] This confusion is due in part to the use of the term "criterion," which has both an epistemological and metaphysical sense. Kant is also a victim of confusion. He conflates the theorist's problem of specifying and defending a view of the connections that unite cognitive states in individual minds (and so the metaphysical problem, although he would not like that term), with agents' problems in knowing which cognitive states are their own. Hence, the recurring references to synthesis watching. Since these issues are separable, his inability to explain how we come to recognize our own states does not compromise his defense of synthesis as the ground of mental unity.

Modern Mentalism, Wiggins, and Parfit

Modern Mentalism

Kant's cognitive criterion is, I have argued, a sound reply to Hume, and a far better account of mental unity than those provided by Locke or Leibniz. I turn to contemporary theories. The last 30 years have produced a number of important studies on personal identity. Current work may be divided into three positions: modern mentalism, which has been the dominant trend, and the important dissenting views of David Wiggins and Derek Parfit.[25] Wiggins opposes mentalist criteria on the grounds that they yield incorrect answers in "puzzle" cases; Parfit's disagreement is more fundamental. He denies that there is any deep fact about personal identity about which criteria can be correct or incorrect.

Many recent writers, including Paul Grice, Anthony Quinton, Terrence Penelhum, Sydney Shoemaker, John Perry, and David Lewis[26] (among others), have argued for broadly mentalistic accounts of mental unity. Although these accounts differ in details, the fundamental idea is that the unity relation for minds includes some combination of continuity of memory, belief, and desire. Oddly, the contemporary impetus for this consensus comes from Sydney Shoemaker's classic retelling of Locke's tale of the prince and the cobbler.[27] In the original version, the two are said to switch souls, whatever that is supposed to amount to.

Shoemaker made Locke's point immediately clear and compelling for modern audiences by moving Mr. Brown's brain to Mr. Robinson's body and then inquiring who the resulting person ("Brownson," to preserve neutrality) is, Brown or Robinson. As Shoemaker argued, because Brownson would believe that he was Brown, be devoted to Brown's wife and children, be able to recall details of Brown's life, display Brown's personality traits, likes, dislikes, mannerisms, and the like (or at least those that don't depend on having a certain kind of body), and because these psychological affinities could hardly be dismissed as co-incidental, there is a strong inclination to say that he is Brown. That is, there is strong reason to believe that the unity relation for persons involves not bodily continuity but mental continuity.

Mental continuity is fairly similar to Kant's criterion of synthetic connection, although it includes emotional as well as cognitive factors. Nevertheless, many of the variations and amplifications of Shoemaker's argument that have been offered over the years also provide support for the cognitive criterion. Still, there are two salient differences between Kant's view and contemporary accounts. One concerns how we understand mental continuity; the other, how we understand the project of finding the unity relation for minds. In both cases I will argue for the surprising thesis that the older view is the better.

Modern mentalists take memory, belief, and desire continuity to involve causal connections among mental states. So this aspect of mental continuity is like Kant's relation of synthesis, except that synthesis only concerns cognitive states.[28] Current accounts differ in stressing the *similarity* of a person's beliefs and desires across time.[29] What justifies the claim that mental unity requires similarity of beliefs and desires, in addition to causal connection, however? No one knows how much similarity in belief and desire people have over a lifetime. Perhaps there is no similarity of belief and desire between the child's mind and that of the adult, even though one evolved from the other.[30] Causal dependence might produce a large amount of similarity, so Kant's position is compatible with the idea that different stages of a person are psychologically similar. His criterion does not prejudge the issue, however, and is for that reason preferable to many contemporary accounts.

The second disagreement concerns the nature of the project. Kant is trying to figure out what persons must be like—in particular, what connections must exist among their cognitive states—for them to have the cognitive capacities we recognize them to have. Recent studies have often borne the stamp of linguistic philosophy. John Perry express the prevailing understanding in the introduction to his collection, *Personal*

Identity: "In studying the problem of personal identity, we are learning about our own concept of a person, trying to articulate and analyze knowledge we in a sense already have."[31] Thus, Kant and our contemporaries seem to be addressing different questions. What relations must obtain among cognitive states for persons to have certain capacities? What relations must obtain among mental states for us to employ our concept "same person"?[32]

In fact, these questions are intimately related and Kant's is the more fundamental. Despite the frequent appeals to "what we would say" about bizarre cases in the literature, contemporary work is not a protracted exegesis of the English expression "same person." The question of personal identity concerns not the word "person" but the classification 'person', and so, what persons are like.[33] To address this question, we must first consider why we have two classifications, 'person' and 'human being', that apply to pretty much the same organisms.[34] Presumably, the answer is that we use the classification 'person' to explain and predict current behaviors, and the beliefs and desires that underlie them, on the basis of past beliefs and desires. We need an additional classification, beyond the biological one, because, tragically, some human beings never exhibit the psychological regularities on which such predictions and explanations are based, or only exhibit them for part of their lives. In addition, "person" is used to indicate the presence of cognitive capacities that make human beings moral agents. Given the point of the classification—to indicate psychological regularities and capacities—we can see, on reflection, that when we regard individuals as persons, we must regard their mental states as connected by mental continuity. Puzzle cases are one means of carrying out such reflections. When presented with extraordinary cases, we realize that unless we regard the mental states that are united by mental continuity as states of continuing persons, then *no* individual in the case would have the properties and capacities that are essential to being a person. So we say "same person" where there is mental continuity. What we say is, however, a reflection of what we believe about the traits and capacities distinctive of persons, and about the relations that must unite states for an individual to have those traits and capacities. That is, what we say depends on the answer we give to Kant's question. Given the traits and abilities we acknowledge persons to have, what relations must unite their cognitive states?

Wiggins's Argument Against Mentalism

Kant's cognitive criterion can receive additional support from arguments for modern mentalism; equally, it is threatened by critics of this position.

David Wiggins has argued that all mentalist criteria are fatally flawed, because they would permit "branching" persons in unusual circumstances. For example, if a brain were duplicated or split by commisurotomy and the two organs were implanted in different bodies, then mental continuity criteria (including Kant's) would imply that each of the resulting individuals was the same person as the original individual. So someone might branch into two streams, while remaining the same person.[35]

To avoid this result, Wiggins argues that we must use a hybrid criterion that involves mental and physical factors. He suggests that "person" be understood as a nonbiological qualification of "animal". Thus, there might be different kinds of persons—human-persons, dolphin-person, and so forth. The unity relation for person could then ride piggyback on the unity relation for the particular kind of animal. If we have a human being who has and retains the extra qualities that make him a person, then he will continue to be the same person by virtue of continuing to be the same human being. The pure mentalist criterion would be replaced by a hybrid: person capacities, plus the unity relation for the relevant animal.

How does this proposal meet the difficulty, however? The same worries that have been raised about splitting persons could be raised about splitting human beings. If science fiction is to be our guide,then we can clone human beings, and so end up with branching persons *cum* human beings. We do not seem to have made any progress. The salient response to such fanciful considerations is that (almost) given by Lewis Carroll. If pigs *could* fly, then we would use a different set of classifications for describing the world. (Oddly, Wiggins offered a similar response himself in an earlier discussion of the problem.[36]) More formally, Kant's criterion can be adequately defended by noting that these considerations are not relevant. As long as the problem of personal identity is understood in terms of examining the limits of our concept 'same person', then it might be necessary to probe those limits by asking what we would say in extraordinary cases. As I have argued, however, this is not the best approach and it is not Kant's approach. He wants to consider how the cognitive states of people, *constituted as we are*, must be related to ensure the functioning of basic cognitive capacities.

Parfit's Denial of Personal Identity

Derek Parfit has argued,in a series of writings, that we should no longer think in terms of personal *identity* at all.[37] His point is that even when later mental states are psychologically connected to earlier ones, the similarities in views and values between the two person-stages may be too feeble to justify a claim of identity and all that that entails. Thus, he would reject the cognitive criterion. The ability of two cognitive states to be connected by synthesis would not be sufficient to make them states of a continuing person. On Parfit's view, we are wrong to fasten the yes-or-no question of identity; what matters are the psychological connections themselves, and these can hold to a greater or lesser degree. The disagreement between Kant and Parfit seems to be verbal. Parfit would agree with Kant that earlier states can and do influence the contents of later ones. Further, he thinks that these relations of influence are what is important. In cases where the psychological traits of a human being have changed markedly over time, however, he would withhold the label "same person."

Parfit would regard the difference not as verbal but as substantive, for two sorts of reasons. First, he makes the common error noted earlier. He construes personal identity as a matter of identity, not individuation.[38] If the issue is cast in terms of individuation, then his concerns are eased considerably. Since individuals can alter with time, in talking about a later stage of an individual, we are not attributing sameness in the face of obvious differences. Parfit's second reason, or cluster of reasons, focuses on the implications of saying "same person." These range from legal punishment in finding the perpetrator of a long past crime to terror in recognizing one's own nonimminent mortality.[39] If we are absolutists about identity, then, Parfit reasons, we may be too harsh in reacting to distant misdeeds, and too frightened in contemplating the death of someone who may not be very like us now, either physically or mentally. Such worries are irrelevant to Kant's doctrine. He does not construe mental unity as involving the continuity of a mystical Cartesian ego, but in terms of a relation of contentual connection across states. Since contentual connection need not imply great psychological similarity, it would be perfectly consistent with his analysis in the First Critique to appeal to facts about human psychology in setting up appropriate social institutions, and in developing reasonable personal expectations. Given such research, we might not punish someone for a past misdeed, even though we acknowledge that we are confronting the same mind. Locke himself realized that although "person" is a forensic term, our legal practices do not invariably accord with our views about the continuity of persons.[40]

Although Kant is an absolutist, he has nothing to fear from Parfit's recent critique of absolutism. His position does not rest on metaphysical error, nor need it lead to practical error. Conversely, the Critical investigations into the unity of apperception raise serious doubts about Parfit's claim that there is no fact of the matter about personal identity. Kant advocates the cognitive criterion for theoretical reasons: Synthetic connection is essential for basic cognitive capacities, so cognitive states are parts of one mind if and only if they can be synthetically connected.[41] Synthetic connection is a deep fact about mental life; it underlies mental capacities that enable us to be persons. Further, it sets up a particularly intimate relationship between past and present mental states. For the past states that can be synthesized with present states exhaust our inner cognitive resources for dealing with present problems. Given this theoretical justification for using 'same mind', and the absence of untoward practical consequences, Parfit's basic contention that judgments of personal identity must be arbitrary (and can be pernicious) seems less compelling.[42,43]

Objections Considered

Is the Cognitive Criterion Too Weak?

I conclude my argument for introducing apperception into contemporary dialogues about personal identity and mental unity by examining three likely objections. The doctrine that cognitive states belong to one mind if and only if they can be synthetically connected to each other offers a criterion of mental unity that is too weak, too strong, or too "*a priori.*"

The criterion may seem too weak, because comentality is defined in terms of which cognitive states *can* be synthesized with others. Can under what circumstances? If we are willing to do enough tinkering, strange things can happen. So, for example, we might carefully remove a small piece of Brown's brain and place it in a corresponding location in Robinson's head, so that the cognitive states whose memory traces were in that bit of gray matter might be synthesized with Robinson's current states. The criterion is too weak, because Brown's and Robinson's (and everybody else's) states *can* be synthesized.

This implication is avoided by making explicit what the previous formulation leaves implicit: can under fairly normal circumstances, or, in Kant's preferred terminology, can constituted as we are. He does not know how to add any details, however. The *Critique*'s central negative teaching about the thinking self is that we cannot determine the material or immaterial medium of thinking or information

storage merely by analyzing the capacities required for cognition.[44]
The amended criterion may appear circular, because "normal" can
only be understood by reference to the way(s) that states of one
mind can be connected by synthesis. Cognitive states would belong to
the same mind if and only if they can be synthesized in the way(s)
that cognitive states that are states of one mind are synthesized. The
circularity is not vicious, however, because Kant is not trying to provide an epistemological criterion for telling which states belong to
one mind. He is addressing the theoretical or metaphysical question
of what the unity of a mind consists in. Given the capacities that we
attribute to minds, he argues, the states of individual minds must be
bound together by relations of contentual connection, however those
connections are normally brought about. This account is very preliminary, but not circular.

Is It Too Strong?

From a different perspective, the cognitive criterion may appear too
strong. Cognitive states are comental if and only if they can be synthetically connected, but that implies that each of a person's cognitive
states is synthesizable with all the rest. Kant does not shrink from this
implication, but stresses it: "cognitive states [must] belong *with all others
to one consciousness*, and therefore must be at least capable of being
so connected" (A116, amended translation my emphasis). At other
points he refers to apperception as "all-comprehensive" (A123),
"thorough-going"(B133, A112), and "universal" (B132). Although this
is a stringent requirement, Kant has good reasons for insisting upon it,
and a strong motive to do so: Leibniz's wild proliferation of *petites
perceptions*.[45]

Our mental life is spread out in time (A98–99). Some states are simultaneous, but the vast majority occur at different times. We may
think of a mind as a series of cognitive states, each with a temporal
parameter. To see the force of Kant's position, consider going through
the states in their temporal order. Suppose we are at state 492. The
cognitive criterion requires that for an earlier cognitive state to be comental with 492, it must be possible for elements from that state to be
combined with elements in 492 to form a subsequent state. This could
occur directly or indirectly, if elements from the earlier state had been
combined in an intermediate state that could in turn be synthetically
combined with 492.[46] Suppose, however, that this relation fails for some
state, 49. Kant's point is that if state 49 can make no epistemic contri-

bution at all to a present state, then it is for the individual *qua* knower as good as nothing (A116, B132). There is no point in assigning it to the same mind as 492, because that assignment cannot explain any cognitive attributes. We may now turn to the states that follow 492. State 492 will be comental with these states if and only if elements from 492 can be directly or indirectly combined with elements of each one to form some subsequent state. Again, let us suppose that this relation fails for some later state, 5118. Kant's point would be the same. We go forward to state 5118. If state 492 can have no epistemic impact on the now present state, then the states are nothing to each other. Finally, consider simultaneous states, 492 and 492a. If the existence of 492a is epistemically irrelevant to 492, then it is, Kant claims, misleading to place them in the same mind. Such an assignment is completely idle in accounting for the cognitive attributes of any mind. Thus, for any arbitrary state, that state will be comental with only those earlier, later, or simultaneous states with which it is connected or connectible by synthesis.

Is It Too A Priori?

Although Kant has a rationale for his stringent criterion, it may lead to a different charge—the familiar charge that his theory is excessively *a priori* (i.e., too far removed from actual or potential empirical data). In evaluating this charge, it will be helpful to have a less abstract version of the doctrine. Kant regarded it as an open question whether thinking is carried out by an immaterial or material substance or by a series of such substances. However, he presumably believed that earlier mental states influence later states, because they leave a trace in some medium or other. As we saw earlier, Leibniz speculated that every perception leaves a permanent trace.[47] Tetens drones on incessantly about the *spüren* (traces) left by previous mental states. So presumably Kant thinks that a cognitive state has a potential influence on later states through some sort of material or immaterial trace.[48] Given this somewhat more concrete model, we can evaluate the charge of excessive apriority by imagining future scientific discoveries that might threaten his doctrine.

Three possible results seem problematic. First, suppose it turns out that not all cognitive states leave permanent traces. In fact, a number of psychologists have speculated that information taken in by the senses only reaches long-term memory through rehearsal (e.g., repeating the phone number you just heard several times) or through "deep process-ing" (i.e., by being integrated with information that is already in long-term memory).[49] Consider the moment when someone hears a phone number. Since that number might be rehearsed or might simply fit into previous information, that intuition could be synthesized with previous mental states. Thus, it would be comental with those states. Suppose, however, that no further processing does occur and that no trace is laid up. Two days later, that intuition will not be connectible by synthesis with previous cognitive states.

Although this discovery would refute Leibniz's metaphysical specu-lation, Kant does not prejudge the issue. His theory could accommodate this development in either of two ways. First, it would be reasonable to deny that ephemeral states that fail to leave traces are cognitive states. In that case, they would not be included in the scope of his definition of synthetic connection. Such states might have become functioning parts of minds, but failed to and so should not be regarded as cognitive states. A second response would be to relativize comentality to a time. Two states would belong to the same mind, at a time, if, at that time, they could be connected by synthesis. The set of cognitive states that belong to the unity of apperception is constantly changing (by expansion) through time. If there are traceless states, then that set would constantly expand and contract. Since both options are reasonable, the discovery that presumed cognitive states do not always leave traces would not require us to reject the cognitive criterion.

Second, suppose that we discover that after 25 years, 38 percent of brain traces disappear. Taking the set of traces laid down in human brains in 1965, only 62 percent remain today. We may consider a par-ticular cognitive state, 49, whose trace has vanished. Let us assume further that although 49 could have been synthesized with other states, it was inert. It has no trace and no derivatives. Now consider state 492 that occurred in 1970. For a long period of time these states were com-ental, but they are no longer. Further, 492 was comental with 49 and is comental with the current state, 5118, but 49 and 5118 are never comental. Although this may seem perplexing, the cognitive account can be defended by repeating the second response to the question of traceless mental states. The set of states that belong to the unity of apperception expands and contracts over time. Thus, states that are comental at some times need not be comental at all times. This is both logically sound and a natural response to the alleged discovery, inde-pendently of prior theoretical commitments. For how else would we interpret the discovery of impermanent traces except in terms of temporary constituents of minds or brains?

Modularity

Although the cognitive criterion could handle both these discoveries, a third possible development raises serious questions. In recent years there has been much discussion of the modular structure of the mind. [50] Modularity means that the mind is composed of a group of independent systems for dealing with different kinds of data. A central tenet of the modularity hypothesis is that different modules do not share information back and forth. In Zenon Pylyshyn's phrase, they are " informationally encapsulated."[51] Seemingly, the establishment of the modularity thesis would refute Kant's view that the states of one mind can all enter into relations of synthesis. But the situation is quite complex. First, some versions of modularity are compatible with Kant's position. For example, Jerry Fodor suggests that sensory systems are modular, but they feed information forward into a central processing system.[52] Information about stereoscopic depth might be processed by a module in the visual system but then forwarded to the central processing system, where it can be combined with information from other modules. Since states within that module will have contributed information to the state that is forwarded, they will be connectible by synthesis with states from other modules. Still, other possible versions of modularity would be more problematic. Suppose that different modules affect behavior directly, without pooling their information at any stage. How should this situation be characterized? Is one body being directed by different minds? Both Plato and Freud present this type of picture (although neither should be thought of as a protomodularity theorist). Although this option seems possible, in advance of knowing specific details, it is hardly forced.

This objection reveals both the strength and weakness of Kant's account. He develops the doctrine of apperception by carrying out a transcendental psychology of *cognition*. If the problem is cast in those terms, then I believe that his analysis is sound. Synthetic connection is necessary for basic cognitive capacities, and therefore the foundation of a necessary unity of apperception. Insofar as we consider the mind exclusively in terms of its cognitive abilities, there is no reason to classify states that can have no cognitive bearing on one another as belonging to the same mind. So Kant concludes that such states would be "nothing to me." What the modularity objection shows is that this may be the wrong way to conceptualize the problem. Perhaps a mind should not be considered exclusively in terms of its cognitive abilities; perhaps it should be regarded as that which directs the behavior of a particular body; or perhaps it should be considered as a source of interests and intentions.

On the other hand, there is value in Kant's single-mindedness. Because he focuses exclusively on cognition, he is able to offer a rich analysis that reveals that many cognitive tasks require certain connections across the states of a mind. Since a mind is engaged in cognition, it is extremely important to have an account that explores the unity of consciousness from this direction, even if that is not the only possible or useful direction. Kant's account may well need to be augmented by noncognitive factors, and so revised. This scenario hardly upholds the charge of excessive apriority, however. It shows only that his analysis is a function of his way of conceptualizing the problem—just as anyone's analysis will be.

Summary of the Account

Chapter 4 and the first four sections of this chapter present an interpretation of the transcendental unity of apperception that diverges from the accepted wisdom on every major count. On my reading, apperception is neither the first premise of the transcendental deduction, nor a version of the *cogito*, nor about the self-ascription of cognitive states, nor about self-awareness, nor (in the pejorative sense) a metaphysical doctrine. On the contrary, it is an adequate reply to Hume's skepticism about personal identity that has much of Hume in it. It presents a theoretical account of the unity of a mind that is grounded in the attempt to understand how basic cognitive capacities are possible. As such, it goes far beyond the frequently cited work of Locke and Leibniz on personal identity and can also illuminate contemporary debates. This may seem too good to be true, but considerable internal and external evidence reveals that the doctrine I attribute to Kant is a central theme of the Deduction chapter. Were that chapter read on its own, apperception would probably have a much less negative reputation. But, of course, it never is. When considered in light of Kant's other remarks about the self, and in light of another feature of transcendental idealism, both the doctrine of apperception and transcendental psychology generally begin to look like transcendental doubletalk. In the last section, I confront these problems and suggest how this valuable work may be preserved. As noted earlier, this calls for some fairly revisionary steps.

Apperception and Kant's System

Too Many Selves

I discussed the problem of "too many selves" briefly in Chapter 1.[53] Officially, the *Critique* maintains that there are two selves or that the self may be viewed from two perspectives.[54] From one perspective, it is understood as "phenomenal" or "empirical," "passive," subject to natural laws, and hence unfit to be the object of moral criticism. According to the other, the self is "noumenal," completely unknown and unknowable, but morally evaluable (Bxxvii–xxix). As noted, the problem is that it is not clear how the I of apperception can be fitted into this scheme. Kant is staggeringly ambivalent on this fundamental point, and in the end he refuses to categorize it as either phenomenal or noumenal:

> The I think expresses an indeterminate empirical intuition, i.e., perception. Something real that is given, given indeed to thought in general, and so not as appearance [phenomenon], nor as thing in itself (*noumenon*), but as something which actually exists, and which in the proposition I think is denoted as such . . . [B422–23n, my underscoring].

It is not hard to guess what is driving Kant to a position that is incoherent in his own system. As we saw in Chapter 4, he occasionally entertained hopes of using the spontaneity of apperception to make a case for transcendental freedom. Although that project is abandoned in the *Critique*, the possibility of transcendental freedom is still supposed to be established by the phenomenal–noumenal distinction. The problem is that apperception falls on the wrong side of this distinction, and so threatens to undermine its point.

Given the impossibility of noumenal knowledge, the doctrine of apperception must present a phenomenal, if highly abstract, aspect of the self. If Kant is right that anything of which we can have knowledge must be governed by causal laws, then synthetic connection will be lawful. Imagination, understanding, and reason will all have their own laws. The I that thinks will be phenomenal and causally determined. This I is, however, too close to us. It is the I with which we identify. What possible comfort—or even interest—could we have in knowing that some noumenal self is free and potentially immortal, when the self with which we identify, the thinker, is phenomenal? I believe that Kant refuses to acknowledge the phenomenal character of the doctrine of apperception to avoid this devastating implication. I see no coherent alternative, however. The doctrine of apperception can only be phenomenal, and so we might as well admit this fact,[55] whatever the fallout for doctrines in the later Critiques.

The Ideality of Time

Within the context of Kant's system, a second, major problem for the doctrine of apperception, and transcendental psychology generally, is the ideality of time thesis. Strawson gives the essential outlines of this issue in his argument for the fundamental incoherence of transcendental idealism.[56] The various activities that are described in the Deduction's account of how the mind influences (or might influence) what we know can only be understood temporally. They are processes and so take time.[57] According to the Aesthetic, however, the mind's activities *produce* time. So they cannot take place in time.

I agree with Strawson that trying to understand the activities described by transcendental psychology atemporally requires "traversing the limits of intelligibility."[58] I also agree that central tenets of Kant's philosophy produce intractable inconsistency.[59] Not surprisingly, I demur on the point that the incoherence is largely the fault of transcendental psychology.[60]

Transcendental psychology is consistent with itself. There is no conflict between the transcendental psychology of the Deduction and that of the Aesthetic. The psychology of perception in the Aesthetic establishes, for example, that we can perceive space only because our senses can construct three-dimensional percepts from two-dimensional retinal data. This hardly implies that space is not three-dimensional, however. It shows only that we cannot infer that space is three-dimensional from what we perceive (without further argument). Kant's arguments that space and time are forms of intuition do not establish that they are not real; and they are certainly not what convinced him that they are not real. The reasoning runs in the opposite direction. He was convinced of the unreality of space and time on metaphysical and scientific grounds. In the Antinomies, he presents the metaphysical considerations. Typically, the obvious scientific background is left implicit. The lengthy, brilliant, but fundamentally inconclusive debates over the nature of space and time convinced Kant, I believe, that science (i.e., Newtonian physics) could not assign any determinate character to space or time.[61] Since any real thing must have a determinate character, however (A39/B56), space and time are not real, as far as science is concerned. Given this conviction, and the contemporary puzzles about how we perceive space, Kant then argued that the space we perceive only reflects the way we perceive.

In one guise, the point that I have been arguing has been familiar since the nineteenth century.[62] It does not follow from the fact that space and time are forms of intuition that they are not also real.[63] Even though the character of our perceptions is not evidence for time, time could be shown to be real on theoretical grounds. Its reality could be established if a well-supported theory required us to assume the passage of time. Kant nearly considers this type of argument. Intelligent people unanimously object to the ideality of time thesis on the grounds that alterations are real (A36–37/B53–54). At this point, what is needed is some good theoretical explanation that requires alterations. Kant's own theory of synthetic connection would do, but maddeningly he does not pursue the objection in this or any other fruitful direction. Instead, he turns it into a straw man. Intelligent people are not confident about alteration on theoretical grounds, but because of the changes in their cognitive states. But our perceptions only reflect the forms of intuition, so the objection fizzles. Again, I suspect that Kant is unwilling to reintroduce theoretical arguments about time, because the most sophisticated and fundamental arguments (from physics) had already proved inconclusive.

In any case, Kant's transcendental psychology does not suffer from internal inconsistency.[64] The inconsistency is between the theory of apperception and transcendental psychology generally and the doctrine of the ideality of time. If time is not real, then the accounts of the identify of a mind through time, and of the cognitive processes that enable us to have knowledge, are incoherent. Conversely, if the theories of synthetic processing and apperception are true, then time is real.

Under these circumstances I see no choice but to reject the metaphysical claim, which is, in any case, independently problematic. This is a drastic move within Kant's system. Still, it does not mean a total rejection of transcendental idealism. For in keeping transcendental psychology, we also keep the source of all the arguments that our knowledge is influenced by the structure of our minds. And that doctrine is at least as central to transcendental idealism as the theses of the ideality of space and time. Although more devout Kantians will undoubtedly find my proposals extreme, I see no other way to preserve Kant's important work on apperception and the prerequisites of cognition generally.

6

Perceiving Times and Spaces: The Cognitive Capacity at the Center of the Deduction

Cognitive Tasks, Apperception, and the Deduction of the Categories

Chapters 3 and 4 followed Kant's explorations of three cognitive tasks:

How can we represent objects?
How can we make judgments about objects?
How can cognitive states be representational for a subject?

Chapters 4 and 5 showed how these analyses led to the development of a persuasive account of mental unity, the unity of apperception. This material constitutes a substantial part of the objective and subjective sides of the Deduction chapter. What is missing from the account so far is what is missing for most of the chapter itself: the connection between these task analyses and apperception, and Kant's goal of establishing a special status for the 12 categorial concepts. That is the project for this chapter. I will use these task analyses and the account of apperception, plus a more specific analysis—the analysis of perceiving spatial and temporal arrays—to show how Kant's transcendental psychology enables him to construct one long argument for the universal applicability and indispensability of the categories, an argument that stretches from the Aesthetic through the Principles.

In the prefatory material to the Deduction chapter, Kant describes his goal. The deduction of the categories must show, "how *subjective conditions of thought* can have *objective validity*, that is, can furnish conditions of the possibility of all cognition of objects" (A90/B122, amended translation). Since the subjective conditions of thought are the categories, the goal is to show how the categories furnish conditions for the possibility of all cognition of objects. Those conditions are explored in the objective deduction. Among other factors, knowledge of objects is possible only if we can represent objects and make judgments about them. As we saw in Chapter 3,[1] we can represent objects on the basis of our constantly changing stream of sensory inputs only if we have a productive imagination that can synthesize representations from cognitive states. At this point, we need to be explicit about a requirement that was only implicit in the earlier discussion. Cognizers must have rules of synthesis through which actual cognitive states can be combined to form representations of objects. More formally, individuals can achieve representations of objects only if one of their functions of synthesis is defined over the cognitive states that objects produce in them. Here is the problem. The states produced would seem to depend on the particular objects encountered. How, then, could we ever be sure that we can have knowledge of all, or any, of the objects we will encounter? Kant believes that the categories solve this problem by providing universal functions of synthesis. Had he a sound argument for this view, then he would be able to show that the categories supply a crucial condition for the possibility of cognition.[2] His first attempt at this line of argument, in the A edition, is quite unpersuasive, however. As noted,[3] he assumes that the functions that permit the construction of representations of objects also permit the representations to be brought under a concept (A105). He then assumes that the categories supply the universal functions of synthesis that permit thought (and concept application) (A111).[4] So he may conclude that the categories make it possible to construct representations of objects and so supply a critical condition for the possibility of knowledge.

The objective side of the B deduction focuses on judgment. Knowledge of objects requires being able to make judgments about objects. In turn, as we have seen,[5] judgment presupposes a synthesis that constructs representations of objects and then requires a further synthesis of those representations. Kant believed that judgment provided a more direct argument for the special status of the categories. But this argument is much too quick. He takes as given the assertion of the Metaphysical Deduction that the synthetic functions that permit judgment are functions associated with the categories (B143). Thus, once again, he can claim that the categories supply a condition for the possibility of knowledge. He has yet to provide a convincing argument for this view, however.

Kant's reliance on the Metaphysical Deduction's inadequately supported identification of the basic forms of judgment with the categories distorts the argument of the Deduction chapter. To show that the categories have objective validity (i.e., furnish the conditions for the possibility of *all* cognition of objects), he would have to show that they must be involved in all our perceptions and thoughts or judgments of objects. Given this identification, however, he feels no obligation to explain how the categories make judgments possible. Instead, all his efforts to justify the categories are concentrated on explaining the "by no means obvious," fact that "objects of sensible intuition . . . must conform to the conditions which the understanding requires for . . . thought [i.e., the categories]" (A90/B123). Only when he returns to the consideration of individual categories in the Principles can we entertain any hopes of finding arguments that thoughts or judgments are also subject to the "conditions required for thought."

Kant does not try to establish a special status for the categories just by examining the conditions required for cognition of objects in general. Either because he realized the lameness of the arguments just presented or because he wanted to convince skeptical opponents and so could not assume that we have knowledge, or for both reasons, he also offers an argument from apperception. In this case, the argument is to show that the categories are indispensable, because they furnish conditions that make apperception possible. This is one point on which all commentators agree. Somewhere in the Deduction chapter is an argument from apperception, and it is supposed to bear much of the burden of establishing the special status of the categories. This clue only helps us to understand the structure of the deduction, however, if we have a clear understanding of the doctrine of apperception. In the preceding chapters I have argued that apperception does not concern the ascription of cognitive states; it is a theory about what must be true of cognitive states for them to *be* states of one mind.[6] They must be connected or connectible by synthesis with one another. It is further confirmation of this interpretation of apperception that it enables us to see quite clearly how the argument from apperception for the categories is supposed to go.

If the unity of apperception is a matter of synthetic connections across cognitive states, then it is fairly obvious what conditions are necessary for the *possibility* of apperception. Apperception is possible only if a thoroughgoing connection of cognitive states by synthesis is possible. Once again, there is a potential problem. Cognitive states will be connectible by synthesis only if there are functions of synthesis that are defined over them, indeed, defined over any pair of them (since all states that belong to the unity of apperception must be connectible with each other). But how could we ever be sure that rules of synthesis are available to produce the unity of apperception? This problem is simplified for Kant, because he has already handled the case of thoughts or judgments. These are subject to the rules of thought, which reflect or are associated with the categories. Once judgments are constructed, they can be combined in further judgments by the logical connectives.[7] For example, the elements of "I am cold" and "The cat is on the mat" can be combined into a further judgment, "I am cold and the cat is on the mat." So when he raises the issue of the possibility of apperception, he casts the problem in terms of intuition:

> For the diverse cognitive states that are given in a certain intuition would not be one and all *my* cognitive states if they did not all belong to one self-consciousness. As *my* mental states . . . they must conform to the condition under which alone they *can* stand together in one universal self-consciousness . . . [B132, amended translation; see also A122].

The problem of the possibility of apperception thus comes down to the problem of how we can ever know that all our actual intuitions are connectible by synthesis with each other. Again, the argument Kant wants to make is that this condition on the possibility of apperception can be fulfilled by the categories. They provide universal functions of synthesis that can guarantee mental unity (A125).

The task analyses of the objective Deduction and the subjective Deduction's doctrine of apperception thus prepare the ground for similar arguments for a special status for the categories. Representing objects and judging objects required functions of synthesis that can be applied to cognitive states produced by whatever our senses present us with; the possibility of apperception requires functions of synthesis that allow us to unite all our intuitions in a single self-consciousness. In both cases, these conditions can be supplied by functions of synthesis associated with the categories. Or so Kant wants to argue. Although the requirements for objective knowledge and apperception can both be satisfied by the categories, the assumptions behind these arguments are importantly different. In one case the possibility of cognition is assumed, and it is taken to involve perceiving objects and bringing them under concepts. This is clear as Kant sums up this side of the argument in the A Deduction:

> Actual [cognitive] experience, which is constituted by apprehension, association (reproduction), and finally recognition of appearances, contains in the last and highest of these merely empirical elements of experience, certain concepts which render possible the formal unity of experience,

and therewith all objective validity (truth) of empirical knowledge . . .
[A125].[8]

This is a very rich notion of cognitive experience, and the argument
that the categories render experience possible threatens to become vacuous. Since experience involves thinking about objects, it must be
subject to rules of thought which are allegedly associated with the categories. By contrast, the argument from apperception begins with the
most minimal cognitive task: the ability to have cognitive states that
represent some content to the subject. From this minimal assumption,
Kant argues for the necessary unity of apperception, and then from
apperception to the special status of the categories. The categories are
required for the possibility of apperception, and that is required even
to have cognitive states that are representational for the subject.

As already indicated, Kant makes several attempts to argue from the
necessity of syntheses to a special status for the categories, attempts that
fall short of their goal. At ¶ 26 of the B Deduction, he tries again, by analyzing yet another cognitive task, our ability to perceive times and places,
to perceive A following B, or C above and to the left of D. This analysis allows Kant to forge a link between the Aesthetic's doctrine of the forms of
intuition and the arguments about our ability to assign temporal and spatial position to objects and events in the Principles, and thus to construct
one long argument to show that the categories can furnish conditions for
the possibility of knowledge and for the possibility of apperception.

In the end, I will argue that Kant's analysis—and so his best argument
for the categories—fails. Like his contemporaries and our own, he has
great difficulty understanding the relation between perception and cognition, and so makes an error in transcendental psychology. Still, this
analysis offers valuable insights into the tensions and issues that must be
dealt with by any adequate theory of perception or cognition. At the end
of the chapter, I examine yet another cognitive task, the Second Analogy's investigation of our ability to perceive temporal order. I consider this
task, because (as I shall argue) the best version of the deduction of the
categories is not completed until the argument of the Principles, and this
is the critical example. In this case, I argue again that the analysis provides important insights. Although both these analyses are independently
valuable, the central purpose of this chapter is exegetical. I try to show
that by taking a psychological approach to apperception and by considering the analyses of various cognitive tasks, especially the analysis of
perceiving times and spaces, we can see Kant as offering a fairly clean line
of argument for a special status for the categories. Even though the de-

duction contains mistakes, it brings together a number of important considerations about cognition in a powerful and coherent case for a special set of concepts. The deduction is neither a patchwork nor a botch, but a bold and clever attempt to carry out a sensible and potentially very important project: Given the cognitive capacities that we have and the resources that we bring to them, are there any necessary and invariant features of human cognition? This is why, after 200 years, the deduction of the categories is still a fascinating and important piece of work.

Paragraph 26 of the B Deduction is about perception. Kant begins by drawing attention to the fact that by "*synthesis of apprehension* I understand the combination of the manifold in an empirical intuition, whereby <u>perception</u>, that is, empirical consciousness of the intuition (as appearance) is possible" (B160, my underscoring). He concludes the main body of the section with the observation that, "All synthesis, therefore, <u>even that which renders perception possible</u>, is subject to the categories" (B161, my underscoring). This paragraph is difficult to follow, because, although Kant tells us that his topic is perception, he does not inform us about his own or his contemporaries' assumptions about perception. ("Empirical consciousness of the intuition as appearance" merely replaces one difficult concept with four difficult concepts.) In the next three sections, I fill in four key pieces of the background. "Perception: The Eighteenth-Century Background" briefly presents some widespread scientific and philosophical assumptions about perception. In "The Synthesis of Apprehension in A," I consider the A edition's argument for constructivism in perception, specifically, for the synthesis of apprehension. "A Role for Concepts in Perception in A" follows Kant's exploration of the relation between concepts and perception in perceptual recognition. With this material in hand, I return to the crucial arguments of ¶ 26. Once we have seen where Kant (and others) have been, it will be much easier to see where he is going, and why.

Perception: The Eighteenth-Century Background

The Standard View

The standard eighteenth-century view of perception included the following elements. As always, the central case was vision. We see by the light reflected from objects causing images on the fundament or retina of the eye. As William Porterfield put the point in his widely read *A Treatise on the Eye*, we do not, however, "see any pictures painted on the retina.''[9] From the retina, nerves travel up through the optic chiasma to the thalamus. Many believed that because of the order of the nerves, when sensations are finally produced in the sensorium—when the neural signals somehow become mental and conscious—the images are isomorphic to retinal images. These elements of the standard view were all presented in Johann Gehler's encyclopedic *Physikalisches Wörterbuch, oder Versuch einer Erklärung der vornehmsten Begriffe und Kunstwörter der Naturlehre*, which was being prepared as Kant wrote the editions of the *Critique*.[10]

Intellectual Theories of Perception

As noted in Chapter 3, Thomas Reid's influential theory proposed an important distinction between sensations and perceptions. According to Reid, we do not usually take note of our sensations, but overlook them. Kant seems to endorse this view in the *Anthropology*, when he claims that, if we are more conscious of the organ being affected than of the reference to an external object, then cognitive states that belong to outer sense become inner cognitive states.[11] Reid was also well known for maintaining that perception involves a conception of the object and a belief in its present existence.[12] Since he first proposed it, the belief account of perception has attracted many psychologists and philosophers, including Kant's sometime opponent, Johann August Eberhard.[13] Oddly, it has a much stronger etymological warrant in German than in English, for the literal meaning of "*Wahrnehmung*" is "taking [for] true."

Although Reid goes further in proposing that perception actually involves belief, both Locke and Condillac had taken perception to have an intellectual component. Locke described perception as "the first operation of all our intellectual faculties. . . ."[14] Condillac echoed the sentiments: "The perception or the impression caused in the mind by the agitation of the senses, is the first operation of the understanding."[15] On the other hand, if Tetens is a reliable witness, then the question of whether there was a recognitional–intellectual–conceptual element in 'l representations that allow us to differentiate objects was a major and dis,puted one.[16]

The Synthesis of Apprehension in A

A99

Turning to Kant's own views, ¶ 26 focuses on the "synthesis of apprehension that makes perception possible." Because this synthesis is not mentioned previously in the B Deduction, it is hard to see how we can understand the phrase except by looking at the first edition, where it occurs twice. The first reference comes as Kant prepares the reader for the transcendental deduction. He tries to explain the need for a *synthesis of apprehension*. Although our senses supply us with diverse elements, these cannot be represented as a diversity and contained in a single cognitive state without a synthesis of apprehension (A99). He gives the example of constructing a representation of space and notes that, because the contents of this representation include *a priori*$_O$ elements, the synthesis of apprehension must be pure and *a priori*$_O$.

Kant's reasoning in this passage is very dark. He claims, enigmatically, that insofar as it is contained in a single moment of time, a moment that can be distinguished from the moments it follows and precedes, a cognitive state [or its contents] must be an absolute unity. At this point, it is important—indeed essential—to recall where this is leading. Kant is preparing us for the discussion of perception that occurs at A119–20.[17] The single representation that we are being asked to consider is a single *perception*.

A119–20

The second discussion of the synthesis of apprehension in A is vastly clearer. This synthesis is needed to produce an *image* from the sensory data (A120). Kant repeats the point, with some elaboration, in a footnote:

> That imagination is a necessary ingredient in perception itself, no psychologist has yet realised. . . . This is due partly to the fact that that faculty has been limited to reproduction, partly to the belief that the senses not only supply impressions but also combine them so as to generate images of objects. For that purpose, something more than the mere receptivity of impressions is required, namely, a function for the synthesis of them [A120a; first sentence, my translation].

Why have psychologists failed to see the crucial role of imagination in perception? One explanation may be that they subscribe to the standard view presented in Gehler's *Wörterbuch*. What we see corresponds to—indeed is isomorphic to—the retinal image, either because of the arrangement of nerves or for some other reason. Kant's objection to this position is not that it is false, but that it is much less than the entire account. Although they differed over the possibility of unconscious perception, Locke, Leibniz, Reid, Condillac, and Tetens—and Kant—all acknowledged that innumerable retinal images never reach perceptual awareness. Hume misstated the case in claiming that (conscious) mental life is nothing but a stream of perceptions in constant and incredibly rapid flux; but his point is correct for unconscious retinal images. Under these circumstances the claim that mental representations replicate the topology of retinal images provides only a small piece of the account of how we have stable and coherent visual images.

A common gesture in the direction of a solution was to suggest that we *attend* to some mental representations and not to others. Condillac, Reid, and Tetens all appeal to attention[18]; in the *Anthropology*, Kant characterizes the power of apprehending given ideas to produce an intuition as *attentio* (attention).[19] This notion cannot bear much weight, however. It is only a place holder to indicate some means of selecting some elements of some cognitive states and discarding others. But selecting and discarding is not enough, and this is Kant's point. If a stable visual image of a scene is to be produced, then el_ments from the selected representations must be combined.

Examples from the Pölitz Lectures

The student lecture notes published by Pölitz[20] contain a remarkably clear discussion of this issue, complete with three helpful examples:

> My mind is always occupied forming itself an image of the diverse elements by running through them. For example, when I see a city, my mind forms itself an image of the object that it has before it by running through the diverse elements. When later, a person comes into a room that is loaded with pictures and adornments, he cannot make himself an image of it, because the mind cannot run through it. He does not know where to begin in order to make himself a likeness of the object. It has been reported that when a stranger comes into St. Peter's in Rome, he becomes totally confused because of the multiplicity of the splendors. The cause is: his mind cannot run through the diverse elements to make a likeness of them. The imitative faculty is the formative faculty of intuition. The mind must employ many observations in order to make itself a likeness of an object, by representing [for] itself the object from every other side. For example, a city appears differently in the morning and in the evening. There are thus many appearances of a thing according to different sides and points of view. From all these appearances, the mind must make itself a likeness, by taking them all together.[21]

That is, we achieve perceptual images by the formative imagination selecting and combining the data of sense. The Pölitz lectures must be used with care. Few professors would want student notes to be taken as definitive of their views, Kant included.[22] It seems reasonable to use this material to illustrate doctrines that appear in the published writings, however. Besides the discussion at A120 and A120a, the formative (*bildende*) synthesis itself appears in the *Critique* in a highly relevant context: "the formative synthesis through which we construct a triangle in imagination is precisely the *same as that which we exercise in the apprehension of an appearance* . . . " (A224/B271, my emphasis).[23] That is, the synthesis of apprehension is a formative synthesis.

The Case for the Synthesis of Apprehension

Kant's defense of the synthesis of apprehension, and so of a constructivist view of perception, rests on three solid points. First, the task to be explained is how we are able to achieve stable visual images on the basis of an incredibly rapid flux of retinal images. This assumes only what all will grant: We have stable visual images; the retinal data are remarkably fluid. Second, insofar as the senses are understood as *recipients* of information from the ambient environment, the creation of visual images cannot be attributed to the senses. Descartes had introduced the notion of a "common sense" (which was also taken up by Locke) where data from the various senses were to be combined to produce a common representation of the object. This doctrine may be part of (or much of) the explanation of why psychologists have failed to appreciate the need for imagination in perception. Kant's objection to it is straightforward. If sensibility is characterized as the faculty that receives information, then, in the absence of empirical investigation, it cannot *also* be characterized as the faculty that combines information. Finally, insofar as imagination is understood merely as a faculty for reproducing the data of sense, it is not up to the task. Reproducing the order of sense would simply reproduce the flux from the retina. Since copying and reproducing are inadequate to the demands of the task, Kant reasons that we must have a constructive faculty. The perceptual image represents together aspects of the object that coexist in it but that were not sensed together. As he notes explicitly in B, the imagination is commonly characterized as the faculty of representing in intuition an object that is not present (B151). So he assigns the construction to a constructive or productive imagination.

This analysis of perception is a special case of problem of constructing a representation from diverse cognitive states that we considered in Chapter 3. And it shares strengths and weaknesses of the general analysis. Although Kant defends the need for a synthesis of apprehension, he does not justify the claim that it is *a priori*$_O$. Again, all he shows is that the law of association is inadequate. If he could support the assertion at A99 that the synthesis of apprehension is responsible for the construction of representations of space (or time), then he would have a more reasonable claim that it is *a priori*$_O$.

A99 Revisited

This interpretation of A120 and A120a receives some additional confirmation from the fact that it allows us to make some sense of the earlier discussion at A99. Kant's claim that a synthesis of apprehension is necessary if diverse elements are to be contained in a single state representing that diversity is given considerable support by the later discussion. By reflecting on the implications of that discussion, I believe that we can also begin to see what Kant is driving at when he claims that insofar as it is contained in a single moment, a cognitive state contains an absolute unity. The point is easier to grasp by starting with an example of perceiving a temporally extended event. Suppose we are listening to the first few measures of *"Für Elise."* We do not merely hear the notes, we hear the melody. For this to happen, our awareness of individual notes must enable us to construct a state that represents the relations among those notes. The playing of the melody occurs in time, and we take in auditory information about it in time, but to hear the melody, we must bring that temporally disparate information together at some point.[24] That is, we must represent information that is temporally disparate in two senses—we receive it at different times, and it informs us about different times—in a single moment. Although not all objects of perception are spread out in time, our perceiving of them is, because perceptual images are constructed from diverse sensory data. That is the point made forcefully by A120 and A120a. Even though we perceive very quickly, data are received at slightly different moments. For us to form a perceptual image of the object, diverse elements taken in at different times must be represented together in some single moment. We might have a perceptual image that endures for some time. However, that time will be made up of moments, each one of which contains information gathered at diverse times. Given Kant's constructive account of perception, it follows that cognition is possible only if our cognitive lives are made up of such moments. I believe that this is at least part of what he is trying to get at in stressing the unity of momentary cognitive states, and the need to differentiate such moments from each other.

A Role for Concepts in Perception in A

The Need for Nonreproductive Synthesis

The first edition thus provides a clear and convincing defense of the need for a constructive synthesis in perception. This synthesis is attributed to a productive imagination, as opposed to the reproductive, which merely follows the law of association. But what does the productive imagination follow? As noted in Chapter 3, in the A edition, Kant assumes that there is some intellectual element involved in any representation or perception.[25] I objected that this point was too controversial to be assumed. The A edition makes another connection between concepts and perception, however, and this connection seems sound. In perceptions that lead to recognition in a concept, the imagination follows rules of synthesis associated with concepts.

Perceptual Recognition

As he prepares the reader for the A deduction, Kant examines the "synthesis of recognition in a concept." His point is that for perception to lead to recognition—subsuming the perceived item under a concept—there must be a synthesis of the diverse elements gathered by sense, and that synthesis must be associated with the concept (A103). The discussion of this passage is rather convoluted, and in the end, he only manages to link the imagination to the faculty of concepts, the understanding, through an intermediary discussion of apperception. We can appreciate his point about the role of concepts in perceptual recognition more easily by turning to the discussion of concept application in the Schematism.

Concept Application

Kant believes that concepts are associated with schemata, or rules for producing different kinds of images. We apply concepts to presented objects by noting in some unconscious way that the imagination followed the same procedure in constructing a present image that it followed in previous cases (A140/B179–80). That is, concept application involves a comparison of procedures for constructing representations, rather than a comparison of images themselves. How is this possible?[26] We have a finite store of concepts and associated schemata with which the procedure for generating an image of a current scene may be compared. If the imagination tried all possible ways of selecting, discarding, and combining the diverse elements provided by the senses in order to find a match with one of the stored schemata, the process would be endless. There are too many possible permutations and combinations. To yield matches, one of three possibilities must be realized. (1) The selecting and combining is directed from the top down, so that the imagination tries various procedures, taken from our repertoire of stored schemata. (2) Because it operates according to innate or acquired principles that are well coordinated with our conceptual repertoire, the imagination automatically uses procedures to generate images, images that permit matches. That is, there is something like a preestablished harmony between the faculties, so that the imagination uses procedures that permit matches with stored schemata. (3) There is some combination of top–down direction, and coordination between the faculties.

Although I have cast the issue in terms of Kant's specific theory of concept application, the range of options is the same on more standard theories, just as long as perception is taken to be constructive. Concept application requires us to compare either a current representation or something like a procedure for generating that representation, with stored representations of concepts, whether they be schemata, images, or whatever. So for concept application to be possible, the imagination must generate something—its own procedure or a product of its procedures—that can be compared with stored representations of concepts. In which case, the processes that subserve perception must be subordinate to or coordinate with the processes involved in concept application. Otherwise, the perceptual processes might synthesize endlessly without ever permitting the application of a concept.

The crucial point is not the particular theory of concept application, but the argument that perception is constructive. Without this assumption the argument collapses, because the entire system could be data driven. We would not select among sensory representations, but merely forward them to some location in the mind–brain where they are compared with stored copies of previous sensory representations. In these circumstances neither subordination nor coordination would be required. Once perception is shown to be constructive, however, it follows that, in concept application, the imagination and the understanding must be related by subordination or coordination. The discussion in ¶ 24 of the B edition suggests that Kant leans toward subordination, but a passage from the *Anthropology* employs a coordination model.[27] For the purpose of understanding the argument in ¶ 26, we need not choose among these options. Whether through coordination, subordination, or some combination of the two, in concept application, the imagination is able to produce representations or procedures that match stored representations of concepts. I will refer to the syntheses of the imagination that produce these representations as "C-functions," because they subserve concept application. Since we can apply concepts to objects through perception, we know that the imagination can construct perceptions on the basis of sensory data through the use of C-functions.

With some understanding of current assumptions about perception, particularly Kant's own views about the necessity of a synthesis of apperception and the role of concepts in perceptual recognition, I believe that we can make considerable sense of the dense argumentation in ¶ 26.

¶ 26 in the B Deduction

The Centrality of ¶ 26

Kant is explicit about his goals for this section:

> We have now to explain the possibility of knowing *a priori*, by means of *categories*, whatever objects may *present themselves to our senses*, not indeed in respect of the form of their intuition, but in respect of the laws of their combination. . . . For unless the categories discharged this function, there could be no explaining why everything that can be presented to our senses must be subject to laws which have their origin *a priori* in the understanding alone [B159–60, original emphasis].

That is, this section is going to explain the by no means obvious fact that objects of sensible intuition must conform to the categories. But this was a major goal that Kant announced right at the beginning of the Deduction (compare A90/B123)! Presumably, he thinks that it has not yet been attained. The final section of the chapter (¶ 27) merely recapitulates the argument and relates the conclusion to other possible solutions to this set of problems. Clearly, ¶ 26 is intended to make a crucial contribution to the deduction of the categories.

In a classic study, Dieter Henrich argued for the importance of this section from a slightly different perspective.[28] Henrich drew attention to a striking textual puzzle. At both ¶ 20 and ¶ 26, Kant announces that he has now completed the deduction of the categories. The inconsistency is mitigated somewhat by the immediate observation in ¶ 21 that he has really only begun the deduction; more work remains to be done. On the basis of these comments, Henrich proclaims that any acceptable interpretation of the deduction must explain what is new in ¶ 26, or between ¶ 20 and ¶ 26, which permits the completion of the deduction. He calls this interpretive criterion the problem of the "two-steps-in-one-proof." Although this constraint on interpretations seems persuasive, I shall disagree with his own solution to the problem later.

Perception as "Scanning an Image"

After introductory remarks about his goals for the section, Kant presents his broad topic: the synthesis of apprehension required for perception. As noted, he then characterizes perception as the "empirical consciousness of the intuition (as appearance)" (B160). Of course, Leibniz had denied that perceptions are always conscious, but Kant's usage does not appear to beg any substantive questions about the existence of *petites perceptions*. As we have seen, Kant allows for the existence of unconscious cognitive states (*Vorstellungen*).[29] He simply reserves the term "perception" for states of which we are aware.[30] Although this section does not offer further explicit characterizations, some examples are appended to the main discussion that clarify Kant's understanding of perception. In particular, the example of perceiving a house gives a fairly clear sense of how he conceives of the central case of visual perception:

> When, for instance, by apprehension[31] of the diverse elements of a house I make the empirical intuition of it into a perception, the *necessary unity* of space and of outer sensible intuition in general lies at the basis of my apprehension, and I draw as it were the outline of the house in conformity with this synthetic unity of the diverse elements in space [B162, amended translation, my underscoring].

The passage I underscore suggests that Kant takes perception to involve something like scanning the contours and boundaries of perceived objects. We perceive when we draw a line around the objects boundaries and other salient geometrical features with our mind's eye. If we cannot do this much, then it is not clear that we are even differentiating an object from its background, so this is quite a minimal sense of perceiving. With some trepidation, I will describe this model of perception in terms of "scanning an image." "Scanning an image" is an abbreviation for "scanning the visible contours of an object represented in an image." (We don't see—*a fortiori*, we don't scan—our perceptual images themselves.)

Given this model of perception, we can sharpen the characterization of Kant's goals. He will try to explain how the categories apply to all objects that we can perceive, in the minimal sense of being able to scan images of them. Or to return to another formulation (to which he returns at the end of the section): The goal is to establish the objective validity of the categories by showing how they furnish conditions for the possibility of all cognition of objects—even this very minimal cognitive task of scanning the image of an object.[32] Since it is not obvious how the categories might contribute to the possibility of scanning an image, and so why this type of perception might be governed by them, Kant has set himself a challenging project.

Perceiving Times and Spaces

Kant argues that the categories are needed for, and involved in, the perception of all objects in space and time—even in this minimal sense— by arguing that they are needed for, and involved in, perceiving times and spaces. This essential lemma is established by analyzing the task of perceiving times and spaces. Space and time are not merely the forms of intuition, but themselves intuitions. "[They are also represented *a priori*] as themselves *intuitions* which contain a diversity of elements and therefore are represented with the unity of this diversity" (B160). We perceive spatial and temporal arrays. We perceive A before B and C above and to the left of D. How are we able to do this? This discussion draws on a point that Kant adds to the B edition:

> The mere form of outer sensible intuition, space, is not yet cognition; it supplies only the diverse elements of *a priori* intuition for a possible cognition. To know anything in space (for instance, a line), I must *draw it, and thus synthetically bring into being a determinate combination of the given* diverse elements . . . ; and it is through this unity of consciousness that an object (a determinate space) is first known [B137–38, amended translation, my underscoring].

The form of outer intuition guarantees that whatever two-dimensional data we take in will be represented in a spatial grid. In and of itself, however, the process form does not produce a representation of any particular (or determinate) spatial region. To perceive spatial [and temporal] regions, we must perceive (or imagine) objects and events in spatial [and temporal] arrays.

Kant repeats this point, and expands upon it, in a notoriously convoluted note that appears in the middle of ¶ 26.

> Space, represented as *object* (as we are required to do in geometry[33]), contains more than mere form of intuition; it also contains *combination*

of the diverse elements, given according to the form of sensibility, in a cognitive state whose contents are *intuitive*, so that the *form of intuition* gives only the diverse elements, the *formal intuition* gives unity of the contents of a cognitive state. In the Aesthetic I have treated this unity as belonging merely to sensibility, simply in order to emphasize that it precedes any concept, <u>although, as a matter of fact, it presupposes a synthesis which does not belong to the senses but through which all concepts of space and time first become possible</u>. For since by its means (in that understanding determines the sensibility) space and time are first given as intuitions, the unity of this *a priori* intuition belongs to space and time and not to the concept of the understanding [B160a; amended translation, my underscoring].

That is, again, we have representations of particular or determinate spaces and times, and these cannot be accounted for by the existence of forms of intuition alone. (Or at least, not by what we have so far learned about the forms of intuition.) They presuppose a synthesis that makes determinate or unified representations possible. What is so confusing is that Kant first attributes the unified representation to the senses, then he notes that it requires a synthesis that belongs to the understanding, and finally he claims again that the unity belongs to the senses!

Differences Between the Editions

It is clear from the texts preceding and following the note that the synthesis at issue is the synthesis of apprehension. To begin to get a handle on this text, we must recall Kant's earlier discussions of this synthesis. As noted, the first edition provides a solid argument for the need for a constructive synthesis in perception, which is attributed to the productive imagination. The dramatic opening of the B Deduction signals a change. He proclaims that all combining or synthesizing must be attributed to the understanding (B130). At the time of the first edition, he had realized that merely reproducing the data of sense in the order in which they came would never lead to stable and coherent images, but he did not elaborate (A120–21, A120a). Between editions he must have seen the implications of this discussion more clearly. We need a faculty of imagination even to achieve the level of perception, and if a reproductive imagination is inadequate, a faculty of imagination that is unguided would be worse. So he assumes that perceptual syntheses must be carried out by the imagination guided by the understanding, or just by the understanding itself. Let us call the syntheses required for perception "P-functions." In the preceding section we saw that Kant also had a solid argument that perceptual recognition (in a concept) required the use of C-functions.

The second important change is that Kant finally makes up his mind on the issue of one versus two sets of synthesizing functions. In a well-known passage common to both editions, he had claimed:

> The same function which gives unity to the contents of various cognitive states *in a judgment* also gives unity to the mere synthesis of the contents of various cognitive states *in an intuition*; and this unity, in its most general expression, we entitle the pure concept of the understanding [A79/B105, amended translation].

Since Kant never supplies any backing for this claim in the first edition, it has the look of an argument by fiat and does not play a prominent role in the deduction. Further, he explicitly rejects the claim in the *Prolegomena*, where he distinguishes between *judgments of experience* and *judgments of perception*.[34] "The latter require no pure concept of the understanding, but only the [psycho]logical connection of perceptions in a thinking subject."[35] By 1787, Kant has obviously rejected this view. All combination is carried out by the understanding [which is governed by the categories]. The question is: Why does he change his mind?

As noted, what is totally new in the B Deduction is the discussion of perceiving spatial and temporal arrays, and the point that the forms of intuition do not, by themselves, supply any cognition of determinate objects, including spaces and times. I believe that we can gain insight into Kant's new position by backing up and considering why it would be natural to hold that perception does not involve the use of concepts, *a fortiori*, not the use of *a priori*$_{\mathrm{O}}$ concepts. In the A edition Kant had been tempted by the idea that all representing or perceiving involves the use of a concept, as we have seen. Consider an obvious counter-example, looking at a crumpled newspaper. You can look at the paper and scan its contours and yet have no concept for its shape. Since perception is constructive, however, you must have some function or functions that select and combine sensory data to produce a stable image. Notice, however, that as you perceive the paper, as you scan its image, you scan edges, curves, straight pieces, folds, and other local geometrical features. This is, I believe, the crucial point. Concepts for the local spatial features of the object can provide the needed synthetic functions (even in the absence of any concept for the whole object), and these appear to be always available to do so, regardless of what concepts you have or have not acquired. For Kant has already argued that spatial concepts are not acquired, because space was never in the senses.[36] If you can perceive at all, then you can construct perceptual images of whatever objects you confront by constructing their surface geometry in Euclidean space, and seemingly concepts for governing these syntheses are always available to you.

P-Functions as Spatial and Temporal C-Functions

Kant makes the crucial identification—of the syntheses that permit concept application with the syntheses that produce intuitions that contain a unity of diverse elements—for the case of spatial and temporal concepts in the note to B160: "although, as a matter of fact, it [the unity of the intuitive contents of representations of spaces and times] presupposes a synthesis which does not belong to the senses, but through which all concepts of space and time first become possible." That is, the syntheses that permit us to perceive spatial arrays, for example, in the minimal sense of being able to scan images of them, are the syntheses that permit us to apply spatial concepts to the arrays.

Although this claim is reasonably clear, what about the apparent vacillation about whether the unity that characterizes the contents of intuitions is conceptual or not? I start with the sudden shift back to sense in the last sentence: This unity really belongs not to concepts but to space and time. In ¶ 24, to which we are referred at the end of the note, Kant states that intuitions produced by imagination belong to sensibility, because all intuitions belong to sensibility (B152). The point of this final sentence is merely to stress that, despite the use of C-functions in constructing spatial and temporal arrays, *what* are constructed are perceptions or conscious intuitions.

How can Kant claim that the P-functions involved in constructing images of spatial and temporal arrays both presuppose syntheses associated with spatial and temporal concepts and yet precede all concepts? Although this claim is perplexing, we can make some sense of it by reflecting on the special status of spatial concepts. Whatever modifications experience might make in the process forms of intuitions, we do not acquire spatial and temporal concepts from experience, because space and time are never in the senses. Thus, I believe that he is claiming that our perceiving of determinate spatial and temporal arrays precedes all concepts, as concepts are normally understood. It precedes all acquired concepts. Finally, Kant presumably attributes the unity of spatial and temporal arrays to the senses in the Aesthetic, because he has not yet presented the constructive account of perception, without which the question of the source of unity in perceptions does not arise. How are we able to perceive spatial and temporal arrays? The forms of intuition themselves are inadequate. To perceive a spatial array, for example, we must perceive something arrayed in space. And when we perceive something arrayed in space, we can construct the perception of that object by employing syntheses associated with our *a priori*$_O$ spatial [or temporal] concepts, concepts like 'straight', 'curved', 'above', 'to the left of', 'larger than', 'congruent with'. This simple task thus requires three different factors: forms of intuition, objects to supply the diverse elements in cognitive states to be united in perceptions, and syntheses associated with *a priori*$_O$ spatial concepts to do the uniting.

Perceiving Objects by Perceiving Spatial and Temporal Arrays

Despite its apparent simplicity, this task has immense theoretical importance, in part, because of the reciprocity between perceiving spatial and temporal arrays and perceiving objects arrayed in space and time. We can only perceive spatial arrays, for example, by perceiving objects arrayed in space, but conversely, *whenever we perceive an object arrayed in space, we also perceive a spatial array, and so can synthesize the perception by employing a priori*$_O$ *spatial concepts.* I take it that this is what Kant means when he says in the sentence right after the one to which the note is appended:

> Thus *unity of the synthesis* of the diverse elements, without [in space] or within us [in time], and consequently also a *combination* to which everything that is to be represented as determined in space or time must conform, is given *a priori* as the condition of the synthesis of all *apprehension*—not indeed in, but with these intuitions [B160–61, amended translation].

That is, the perception of a determinate object in space is given along with the perception of a determinate spatial array.

We can perceive something without knowing what it is. So we need not have a concept for everything that we perceive, but only for those things that we recognize in a concept through perception. On the other hand, everything that we perceive is a spatial and/or temporal array. And, Kant argues, in perceiving spatial and temporal arrays, we use syntheses that make application of spatiotemporal concepts possible. So even in cases where we do not recognize the perceived item in a concept, our perceptual synthesis is still guided by rules associated with spatial and temporal concepts. Further, since space and time are the forms of intuition, everything that we perceive is subject to them. Thus, even in cases where we recognize an item in a (nonspatial and nontemporal) concept, the rules governing the synthesis of the perception are still subject to rules associated with spatial and temporal concepts (B160). It follows that all perceptual syntheses are guided by rules associated with spatial and temporal, and perhaps further concepts. After this intricate discussion and the illustration of its general point in the case of perceiving a house, Kant can finally, [and presumably happily] conclude: "It is one and the same spontaneity, which, in one case, under the title of imagination, and in the other case, under the title of understanding, brings combination in the diverse elements of intuition," (B161n, amended translation).

Kant's Long Argument

Additional Considerations

How does the analysis of perceiving spatial and temporal arrays provide an argument for the categories? So far, Kant claims only that such perceptions are constructed by syntheses that permit application of spatial and temporal concepts. The categories are not mentioned. The centrality of this ability depends on two further considerations. Since space and time are the forms of intuition, *all* our perceptions are of objects and events in spatial and temporal arrays. Second, in the Principles, Kant will argue that applying spatial and temporal concepts requires applying the categories, so that any perception that can be subsumed under spatial and temporal concepts can also be subsumed under at least one of the categories.[37] Thus, whatever syntheses permit application of spatiotemporal concepts also permit application of the categories.

The Basic Argument

With these two additional considerations, Kant's analysis of perceiving spaces and times becomes part of a long argument for the universal applicability of the categories to everything that we can perceive. Since this reasoning is both critical to an understanding of the structure of the transcendental deduction and somewhat complex, I will display it:

*1. Perception of spatial and temporal arrays requires that a C-function, which would permit application of spatial and temporal concepts to perceived objects and events, synthesize the diverse elements of intuitive cognitive states into an image. [Kant's analysis of perception and B160n.]

  2. Space and time are the forms of intuition, so all our perceptions are of objects and events in spatial and temporal arrays. [Transcendental Aesthetic]

  3. In all our perceptions, we produce stable images by synthesizing data according to C-functions that would permit application of spatial and temporal concepts. [1 & 2]

  4. We can apply spatial and temporal concepts to objects and events only if we can also apply the categories to them. [The Principles]

  5. Thus, whatever syntheses permit application of spatiotemporal concepts also permit application of the categories. [4]

  6. Thus, the categories apply to everything that we can perceive, in the minimal sense of being able to scan an image. [3 & 5]

Although this argument is not set out formally in ¶ 26, all its major pieces are presented. (*1) occurs in the passage just cited from B160n; Kant reminds us that space and time are the forms of intuition, and he infers that the syntheses that govern spaces and times also apply to everything that is represented as determined in space and time (B160, B161) (2); and, most importantly, he appends discussions of the house and freezing water examples that offer previews of the arguments about quantity and causation that are to come in the Principles (B162) (foreshadowing 4). Finally, he draws the conclusion (6): "All synthesis, therefore, even that which renders perception possible, is subject to the categories . . . " (B161).

Universal Applicability and Objective Validity

If sound, this argument would establish the universal applicability of the categories. It would also show that *a priori*$_\mathrm{O}$ elements must be involved in very basic cognitive tasks. This argument is a significant improvement over Kant's previous attempts to argue for the special status of the categories, both in the A edition and in earlier sections of the B Deduction. The discussion in A suffered from two related problems. First, the doctrine of the three distinct syntheses suggested that perception requires only sense and imagination; concepts enter only when we reach the level of recognition and knowledge. Kant avoided this implication by assuming that perception, or any cognition, involves concepts or some intellectual component. So, presumably, perceiving a house involved the concept 'house'. This view had prominent supporters, including Reid and Locke. As we have seen, however, it could not be assumed as an uncontroversial premise. In ¶ 26, Kant makes the much more modest assumption that perception only involves scanning an image. He then argues that even this requires an intellectual component, but a much more general component that is common to all cases and always available, syntheses associated with spatial and temporal concepts. Second, the A Deduction claimed that we do not reach the level of experience until all three syntheses, including the conceptual, have organized the data of sense. In relying on this rich notion of cognitive experience, Kant was in serious danger of trivializing his conclusion. Again, the modest assumption involved in ¶ 26 avoids this problem, because it is far from obvious that the categories, or any rules of thought, should be related to the construction of perceptual images.

The argument of ¶ 26 also has the advantage of making a direct link between the categories and what we perceive. A number of passages in both editions try to link objects of intuition to the categories through the necessity of apperception. (In fact, this move also appears at B161.) The serious drawback of all such arguments is that they rest on the unsupported contention that the categories are, in fact, required for the unity of apperception, or that they are, in fact, the laws of thought or are associated with the laws of thought. This is the great advance of ¶ 26, and so the "second step" in the argument for the categories. Prior to this section, Kant had argued that all cognitive states, judgments and intuitions, must be able to belong to the unity of apperception and that the categories somehow made this possible. Hence, all judgments and intuitions are made possible by the categories, and so are subject to them. As Kant wisely observes in ¶ 21, this can only be a beginning of a deduction of the categories. With the argument sketched in ¶ 26, there is some hope of actually demonstrating an important role for the categories in cognition.

This was another major goal of the deduction of the categories. The categories were going to be shown to be objectively valid, by demonstrating that they supply conditions that are necessary for the possibility of any cognition of objects at all. Kant extends the argument of ¶ 26 to include a demonstration of objective validity. After noting that the categories must be involved in perception, he continues: "and since experience is knowledge by means of connected perceptions, the categories are conditions of the possibility of experience, and are therefore valid *a priori* for all objects of experience" (B161). In A the objective Deduction had shown that knowledge of objects is possible only if we have rules of synthesis that enable us to construct representations from the cognitive states that objects produce in us. Here the point is put more perspicuously, in terms of perception. Knowledge requires the construction of perceptions. Whatever sensory data we take in, we know that, thanks to the forms of intuition, those data will be converted into intuitions involving temporal and spatial properties. By the argument just given, however, the syntheses that enable us to construct perceptions of spatiotemporal arrays are also the syntheses that allow us to apply the categories. Thus, so long as we are able to apply the categories, we will be able to construct perceptions on the basis of whatever sensory data we take in.

To see the force of the claim for objective validity, we need to recall that Kant believes that the rules of synthesis for constructing either representations or perceptions must involve *a priori*$_o$ elements. The data of sense are too numerous and too jumbled to supply any useful principles themselves. Given this assumption (which as I argued in Chapter 3 and above is inadequately supported), Kant's argument for objective validity can be represented as a continuation of the previous chain of reasoning:

7. Knowledge of objects is possible only if we can find some rule of synthesis to unite cognitive states in a representation or perception. [Objective Deduction in A]
8. All our intuitions involve temporal and spatial properties. [Transcendental Aesthetic]
9. The syntheses that enable us to apply the categories enable us to construct perceptions of spatial and temporal arrays. [1 & 5]
10. Thus, so long as we can apply the categories, we can construct perceptions, whatever the data of intuition. [8 & 9]
11. Since the rules needed for the synthesis of representations or perceptions cannot be supplied by sense, and we have no other *a priori*$_o$ candidates, the syntheses associated with the categories make perception possible. Hence, they make knowledge possible, and are objectively valid. [10]

While Kant does not return to the issue of judgment at this point, it is easy to see how to construct a parallel continuation that begins with the result of the objective Deduction in B. Knowledge requires judgments, and judgments require that cognitive states be synthesized in representations (which will themselves by synthesized in judgments). So we could continue the displayed argument:

12. For knowledge to be possible, cognitive states must be united by syntheses in representations that will themselves be synthesized in judgments. [Objective Deduction in B]

13. Regardless of what other information they contain, all intuitions include spatial and temporal properties, and so can be synthesized in perceptions by functions that are associated with the categories. [6 above]
14. Thus, so long as we can apply the categories, this requirement for knowledge will be met. [12 & 13]
15. Since the rules needed for the synthesis of representations cannot be supplied by sense, and we have no other a $priori_O$ candidates, the syntheses associated with the categories supply a necessary precondition for judgment. Further, since the syntheses that permit the construction of judgments from representations are associated with the categories, the categories supply a second condition that is necessary for judgment. And since judgment is necessary for knowledge, the categories make knowledge possible and are objectively valid. [14]

As already noted,[38] the assumption about the connection between the syntheses involved in judgments and the categories is inadequately defended, as is the claim that the rules of synthesis must be a $priori_O$. Nevertheless, if these points are granted for a moment, then we can see why Kant believes that the categories make cognition possible. They make perception possible and they make judgment possible. Further, the line of reasoning just presented applies to all knowers, constituted as we are and having space and time as the form of their sensibility. Hence, the categories would also be objectively valid in the sense that they are uniform across subjects. And the intersubjective validity of the categories would not be a contingent matter, like the (more or less) uniform perception of secondary qualities. Rather, it would be established on the basis of a transcendental psychology of cognition itself.

The Argument from Apperception

Arguments that try to establish the objective validity of the categories by showing how they make knowledge possible beg the question against the skeptic, since they presume that knowledge is possible. To the skeptic, Kant claims, again and again, that the categories are required for the possibility of apperception. Although he does not return to the theme of apperception at the end of the B deduction, it is fairly clear how the argument sketched at ¶ 26 can be extended to demonstrate that the categories supply a necessary condition for apperception. The subjective Deduction has shown that cognitive state can belong to the unity of self-consciousness only if they are connected or connectible by synthesis with each other. These states include thoughts and perceptions, and for reasons noted earlier, the potentially problematic cases are perceptions.

To show the relation between the categories and the possibility of apperception, the argument may be continued as follows:

16. Apperception is possible only if all my perceptions are connected or connectible by synthesis with each other. [Subjective Deduction]

17. Regardless of what other information they contain, the contents of all my perceptions can be subsumed under the categorial concepts and spatial or temporal concepts. [6]

18. Once cognitive states have been united in representations (perceptions or concepts), they can be united in judgments. [Analysis of Judgment]

19. However, judgments can be combined in further judgments by the logical connectives. [Once we have judgmental representations, they are subject to the laws of logic.[39]]

20. Hence, a thoroughgoing unity of apperception is possible, all my perceptions are connectible by synthesis with each other, and all my other cognitive states, because they are synthetic progenitors of conceptual states that can be directly synthesized with each other. [Account of Synthesis[40]]

21. Through the categories, all perceptions and judgments can belong to a thoroughgoing unity of apperception. Since the rules needed for the synthesis of cognitive states that is necessary for apperception cannot be supplied by sense, and there are no other *a priori*$_o$ candidates, the syntheses associated with the categories supply a necessary condition for the possibility of apperception. [16 & 20]

But for the categories, mental life would not be unified; rather, "appearances might crowd in upon the soul . . . and would be for us as good as nothing (A111); much might arise in empirical consciousness . . . in a state of separation, and without belonging to a consciousness of myself . . . " (A122). Hence, the categories would be necessary for the unity of apperception, which is, in turn, necessary for us even to have cognitive states that represent something to a subject. So even the skeptic must concede the indispensability of the categories.

How the Argument Fails

This is, I believe, Kant's best argument for the various claims that he seeks to establish about the categories. They are universally applicable and objectively valid; they make apperception possible. It achieves startling results from minimal premises. If sound, it would show that we cannot even have perceptual images unless we can, for example, apply the categories of cause and effect to the objects and events we perceive! This result is so startling that we might wonder whether Kant could have believed that he had an argument to support it. However, the argument derives its force from two principal sources: the analyses of cognitive tasks, including the doctrine of the forms of intuition, and the arguments of the Principles, in particular the careful reasoning of the Analogies. As we have seen in Chapters 2–5, and will see later, these are surprisingly strong anchors. This long argument unites key aspects of Kant's position in a single argument and places the burden of establishing the categories on its strongest parts. It also rests on the best available scientific or protoscientific discussions of its central topics.

For all that, the argument fails. Even if the arguments in the Principles were completely successful, the central link given in ¶ 26 is too weak for Kant's purposes. That link is the claim that in perceiving spatial and temporal arrays, the syntheses that enable us to construct perceptions also permit the application of spatial and temporal concepts, that is, the P-functions are the C-functions. Although there are strong reasons to believe that this is true *for cases where perception leads to conception*, those are not the relevant cases. Kant is trying to rule out the possibility that we might have perceptions that could not be conceptualized. For all he has shown, P-functions that permit concept application could be but a fraction of the functions that subserve perception.[41]

There are two problems with the argument. Even if space and time are not in the senses, so that our spatial and temporal concepts are not acquired in any straightforward sense, it does not follow that such concepts must be available to us in advance of any [other] concepts. Further, even when we clearly have spatial concepts, for example, and can recognize instances through the use of C-functions, it still does not follow that *whenever* we perceive a spatial array, we connect its diverse elements via the same rule of synthesis that we use when we apply a concept to the array. Kant's general project was to reveal the preconditions of knowledge, so he takes perceptions culminating in recognition in a concept as paradigmatic, rather than, for example, perceptions guiding movement. Further, his analysis of perception shows that we must construct perceptual images by using some nonarbitrary functions of synthesis. Further still, his analysis of the necessity of coordination or subordination between the faculties in cases of applying concepts shows that there must be C-functions that can construct perceptual images. Finally, the view that perception involves concepts, or some intellectual element, was widely held. Under these circumstances, Kant's analysis of perceiving times and spaces would seem extremely plausible. Nevertheless, for his purposes, he has picked up the wrong end of the stick. Even in ¶ 26, he errs in regarding perceptions that lead to conception as central cases. When he generalizes to all perception (*1), he ends up begging the question he wants to address: Could there be perceptions that cannot be synthesized with other cognitive states?

Two hundred years after the B Deduction, the verdict is still out on the relation between perception and cognition. Since we apply concepts to objects on the basis of perception, perception must be coordinated with or subordinate to conception in some instances. Further, perception is at an entirely different, and apparently more cognitive level, than mere sensation. These facts have led many—Thomas Reid, Hermann Helmholtz, Jerome Bruner, Richard Gregory, and contemporary computer modelers,[42] among others—to believe that concepts, or even belief and inference, are involved in constructing perceptions. Kant may well be right that the same processes underlie perception and concept application. He has no argument that this must be so, however. He has not shown that this is a necessary feature of any adequate theory of perception.

Defending the Long Argument Interpretation

Some Advantages

On my interpretation, Kant's best argument for the categories has subjective and objective elements; it is both regressive or analytic (because it presupposes some cognitive capacities) and progressive or synthetic (because it argues from the presupposition of fairly minimal capacities to very strong claims about the categories); and it employs a rich and suitably weak notion of [cognitive] experience at different points, and so does not rest on an equivocation on the term "experience." Although significant improvements are made in the second version, much of the analysis that justifies Kant's position is provided only in A. As promised, it is also a fairly clean line of argument. Many themes criss-cross and interrelate, but they all revolve around the central issue of the prerequisites for the various cognitive tasks that make up experience. For obvious reasons, I cannot show that an equally coherent argument cannot be constructed if the transcendental psychology is omitted. I will try to illustrate the virtues of using this material, however, by contrasting my interpretation with two influential accounts that also focus on ¶ 26, those of Dieter Henrich and Henry Allison.

Henrich's Antipsychological Reading

I have already presented Henrich's textual argument for the two-steps-in-one-proof constraint on interpretations of the deduction.[43] Plausible readings must explain how ¶ 26 is supposed to complete the proof of the categories that is only partially completed by ¶ 20. His own proposal is straightforward: By ¶ 20 Kant has shown that intuitions, insofar as they are given in a unified intuition [*in Einer Anschauung*], are subject to logical functions of judgment (i.e., the categories). At ¶ 26 he introduces the factual claim that we have unified representations of space and time. When this fact is combined with the conclusion established in the Aesthetic, that our representations of space and time "include *everything* that can be present to our senses," it follows that "every given manifold without exception is subject to the categories."[44]

The most obvious objection to Henrich's reading of ¶ 26 is that it gives no explanation of the fact that, in apposition to the main discussion, Kant offers previews of the arguments about homogeneous parts and about causation that are to come in the Principles. Why does Kant feel that it is necessary or appropriate to foreshadow those discussion here, unless the argument of this section is to be completed in the Principles? Further, five pages later, Kant says explicitly that the case for the categories will be completed in the Principles:

> How they [the categories] make experience possible, and what are the principles of the possibility of experience that they supply in their application to appearances, will be shown more fully in the following chapter on the transcendental employment of the faculty of judgment [B167].

Further, Henrich does not deal adequately with Kant's specific description in ¶ 21 of what he is going to show in ¶ 26:

> In what follows (cf. ¶ 26) it will be shown, from the way [*aus der Art*] in which the empirical intuition is given in sensibility, that its unity is no other than that which the category (according to ¶ 20) prescribes to the diverse elements of a given intuition in general [B144–45, amended translation].

Here Kant seems to be echoing his summary of the first edition Deduction chapter:

> This is all that we were called upon to establish in the transcendental deduction of the categories, namely, to render comprehensible this relation of understanding to sensibility, and, by means of sensibility, to all objects of experience [A128].

Henrich acknowledges that, besides establishing the categories, the deduction is supposed to clarify the relation of understanding to sensibility. His proposal is that Kant carries out this mission by first showing that the categories govern all unification by the understanding and then noting that space and time are unified intuitions.

> [In this way] we find in the second edition . . . a proof of the validity of the categories which is at one and the same time an explanation of the possibility of their relation to sensibility, *a proof which avoids taking up the problems of an analysis of the cognitive faculties* [my emphasis].[45]

That is, Henrich tries to deal with Kant's interest in relating understanding to sensibility apsychologically. In ¶ 24, however (to which the reader is referred in ¶ 26), it is clear that Kant proposes to show how the understanding relates to sensibility, via a third faculty, the imagination (B151–52).

Henrich's antipsychological reading also directs attention away from the synthesis of apprehension, which Kant highlights. On my interpretation, the doctrine of the synthesis of apprehension embodies Kant's recognition that perceptions must be constructed, and hence can be described as unified. Without this material, what is the basis of the crucial claim that our intuitions of space and time are unified? In the Aesthetic, in the third metaphysical exposition of space (in B) and the fourth of time, Kant claims that we represent to ourselves one space and one time (B39, A31–32/B47). However, his point in those passages is that particular spaces or times are regarded as parts of one space and one time. The Aesthetic provides no support for the claim that our perceptions of determinate spatial and temporal arrays are unified, but that is the topic of ¶ 26.

Allison's Apsychological Reading

I turn to Allison's careful study of the same passage.[46] He takes the second step of the deduction, which culminates at ¶ 26, to involve two projects: Kant needs to show how the categories relate to actual empirical intuitions and how they make experience possible. The first project succeeds, according to Allison, because the synthesis of imagination that governs the synthesis of apprehension is in turn governed by the conditions required by the unity of apperception, and those conditions are the categories.[47] As already noted, the problem with any account that links the objects of perception to the categories through apperception as an intermediary is that it must simply take Kant's word that the categories are required for the unity of apperception. However, the real contrast I wish to draw with Allison's account centers on the second project.

Allison reluctantly concedes that Kant has not shown that [*a fortiori*, how] the categories make experience possible. I believe that even Kant's best argument contains mistakes and so does not establish a special status for the categories. However, on my interpretation, it is clear why Kant *thought* that the categories supplied necessary conditions for various aspects of cognitive experience, and hence why he thought that he could carry out a deduction that established their objective validity. Allison regards the first part of the Deduction as an analytic argument. It considers what is implicitly contained in the concept of 'objective experience' and in the concept of a 'subject of knowledge'. The second part of the argument is synthetic and tries to show that the categories make experience possible.[48] If the first part of the Deduction is merely an analytic argument, however, then it could never make a contribution to the second, synthetic step, as Kant would be the first to point out. Further, although Allison considers the examples of perceiving a house and the freezing of water, he believes that Kant's discussions are completely muddled. The categories are supposed to be necessary conditions for distinguishing mere subjective perceptions from the objective order of things and events; they are "objectifying conditions." In these passages, however, Kant seems to be saying that the categories are needed just to perceive a house or the freezing of water.[49]

In fairly sharp contrast to Allison's account, I take the entire Deduction to be a synthetic argument. Further, I take it—and not just the Principles—to offer arguments about how the categories make cognitive experience possible. Kant assumes that we can perform various cognitive tasks and then argues that these tasks require rule-governed syntheses. In this way, he is constantly trying to show how various aspects of cognitive experience may require special rules of synthesis that are connected with the categories. Paragraph 26 is a major step forward, because it shows that we need syntheses even to perceive spatial and temporal arrays, a point that is clearly illustrated in the examples. Presumably, that is why he concludes the section by returning to the claim that the categories make [cognitive] experience possible. Further aspects of cognitive experience, including the ability to perceive an objective time order, are explored in the Principles. On my reading, however, it is clear how the Deduction chapter itself is supposed to advance the project of showing that, and how, the categories make cognitive experience possible.

The Loss of Generality

I conclude my defense of this interpretation by considering an obvious objection. Even if sound, the long argument could not establish Kant's general thesis that the categories are valid for every understanding, regardless of mode of sensibility (A88/B121, B144). This point is correct, for the argument depends on assuming that space and time are the forms of intuition. Still, I believe that it is his best argument. As noted in Chapter 3, individual categories are not discussed in the Deduction chapter, but only in the Metaphysical Deduction and in the Principles. So any argument for the 12 specific categorial concepts must draw from one of these sections. Kant does not seem to have any reasonable way of linking the forms of judgment to the categories, however. On the other hand, the arguments of the Principles make explicit and essential use of the spatiotemporal character of human experience. So any interpretation that does not wish to rely on the Metaphysical Deduction must forfeit generality, so this objection does not raise a special problem for mine.

¶ 26 as Completing the Argument of the Metaphysical Deduction

I should add that although I believe that the long argument is the best Kant has, there are obviously many elements in the Deduction and in ¶ 26 that look back to the Metaphysical Deduction—most notably its opening statement. This passage is the juncture of two very different arguments. As I have shown, the analysis of perceiving spatial and temporal arrays is the centerpiece of a long argument that anticipates the results of the Principles. However, it also provides an essential premise for an argument that draws on the Metaphysical Deduction. If Kant assumes the results of the Metaphysical Deduction, then he has a very compact argument for the universal applicability of the categories:

> 1. Since space and time are the forms of intuition, all our perceptions are of objects and events in spatial and temporal arrays. [Transcendental Aesthetic]
> 2. We can perceive spatial and temporal arrays only by synthesizing [hence unifying] images from sensory data. [¶ 26 and analysis of task of perception]
> 3. All synthesis is carried out by the understanding. [Opening of B Deduction]

4. The functions by which the understanding combines information are associated with the categories. [Metaphysical Deduction]

5. Therefore, one of the categories can be applied to the contents of all our perceptions and the categories make experience possible.

In defending the long argument, I do not mean to suggest that it is the *only* argument that Kant offers, or even that it is the only argument that he offers at ¶ 26.

How Serious Is the Loss of Generality?

Finally, how important is the loss of generality in the long argument? As Walsh notes, "[Kant] . . . retains the idea of the pure category for theoretical purposes . . . , but it plays no real part in his account of human cognition."[50] Paul Guyer rightly observes that *the* category for Kant is causation. His earliest theory of experience consisted of a sketch of the Analogies of Experience, and this is the most carefully argued section of the *Critique*.[51] Further, as DeVleeschauwer has pointed out, Kant was committed to the categories, prior to the discovery of the Clue.[52] If the arguments of the Principles are sound, particularly if the Analogies succeed in establishing the necessity of the concept of cause for human spatiotemporal experience, then Kant would have no reason to mourn the loss of a more general conclusion.

I will conclude my discussion of the deduction of the categories and my defense of the long argument interpretation with a brief account of the Second Analogy. Although it has not been approached this way, I will argue that the reasoning in this section is an obvious—and outstanding—example of transcendental psychology. By presenting Kant's closely reasoned analysis of the prerequisites for assigning temporal position to objects and events, I will also support my claim that the long argument is the best he has.

Transcendental Psychology in the Second Analogy

Guyer's Interpretation

The Second Analogy has been dissected and reconstructed more than any other section of the *Critique*. On the basis of a comprehensive review of the secondary literature and of Kant's early writings, Paul Guyer has offered an interpretation of the basic structure of the argument that will, I believe, prove to be definitive. Guyer is determined to shield this reasoning from any taint of psychology, however. Contrary to his intentions, I will use his interpretation to present the task analysis that is at the center of the Second Analogy. Then I will explain why Guyer's belief that a psychological approach must end in circularity is unfounded.

Hume demonstrated that the necessity involved in the concept of causation cannot be based on experience. The Second Analogy is to demonstrate that the causal concept is nevertheless objectively valid. It is objectively valid, because it makes knowledge of objects possible. Among other conditions, knowledge of objects is possible only if we are able to unite the elements of various cognitive states in perceptions. The argument of ¶ 26 showed that we can form perceptions of all spatial and temporal arrays, and hence of all objects and events arrayed in space and time, by using syntheses that enable us to apply spatial and temporal concepts. The project of the Analogies is to show that we can apply temporal concepts to objects—we can assign them determinate places in time—only if we can apply the concepts of substance, cause, and community to them. Hence, the syntheses that enable us to apply temporal concepts are the same syntheses that enable us to apply certain categories. Since these syntheses are allegedly necessary conditions for the possibility of cognition, so are the categories. Although I accept Guyer's view that a fully adequate treatment needs to consider all the Analogies, I will only deal with the argument of the Second Analogy, since that is sufficient to make my point.

This section focuses on the cognitive task of determining temporal position. To recognize any alteration in a substance, we must recognize an objective succession, one condition of a substance succeeding another. Guyer delineates the basic structure of Kant's reasoning.[53] The starting assumption is that time itself cannot be perceived. We cannot perceive empty time, but only states of affairs in temporal arrays (cf. B138). Even in the latter case, however, we cannot directly see when a state of affairs obtained. As Guyer notes, our perceptions of scenes do not come replete with a time clock in the corner to inform us of the time of the action. The problem arises because our perceptions are successive—all of them. Whether we are perceiving the diverse, but coexisting parts, of a house or the movement of a ship downstream, our perceptions are successive. For this reason, we could not consciously or unconsciously appeal to succession in our perceptions to determine succession in the object. So how can we recognize that one condition of an object occurred after another?

Kant reasons as follows (using "A*" and "B*" to indicate our perceptions, and plain letters for the objects of the perceptions, rather than

Kant's ambiguous notation): "in a happening . . . B can be apprehended only after A; the perception A* cannot follow upon B* but only precede it" (A192/B237). But how could we ever know that B* has to follow A*? Nothing in the individual cognitive state *qua* cognitive state can provide that information. Hence, we can only recognize objective succession—*and* that B* had to follow A*—if something in the contents of A* and B* informs us that B had to follow A. What could that be except our recognition that A is a particular state of affairs and that states of affairs of this type are invariably followed by states of affairs of the type exemplified by B? That is, we can recognize that B* had to follow A*, if and only if we have a rule stating that B's have to follow A's. This is a very important point and Kant makes it twice in three pages:

> In our case I must therefore derive the *subjective succession* of apprehension from the *objective succession* of appearances, since the former is otherwise entirely undetermined and distinguishes no appearance from any other. The former [succession] alone proves nothing about the connection in the manifold, because it is entirely arbitrary. The latter [succession] will therefore consist in the order of the manifold of appearance according to which the apprehension of the one [state] (that which happens) follows on that of the other (which precedes), *according to a rule.* Only by that means can I be justified in saying of the appearance itself, and not merely of my apprehension, that in it a succession is to be found, which means as much as that I cannot order the apprehension otherwise than in this very succession [A193/B238, Guyer's translation].

> It is therefore only in respect of a rule according to which appearances [objects] in *their* succession, that is, as *they* occur, are determined by the preceding state that I make my subjective synthesis (of apprehension) objective, and it is only under this presupposition that the experience itself of something that happens is possible [A195/B240, Guyer's translation and emphasis].

The celebrated reply to Hume is that if we did not apply a concept of 'cause' (that includes necessary succession) to states of affairs, then we would not be able to determine temporal relations.[54] This is Guyer's account of the basic logic of Kant's argument. So far, nothing precludes interpreting the Second Analogy as a task analysis in transcendental psychology, as I have done. Further, this reasoning can be added to the arguments considered earlier to show the universality of the causal principle. We can apply temporal concepts to objects if and only if we can also apply the concepts of 'cause' and 'effect' to them. Thus, causal reasoning applies to all states of affairs that we can recognize to stand in temporal relations. And, by the long argument, that includes all the objects and events that we perceive.

Guyer's Objection to a Psychological Reading

It is the next step in Guyer's analysis that allegedly rules out a psychological reading. We cannot recognize temporal relations unless we can appeal to causal rules. But where do we get particular causal rules? Guyer believes that Kant must assume that we establish them inductively, just as Hume claims.[55] I agree. He then infers that under these circumstances we cannot regard Kant's "theory of judgment—or time-determination . . . [on] a psychological model of the generation of beliefs but [must regard it] as an epistemological model of the confirmation of beliefs."[56] On a psychological reading, Kant would allegedly be caught in a vicious circle. We cannot recognize temporal relations unless we appeal to causal rules, but how could we establish causal rules unless we can recognize temporal relations? To avoid this difficulty, Guyer maintains that Kant's point is really about justification. Only causal reasoning can *justify* our temporal claims.

Versus Guyer's Antipsychologism

I have three objections to Guyer's antipsychologism. First, there are numerous passages where it is clear that Kant's point is that we could not *make* temporal assignments in the absence of a causal interpretation, and not merely that we could not *justify* such assignments—for example (B234), "In other words, the *objective relation* of appearances that follow upon one another is not to be determined through mere perception." In fact, the first part of the text Guyer cites in support of the justificatory interpretation makes this point:

> In our case I must therefore derive the *subjective succession* of appre- hension from the *objective succession* of appearances, since the former is otherwise entirely undetermined and distinguishes no appearance from any other. The former [succession] alone proves nothing about the con- nection in the manifold, because it is entirely arbitrary [A193/B238, Guy- er's translation, my underscoring].

Second, Guyer's interpretation gives Kant a weak reply to Hume. Hume would have an easy counter: claims about temporal order, like most of our putative knowledge claims, are not justified. Guyer tries to escape this difficulty by suggesting that the argument of the Second

Analogy is not completed until the Refutation of Idealism. If the Refutation shows that we cannot be justified in assigning temporal location to our own cognitive states unless we are justified in assigning temporal position to "outer" events, then he thinks the skeptic is beaten. I don't see why. Why shouldn't Hume simply admit that we are not *justified* in this either? Further, the Refutation of Idealism was not added until the second edition and there is no reference to it in the B version of the Second Analogy. Hence, it seems somewhat far-fetched to think that Kant saw it as completing this very important argument.[57]

Finally, and for my purposes, most importantly, Guyer's rejection of a psychological interpretation depends entirely on his equation of transcendental psychology with developmental psychology. As I argued in Chapter 1, Kant was extremely interested in the question of origins. Transcendental psychology is an attempt to determine the necessary conditions for cognitive tasks—especially any conditions that require *a priori*$_O$ elements. And, of course, 'cause' is *the a priori*$_O$ concept. Interestingly, Kant does not argue that 'cause' cannot be extracted from sensory experience in the Second Analogy. That result was established independently by Hume and is presupposed. Rather, Kant examines the task of assigning position in time and argues that we can only make such judgments if we can make judgments of causal relations. Presumably, he would also claim the converse dependency. For he is trying to show that the very syntheses that enable us to apply temporal concepts also enable us to apply causal concepts. That is why the concept of cause is objectively valid—because allegedly these syntheses are required for any cognition (perceptual or conceptual) of objects.

There is no circularity in this analysis, however. Kant is interested in origins, not development. The claim is not that we must employ causal concepts *before* we can order states of affairs in time but that we can only do one by doing the other, and that 'cause' cannot be gotten out of the senses. Although this analysis would put constraints on developmental psychology, it is not itself developmental. From the point of view of transcendental psychology, how exactly we develop the capacities and stocks of rules required for cognition is not an interesting question.

What Kant Has Shown

In the Second Analogy, Kant discovers a truly puzzling fact about human cognition.[58] States of affairs do not wear temporal locations on their sleeves and all our perceptions are successive, so how do we tell when we are observing succession in the world? Kant's transcendental psychology is sound in laying out the problem, but is he right in the claim he most wants to establish, that the recognition of temporal position depends on interpreting the world causally? Here, as in the case of the Euclidean nature of spatial perception, his positive suggestion is less compelling than his basic account of the task. Although we must have some way of making temporal determinations, "the" way may be an aggregate of many ways.

There is an obvious logic to Kant's suggestion. We need a mark or symptom of succession in time, and since effects follow their causes, establishing causal relations would do the job. However, there appear to be other low-level and high-level ways to accomplish the same task. At the lower level, the discovery of motion detectors suggests that we need not appeal to the contents of states at all. Given a particular arrangement of neurons, it is possible for a slightly higher-level neuron, M, to fire if and only if a stimulus registers sequentially on an array of adjacent receptor level neurons, $n_1, n_2, \ldots, n_i$. Very roughly, some neural assemblies in the visual system operate in accordance with the rule "M iff n_2 a given interval after n_1, n_3 the same interval after n_2, and so forth."[59] With such assemblies we could tell, for example, that a light moved from left to right in our visual field, and so that it occupied one position after another.

We also appear to make temporal judgments by tacitly appealing to ordering principles that involve content but not causal relations. In a fascinating series of experiments, Fodor, Bever, and Garrett showed that grammatical considerations can affect temporal judgments. Subjects listened to tapes of sentences that were interrupted by "clicks" (short bursts of noise) at various locations in the sentence. For our purposes, two interesting results emerged. Subjects are surprisingly inaccurate about when the click occurred in the sentence. Consider the sentence "That he was happy^ was evident from the way he smiled." According to the grammatical theory Fodor et al. were trying to test, the caret is located at the major constituent break in this sentence. Now if the click is placed right here, subjects will locate it correctly. For other objective placements, subjects still tend to locate it at this boundary.[60] Although grammatical structure does not yield accurate temporal information (at least in this experimental design), it does affect temporal judgment.

Interestingly, although the "click" experiment suggests that Kant's claims for the ubiquity of causal interpretation are too strong, it gives him a reply to a standard and potentially devastating objection to his whole line of reasoning in the Second Analogy. Arthur Melnick offers a recent version. He suggests that we can be directly aware of succession, because two states of affairs could succeed each other in the "specious" present.[61] Kant wrote over 100 years before the specious present became part of psychological landscape.[62] Thus, it might appear that his argument rests on ignorance of this phenomenon. Some of the force of this criticism can be blunted by recalling that the specious present is so named because it is specious. As I noted earlier, we can recognize melodies by constructing a single representation of the relations among the individual notes. However, we cannot literally hear the familiar E–D#–E–D#–E–B–D–C–A opening of "*Für Elise*" all together in one moment, even though it seems as if we do. Introspection—as Kant was well aware—is not a reliable guide to psychology. The click experiment provides useful support for this reply. We hear sentences in the specious present, but that does not mean that even in these brief time intervals, we operate as a tape recorder. We do not simply replicate the data of sense. On the contrary, what this experiment shows is that we construct our perception of the sentence and the click.

The surprising claim of the Second Analogy—that we assign temporal position to states of affairs only by interpreting them causally—is almost certainly false. Still, Kant's careful reasoning has uncovered a major research area: What are the means by which we recognize temporal order? Given their limited range of operation, motion detectors cannot be the whole story. The click experiment suggests that if we ever do find answers that would enable us to complete the argument of the Second Analogy correctly, they may be as surprising as Kant's own premature solution. Finally, although Kant badly overrated the generality of his solution, it will undoubtedly be among the answers to his problem.

7

The Limits of Transcendental Psychology

Kant's Paralogisms

Like the *Critique* as a whole, transcendental psychology offers both positive and negative doctrines. To this point, I have considered only the positive results of Kant's explorations of cognition. He also drew important negative conclusions about what philosophy could *not* tell us about the mind in the "Paralogisms of Pure Reason."

The Paralogisms chapter is standardly regarded as an extremely successful critique of Kant's predecessors' pretensions to pneumatology. Robert J. Richards's summation is typical:

> [Kant's] incisive exposition of the paralogisms of rational psychology—the uncritical, *a priori* deductions asserting the ego to be a substance, a simple entity, an enduring personality, and related in specific ways to the external world—slashed the roots of Wolffian rational psychology and withered its derivative claims about the soul's immateriality, spirituality, and immortality.[1]

Although this account is not incorrect, it is importantly incomplete.

There can be no question that the criticisms of this chapter are directed against Rational Psychology. Kant says so, even though he does not name names, or not enough names. Only Descartes is mentioned explicitly, but, as Margaret Wilson has argued, Leibniz was undoubtedly another target.[2] So was Christian Wolff. The discipline of Rational Psychology that was formally introduced in Wolff's *Psychologia rationalis* appears to be the focus of Kant's objections. As noted in Chapter 1, Rational Psychology begins with propositions from Empirical Psychology. Through analysis and demonstration, it then deduces the essential properties of the soul, from which its more superficial properties flow.[3] One of the constant themes of the Paralogisms is that no amount of analysis or demonstration can establish the type of synthetic doctrines that Rational Psychology puts forward (e.g., the soul is a simple substance). In the simpler and more compact 1787 version, virtually the entire critique is compressed into this one point: If we are dealing with identical propositions, then no substantive or synthetic claims about the soul can be extracted from them.

Criticizing the mistakes of others is only one purpose of the Paralogisms, however. As Wilfrid Sellars, among others, has observed, the I that thinks that is the topic of this chapter is the Deduction's I of apperception (see, e.g., A400).[4] Although this identification is often acknowledged, the chapter has not been read in light of the transcendental psychology of the Deduction.[5] Rather, it is usually offered as evidence of a sensible antipsychological approach to philosophy. This is partly because Kant contrasts his "logical," "formal" account of apperception with the claims of Rational Psychology (e.g., A350). As we have seen, however, these labels do not mean what twentieth-century readers take them to mean. Transcendental logic is no branch of formal logic, as we know it, but a study of the sources and prerequisites of cognition.

In this chapter I argue that we can only make sense of the details of Kant's criticisms if we see the Paralogisms as a continuation of the transcendental psychology of the subjective Deduction. The earlier text offered the positive case for a unity of apperception; here Kant strives to clarify what the doctrine of apperception does not say, by explaining the inherent limitations of the analyses that transcendental philosophy can provide. He undercuts the discipline of Rational Psychology, partly by exposing its own fallacious reasoning and partly by reflecting on the sorts of conclusions about the self that philosophy is and is not capable of establishing.

This is why the Paralogisms of Pure Reason has more than historical interest. It is not just an elegant methodological critique of a now long-forgotten discipline. By examining the implications of his own work on apperception, Kant discovered that there are important limitations to any purely philosophical study of the mind. These limitations apply equally to current efforts. I argue later that the claims of major contemporary philosophers (Thomas Nagel, Zeno Vendler, and John Searle will be my examples) involve the very confusions and overstatements that Kant warned against. Thus, I will argue that negative teachings of transcendental psychology still have an important role to play in curbing illegitimate philosophical speculation about the mind.

The Paralogisms chapter is the only section of the Dialectic that was rewritten for the second edition of the *Critique*. I believe that Kant abbreviated his presentation for two reasons. As I indicate later, the B Deduction incorporated many negative points about apperception that had been dealt with in the first version of the Paralogisms. With this material already covered, Kant could present a much simpler line of criticism: The Rational Psychologists err in trying to extract substantive conclusions from analytic premises. (Even in the B version, however, we cannot understand the opening discussion of the limitations of self-knowledge without looking back to the transcendental psychology of the Deduction.) Because it offers richer discussions, my interpretation will focus on the original version. Specifically, I will consider the first three Paralogisms in A, which concern the substance, simplicity, and persistence of the soul. The Fourth Paralogism in A is a defense of transcendental idealism that was reworked and relocated in the second edition. Its place in B is occupied by cursory reflections about materialism that I treat only in passing.

Like the chapter itself, I take the First Paralogism as a model for the rest. I argue that we cannot follow Kant's discussion of this paralogism unless we recognize that it is not just someone *else's* mistaken argument; it is a possible misreading of the doctrine of apperception itself. Kant's critique is simultaneously a criticism of the methods of Rational Psychology, a *caveat* about possible misunderstandings of apperception, and a lesson in the limits of transcendental psychology.

Puzzles of the First Paralogism

Kant's official account of his critique of Rational Psychology is not very helpful. Paralogisms are formally invalid arguments. Both editions claim that the First Paralogism exemplifies the fallacy found in all the Paralogisms, ambiguous middle (A402, B411):

> That, which is represented in the contents of cognitive states[6] as the *absolute subject* of our judgments and cannot therefore be employed as determination of another thing is *substance*.
>
> I, as a thinking being, am the *absolute subject* of all my possible judgments, and this content representing me cannot be employed as predicate of any other thing.

Therefore, I, as a thinking being (soul), am *substance* [A348, amended translation; cf. B410–11].

In the first edition, this criticism is elaborated by the suggestion that terms are used "transcendentally" in the major premise and "empirically" in the minor premise and conclusion (A402–3). We have already encountered Kant's primary meaning of "transcendental" Something is transcendental if it concerns our manner of knowing objects, in particular, the nonempirical origins of cognition.[7] An alternative meaning for "transcendental" is introduced at the beginning of the Dialectic, however, and that would seem more appropriate in this context. A category is employed "transcendentally" if it is employed beyond the limits of experience, or without heed to the limits of experience (A296/B352–53). (For ease in reference, I will tag the first sense "transcendental$_1$" and the second, "transcendental$_2$.") Kant's criticism appears to be that the category ["substance" and related terms] is used "transcendentally$_2$," in the major premise, because it is used independently of conditions that would enable us to tell whether objects that we encounter fall under the concept (see A349). By contrast, it is used "empirically" if used in conjunction with a "schema" that enables us to tell which objects should be classified as substances. At a number of places Kant says that the "pure" category is just the empirical category without its schema (A241–42, A242–43/B300–301, A248/B305). Or, reversing the point, he regards the "schematized" category as including a (needed) further specification of the "pure" category. Thus, empirical substances would be a subset of transcendental$_2$ substances, empirical subjects a subset of transcendental$_2$ subjects, and so forth. The First Paralogism is invalid, because although all transcendental$_2$ subjects might be transcendental$_2$ substances, that does not guarantee that a particular empirical subject also belongs to the subset of empirical substances.

The criticism of ambiguous middle through a confusion of empirical and transcendental$_2$ concepts is superficially clear. As we probe more deeply, however, Kant's position becomes murky. In the second edition, he elaborates the charge of ambiguous middle by claiming that the *minor* premise involves a peculiar use of terminology (B411a). Whether the major premise employs transcendental$_2$ concepts and the minor involves empirical concepts or vice versa, the argument would still be invalid by virtue of ambiguous middle. Nevertheless, the unheralded reversal on how the error occurs is puzzling.

Besides the confusion about how exactly the transcendental–empirical mix-up occurs, the diagnosis of ambiguous middle is unsatisfactory for another reason. It provides no justification for Kant's claim that the arguments of the Dialectic are "natural," "inevitable," and can entrap "even the wisest of men" (A298/B355, A339/B397). To fulfill the stated mission of the Dialectic, and even to justify his own interest in these arguments, he needs to make clear why these particular arguments are so attractive and so treacherous.

Thus far we have only a confusing account of why we draw the conclusion given the premises, namely, because we fail to notice or understand the ambiguous terminology. Why would anyone (or everyone) accept the premises? Kant regards the major premise as compelling I believe, because it merely states a standard definition of "substance." He mentions the definition several times prior to the Paralogisms chapter, without providing any explanation or defense (B149, B288, A241/B300). This definition also occurs in the writings of Leibniz, also without explanation or defense, suggesting that it was commonly accepted at the time.[8] Thus, presumably, we are all supposed to grant the major premise, because it is merely a definition. (The same is true for the major premise of the Third Paralogism.)

What about the minor premise? The crucial interpretive fact about this chapter is that Kant endorses, on some reading, the minor premises (and conclusions) of all three Paralogisms (A349, A350, A354, A356, A363, A365). If we can figure out the basis of his support for these claims, then that should tell us why he regards these arguments as compelling and important. Presumably, it will also shed some light on the empirical or transcendental status of the minor premises.

In the A edition, Kant endorses the First Paralogism's minor premise in an unequivocal but rather confusing statement: "Now in all our thought the I is the subject (in which thoughts inhere only as determinations) [and this I cannot be employed as the determination of another thing]" (A349, my parentheses and brackets).[9] This is an odd passage, because the minor premise is an odd claim. In the first phrase, it is not clear whether Kant is describing the I as a subject, or "I" as the subject of thoughts or sentences. The latter reading is suggested by the wording of the paralogism itself.[10] The phrase I put in parentheses appears to be part of a claim that thoughts (themselves) are modifications of, or belong to, an I (itself). Finally, the bracketed clause may also conflate talk of representations and talk of things.

After A349 Kant reiterates the point that different thoughts belong to a common I four times at A350: "I [is] the common subject in which it [all thought] inheres," "The I is indeed in all thoughts," "[the I] is the constant logical subject of thought . . . ," "in it [consciousness] all our perceptions must be found." Despite the barrage, commentators have tended to ignore this point, for a reason suggested by Jonathan Bennett. The claim that all my judgments are mine is true but trivial.[11] This dismissal is encouraged by remarks in the B Deduction and in the B version of the Paralogisms chapter that the doctrine of the I think is "identical," "analytic." If any proposition is analytic, "all my judgments are mine" is analytic. However, it is important to look closely at Kant's statements about the analytic or synthetic status of the apperception principle. Wolff and his followers took Rational Psychology to be a demonstrative science. Thus, *for them*, its propositions are analytic. When Kant emphasizes analytic formulations of apperception, he makes the point that no substantive claims about the thinker can be extracted from analytic propositions (see B135, B407). That is, these remarks are intended as explicit or implicit criticism of the methods of Rational Psychology.

In the Deduction and in the Paralogisms, Kant's own position on the synthetic nature of the doctrine of apperception is clear. He explicitly characterizes his principle of apperception as "synthetic" at A117a and at B134a. He even indulges in a bit of word play, presumably at the expense of the Wolffians: "the *analytic* unity of apperception is possible only under the presupposition of a certain *synthetic* unity" (B133). Further, if we examine the texts of A349 and A350, what he endorses is not the minor premise itself, "I am the subject of my judgments," but a related synthetic claim, "different judgments belong to a common subject." If the latter claim is true, then the former will not only be true (by identity of subject and predicate), but true of actual subjects and judgments.

Counting the minor premise itself, Kant repeats the point that different thoughts, judgments, or perceptions belong to a common subject five times in the space of two pages. Why? This is hardly a point that he needs to press *against* the Rational Psychologists. After all, they believe that all perceptions belong to a simple, numerically identical soul that endures throughout life and considerably beyond. I do not see how these repeated claims can be understood, except as reminders of his own anti-Humean argument for the unity of apperception.

We have encountered five textual puzzles in Kant's discussion of the First Paralogism. What exactly is the transcendental–empirical confusion that is supposed to be the root of the paralogism? Why does he take this argument to be compelling? Why does he support, and believe all must support, its minor premise? Why does he conflate I's with the representation "I"? Why does he insist over and over again that different cognitive states belong to a common subject? The relatively obvious solution to the last puzzle will also yield solutions to the other four. If we go back and reflect on Kant's reaction to Hume's denial of mental unity, two key points emerge that will enable us to follow the twists and turns of this text. First, he is in complete agreement with his predecessor about the failure of introspection to divulge a continuing self. This point is made clearly in both editions of the Deduction—and reiterated in the Paralogisms chapter, twice in A and once in B (A107, B133–34, A350, A381, B413). Second, Kant believes that by analyzing the prerequisites of cognition, he has demonstrated that diverse cognitive states must stand in real, synthetic connection with each other, and so belong to the same consciousness. That is why he thinks the minor premise is compelling. Its central claim, that all possible judgments belong to one I, is the conclusion of his own argument in the subjective Deduction.

Understanding the First Paralogism

To follow Kant's reasoning about the First Paralogism, we need to disentangle the complex relations to his predecessors in these passages. Like Descartes, he believes that any cognitive state, *a fortiori* any judgment, must belong to a self, which we may call the "subject of the judgment." Unlike Descartes, he does not conceive of this self as a simple substance, but only as a system of synthetically connected or connectible states. And unlike Descartes, he believes in this self, because he has analyzed the prerequisites for various cognitive tasks. Against the background of the subjective Deduction, we can understand how Kant interprets the first clause of the minor premise and why he accepts it: "I, as a thinking being, am the *absolute subject* of all my possible judgments, and this content representing me cannot be employed as predicate of any other thing" (A348, amended translation). It means that any possible judgment must be regarded as belonging to an I [to me or to another], that is, to a synthetically connected system of states, and he supports this claim on the basis of his own argument against Hume.

If we look back to prominent statements of the unity of apperception thesis in the Deduction, then we can also clear up the representation-object confusion (the "I"–I confusion) in these texts. The first edition Deduction makes the claim that all judgments [actually, all cognitive states] must belong to a self in the material mode (A107, A116, A122, etc.). In the second edition this claim is expressed by saying that the representation "I think" can be attached to all my judgments (B131–32). This manner of expression may court confusion, but the claims are materially equivalent: If and only if for any judgment J, it must belong to some subject, then it must be possible (for someone) to construct a true sentence "I think (that) J."[12] That is, given that all judgments must belong to some subject, it must be possible for some "I think" to be the subject of every judgment. Presumably, Kant adopted the second formulation in the later edition, because it enables him to provide a partial explanation of why we mistakenly believe that the self is a substance. One criticism of the First Paralogism is that we confuse the fact that the representation "I think" could be an invariant feature of all judgments with the notion that the self is perpetually intuitable (A350).

The second clause of the minor premise is more difficult, because Kant never says why the "I" cannot occur as a predicate. Further, he points out that any concept can occur in either the subject or the predicate position in a sentence (cf. A349, B128–29, A242–43/B300–301). One obvious possibility is that he simply throws in the second clause, because of its occurrence in the standardly accepted definition of "substance" that occurs as the major premise. (Another, complementary, possibility is that he uses this definition because it presents substances as somehow basic and he wants to build at least a verbal bridge between the Paralogisms chapter and his introductory remarks about reason's need for ultimates.) In any case, all Kant is really serious about in this premise is the claim that we must attribute all judgments to a self. This is the claim that is repeatedly asserted in his discussion of the Paralogism.[13]

How do the Rational Psychologists err? Kant's ultimate diagnosis of the error is the same in both editions: "From all this it is evident that Rational Psychology owes its origin simply to misunderstanding. The Unity of consciousness . . . is here mistaken for the intuition of subject as object, and the category of substance is then applied to it" (B241–22; cf. A402). Given the background of Kant's response to Hume, we can understand one way that he thinks Rational Psychologists have been led astray. As Hume noted, we do not have an intuition of the self. On the other hand, in trying to understand our cognitive capacities, we must recognize that cognitive states all belong to one consciousness. Hence, contrary to Hume, we must talk about a continuing consciousness or an I. We use the representation "I." The problem is that Rational Psychologists recognize that we use the representation "I" without clearly understanding the proper foundation of this usage. So they assume that it rests on the deliverances of inner sense. Since there is, in fact, no inner intuition of self, we do not perceive the self as an attribute, a complex, or a series. The error arises because they expect to find an intuition of the self and so mistake the absence of any intuition for the intuition of something with remarkable properties: "in what we entitle soul everything is in continual flux and there is nothing abiding except (if we must so express ourselves) the I, which is simple solely because its representation has no content, and therefore no diverse elements, and for this reason seems to represent, or (to use a more correct word) denote, a simple object" (A381–82, amended translation).

Who perpetrates this error of Rational Psychology? Seemingly not Leibniz. He claims that we think of ourselves as being "of substance, of the simple . . . of the immaterial" "by the knowledge of necessary truths and by their abstractions [that enable us to rise to] reflective acts, which enable us to think of what is called *I*."[14] Without considering exactly what these reflective acts are supposed to be, they are clearly not simple introspectings. Conversely, Descartes seems to be guilty of something very like the error that Kant describes in the following passage: "when I consider the mind . . . I cannot distinguish in myself any parts, but apprehend myself to be clearly one and entire. . . ."[15] This is also a direct criticism of the basic assumption of Wolff's empirical psychology. In every act of consciousness we are aware of ourselves, as well as of the object of our consciousness.[16]

This general criticism of Rational Psychology reveals an important source of confusion about the mind. We have various beliefs about the mind and its states. The Cartesian picture, which represents us as directly aware of thoughts and thinking, provides a seductive explanation for the source of those beliefs that leads us to overestimate our epistemic situation with respect to the mind. We think that we know more than we do about the mind and we think of our knowledge as resting on direct evidence. The explanation is seductive because the Cartesian "source of evidence" about the mind can never provide any counterevidence to our preconceived notions, because it presents no diverse elements of intuition [data] at all. Kant tries to prevent these confusions by repeating and extending Hume's original objection to Descartes: We have no knowledge of the thing that thinks "through awareness or through reasoning" (A355, my translation).[17]

Although this criticism strikes at the heart of the Empirical Psychology on which Rational Psychology rests, it bears no relation to the official account of what goes wrong: a confusion of empirical and transcendental claims. To understand this diagnosis, we must again look back to the Deduction's argument for the unity of apperception. As noted, Kant uses "transcendental" in two quite different senses. The appropriate sense for understanding the Paralogisms would appear to be that introduced at the beginning of the Dialectic. A concept is used "transcendentally$_2$" if it is used without its schema. However, Kant's argument that diverse cognitive states must belong to the unity of apperception—the argument that stands behind his support for the minor premise—reveals that this unity is a prerequisite for cognition. That is, his argument establishes a transcendental$_1$ status for the principle of apperception. Hence, in the Paralogisms, he legitimately refers to the subject of judgment as "transcendental$_1$" (A346/B404, A340; see also B411 and B411a). As he points out, the difficulty is that in order to infer that the self is an empirical substance, the minor premise would have to be asserted on the basis of empirical intuition, presumably the perceiving through inner sense of a permanent self (A403–404), and it lacks this kind of empirical support; it is a transcendental$_1$ claim. That is why in proffering the minor premise as support for the conclusion, "this syllogism . . . puts forward the constant [transcendental] logical subject of thought as being knowledge of the real subject . . . [and so palms] off upon us what is a mere pretense of new insight" (A350). Since one way to describe this misstep would be as a result of confusing transcendental$_1$ and empirical claims, Kant's ambiguous usage provides a verbal victory for the doctrine that all metaphysical errors rest on empirical–transcendental$_2$ confusions.

Since the diagnosis of a transcendental–empirical slide is itself the product of a terminological slide, what is the real error in this reasoning? What mistake does one make in confounding empirical and transcendental$_1$ claims? Kant's analysis of this error is critical to understanding transcendental psychology, because it clarifies the limits of the enterprise. It is also important to philosophy of mind more generally, because it reveals that certain kinds of inferences are invalid. In the Deduction Kant engages in transcendental psychology to determine the prerequisites of cognition; on the subjective side, to determine what properties thinking beings must have in order to perform cognitive tasks. One result is that the states of thinking beings must be synthetically connected or connectible. The mistake comes in believing that this type of analysis of the abstract properties or faculties required for cognition provides information about what sort of thing a thinking being is.

The analysis, then, of the consciousness of myself in thought in general, yields nothing whatsoever towards the knowledge of myself as object. The [transcendental] logical exposition of thought in general has been mistaken for a metaphysical determination of the object [B409].

The point is made even more clearly at A398:

> If anyone propounds to me the question, 'What is the constitution of a thing which thinks?' I have no *a priori* knowledge wherewith to reply. For the answer has to be synthetic—an analytic answer will perhaps explain what is meant by thought, but beyond this cannot yield any knowledge of that upon which this thought depends for its possibility . . . intuition [would be] required; and owing to the highly general character of the problem, intuition has been left entirely out of account. Similarly no one can answer in all its generality the question, 'What must a thing be, to be movable?'

Transcendental psychology is an abstract study; it addresses only very general questions. What faculties are required for representation, judgment, and other tasks involved in cognition? Despite the importance of these analyses, Kant realizes clearly that they furnish no serious clues about what the soul is like.[18] This discovery came as a surprise: "Suspicion is thus thrown on the view, which at first seemed to me so plausible, that we can form judgments about the nature of the thinking being, and can do so from concepts alone" (A399). "From concepts alone" does not mean that he ever believed that we could determine what the soul is like through what we now call "conceptual analysis," that is, either by figuring out what the ordinary person means by "thought" or by giving necessary and sufficient conditions for the (correct) application of the concept.[19] Rather, Kant once believed that we could figure out what a thinking thing was like by determining what characteristics were necessary for a thinking thing (or thought) to be possible.[20] He now realizes that this is a mistake. To determine what something is made of, its constitution, we need intuition (or observation). Understanding the abstract subtasks that must be performed in cognitive tasks cannot substitute for observation in determining constitution. This surprising realization is an important insight. With the aid of reflecting on the differences between the hardware and software in computers, it has reemerged in recent years as the principle that function does not determine form.[21]

When we turn to the Second Paralogism, I shall argue that Leibniz seems to make the false step from a highly abstract description to a claim about constitution just described. With this Paralogism, however, the argument for imputing diverse judgments or perceptions to a transcendental₁ subject that stands behind the acceptability of the minor premise is Kant's defense of transcendental synthesis in the Deduction (see A350). There appears to be nothing in the doctrines of Rational Psychology that could provide any legitimate support for the claim. Further, although the announced purpose of the chapter is to study the fallacies that flow from the doctrine of the I think, that is, from the *cogito*, this model Paralogism is plainly not the *cogito*. Kant mentions the *cogito* in the Second Paralogism (A355), but only discusses it, or Wolff's syllogistic version of it, in a footnote to the B version.[22]

Thus, the First Paralogism is best understood as Kant's own potential paralogism. Presumably, he came to understand the general problem of moving from certain kinds of abstract descriptions to substantive descriptions by reflecting on his own efforts in transcendental psychology and then noting similarities between these analyses and some of the work of his predecessors, in particular, Leibniz. In any case, many of his general warnings about moving from highly abstract analyses to substantive claims about the self, and his particular objections in the First Paralogism, are more easily understood as *caveats* about his own position than as criticisms of his predecessors. One error that the First Paralogism warns us against is inferring from the fact that we must regard different judgments as belonging to a common subject to the position that "the soul is substance," unless the latter "does not carry us a single step further," that is, unless we intend the conclusion of the Paralogism to assert no more than the minor premise itself (A350; see also A365). The view that this is a caution about his own doctrines is further confirmed by the fact that similar warnings appear in the B Deduction itself—for example, "in the synthetic original unity of apperception, I am conscious of myself, not as I appear to myself, nor as I am in myself, but only that I am . . ." (B157), and "The I think expresses the act of determining my existence. Existence is already given thereby, but the mode in which I am to determine this existence . . . is not thereby given" (B157–58a).

There is a further reason behind Kant's conviction that the First Paralogism is rooted in transcendental–empirical confusions. As noted earlier, he changes his mind about how to classify the minor premise. This vacillation reflects genuine perplexity. We have already seen why he suggests a transcendental₁ status for this claim in the second edition (B411a) and why he sometimes describes the subject of judgment as "transcendental₁" in the first edition. Yet, in the second edition, he also describes the claim as "empirical," on the grounds that it imputes existence (B157a, B422a). He has difficulty expressing this point because he lacks the crucial concepts 'theoretical entity' and 'functional description,' but he gets the idea across:

> The I think expresses an indeterminate empirical intuition, i.e. perception. [It] signifies only something real that is given, given indeed to thought in general, and so not as appearance, nor as thing in itself (*noumenon*), but as something which actually exists . . . [B423a].[23]

Thus, Kant himself regards the minor premise as both empirical and transcendental₁. Small wonder that he thinks it is extraordinarily easy to fall into thinking that this premise is "empirical," in the sense that it rests on awareness of an I, or that he thinks this argument has a wickedly ambiguous middle term.

Tying these points together, this is Kant's analysis of the First Paralogism. The argument is compelling, because we must accept the major premise (because it is a definition), and we must accept the minor premise on the basis of his own argument for the unity of apperception in the Deduction. The Deduction establishes that basic cognitive tasks require that diverse states be synthetically connected in a single consciousness. Hence, the minor premise is a transcendental₁ claim, "I" is a transcendental₁ representation, I's are transcendental₁ subjects. Confusion sets in because we do not know how to handle the minor premise, and so fall into transcendental–empirical confusions. These can occur in two different ways. We may not recognize the actual support for the claim at all, and so assume that it is an empirical claim resting on intuition, since it imputes existence. We then expect to find an intuition of the self and the absence of such an intuition leads us to peculiar views about what inner sense is disclosing. Alternatively, we may recognize that the minor premise derives its support from analyses of the abstract properties of the mind required for basic cognitive tasks, but not understand the limitations of these analyses. So we assume that they can support descriptions of the nature of a mind. Both these confusions lead us to believe that we can move beyond the minor premise and assert that the self is a substance. In fact, this conclusion can be maintained only if it merely restates the minor premise interpreted to mean that there is a transcendental₁ subject of judgment.

The mistakes involved in this reasoning about the self are hardly jejune. Rational psychologists—and their modern counterparts— err, because they fail to grasp two surprising limitations on our self-knowledge. Even though we can provide abstract descriptions of necessary features of minds for various cognitive tasks, we cannot move from this level of description to a description of the stuff of which thinking things are made. In "Leibniz and the Simplicity of the Soul" I will consider a modern example of this failing.

The other limitation seems even harder to accept. Despite its "proximity" to us, we have no direct acquaintance with the thing that thinks. In believing that we do, philosophers overestimate what we know about the self. Often this overestimation is disguised by the apparently negative character of the claims. So, for example, Zeno Vendler writes:

> My claims, therefore, that it is the *same* "I" that underlies transference [imagining yourself to be another], and the *same* "I" that could be in another state [that is, the state of being another mind], have to be understood entirely *via negativa*: not distinct, not different. Thus, the unity of this "I" is not like the unity of material things . . . for all these things can be named and identified in many ways. Thus we are driven back to the desperate analogy of the "prime matter." . . . One more instance of the great strain under which our concepts labour in these matters.[24]

Although Vendler sees himself as accepting the negative teachings of the Paralogisms, I doubt that Kant would agree. Our knowledge of the self does not rise to the level of knowing that it is an ineffable something that remains the same in transference. The point against Descartes works equally well against Vendler: "the I, which is simple [ineffable] solely because its representation has no content, and therefore no diverse elements, and for this reason seems to represent, or (to use a more correct word) denote, a simple [ineffable] object" (A381–82).

Thomas Nagel also implies that the lesson of the Paralogisms is merely that the self "cannot be defined as a kind of object, either physical or non-physical, but must be understood as the same subjective consciousness."[25] Later, he asserts that, "The concept of the self . . . implies only that if it refers at all, it must refer to something essentially subjective, often identifiable nonobservationally in the first person and observationally in the third."[26] The essential subjectivity of the subject of thoughts is the puzzle Nagel wishes to examine in *The View from Nowhere*. Given Kant's analysis, however, this puzzle seems to be built out of confusions. The claim that the subjective self is identifiable "nonobservationally" simply substitutes a mysterious process—nonobservational "observation"—for introspection. The eighteenth-century doctrine of inner sense is preferable, because we understand it well enough to recognize with Hume and Kant that it does not disclose a self, subjective or otherwise. Again, Kant's central objection would be that our knowledge of the self does not rise to the level of recognizing it to be subjective or mysterious. Philosophers attribute remarkable properties to it, because there is no intuition of something unremarkable—because there is no intuition of anything at all. Our belief in the self has a totally different foundation.

Identity Through Time

Because the First and Third Paralogisms have many similarities, I skip to the Third Paralogism: "That which is conscious of the numerical identity of itself at different times is in so far a *person*. Now the soul is conscious, etc. Therefore it is a person"(A361). The topic of the Third Paralogism is the identity of the self through time. Like Hume, Kant construes identity as requiring a permanent element that persists throughout the changes in attributes (A361–62). He also uses that which is permanently available to perception, or that which abides while other things change, as the schema of substance, however (A143/B183, A349). Thus, the First and Third Paralogisms appear to cover exactly the same territory, the permanence of the I.

These arguments are also similar in that their major premises are acceptable, because they merely state commonly accepted definitions. Here the major premise is the definition of "person" employed by Leibniz and Locke.[27] Again, the central interpretive problem is to determine why anyone, or everyone, would accept the minor premise. Despite the problems commentators have had with this passage, the logic of Kant's argument is fairly clear, if we bear in mind his own earlier results.[28] The subjective Deduction showed that cognitive states must belong to a synthetically connected system of diverse states, an I. Thus, it showed that we must recognize that a present cognitive state belongs to a system that includes cognitive states occurring at different times. We must be conscious of [or, better, cognizant of] the identity of the I at different times.

So far, the support for the minor premise is exactly the same as that for the minor premise in the First Paralogism. What is new in this Paralogism is the injection of a second distinctive Kantian doctrine: time as the form of inner sense. This is explicit in the text:

all time is merely the *form of inner sense*. Consequently, I refer each and all of my successive determinations to the numerically identical self, and do so throughout time, that is, in *the form of the inner intuition of myself* [A362, my emphasis].

How does the addition of this doctrine bolster, or appear to bolster, the case for a permanent I? If the results of the Aesthetic are combined with those of the Deduction, then we construct an argument for the minor premise, "Now the soul is conscious of the identity of itself at different times." In fact, we can construct an argument for the stronger claim that Kant takes to be the core of the Paralogism: The soul is conscious of the identity of itself at all times ("in the whole time in which I am conscious of myself... I am to be found as numerically identical in all this time") [A362].
This is the argument. Time is the form of inner sense. For me, therefore, moments of time exist when and only when I am aware of a cognitive state through inner sense. Whenever I am conscious of a cognitive state, however, I must attribute that state to an I. Thus, from my own point of view, I am conscious of, or better, cognizant of an I, at all moments of time. That is to say, I am cognizant of the unbroken continuity of myself. In Kant's words:

> all time is merely the form of inner sense. Consequently, I refer each and all of my successive determinations [cognitive states] to the numerically identical self, and do so throughout time, that is, in the form of inner sense.... This being so, the personality of the soul has to be regarded not as inferred but as a completely identical proposition of self-consciousness in time; and this, indeed, is why it is valid *a priori*... [A362].

Thus, to the consternation and confusion of some of his readers,[29] Kant maintains that [permanence] and identity are "necessarily bound up with my consciousness" (A363) and that "we must necessarily judge that we are one and the same throughout the whole time of which we are conscious" (A364). In a certain sense, the proposition that the thinker exists continuously is true, and *a priori*$_O$, because it follows from what Kant takes to be the *a priori*$_O$, form of inner sense, and the *a priori*$_O$ unity of apperception.[30]
Despite the overlap between the First and Third Paralogisms, the reasoning turns on very different considerations. In the First Paralogism, the argument tries to move from the soul as that to which judgments belong, and hence the subject of judgments, to the soul as substance; here there is a direct attempt to establish substantiality, by appealing to unbroken continuity and permanence. What is the error in this reasoning? It does not concern the self, but time.[31] Although it is true we must attribute all cognitive states to an I, and thus, that we must be cognizant of an I throughout all the times that we are conscious (A364), we cannot infer that the I exists at all times, *simpliciter*. To dramatize

the impossibility of regarding these reflections as establishing an objectively (i.e., intersubjectively) valid claim about identity and continuity, Kant invites us to consider our own "permanence" from the point of view of an outside observer. Whenever he attributes a cognitive state to the person he observes, he must regard that state as belonging to a continuing I for reasons that are by now familiar (A363). He will not infer the unbroken continuity or permanence of this, however, for the simple reason that there will be times when he does not, or cannot, attribute a conscious state to the person at all.[32] So this I will not be a permanent element in his experience (A362–63). Thus, the claim that I exist at every moment in time is not intersubjectively valid.

If the conclusion of the Paralogism, "I am a person" is construed to mean "I exist at every moment in time," then it cannot be validly inferred from considerations about time and apperception. As in the case of the First Paralogism, however, the conclusion is assertible if it merely restates the minor premise claim that I am cognizant of the identity of my consciousness at all different times at which I am conscious of anything through inner sense. More bluntly, this conclusion is assertible if it is interpreted as materially equivalent to the doctrine of apperception plus the doctrine that time is the form of inner sense (A365). After noting that uninterrupted continuity cannot be established in the way just described, Kant reiterates his claim that substantiality [and permanence] cannot be established by inferring the constitution of the soul from the formal requirements for thought (A363–65). In a footnote, he argues, via an analogy with the momentum of billiard balls, that a present self may bear all the necessary connections of continuity of thought and memory to earlier selves even though there is no continuity of substance among them (A363–64a).

To whom is this Paralogism compelling? The issue of whether thinking beings think continuously or exist continuously was hotly debated among Descartes, Locke, and Leibniz. Recently, R. I G. Hughes has suggested that this Paralogism offers a criticism of the "notion of time available to a Cartesian thinking being."[33] I do not see how this reading can be squared with the direct references to Kant's own doctrines of the form of inner sense that I highlighted earlier however. Descartes has no special views about time that lead him to infer that thinking beings think at all times. He is led into the view that we think continuously, because thought is the defining attribute of minds; hence, if minds cease to think, they would cease to be. I suspect that Kant deliberately scouts the reasoning in the Third Paralogism to prevent his views about time and apperception from being co-opted into the tedious metaphysical debate about whether souls always think. In any case, the support he offers for the minor premise would only convince someone who accepts his views about apperception and inner sense. Even more than the First Paralogism, this argument is Kant's potential paralogism. His warnings about the illusions of Rational Psychology are *caveats* about his own doctrine of apperception: This theory and the doctrine of the ideality of time only appear to provide knowledge about the mode in which a thinking thing exists.

Leibniz and the Simplicity of the Soul

That, the action of which can never be regarded as the concurrence of several things acting, is *simple*.

Now the soul or the thinking I is such a being. Therefore, etc. [A351].

The Second Paralogism deviates from the pattern of the First and Third in significant respects. The major premise does not state a widely accepted definition of "simple." "Simple" had a standard definition, "without parts," but the major premise makes a different claim. Further, this argument seems to derive from one of Kant's Rationalist predecessors. Margaret Wilson argues persuasively that a similar line of reasoning can be found in the writings of Leibniz.[34] Her hypothesis about the source of the argument is strongly confirmed by the fact that Kant repeats the central line of reasoning of the Second Paralogism in discussing Leibniz's and Wolff's views in *On the Progress of Metaphysics*.[35]

Although I will disagree with Wilson's interpretation of Kant's evaluation of Second Paralogism, her account of its topic seems correct. On her view, Leibniz argued against materialism through the following *reductio*. If the thinking thing were a body or a machine, then it would have parts. Imagine enlarging such a thinking machine, so that we could enter it, as we can a mill. Leibniz continues:

If we did this, we should find nothing within but parts which push upon each other; we should never see anything which would explain a perception. So it is in the simple substance, and not in the composite substance or machine, that perception must be sought.[36]

As Wilson observes, this argument is hopelessly cryptic as it stands. She offers a very plausible interpolation, however: the feature of thought that could find no correlate in a machine is the unity that binds the different elements into one thought.[37] What is not entirely clear from the passages she cites is the direction of Leibniz's argument. Does he argue that thoughts must have a special unity because they belong to the I which has a true unity (and whose unity is established through quite general metaphysical considerations)?[38] Or does he try to prove the unity of the I *from* the unity of thought? Leibniz seems to argue in both directions. An argument from the simplicity of the soul to the unity of thought holds no interest for Kant, however, since he would reject the metaphysical supports for the simplicity claim. The argument that he considers tries to move from the unity of particular thoughts or representations to the simplicity of the thinking thing, or from the unity that characterizes thinking to the simplicity of the thinker. This is the move that would be sanctioned by the major premise. Presumably, he supplies this premise to bring out the hidden assumption in this reasoning. He does not and cannot endorse the major premise. He cannot endorse it, because it is flatly inconsistent with his general claim that the [transcendental] logical exposition of thought in general can yield nothing whatsoever toward the knowledge of myself as object (B409). In the text of this Paralogism, he does not endorse it, even when explaining how we reach the conclusion. We do not conclude that "I am simple" through an inference at all. Rather, "I am simple" is a direct expression of apperception (A355; see later).

Nevertheless, he does accept two pieces of this Paralogism—the minor premise and the conclusion. Since we have no intuition of the self, the representation "I think" cannot be associated with any diverse elements of intuition at all; *a fortiori*, it cannot be associated with complex contents. The representation "I think" can be regarded as designating something simple (i.e., without parts) in the purely negative sense that it does not designate complex sensory data (A355, A356). Thus, Kant grants the conclusion that the soul is simple, if "simple" is so understood that the conclusion merely expresses his own view about the absence of any intuition of the I:

> The proposition, 'I am simple', must be regarded as an immediate expression of apperception. . . . 'I am simple' means nothing more than that this content of cognitive states, I, does not contain in itself the least diversity of elements, and that it is absolute (although merely logical) unity [A354–55, amended translation].

This point is familiar from the First Paralogism. His rationale for the minor premise introduces an important new line of thought. Like the First and Third Paralogisms, the key to understanding this discussion is his support of the minor premise: "The soul, or the thinking I, is such that, its action can never be regarded as the concurrence of several things acting." More simply, thinking can never be regarded as the concurrence of several things acting. He supports this premise in passage strikingly like William James's better-known discussion of the topic:

> For suppose it be the composite that thinks: then every part of it would be a part of the thought, and only all of them taken together would contain the whole thought. But this cannot consistently be maintained. For contents of cognitive states (for instance, the single words of a verse), distributed among different beings, never make up a whole thought... [A352, amended translation].[39]

Kant's presentation almost makes the argument appear trivial. One thought cannot be realized in different beings, because then there would be no one being who had the whole thought. His first sentence rules out this reading, however, by conceding that the *collection* of different beings would contain the whole thought. His point must be that a collection of different beings is just not the right sort of thing to realize a complex thought. Unfortunately, the last sentence simply states that representations distributed among different beings cannot make up a thought without explaining why this is so.

Wilson reads Kant as subscribing to the view that the elements of a thought must stand in the appropriate "conceptual connection."[40] By this I assume that she means that the elements of the thought must stand in the appropriate syntactic and semantic relations to one another. So, for example, the verb not only must agree with the subject, but must denote an activity that is possible for the subject. As already noted, "*Vorstellung*" is ambiguous between the content of a cognitive state and the cognitive state itself. In terms of this distinction, Wilson interprets the claim about the "indivisible unity of a *Vorstellung*" (A355) to refer only to the unity of its content, and not to its unity *qua* cognitive state. She thinks that Kant criticizes the Second Paralogism by rejecting the datum of the "true unity of consciousness" of cognitive states.[41]

This interpretive issue is difficult to settle within the confines of the Second Paralogism, because Kant is very cryptic. Even in these passages, however, he clearly identifies the I think with his own doctrine of apperception (as in the preceding citation about simplicity). And since apperception is a doctrine about the unity of consciousness, it is doubtful that this is what he means to deny.

Further, the most prominent passage in the text of the Paralogism echoes a number of Deduction themes about the unity of representations, synthesis, and the unity of consciousness.

The so-called *nervus probandi* of this argument lies in the proposition, that if many contents of cognitive states are to form a single thought, they must be contained in the absolute unity of the thinking subject [A352, amended translation].

As we have seen, Kant claimed at A99 that although intuition supplies us with diverse elements, these cannot be represented as a diversity and contained *in a single cognitive state* without a synthesis. Further, at A116 and B132, he maintained that unless cognitive states can be synthetically connected to each other, and so belong to a unified consciousness, they could not represent anything. And, finally, at B137, he concluded that "all unification of cognitive states or their contents demands unity of consciousness in the synthesis of them" (see also A102, A103, A108, A113, A123–24, B131a). Given these propositions, it follows that a thought with a complex content must be produced by a synthesis of cognitive states and that these states must all belong to a unity of apperception. This point is perfectly illustrated in the case of a verse. The speaker must produce a verse sequentially, and the listener must hear it that way. For either to comprehend it, however, the different pieces must be combined in a single representational state occurring at a single moment in time. And the content of that state must be the synthetic product of the contents of the states containing the elements.

Thus, Kant does not deny the unity of consciousness. He has, however, a particular understanding of it: his own theory of the synthetic unity apperception. Again, he accepts the minor premise, insofar as it expresses the unity of apperception. Thinking cannot be regarded as the concurrence of several distinct, unconnected things acting. Thought is possible only where synthetic connection allows the different parts of a thought to be united in a single thought, or representational state. He expresses this point as the view that the "subjective I can never be . . . divided and distributed" (A354). For otherwise, we could not say, "I think (the diverse elements in a single cognitive state)" (A354, my translation). Since the subjective I comprises the synthetic connections across cognitive states, it cannot be divided. For were these connections severed, there could be no content in a thought.

What is the error perpetrated by this Paralogism? Once again the crucial mistake comes in the attempt to move from abstract descriptions of the necessary conditions for thinking, to claims about the constitution of the self: "This much, then, is certain, that through the I, I always entertain the thought of an absolute, but [transcendental] logical, unity of the subject (simplicity). It does not, however, follow that I thereby

know the actual simplicity of my subject" (A356; see also B408). Kant
spells out exactly what is wrong with the attempted inference from an
abstract analysis to a characterization of the specific nature of the soul:

> For the unity of the thought, which consists of many cognitive states or
> their contents, is collective, and as far as mere concepts can show, may
> relate just as well to the collective unity of different substances acting
> together . . . [A353, amended translation].

Although thinking requires synthetic connections among the temporally
distinct states that contain parts of the thought, this does not imply that
only simple beings can have thoughts. All it implies is that a collection
of different beings can have a thought only if their states are synthetically
or contentually interconnected. This may rule out some materialist accounts of thought—those that provide no explanation of synthetic connection.[42] However, this abstract description provides no serious clues
about the kinds of physical or nonphysical systems that might realize
the unity of thought.

Just in case Rational Psychologists try to resist this criticism, Kant
drives the point home in the second edition. It is not merely fallacious
to try to adjudicate among possible characterizations of the soul by
appealing to abstract analyses, it is potentially dangerous to the cause.
If Rational Psychologists are permitted to argue for the simplicity and
immateriality of the soul by claiming that they do not see how a material
substance could realize the unity of thought, then materialists would be
free to employ the same strategy to "establish" the opposite conclusion.
Since the latter do not understand how an immaterial substance could
realize the unity of thought, they may claim that the soul is material
(B418a).

There are important differences between Kant's First and Third Paralogisms and the Second Paralogism. Only in this Paralogism does he
appear to carry out the stated purpose of the chapter, namely, to criticize
arguments of his Rationalist predecessors. Further, this may be a case
where an argument of one of his predecessors makes a positive contribution to the doctrine of the unity of apperception. Nevertheless, the
evaluation of this argument turns on exactly the same considerations as
his evaluation of the First Paralogism. Both arguments are related to
genuine insights about the lack of intuition of the self and about the
necessary unity of thinking things. These insights are extremely slippery,
however, and can lead to totally unwarranted claims about thinking
selves. We misconstrue the absence of an intuition of the I as an intuition
of something with remarkable properties, and we falsely assume that

we can move from abstract analyses to descriptions of the nature of thinking things. In discussing the First Paralogism, I noted that major contemporary philosophers still mistake the absence of an intuition of the I for the intuition of something mysterious. Kant's second important *caveat*— that we cannot move from the sort of abstract analyses provided by transcendental psychology to claims about the intrinsic properties of thinking things—can also provide needed discipline to contemporary discussions. In a well-known article John Searle makes the following claim:

> It is not because I am the instantiation of a computer program that I am able to understand English and have other forms of intentionality . . . but as far as we know it is because I am a certain sort of organism with a certain biological (i.e., chemical and physical) structure, and this structure under certain conditions is causally capable of producing perception, action, understanding, learning, and other intentional phenomena.[43]

In this passage Searle indulges in exactly the sort of argument from ignorance that Kant warns Rational Psychologists against. Thinking exhibits intentionality; that is, our thoughts are *about* things. It is not at all clear how a computer can have states that exhibit intentionality. Since people do have intentional states and since *obviously* they think with their brains, then brains must be so constituted (have a particular physical and chemical structure) as to be capable of having intentional states.

If we substitute "unity" for "intentionality" and "immaterial soul" for "brain," this is exactly the Rational Psychologists' argument. It is not clear how machines can have states that exhibit unity. Since people do have unified mental states, and since mental states are *obviously* states of their immaterial souls, immaterial souls are so constituted as to be able to have unified states. Kant's critique is equally apt. If Searle is permitted to run this argument, then we should also permit immaterialists to point out that we do not currently understand how brains can have intentional states, and then to draw their own conclusions. The problem with both arguments is that, although we have certain abstract descriptions of thoughts (they must be unified, they must be intentional), we do not have the slightest idea what kinds of things might be able to instantiate those properties. Proponents of such arguments disguise this fact, by announcing that souls possess the requisite unity or that brains possess the requisite intentionality. But these bold claims do not rest on an understanding of how anything could possess such properties;

they are supported entirely by the *antecedent* conviction that it is brains or immaterial souls that do the thinking. Searle's conviction that brains think is certainly more plausible than Leibniz's speculations about monads. As Kant's analysis shows, however, the arguments of these clever philosophers are equally fallacious.[44]

8

Cognitive Constraints on Empirical Concepts

Kant and Cognitive Science

At the beginning I claimed that denying the transcendental psychology of the *Critique* has two harmful effects. Kant scholars must try to interpret a difficult text without engaging one of its central themes. By this point I hope to have shown that taking transcendental psychology seriously does not lead to embarrassment. Rather, it allows us to make better sense of the Aesthetic's doctrine that space is the form of outer sense, better sense of the complex role of the principle of apperception in the Deduction, better sense of the argument for the indispensability of the categories, and better sense of the critique of Rational Psychology.

I have been less systematic in illustrating the second disadvantage. By ignoring transcendental psychology, historians forego the opportunity to contribute to contemporary debates. Chapters 4 and 5 show how the theory of mental unity that emerges from Kant's analyses of cognitive tasks provides an attractive solution to a philosophical problem of great current interest: personal identity. But I have not shown, in any detail, how this work might contribute to current struggles to understand cognition. I conclude by looking at a very important debate in cognitive science. This will provide an extended example of how the *Critique*'s analyses of the psychological faculties required for cognition can inform contemporary work. An opportunity is being lost.

Kant was uncertain about the status of a science of the higher faculties, what we would call a "cognitive psychology" but he called "applied logic" (see A54/B78). In the *Logic*, he claimed that such a science must be possible, because like everything else in nature, the exercise of our own faculties must operate by laws.[1] The *Critique* maintained that applied logic could not aspire to be a *demonstrated* science, because it must appeal to empirical principles (A55/B79). And in *The Metaphysical Foundations of Natural Science*, he seemed to deny that any science of the soul could be a proper, mathematical science.[2]

Nevertheless, Kant realized that general logic, and so transcendental logic (or transcendental psychology), bore an important relation to a possible cognitive psychology or applied logic. He suggests two somewhat different models in the *Critique*. General logic describes the way in which the understanding itself operates; but in characterizing the way people actually think, we must factor in the "accidental subjective conditions which may hinder or help its application" (A55/B79). Just before, he had presented applied logic as characterizing the "rules of the employment of understanding under the subjective empirical conditions dealt with by psychology" (A53/B77; see also B140). On the former model, the normal operation of the understanding is *interfered* with by other faculties; in the latter, the ideally characterized faculty of understanding is *realized* by faculties that only approximate its ideal functioning, regardless of the influence of other factors. Either way, Kant clearly recognized that his work must have a bearing on empirical research, even while he doubted the ultimate status of that research.[3] Transcendental psychology offers an idealization of cognitive functioning; as such, it can provide guidance about the sorts of mental equipment that empirical researchers need to look for.

Concepts have become an important topic in cognitive science. Eleanor Rosch's discovery of the apparent "prototype" structure of concepts inspired many follow-up studies aimed at determining how concepts are represented in us.[4] Concepts have also been prominent in the developmental literature. How do children's concepts differ from those of adults? What mental equipment is implied by children's uses of concepts?[5] Attempts to simulate knowledge representation in computers have also led theorists to reconsider the nature of concepts. Although the issue of concepts is somewhat amorphous, it can be summed up in two (amorphous) questions: What kinds of concepts do we (or children) use? What kinds of mental representations and/or mental faculties underlie our ability to use the kinds of concepts that we use?

I begin by considering a more limited question, which emerged from Rosch's early work: Do people apply concepts by representing and using necessary and sufficient conditions for membership in a particular category? Although this is obviously an empirical question, the experimental results are fairly confusing. I will argue that Kant's reflections on what concepts *must* be like for knowledge to be possible can provide needed theoretical insight into the issue. Then I take up the broader question of how concepts are realized in us. We cannot turn to Kant and expect to discover that the true theory of concepts has been lying, undetected, in our midst for 200 years. My goals are much more modest (and, I hope, realistic). Kant approached concepts in terms of his general project of transcendental psychology: What must concepts be like, and what faculties must underlie them, for us to be capable of knowledge at all? I argue that his analyses of concepts, and of the faculty of reason, offer a novel suggestion about the kind of mental equipment that underlies concept use. This suggestion has four substantial virtues: It explains a fair bit of experimental data, it is relatively simple, it has clear implications for the direction of empirical research, and it is principled— that is, it is clear, given the way concepts are supposed to function, why they should be supported by this type of mental equipment. Lest I raise expectations too high, I should repeat that Kant's analyses only point in a particular direction. I develop those insights in some obvious ways and show their bearing on current attempts to understand the psychology of concepts.

Do We Employ Necessary and Sufficient Conditions?

Difficulties with the Classical View

The "classical" view of concepts[6] assumes that the items in the extension of a concept all share a manageably small set of salient features. These features are listed in the concept, or mental representation, and that is how items are grouped together under a concept.[7] When an item is presented, the possessor of a concept runs through the list. If the item has all the features listed for the concept, then it is subsumed under the concept. Wittgenstein attacked this notion from the extensional side. In a well-known discussion, he argued there are no common properties that all games, for example, have in common.[8] Rosch's work undermined the psychological assumptions of the necessary and sufficient conditions model of concepts. If this story were correct, then for each item presented, a concept user would run through a list. The same list for the same concept. What Rosch found, contrary to this model, is that different items are treated differently. Some items, "typical" instances of the concept, are classified immediately. Further, other items seem to be classified under the concept, depending on their similarity to typical items, rather than through the use of a checklist. This led her to propose that the mental representation of concepts is not a list but a "prototype," that is, a typical example, some characteristic features, and an explicit list of exceptions (e.g., "Penguins are birds, even though they cannot fly").

Edward Smith and Douglas Medin offer a lengthy review of the literature spawned by Rosch's findings. They conclude with the observation that although the balance of the empirical evidence argues against the presence of necessary and sufficient conditions, it does not really establish one view as correct and rule out all the others.[9] Medin has also noted that the necessary and sufficient conditions model has systematic weaknesses, beyond empirical tests of classification (not all of which are disconfirming).[10] No one, experts included, seems able to list defining features for concepts. Further, there appear to be unclear cases: Is a radio a piece of furniture? If we apply concepts by employing necessary and sufficient conditions, then all cases should be decidable.[11] On the other hand, prototype theories, or more generally, probabilistic theories, also have problems. (Probabilistic views take concepts to be organized around features that are *typical* of members, but not defining.) Probabilistic theories imply that the only information that is stored in mental representations concerns central tendencies. However, empirical evidence suggests that the size of a classification, the variability of examples, and *correlations* among features are also used in classifying instances.[12]

In sum, although the necessary and sufficient conditions view has serious difficulties, the empirical results are not decisive. Smith and Medin note that "there will likely be no crucial experiments or analyses that will establish one view of concepts as correct and rule out others irrevocably." They also predict that elements of the classical view will appear in any complete theory of concepts.[13] I believe that Kant's analyses of empirical concepts shed unanticipated light on this issue. For he offers principled reasons for believing that the necessary and sufficient conditions model cannot be correct, if empirical concepts are going to fill their role in the acquisition of knowledge. Thus, he shows that the classical view cannot be correct for the normal case. Besides its popularity among philosophers and psychologists, a recent study by McNamara and Sternberg reveals that most lay people also hold a necessary and sufficient conditions model (perhaps explaining why it is the classical view).[14] Given the strong intuitive appeal of this view, and the inconclusive empirical evidence, it is important to show why it must ultimately be rejected. In addition, Kant's discussion provides positive clues about what an adequate model of concepts might look like.

Kant on Concepts and Concept Application

Kant's general position on concepts is that they are rules. These rules permit us to unite separately given perceptual materials under one label:

> as regards its form, a concept is always something universal which serves as a rule. The concept of body, for instance, serves as a rule for our representation [*Erkenntniss*] of outer [objects], by unifying the diverse elements which are thought in it. . . . Thus the concept of body requires in the perception of something before us, the content [of a cognitive state], extension, and with this, impenetrability, form, and so forth . . . [A106, amended translation].

Despite the misleading implications of the example, Kant realizes that we cannot explain how we apply the concept 'body', for example, by noting that we first apply the concepts 'extension', 'impenetrability', and so on, because we would be involved in an infinite regress (cf. A133/B172).

In Chapter 6[15] I briefly described Kant's hypothesis about how we apply concepts to objects. In opposition to the image-based accounts of his predecessors, he argued that we do it through the use of *schemata*— not images but *rules for constructing* images. These rules indicate the sequence of operations that the perceptual system goes through in producing images of instances of the concept (A141/B180; see also A103–4, A77–79/B103–4). My chief concern is the question of necessary and sufficient conditions, and so the fixed or changing nature of the rules that enable us to apply concepts. Still, in passing, I will note two advantages of the schemata hypothesis. It avoids the regress problem, because it explains how concepts are applied on the basis of perceptual, not conceptual information. Second, it is plausible to think that what matters in conceptualization is how perceptual data are treated by the cognitive system, and not what they are like in themselves. Thus, the key to applying concepts to objects might well be the perceptual processes that occur when encountering instances.[16]

Empirical Warrant and the Open-Ended Character of Experience

Kant's support for schemata does not have any direct implications for the necessary and sufficient conditions issue. Rules for producing images *could* be treated as necessary and sufficient conditions as easily as feature lists.[17] In the *Methodology* and the *Logic*, however, he explains why all definitional approaches must fail for empirical concepts. He often repeats the point that synthesis must precede analysis (B130, B133). We cannot analyze what features are contained in our concepts before we have synthesized diverse elements into a conceptual whole, before we have taken the diversity provided by sense and united it in a representation. Once we have done this for a number of instances, and abstracted a rule for producing images, however—once we have a functioning concept—it seems that we could draw up lists of features that are crucial to different concepts by working backward from the instances. The problem is that this cannot be done for empirical concepts: "Since the synthesis of empirical concepts is not arbitrary but empirical and as such can never be complete (for in experience ever new characteristics of the concept can be discovered), empirical concepts cannot be defined."[18] Kant's simple point is that since experience is open-ended, we could never work from a complete set of recognized instances.

The deeper point is that if empirical concepts are to play a role in the generation of warranted belief, then they cannot be defined. Kant agrees with his Empiricist predecessors that an empirical concept is one that has been acquired from experience. We have the concept 'dog', because, having encountered a number of dogs, we have abstracted, among other things, a schema for generating perceptual images of dogs. The crucial epistemological point about empirical concepts is that there can be no question about their legitimate applicability to the world.[19] Since we abstract similarities in image processing, for example, from our dealings with instances, we cannot be deluding ourselves into believing that a class of similar objects exists (see A84/B116). This is not to say that empirical concepts cannot be altered or even discarded.[20] As we encounter more and more instances, our grouping of perceptual processes together as similar may change in subtle or dramatic ways. Further, we may analyze the perceptual and other features that seem common to instances, and discover that some concepts group objects together that share only superficial or theoretically unimportant similarities. These corrections to our original conceptual acquisitions are made on the basis of (current) total evidence. For Kant empirical concepts are acquired, refined, rejected, or maintained on the basis of experience. That is why they are legitimate: They are warranted by the very processes that produce and shape them. Since empirical concepts derive their epistemological warrant by being malleable by experience and since experience is open-ended, they cannot be defined.

When Should We Codify Our Concepts?

To see Kant's point consider when it might be appropriate for our conceptual faculty to stop abstracting similarities from instances and codify those similarities in definitions for future use in classifying new instances. Since we continue to have experience, there can be no good moment to stop. For whenever the process stops, it limits the evidence, or at least favors some evidence over other evidence. Suppose that the conceptual faculty shifts from the acquisition mode to the codifying mode on an individual's twenty-first birthday. If the definition is used strictly, then similar cases will be denied membership in the extension of the concept. Since those cases are potential evidence for the adequacy of the classifications, however, the individual's system of concepts would no longer be warranted on the basis of the total evidence. The system of "empirical" concepts would lose its experiential warrant.

To avoid this problem, let us assume that the conceptual faculty codifies concepts at 21 years but that other faculties can override the definitions, under certain circumstances. Standardly, definitions are used to classify new instances. There is another faculty, however, that is able to engage in conscious reflection on new cases and to use systematic considerations about theoretically important similarities to remove old concepts and replace them with more satisfactory concepts. This two-faculty, or "liberal," definition model will avoid the epistemic error of limiting the evidence. Further, this model seems to reflect the practice of scientists in dealing with critical concepts in their disciplines. If we probe a bit deeper, however, there are still epistemic problems with the liberal definition model. First, we should note that it is evidentially biased toward old cases. New cases can get a hearing, but they must prove their importance as data, whereas during the acquisition of the concept, any case was freely admitted to the data base. Favoring old evidence has some epistemic virtues in the context of organized scientific research. If a datum or a theory has been abroad in the scientific community for some time, then there is reason to hope that it has withstood attempts to deny it. This is not the case for data that is old only in the lifetime of a particular individual, however. Yet, in the model, this is the type of old data that is given pride of place.

The second epistemic shortcoming of the liberal definition model is that new data are not admitted automatically, but only on the basis of conscious reflection. Conscious reflection about the adequacy of our concepts is epistemically virtuous, as Kant would be the first to stress. For the perceptual similarities that tend to lead us to group instances together may turn out to be theoretically unimportant. The demands put on conscious reflection by this model seem too high, however. To prevent our concepts from gradually slipping out of alignment with the data experience provides, we would have to exercise constant vigilance over our "automatic" classification system. If empirical concepts are to be reflective of reality, because of the way they are produced, it is far better to have a process that allows for automatic continuous updating. Since we need such a process to explain how we manage to acquire concepts at all, Kant assumed that it continues to mold our concepts to fit the data that we continue to experience.

Implications for Necessary and Sufficient Conditions

Kant's analysis of what empirical concepts must be like for them to yield knowledge has clear implications for the debate over necessary and sufficient conditions. Although the particular spurs to study concepts are varied, in general, concepts are important to cognitive science, because an adequate theory of concepts is necessary for a complete explanation of feats of cognition. Further, the following assumptions about concepts are ubiquitous among cognitive scientists[21]: Most (if not all) concepts are acquired through experience, most concepts are reflective of the experiences that give rise to them, concepts can be used to provide more or less accurate descriptions of reality—and so contribute to cognition—because they are derived from our encounters with reality. Since these views are ubiquitous, they are almost never expressed. Still, I believe that the vast majority of cognitive scientists would be shocked if one of their number denied any of these claims, for more than a small or isolated set of concepts. But if (empirical) concepts are reflective of reality, because of the ways they are produced, then we should not expect them to be represented by necessary and sufficient conditions. A definition model implies rigidity in the face of new experience, but the basic theoretical assumption about concepts is that they are molded by experience. And, as Kant observes, in experience, ever new characteristics of concepts may be discovered. An empirical concept realized by necessary and sufficient conditions is not quite like a soluble fish,[22] but it would not be very serviceable for cognition.

I should note that it is quite consistent with Kant's analysis that some of our concepts *appear* to follow the necessary and sufficient conditions model. This is to be expected if a concept has very few instances, if few instances are encountered, or if there is very little variability across instances. Concept users would appear to be applying necessary and sufficient conditions. Further, Kant is explicit that if a science is ever completed (or believed to be so), then it could have definitions. Hence, the common view that there are definitions in various branches of mathematics would be compatible with this aspect of his philosophy. Thus, Kant's analysis suggests that the data will be somewhat mixed, even though necessary and sufficient conditions would be an inappropriate way to represent empirical concepts, for the normal case.

Further Implications

Kant's attack on definitions has two further implications for work on concepts. First, concept learning would turn out to be something of a fiction. Insofar as this process is standardly understood as taking place over a relatively fixed span of time, before which subjects lack the concept and after which they have it, concept learning does not take place. To meet the requirements for empirically warranted belief, concept learning must be, in the educational cliche, a lifelong experience. The second implication is even more radical. If cognition is possible only because our conceptual repertoire is adaptive to the changing evidence of the environment, then cognitive scientists may not want to appeal to concepts at all, but rather to something like conceptual worms that continually evolve through time. The current confusion about concepts may be caused, in part, by a mistaken attempt to provide a static account of a phenomenon whose essence is the ability to change. Kant's analyses of the prerequisites for cognition reveal that to be the inherent and theoretically fatal weakness of the necessary and sufficient conditions model. Whatever its intuitive appeal, it presents concepts as completed, rigid mental representations. Once the open-ended character of experience is fully appreciated, it becomes apparent that this model is inconsistent with the basic theoretical assumption about empirical concepts—they are central to cognition because they are molded by experience.

Empiricism and "Original Sim"

Quinean Empiricism

If concepts are not represented in us by a list of necessary and sufficient features for category membership, what mental mechanisms do account for our ability to classify under concepts? Many discussions begin with the framework offered by Quine in "Natural Kinds."[23] In the beginning, classification occurs via perceptual similarity. Our sensory systems have innate quality spaces that lead us to experience certain stimulations as similar. Paradigmatically, our visual system has an innate standard of similarity for colors, so that, for example, different shades of yellow will strike us as quite similar. Quine hastens to add that this appeal to innate structures in no way abandons the tenets of Empiricism. We can measure quality spaces empirically, by determining the "generalizations" made by animals conditioned to respond to stimuli of certain colors. And since quality spaces are required for *all* learning, they must be innate.[24] Further, Quine's Empiricist scruples are clearly evident in his account of the second stage of concept acquisition. We start with a color-slanted quality space, but science enables us to rise above it:

> He [man] has risen above it by developing modified systems of kinds, hence modified similarity standards for scientific purposes. *By the trial-and-error process of theorizing* he has regrouped things into new kinds which prove to lend themselves to many inductions better than tne old [my emphasis].[25]

Not surprisingly, this account posits very little mental equipment underlying the use of concepts.[26] Innate quality spaces enable children to get started; through the undefined capacity for ingenuity and trial-and-error learning that produces scientific theories, the race acquires more useful categories, and teaches them to novices.[27]

The "original sim" account, as Frank Keil labels it, has been criticized in several recent empirical studies.[28] Contrary to Quine's speculation, children—even *very* young children—do not appear to group objects together just on the basis of qualitative similarity. Perhaps the most dramatic demonstrations are Gelman and Markman's studies with 3- and 4-year-olds.[29] The design of the study pitted appearance against category membership. (An example of the test materials is illustrated in Figure 8.1.) Having been told that the target (e.g., the cat) had a particular property, children were asked which other items would have the same property: items in the same category but with different ap-

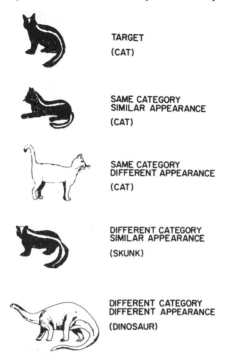

TARGET
(CAT)

SAME CATEGORY
SIMILAR APPEARANCE
(CAT)

SAME CATEGORY
DIFFERENT APPEARANCE
(CAT)

DIFFERENT CATEGORY
SIMILAR APPEARANCE
(SKUNK)

DIFFERENT CATEGORY
DIFFERENT APPEARANCE
(DINOSAUR)

Figure 8.1   One set of pictures used by Gelman and Markman to test category membership versus similar appearance. (Reproduced from *Child Development 58* (1987): 1532–41, by permission.)

pearances or items with similar appearances but in different categories. Both 3- and 4-year-olds infer that the same property will be present significantly more for the same category–different appearance items than for different category–same appearance items. Further, this pattern held for each of the 10 examples used in the study.

These results suggest that there is never a time when perceptual similarity is the sole mechanism that leads children to group objects together.[30] Gelman and Markman's data are consistent with findings of other researchers. Susan Carey has argued that children's use of concepts is tied to theories.[31] Although they disagree over important details, Frank Keil's work also implies that children's concepts are supported by implicit theories.[32] This might suggest that Quine was right about the two elements in concept acquisition—similarity plus instruction in science—but wrong about how early instruction begins.[33]

However, the second part of the similarity-corrected-by-science hypothesis is also at odds with recent empirical work. Douglas Medin and his colleagues have observed that, in experiments on categories, "[p]eople act as if things (e.g., objects) have essences or underlying natures that make them the thing that they are."[34] This would explain why some properties are treated as more important for category membership than others. Further, it might account for the intuitive appeal of the classical position. Medin notes, however, that although positing an "essentialist heuristic" explains much of the data on concepts, it is bad metaphysics [and bad science]. If concept users rely on an essentialist heuristic, it is not because they have internalized the wisdom of science.

Current Directions

Without pretending to summarize the entire literature on concepts, let me bring together some leading ideas about the factors underlying concept use. Perceptual similarity is important, even though it can be overruled by other considerations. Knowledge about the world, couched in explicit or implicit theories, also seems crucial. Although the theoretical knowledge underlying concept use is sometimes available to subjects, often it is not. And in the case of children, it is unreasonable to attribute explicit theories of physics or biology.[35] Perhaps concept users employ an essentialist heuristic that enables them to form coherent concepts. In general, concepts appear to have a great deal more structure than had previously been realized. Hence, it is implausible to represent them simply as lists of correlated features.[36] The features important to classification under a concept are themselves interrelated. Further, some seem more fundamental, and some occur at different levels of abstraction or specificity. Both the essentialist heuristic and theory-driven models are attractive, because they offer ways of explaining the relations among features in a concept.[37]

Medin also favors the essentialist heuristic because it suggests how similarity-based and knowledged-based mechanisms might be integrated. Assuming that perceptual similarity is a *clue* to deeper similarities, then similarity together with the essentialist heuristic could point the way toward classifications that can later be rooted in knowledge.[38] Medin's goal is a coherent account of concepts that is not itself just a list of factors: similarity + theories + central features + different levels of features + heuristics (e.g., essentialism). I shall argue that Kant's reflections about how concepts and theories must be structured for knowledge to be possible provide a coherent framework for understanding these empirical results. Negatively, Kant argued against definitions for empirical concepts. But he also believed that the demands of knowledge had positive implications for the structure of concepts.

Concepts and Reasoning

The Task of Inference

The fundamental cognitive fact about concepts is that they are serviceable only if they so partition objects that we can engage in reasonably successful inductions. This is clear in the concept literature, where discussions often focus on inferences.[39] Approximately 300 pages into the *Critique of Pure Reason*, Kant turns to the topic of reason, the faculty that enables us to make inferences. Previously, we have considered his analyses of relatively basic cognitive tasks. Here his quarry is quite sophisticated: What kind of faculty of reason must we have for it to be capable of producing knowledge through inference?

Contemporary discussions recognize the importance of inference to knowledge but rarely consider the problem in its full generality. Instead, they tend to concentrate on experimental validation of particular models of inference. By contrast, Kant directs all his energies to the abstract analysis of the task itself. He pursues his inquiries into the requirements for making inferences in the Ideal of Reason, the Regulative Use of the Ideas of Reason, and the introductions to the *Critique of Judgment*. This capacity turns out to have surprising implications for the structure of our concepts, and even for the structure of nature itself—or for any nature that could be known by us through our powers of intuition, understanding, and reason.

Analytic and Synthetic Approaches to Concepts

Kant can formulate the problem of the adequacy of concepts for inductive inference with particular clarity and starkness, because he understands representations, concepts, and judgments synthetically. We synthesize concepts and judgments on the basis of materials supplied by experience. Why should there be any connection from one representation or concept or judgment to another? Each is constructed on the basis of data supplied by different objects. So how is even simple instance induction possible? How can we know, for example, that the dog we now confront is unlikely to attack us unless threatened? The difficulty of this problem is missed if concepts and judgments are understood analytically.

This is a common failing of Leibniz and many contemporary cognitive scientists. For Leibniz, all judgments are explicative: The predicate of the judgment merely displays what is implicitly contained in the subject concept. Judgments are made by comparing representations or perceptions to determine if the predicate concept is contained in the subject concept. Now let us consider something apparently very different: the standard paradigm for concept learning experiments. Here subjects or computer programs are "taught" a new concept on basis of "experience." So a person or program is given a new term—"flurg" (to borrow Jerry Fodor's example[40]—and set of instances and foils. In the case of the computer program, the salient features of the examples are described, and the program has to figure out which features must be present or absent for the label to be correctly applied.[41] Similarly, human subjects are told which of the examples are "flurg" or "nonflurg," and they must determine the criterial properties for this concept, say being green or square. To see the affinities with Leibniz's view, consider what would happen after this type of concept learning. A new flurg is encountered. If it is correctly labeled a "flurg," it must be either green or square. So, from the fact that it falls under the concept 'flurg', we may infer that it, like other flurgs, is either green or square. But this inference is vacuous. For on this model of concept learning and concept possession, unless subjects recognized it to be either green or square, they would not label it a "flurg." Although this position is not as strong as Leibniz's claim that all judgments are analytic, it does seem to follow that what is inferred about objects, through the concepts they fall under, are only properties implicit in the concept.

In a note to the First Introduction to the *Critique of Judgment*, Kant points out that empirical cognitions

> cannot be abstracted *analytically*, from a simple comparison of perceptions (as is commonly supposed), because the union of two distinct perceptions by means of the concept of an object (so as to yield knowledge of it) is a synthesis.[42]

To produce knowledge a judgment must be a function of properties that are combined in the object.[43] It can never arise merely by comparing one concept with another. When the synthetic character of concepts and judgments is appreciated, however, the problem of instance induction becomes acute. We apply the label "X" to an object and observe its properties. Then we consider a new X and presume that it will share these properties, not because they are implicit in the concept 'X', but simply because it is an X. How is this kind of inference, so basic to knowledge, possible? What must concepts be like for it to be possible?

How to Carve Nature at the Joints

The standard answer is that concepts must "carve nature at the joints." They must group things together under one label that share deep similarities. Then our inductions will be successful. Unfortunately, like the proverbial market advice to buy low and sell high, this bromide provides no clues about how to find a substantive answer. Kant tries to provide a real answer by considering the requirements of inference itself. Inferences require principles. To infer that the dog before us will not attack if left alone, we must tacitly or explicitly appeal to a higher principle. Previously encountered animals have behaved in this way, so we assume that our judgments about them, and the judgment we are about to make about the dog, fall under a higher principle: In general, animals do not attack unless threatened. In the absence of some such principle, we would not be making an *inference*, but merely a hopeful guess. The appeal to principles raises the puzzle about concept-based inference in a different guise:

> But that objects in themselves, the very nature of things, should stand under principles, and should be determined according to mere concepts, is a demand which, if not impossible, is at least quite contrary to common sense [A301–32/B358].

Despite the misleading hint of "objects in themselves," Kant does not solve this problem by appeal to the phenomenal–noumenal distinction, but in quite a novel fashion. He considers the demands that reason's need for higher principles puts on concepts and on nature itself. Nature must have a certain kind of structure: Its properties must form a hierarchy. "For we can conclude from the universal to the particular, only in so far as universal properties are ascribed to things as being the *foundation* upon which the particular properties rest." (A652/B680, my emphasis). That is, inference will be possible only if it is mediated by principles indicating that some properties are the grounds or foundation of other properties.

Although Kant's position is clear, the argument for it seems vulnerable to straightforward counterexample. Seemingly, we can and do make inferences about new instances merely on the basis of *correlations* between properties—even when there is no relation of ground and dependence between the properties. To borrow a well-known example from Hempel, the presence of Koplick spots inside the mouth enables a physician to infer that the patient will soon run a fever, although there is no presumption that the spots are the ground of the fever.[44] When we reflect on such counterexamples, however, we can see the deep point behind Kant's claim. Although there is no dependency relation between the fever and the Koplick spots, the spots can be used to infer the fever only because we presume that they are indicative of *some further condition*, which *is* the ground of both fever and spots. Kant's statement of his analysis is, as often, excessively cryptic. What he means is that inference must always be mediated by a principle, which is such that either the principle itself, or some further principle that supports it, appeals to properties that are related as ground and dependent.

There remain only two possible classes of counterexample. Through exhaustive enumeration, we know that everything that has the property X also has the property Y. In such cases, the inference is not inductive or ampliative, however, because we would already know of the present instance that it has both properties. The second possibility is that some inferences are mediated by principles stating correlations that are taken to be brute, even in the absence of exhaustive enumeration. "Brute" is meant to signify that we have no reason to believe that anything mediates the correlation between the two properties. The 1980 election provided a classic example. It was noted that from 1820 through 1960, every president elected at the even 20 years died in office. Kant's argument is that this kind of pattern cannot license an inference about new cases, because it provides no justification for the inference. *Ex hypothesi*, previous correlations are not taken to be evidence of any connection between the properties, so nothing but blind chance could be offered in support of the inference. That is, nothing supports it.

Putting the matter positively, instance induction requires the use of a principle that is taken to indicate a relation of ground and dependence among some properties. This does not mean that any inference so mediated produces knowledge. Given the popularity of astrology columns, many people seem to believe that there is a connection between the position of the stars and the course of human events. People who use the stars to make inferences are not justified, even though they take whatever correlations they are able to find as signs of connection. Employing principles that are regarded as indicative of some relation of dependency among properties is a minimal condition. Without it, Kant maintains, we are not engaging in the task of *inferring* from previous experience at all.

He expresses this situation by saying that reason puts a "demand" on nature. It must have not joints, but hierarchical relations, with a few basic properties supporting less fundamental properties, which in turn support even more derivative properties. This "demand" does not establish any metaphysical claims about the actual structure of nature. As Henry Allison has argued in detail, Kant would be the last philosopher to infer from the fact that nature must be hierarchical for us to achieve knowledge, that all nature is hierarchically arranged.[45] His idea is, rather, that we must approach nature in the expectation that it has a hierarchical structure. Given the faculties we bring to the task of cognition, that is the only way that we could acquire knowledge. This approach to nature puts a demand on empirical concepts. "[W]e must seek for a certain systematic unity of all possible empirical concepts, in so far as they can be deduced from higher and more general concepts ... " (A652/B680). We must employ concepts that are related as genera and species.

The Structure of Concepts

Although the relation of genera and species is often mentioned as a criterion for the adequacy of empirical concepts, Kant never fully elaborates. Still, we can fill in some details from the passages in the Regulative Employment of the Ideas just cited and from two discussions in the *Logic*. The *Logic* notes that when concepts are related as genus and species, the higher concept contains the "cognitive ground of the lower."[46] This, I take it, is how the relation of genus and species between concepts reflects the relation of ground and dependence among properties in nature. The genus concept indicates the presence of properties that are the foundation of the properties indicated by the species concept. Notice that the relation of genus and species between concepts is much stronger than the frequently noted relation of superordination and subordination. "Furniture" is a superordinate concept with respect to "chair," but it could not be considered the genus. In describing a chair as a piece of furniture, we do not indicate any properties that underlie (or could be used to explain) its chair properties.

The *Logic* also offers a discussion of the structure of individual concepts.[47] Concepts have both an external and an internal [cognitive] use. In the external use, concepts are used to distinguish objects. For this purpose the characteristics associated with a concept must be sufficient to distinguish one class of things from another.[48] Concepts also have an internal use, however, which "consists in *derivation* in order to cognize the thing itself through characteristics as grounds of its cognition."[49] The characteristics can be coordinate with each other, or constitute a [partial] series of subordinate characteristics, which ascend to ever higher genera and/or descend to ever lower species.[50] I take Kant's point about derivation to be that, when we do have ascending series of subordinate characteristics for the coordinate characteristics, we have characteristics that indicate the relatively more fundamental properties that ground the coordinate characteristics. Hence, we have a concept that contains within itself information about the sorts of properties that underlie more superficial properties associated with the concept.

If characteristics are sufficient for coordination and subordination, then Kant describes the complex of characteristics as the "essence" of the concept. He hastily adds that this is not a real essence, however. It only indicates dependency relations among properties known to be associated with the concept. To get the real essence, we would have to know everything whatsoever that belongs to the existence of the objects[51] and, for reasons we have already seen, this is impossible. Thus, "essence" is something of a misnomer. This complex of characteristics is not fixed and does not provide necessary and sufficient conditions for application of the concept.[52]

The relation of genera and species thus holds between concepts and between characteristics [concepts] within individual concepts. This duality does not indicate inconsistency, but a substantive assumption. The "external" relations of a concept to other concepts are mirrored in the internal structure of the concept. Concepts are adequate to the demands of inference only if they are related as genera and species, and the internal structure of a concept mirrors its external relations. Although the inference is never drawn, it follows that cognitively adequate individual concepts must have a complex inner structure. They cannot be lists of unrelated features. The mental representation of an empirical concept must have a rich structure that captures dependency relations among the different levels of properties associated with the concept. Thus, the concept of an X must be an incomplete theory of X's.

Examples of Dependency Relations

Kant explicates the relation of genera and species in terms of dependency relations. The genus concept indicates properties that are the foundations of properties associated with the species concept. But what are the dependency relations? He can provide no exhaustive specification, for the obvious reason. Until the "end of science," no one can describe all the various ways in which properties depend on more fundamental properties. Still, despite his normal disdain for examples, we are given several illustrations from eighteenth-century science. He considers the hypothesis that all faculties of the human mind stem from a single fundamental power (A649/B677). These faculties have so many different effects that this hypothesis would not even have arisen, but for the fact that reason

requires [us to] . . . reduce, so far as may be possible, this seeming diversity, by comparing these with one another and detecting their hidden identity. We have to enquire whether imagination combined with consciousness may not be the same thing as memory, wit, power of discrimination, and perhaps even identical with understanding and reason [A649/B677].

In a marginal note to the First Introduction to the *Critique of Judgment*, he asks rhetorically whether Linnaeus could have hoped to construct a system of nature had he assumed that each thing had an individual essence, rather than being capable of belonging to a class, "which could be brought under genus-species concepts."[53]

In both these examples, part of Kant's goal seems to be to provide empirical confirmation for the thesis he has already defended through his analysis of the task of inference. For inference to be possible, we must seek principles that relate properties as ground and dependent—and here are two examples where we see this demand of reason in action. In the published discussion of psychology, he elaborates how the grounding is supposed to work: Derivative powers will be resolved into more fundamental powers, until all the powers can perhaps be understood as one power operating under different conditions. That is, the relation of ground and dependent is the relation of constituents to the whole. A complex faculty has the effects that it does, because it is made up of more basic faculties. The same relation is highlighted in Kant's more extended discussion from chemistry. We do not encounter instances of pure earth, pure air, and so forth. Nevertheless, in chemistry, the chemical interactions of bodies are explained by reducing all kinds of matter to more basic substances (earths, salts and inflammable substances, water and air). Again, properties of wholes will be a function of the properties of their microscopic constituents (A646/B674ff).

The *Metaphysical Foundations of Natural Science* offers a further illustration, although not in the context of a discussion of genera and species. This is Kant's well-known argument that solidity is not a fundamental power of matter. Solidity is supposed to account for the fact that objects can keep other objects from entering their current spatial position. This is possible, he maintains, only if all parts of matter have repulsive forces.[54] Kant's belief that dependency relations include the dependence of observable properties on properties of, or forces governing, constituents is hardly surprising in the historical context of trying to extend Newton's ideas to other domains of physical science.

For reasons we have already seen, a complete list of dependency relations cannot be given. Instead, we have some useful pointers. Concepts display the systematic unity that will permit a hierarchy of genera and species when a genus concept indicates (1) properties of, or (2) forces governing, constituents that explain the powers or properties of the phenomenon indicated by the species concept. This, then, is the "demand" that reason puts on empirical concepts. To be adequate to cognition, they must exemplify this type of systematic interconnection.

It is tempting to think that reason has no more ability to enforce this demand than its "demand" for structure in nature. Kant encourages this view by describing the systematizing demand as "subjective" and as "an ideal." However, it is subjective only in the sense that it does not permit the inference to objective hierarchies in nature (e.g., A645/B673); it is an ideal because it aims to bring as much unity to concepts as possible, without knowing how much *is* possible (A647/B675). The demand of reason is not subjective in the sense of being merely apparent or arbitrary, and it is not ideal in the sense of being merely normative. It is psychologically real.[55] "Reason . . . has a real use, since it contains within itself the source of certain concepts and principles [viz., seek systematic unity in concepts]" (A299/B355). For Kant it is not merely a normative doctrine that sound inferential practice requires appeal to principles that indicate a relation of ground and dependence. Our inferential successes and the development of scientific theories are *evidence* that we have a faculty that seeks concepts that are systematically interrelated.

The false impression that the demand of reason is not psychologically real is reinforced by the fact that Kant offers no suggestions about *how* such a demand might be effected. Here he stands by his prefatory pledge not to speculate about how something that is necessary for knowledge actually comes about (Axvii). For my purposes, however, this issue is critical. Although Kant believes in the psychological reality of the demand for system on the basis of successful inferences and scientific practice, the case needs to be strengthened. In the absence of any hints about how such a demand could be implemented, its psychological reality will seem less plausible. The next section tries to fill this gap, by speculating about heuristics that might carry out reason's demand for system. Reflecting on possible heuristics also serves a second purpose. It enables us to see some of the implications of Kant's analysis of empirically adequate concepts for current research on concepts.

Implementing the Demand of Reason

Reason demands that we use concepts that have a systematic unity. Or, less metaphorically, we can acquire knowledge through inferences only if we use such concepts. As already noted, however, empirically adequate concepts are also based on experience. They are constructed and modified on the basis of encounters with objects. So the concepts that we acquire through experience must be subjected to further testing to determine if they can be part of a unified system of concepts. However— and this is the hard part—the testing must precede anything like a complete scientific understanding of the dependency relations among the properties of these objects. That is, we must try to figure out if a concept can fit into a systematic description of the hierarchical structure of nature, without knowing what that structure is (if it has one). Since the end state is not known, it is, to say the least, highly unlikely that we can find an algorithm to determine the systematic potential of concepts. Instead, the hope is to find heuristics that are somewhat reliable in leading us toward more systematic concepts.

Heuristics can be conscious or unconscious. Kant's discussion of genera and species is intended, in part, to be an epistemic recommendation. In the practice of science, we should deliberately set out to find theories with hierarchical structure. However, he describes the demand for system as "natural tendency" of reason (A643/B670). This suggests that he believes that we are prone to look for system, even without trying. The heuristics I consider could have conscious and unconscious versions. Once science has become a conscious activity, it is very easy to see how individuals could pursue the goal of systematic unity in concepts. They could just follow Kant's advice! The earlier stage seems more problematic. Without knowing anything about nature, including our own cognitive powers, how can individuals or the race fasten on concepts that are sufficient to get scientific theorizing started? How can they do this in the face of the enormous variety of forms in nature (e.g., A651/B679)? To solve the problem of early conceptualization, we need to find heuristics that can be unconscious.

The best and most obvious heuristics for finding concepts that might fit into a complete hierarchical system are those that favor concepts that exemplify at least a small piece of this pattern. For example, we might favor concepts that indicate a cluster of correlated attributes. (Here I use "attribute" as the generic term for property, power, or relation.) So if items that bark also regularly engage in a distinctive form of locomotion and also regularly behave toward people in a special way, then we group these items under a concept. Such clusters are good evidence of an underlying attribute or attributes on which members of the cluster depend. In the early stages of conceptualization, this heuristic could be unconscious, however. Leaving off the conscious rationale, the heuristic is just: Fasten on concepts that indicate clusters of correlated attributes.[56] A slightly different aspect of the pattern would be captured by a heuristic that favored concepts that indicate a dependency relation among attributes. So if items get bigger *because* they eat, then they should also be grouped together under a concept.

As Medin noted in defense of the "essentialist" heuristic, superficial similarity can often be a clue to similarity of more fundamental attributes. In fact, perceptual similarity can be understood as a special case of the first heuristic. If we are prone to assign a concept to items that share clusters of correlated attributes, then we will also classify objects together that share a number of *perceptually* similar features. Thus, if Kant is right, we would expect perceptual similarity to play an important role in conceptualization, as it does. But this would not be the role that Quine envisioned for "original similarity." The role is not original, but derivative. Perceptual similarity would only be used in categorization, because it can be indicative of a rich structure of dependency relations among the attributes indicated by the concept. It would have no independent status, but would merely be one of a bag of tricks for detecting complex interrelations among properties. Both Quine and a contemporary Kantian will correctly predict that subjects will group things together that look alike. The latter will add, however, that this heuristic will be overriden where other indicators suggest that dependency relations are to be found elsewhere. I take Gelman and Markman's results that, in the face of richer sources of evidence (but not scientific theories), even 3-year-olds will abandon perceptual similarity to be some confirmation of the Kantian position.

Barbara Landau, Linda Smith, and Susan Jones have recently published some tantalizing results about the importance of shape in learning lexical items.[57] Adults, 2-year-olds, and 3-year-olds favor shape over size and texture in grouping items together that "go together" and in extending novel count nouns to new instances. The bias is greatest in adults, and increases between 2 and 3 years of age. These authors speculate that shape bias develops in the process of learning new words between the ages of 2 and 3, because "the earliest learned words, basic level concrete nouns, do in fact largely divide the world according to shape." Since it is useful here, children generalize to later word learning tasks. There are several obvious objections to this hypothesis. Two-year-olds already know many basic nouns.[58] More importantly, it is not clear how the hypothesis explains the *stronger* bias of adults, who are no longer learning basic nouns, but abstract ones. I offer a different hypothesis. Grouping objects together by shape is a heuristic that serves the systematizing demand of reason. Shape would be a useful heuristic for two different reasons. Many other attributes of objects depend on their shapes. To take a relevant example, balls can be rolled, because they are round. So shape can be viewed as a special case of the second heuristic. Shape can also be understood as a cluster of more local geometric properties of objects, however. For example, the distinctive shapes of cat ears, faces, and paws are part of the overall feline figure; but they can easily be regarded as separate but correlated attributes. That is, using shape exemplifies first heuristic. Thus, similarity in shape would be a good predictor of classifications that will have a rich structure of dependency relations among the attributes of the objects in the classification, and so a good predictor of concepts with high systematic potential.

The preceding arguments are not intended to show that Kant's claims for the systematizing demands of reason offer the best explanation of the empirical data. In this section I have only tried to establish the plausibility of regarding this systematizing demand as psychologically real. Given these four heuristics—correlated attributes, attributes related by dependency, perceptual similarity, and shape—we can see how the demand of reason could be implemented. Extracting cognitively adequate concepts from the abundance of nature, in the absence of scientific understanding, is not easy, but seemingly we can get started without the assistance of any magical abilities. In the final section I try to show that Kant's idea of a "demand" for system provides greater theoretical insight into recent empirical results than the available contemporary proposals.

Theoretical and Experimental Implications

As already noted, recent interest in concepts has produced a plethora of experimental results. Perceptual similarity plays an important role in classifying items under concepts, but not the dominant role sometimes attributed to it. Adults' and even young children's use of concepts seems to imply the presence of implicit or explicit theoretical knowledge. In general, concepts seem to have a great deal of structure. They indicate attributes that are interrelated and that exhibit different levels of abstractness or specificity. Several hypotheses about the mental equipment underlying concept use have been proposed to explain these results, the most popular being the theory theory. Concepts are supported by explicit or implicit theories.

As Murphy and Medin observe, however, to explain a feature of concepts by saying that concepts are backed by theories is not very satisfactory, unless one can say what a theory is.[59] Further, it is clear that the implicit theories attributed to children on this model are not very like scientific theories, so a question arises about how minimal they can be and still be theories. Frank Keil, who defends the importance of theoretical knowledge, has also noted that there appear to be theory-independent principles, such as "properties have purposes" and "properties reflect essences," which guide us in classifying objects together under a concept.[60] Finally, this approach raises an obvious question that is not very easy to answer: How many implicit theories are there?

Medin's proposal of an essentialist heuristic is simpler, because one heuristic is applied across a variety of domains. Essentialism has vices of its own, however. Kant notes that a belief in individual essences would thwart efforts to develop a system of concepts based on genera and species that is necessary to concept-based inference.[61] Inference only works when there are similarities *across* individuals. Even if essences are located in kinds rather than in individuals, essentialism would still block higher-level inferences across kinds. Thus, an essentialist heuristic would be counterproductive in trying to develop a set of concepts that permits the largest number of inferences about new instances. It is bad metaphysics, as Medin points out, and a bad inferential strategy.[62]

Kant employs a very different perspective to answer the two fundamental questions about concepts: What kinds of concepts do we have? What mental equipment underlies our ability to use such concepts? For concepts to be adequate to cognition, in particular to the demands of inference, they must have a complex inner structure that indicates dependency relations among attributes. Given the richness of forms in nature, we can fasten on adequate concepts only if we actively seek concepts with high systematic potential, only if we "approach nature in order to be taught by it" (Bxiii) by "projecting" a "systematic unity" on nature (A647/B675). Hence, we must have psychological mechanisms—the "demand" of "reason" is merely a place holder—that enable us to seek adequate concepts. On Kant's model, concepts require at least the following mental equipment. Individual concepts are represented by complexly interrelated sets of attributes, which amount to partial theories of the dependency relations among objects, properties, and forces; and the whole process is supported by various heuristics. We can fill in some further details by recalling his objections to defining empirical concepts. The representations underlying concepts are constantly updated by the application of conscious and unconscious systematizing heuristics to the individual's expanding body of data.

This model provides a coherent framework for understanding a variety of empirical results. As noted earlier, both the theory theory and the essentialist heuristic are appealing, because they seem to provide some account of the surprising amount of structure that has been discovered in concepts. This is a virtue shared by Kant's model. Concepts must have significant internal structure to be cognitively adequate, and we have various heuristics for acquiring such concepts. Thus, the model retrodicts the discovery of structure in concepts. It is simpler and more plausible than the theory model, however. We do not need a number of implicit theories. More importantly, perhaps, on this picture, we do not attribute *theories* to children and lay adults. The heuristics subserving the demand of reason suggest, instead, that we will adopt concepts that indicate *some* dependency relations among attributes. Concepts would be backed only by theory *fragments*. Besides the problems with essentialism already noted, Kant's model has the advantage of providing a principled explanation for the empirical results. Given his analysis of what concepts must be like for inference to work at all, we can understand why concepts should be expected to have the structure that they do. As noted in passing, the model also offers a unified explanation for the use of perceptual similarity, shape, and [partial] theories in determining classifications.

In addition to theoretical insight, Kant's analysis of what cognitively adequate concepts must be like provides a clear directive for research on concepts. If we are Quineans, then we will try to understand the processes of concept formation by investigating innate quality spaces. Theory theorists will try to uncover the implicit theories that stand behind conceptual practices. An essentialist will look not for theories but for essences. But if we take Kant seriously, then we should try to discover general-purpose heuristics that lead to potentially systematic concepts. What are they? How good are they? Do they show a clear developmental pattern? Do they, as Kant believed, lead to metaphysical excesses in the pursuit of complete scientific understanding?[63]

Conclusion

I have presented only one example of how Kant's attempts to understand the prerequisites of cognition can contribute to current debates, but I think it is a convincing one. Through reflecting on what concepts must be like to serve cognition, Kant develops a model of empirical concepts that can give needed order to chaotic empirical results. In retrospect, I hope that it is no longer surprising to hold that a great theoretician who devoted enormous intellectual efforts to determining what cognition requires of our mental faculties might have had some ideas that are useful to cognitive science. The history of philosophy can be a *philosophical* discipline only if the ideas of the past were so powerful that they can be a continuing source of insight to later theorists. In denying transcendental psychology, we run the risk of turning an intricate and vital study into a museum piece. The great book is much more rewarding—and makes much better sense—when it is read intact.

NOTES

Chapter 1

1. P. F. Strawson, *The Bounds of Sense* (London: Methuen, 1966). The citations are from pages 32 and 16.

2. Ibid., p. 19.

3. Ibid., p. 16.

4. Ibid., p. 96. After presenting interpretations of various Kantian doctrines without recourse to the psychological aspects of the arguments, Strawson gives an interpretation and criticism of transcendental psychology in Part Four. I discuss this argument at the end of Chapter 5.

5. Three important exceptions are Robert Paul Wolff, *Kant's Theory of Mental Activity* (Cambridge, Mass.: Harvard University Press, 1963), Onora O'Neil, "Transcendental Synthesis and Developmental Psychology," *Kant-Studien* 75 (1984): 149–67, and Ralf Meerbote, "Kant's Functionalism," in J. C. Smith, ed., *Historical Foundations of Cognitve Science* (Dordrecht, Holland: Reidel, 1989). One piece of transcendental psychology that has received some attention is Kant's theory of imagination. For references and a very interesting recent discussion, see J. M. Young, "Kant's View of Imagination," *Kant-Studien* 79 (1988): 140–64.

6. Jonathan Bennett, *Kant's Analytic* (Cambridge: Cambridge University Press, 1966), pp. 56, 111ff. I discuss another aspect of Bennett's antipsychologism in Chapter 6, note 26.

7. Paul Guyer, *Kant and the Claims of Knowledge* (New York: Cambridge University Press, 1987), p. 374. Henry Allison, *Kant's Transcendental Idealism: An Interpretation and Defense* (New Haven: Yale University Press, 1983). I discuss one of these efforts at depsychologizing in "The 'Logical' Reading of Apperception" section in Chapter 4.

8. I discuss Henrich's attempt to reconstruct the deduction of the categories while eschewing psychology in "Henrich's Antipsychological Reading" in Chapter 6.

9. Norman Kemp Smith, *A Commentary to Kant's "Critique of Pure Reason"* (New York: Humanities Press, 1962), p. 51. Cohen, Caird, and Riehl were the offenders.

10. Ibid. For the pledge, see p. 270; the account follows. I consider the issue of the noumenal versus the phenomenal self below and again at the end of Chapter 5.

11. H. J. Paton, *Kant's Metaphysics of Experience*, 2 vols. (New York: Humanities Press, 1965), 572ff.

12. W. H. Walsh, "Philosophy and Psychology in Kant's Critique," *Kant-Studien 56* (1966): 186-98, p. 191.

13. My discussion of the early reaction to Kant's psychology draws on four sources: Frederick Beiser's *The Fate of Reason* (Cambridge, Mass.: Harvard University Press, 1987); Gary Hatfield's forthcoming *The Natural and the Normative: Theories of Perception from Kant to Helmholtz* (Cambridge, Mass.: MIT Press); Jürgen Bona Meyer, *Kant's Psychologie* (Berlin: Wilhelm Hertz, 1870); and several articles by David E. Leary, "The Psychology of Jakob Friedrich Fries" (1773–1843): Its Context, Nature, and Historical Significance, *Storia e Critica della Psiscologia 3,* (1982): 217–48, "The Philosophical Development of the Conception of Psychology in Germany, 1780–1850," *Journal of the History of the Behavioral Sciences* XIV (1978): 113–21, "Immanuel Kant and the Development of Modern Psychology," in William R. Woodward and Mitchell G. Ash, *The Problematic Science: Psychology in Nineteenth Century Thought* (New York: Praeger, 1982), pp. 17–42.

14. Johann Georg Hamann also offered a well-known metacritique, but one that was intended to overthrow rather than shore up the Critical philosophy. See Beiser's discussion (op. cit.), Chapter 1.

15. In Chapter 3, "The Probem," I provide a clarificatory regimentation of this concept.

16. Here I draw on Beiser's detailed account of Reinhold's position. Op. cit., Chapter 8, especially pp. 227, 237, 241–55.

17. For further details, see Leary's article on Fries, op. cit.

18. I discuss his arguments in "Apperception as the *Cogito*" in Chapter 4 and in "Understanding the First Paralogism in Chapter 7."

19. Immanuel Kant, *Anthropology from a Pragmatic Point of View*, translated by Mary J. Gregor (The Hague: Martinus Nijhoff, 1974), pp. 14–15 (AA VII:133), 39 (AA VII:161).

20. Hatfield offers this convenient approximation. Op. cit., p. 169.

21. Bona Meyer, op. cit., quoted on p. 5.

22. Ibid., pp. 122, 129.

23. See the discussion of "innate" versus "*a priori*" below. I discuss Kant's views on spatial perception at length in Chapter 2.

24. For a detailed account of Helmholtz's position with respect to Kant, see Hatfield, op. cit., Chapter 5.

25. Strawson discusses this possibility in Part Five of *The Bounds of Sense*, op. cit. See also James Hopkins, "Visual Geometry," *Philosophical Review 82* (1973): 3–34.

26. Dr. G. Frege, *The Foundations of Arithmetic*, translated by J. L. Austin (Oxford: Basil Blackwell, 1968), p. x^e.

27. Ibid., p. vi^e.

28. Beiser, op. cit., p. 249.
29. Quoted in Hatfield, op. cit., Chapter 4, note 16.
30. See Michael Dummett, *Frege: Philosophy of Language* (New York: Harper & Row, 1973), Chapter 19, Richard Rorty, *Philosophy and the Mirror of Nature* (Princeton, N.J.: Princeton University Press, 1979), and, especially, Hans Sluga, *Gottlob Frege* (Boston: Routledge & Kegan Paul, 1980), Introduction.
31. Alvin I. Goldman, *Epistemology and Cognition* (Cambridge, Mass.: Harvard University Press, 1986), p. 6.
32. See Sluga, loc. cit., and Goldman, loc. cit.
33. The most obvious example is Gilbert Ryle's *The Concept of Mind* (New York: Barnes and Noble, 1949). However, much philosophy of mind of the 1950s, 1960s, 1970s, and even 1980s was antipsychologistic. For two clear examples, see Donald Davidson's "Mental Events," reprinted in *Essays on Actions and Events* (Oxford: Clarendon Press, 1980), Zeno Vendler, *The Matter of Minds* (Oxford: Clarendon Press, 1984).
34. Cited in Sluga, op. cit., p. 39.
35. Edmund Husserl, *Logical Investigations*, vol. I., translated by J. N. Findlay (New York: Humanities Press, 1970), pp. 92, 98.
36. Ibid., p. 172.
37. Although Husserl resists acknowledging Frege's influence, it seems very clear. See Sluga's discussion, op. cit., p. 40.
38. Michael Dummett made this interesting observation in a conversation with Philip Kitcher.
39. Kant's Wolffian critics maintained that the principle of sufficient reason is a logical principle. Since the principle of the second analogy can be regarded as Kant's analog for sufficient reason (see Guyer, op. cit., pp. 238, 242), one might try to build a case for psychologism in logic. Given that Kant certainly does not regard his principle as logical—and given that it clearly is not—this case can be rebutted, however. See Beiser, op. cit., pp. 196–201, and Henry Allison, *The Kant–Eberhard Controversy* (Baltimore: The Johns Hopkins University Press, 1973), pp. 95–96.
40. See below, the "Transcendental Psychology" section.
41. See Philip Kitcher, "Kant and the Foundations of Mathematics," *Philosophical Review 84* (1975): 23–50. For further discussion, see the "Transcendental Psychology" section.
42. Goldman, op. cit., Introduction. For a useful discussion of the psychologism issue against the background of recent work in cognitive science, see also Adrian Cussins, "Varieties of Psychologism," *Synthese 70* (1987): 123–54.
43. J. B. Watson, "Psychology as the Behaviorist Views It," reprinted in *A Source Book in the History of Psychology*, edited by Richard J. Hernstein and Edmund G. Boring (Cambridge, Mass.: Harvard University Press, 1965), pp. 513–14.
44. Walsh, op. cit., p. 38.
45. *Metaphysical Foundations of Natural Science*, translated by James Ellington (Indianapolis: Bobbs-Merrill, 1970) (AA IV:471).
46. Loc. cit. For an interesting account of what happened to psychology in

the wake of Kant's criticisms, see Leary, "The Philosophical Development of the Conception of Psychology in Germany," 1780–1850, op. cit.

47. *Anthropology*, op. cit., p. 4 (AA VII:121).

48. Immanuel Kant's *Critique of Pure Reason*, translated by Norman Kemp Smith (New York: St. Martin's, 1965). I shall standardly use Kemp Smith's translation, except where I think it distorts Kant's meaning. In those cases, I will indicate that I have amended this translation, or retranslated the passage myself.

49. *Anthropology*, op. cit., p. 21 (AA VII:140–41).

50. Cited in Robert J. Richards, "Christian Wolff's Prolegomena to Empirical and Rational Psychology: Translation and Commentary," *Proceedings of the American Philosophical Society* 124 (1980): 227–39, (p. 231).

51. Ibid., see p. 236.

52. Ibid., p. 237.

53. In Chapter 7, I argue that many of Kant's putative objections to Rational Psychology are also *caveats* about his own transcendental method.

54. Chapter 3, "The Law of Association," "Association and Apriority."

55. *Immanuel Kant Logic*, translated by Robert S. Hartman and Wolfgang Schwartz (New York: Bobbs-Merrill, 1974), p. 13 (AA IX:10).

56. Ibid., pp. 37, 97, 100 (AA IX:33, 92, 94).

57. Hatfield, op. cit., pp. 18–19. Robert Pippin also notes that Kant's meaning of "logic" is quite different from contemporary usage. See *Kant's Theory of Form* (New Haven: Yale University Press, 1982), p. 153 note. In *The Art of Thinking* (widely known as the "Port Royal Logic"), Arnauld explains that "Logic consists in reflecting on these natural operations [conceiving, judging, reasoning, ordering] . . . [this helps us to reason better, to correct and explain defects in the mind's operation and] . . . we become better aware of the nature of the mind by reflecting on its operations." [Antoine Arnauld, *The Art of Thinking*, translated by James Dickoff and Patricia James (Indianapolis: Bobbs-Merrill, 1964), pp. 29–30.]

58. In Chapter 7 I argue that part of the motivation for the Paralogisms chapter is to distinguish transcendental psychology from Rational Psychology.

59. See the discussion of Wolff's method of philosophical hypotheses in Richard J. Blackwell, "Christian Wolff's Doctrine of the Soul," *Journal of the History of Ideas XXII* (1961): 339–54, pp. 349ff.

60. Allison, *The Kant–Eberhard Controversy*, op. cit., pp. 135–36 (AA VIII:221–23). I'm grateful to Allison for drawing my attention to this passage.

61. I provide a specific example of the distinction between an *a priori*$_\mathrm{o}$ element and an innate mechanism in Chapter 2, "Pure Forms."

62. I discuss Kant's constructive notion of proof briefly in Chapter 2, "Geometry and the Space of Perception."

63. See A56 and the citation from Kant's letter to Fichte below.

64. Philip Kitcher defends this analysis of Kantian necessity in "Kant and the Foundations of Mathematics," op. cit.

65. Paul Guyer has recently suggested a different understanding of "necessity" for Kant. I consider Guyer's position in note 63 of Chapter 5.

66. This is Kant's evaluation. Locke thought that by showing empirical origins for concepts, he could demonstrate the flexibility of the human mind to new ideas.

67. I have presented only some aspects of Kant's account of the *a priori* status of mathematics. Besides claims about the *a priori*$_0$ status of spatial properties, Kant also has a particular view of construction in mathematical proof. See, Chapter 2, "Geometry and the Space of Perception," and Philip Kitcher, "Kant and the Foundations of Mathematics," op. cit.

68. Husserl, op. cit., p. 100.

69. This epistemic analysis is defended by Philip Kitcher in "Kant's Philosophy of Science," in Allen W. Wood, ed., *Self and Nature in Kant's Philosophy* (Ithaca: Cornell University Press, 1984), pp. 185–215. I present the analysis of the relevant empirical capacity in Chapter 8, "Concepts and Reasoning."

70. Because he does not recognize analyses of empirical capacities, Guyer believes that either Kant's arguments are all conditional or they must presuppose that a noumenal mind imposes structure on nature. See, Guyer, op. cit., for example, pp. 53ff., and Paul Guyer, "Kant on Apperception and *A Priori* Synthesis," *American Philosophical Quarterly 17* (1980): 205–12. However, also see the discussion of transcendental proof at the end of his book, pp. 417–18.

71. Immanuel Kant, *Critique of Practical Reason*, translated by Lewis White Beck (Indianapolis: Bobbs-Merrill, 1956), p. 48 (AA V:47).

72. Daniel Dennett suggests the kinship between Kant and contemporary cognitive science on this point in "Artificial Intelligence as Philosophy and as Psychology," in *Brainstorms* (Cambridge, Mass.: Bradford Books, 1978), pp. 109–26. For a further account of the strategy of functional decomposition, see Robert Cummins, "Functional Analysis," *Journal of Philosophy 72* (1975): 741–60.

73. P. F. Strawson, the Sounds chapter of *Individuals* (London: Methuen, 1959).

74. I argue this point in "Discovering the Forms of Intuition," *Philosophical Review XCVI* (1987): 205–48 and later in Chapter 2, "The Isolation Argument."

75. Gary Hatfield offers this helpful way of summarizing one line of objection. Op. cit., p. 133. Later I agree with his answer: Transcendental psychology is the psychology of the knowing mind.

76. I consider Strawson's position in Chapter 5, "Apperception and Kant's System."

77. Perhaps the most prominent advocate of this reading is Wilfrid Sellars. See "Metaphysics and the Concept of a Person," in Karel Lambert, ed., *The Logical Way of Doing Things* (New Haven: Yale University Press, 1969, pp. 219–32, and, especially, "this I or he or it (the thing) which thinks," Sellar's Presidential Address to the Eastern Division of the APA in 1970. I try to disentangle some of the relations among these three selves in "Kant's Real Self," in Allen W. Wood, ed., op. cit., pp. 113–47, and Chapter 5, "Apperception and Kant's System."

78. See Chapter 5, "Apperception and Kant's System."

79. See Chapter 7, "Understanding the First Paralogism."

80. Allen Newell and Herbert Simon, *Human Problem Solving* (Englewood Cliffs, N.J.: Prentice-Hall, 1972), p. 53.

81. These discussions focus on the relation between general (and so transcendental) and applied *logic*, but as I have already noted, given our contemporary understanding of "logic" and "psychology," it is clearer to make Kant's point in terms of the relation between transcendental and applied, or empirical, psychology. In Chapter 8 I show in detail how constraints from transcendental psychology can guide empirical research.

82. W. V. Quine, "Two Dogmas of Empiricism," in *From a Logical Point of View* (New York: Harper, 1961), pp. 20–46. See also "Truth by Convention" and "Carnap on Logical Truth," both in *The Ways of Paradox* (New York: Random House, 1966). For a very clear presentation of Quine's views, see Gilbert Harman, "Quine on Meaning and Existence I," *Review of Metaphysics* *XXI* (1967): 124–51. Quine's attacks on analyticity have not gone unchallenged. Strawson and H. P. Grice tried to defend the notion of analyticity in "In Defense of a Dogma," *Philosophical Review LXV* (1956): 141–58.

83. The similarity is argued in greater detail by Philip Kitcher in "How Kant Almost Wrote 'Two Dogmas of Empiricism,' " in J. N. Mohanty and Robert W. Shahan, eds., *Essays on Kant's Critique of Pure Reason* (Norman, Okla.: University of Oklahoma Press, 1982), pp. 217–49.

84. I discuss his reasons for these claims at some length in Chapter 8.

85. Arnulf Zweig, *Kant Philosophical Correspondence 1759–99* (Chicago: University of Chicago Press, 1967), p. 9.253 (AA XII:370). My attention was drawn to this letter by Derk Pereboom's interesting discussion in "Kant's Notion of the *A Priori* and the Transcendental" ms.

86. Cited in Allison, The *Kant–Eberhard Controversy*, op. cit., p. 175. Allison suggests that Kant approved the letter, p. 13.

87. This description follows the model of transcendental arguments given by Ralph C. S. Walker, in *Kant* (London: Routledge & Kegan Paul, 1982), Chapter II, and discussed by Anthony L. Brueckner in "Transcendental Arguments I," *Nous 17* (1983): 551–75.

88. See Barry Stroud, "Transcendental Arguments," *Journal of Philosophy* 65 (1968): 241–56, and Judith Jarvis Thomson, "Private Languages," *American Philosophical Quarterly 1* (1964): 20–31. Although there have been many arguments back and forth in the literature, the criticisms originally made in these papers still seem completely cogent.

89. Margaret Wilson notes that Kant's target is Humean and not Cartesian skepticism in "Kant and the Refutations of Subjectivism," in L. W. Beck, *Kant's Theory of Knowledge* (Dordrecht: Reidel, 1974), pp. 208–17. I also argue against Descartes being a primary target in "Kant's Patchy Epistemology," *Pacific Philosophical Quarterly 68* (1987): 306–16.

90. Chapter 4, "Troubles with Apperception."

91. The relevance of Kant's work to current research in cognitive science and cognitive psychology has been noted by scholars in these fields. See, for example,

Colin Martindale, "Can We Construct Kantian Mental Machines?" *The Journal of Mind and Behavior* 8 (1987): 261–68.

Chapter 2

1. Hans Vaihinger, *Commentar zu Kants Kritik der reinen Vernunft*, vol. II, (New York: Garland, 1970), pp. 33–263.

2. Norman Kemp Smith, *A Commentary to Kant's "Critique of Pure Reason,"* (New York: Humanities Press, 1962), pp. 85–86.

3. In "On Kant's Notion of Intuition (*Anschauung*)," in T. Penelhum and J. MacIntosh, *The First Critique: Reflections on Kant's Critique of Pure Reason* (Belmont, Calif.: Wadsworth, 1969), pp. 38–53. Hintikka reads "intuition" as marking the *singularity* of a representation, and not its relation to sensibility. He offers this interpretation despite the fact that Kant's introductory discussion of "intuition" links it firmly to sensibility: When the mind is affected in a certain way by objects, the faculty of sensibility supplies us with intuitions (A19/B34). For criticisms of Hintikka's position, see Allison, *Kant's Transcendental Idealism*, op. cit., p. 67, and Manley Thomson, "Singular Terms and Intuitions in Kant's Epistemology," *Review of Metaphysics* 26 (1972): 314–43.

4. Robert Howell seems to presuppose Hintikka's position in "Intuition, Synthesis, and Individuation in the *Critique of Pure Reason*," in *Nous* (1973): 207–32. For critical discussions, see previous note.

5. Kant does not appeal to an "isolation" argument to establish his thesis about time in the Aesthetic. As I argue later, however, this is the heart of his case for his theory of space as the form of outer intuition. See also the special problems raised by the theory of time discussed in Chapter 5, "The Ideality of Time."

6. John Handyside, *Kant's Inaugural Dissertation and Early Writings on Space* (La Salle, Ill.: Open Court, 1929), pp. 3–15; see pp. 11–12 (AA I: 24–25).

7. Ibid., pp. 13–14 (AA I:139–40).

8. For an account of Kant's various senses of "*a priori*," see Chapter 1, "Transcendental Psychology,"

9. In "Apperception and Kant's System" in Chapter 5 I discuss the relation between Kant's theory of the forms of intuition and his metaphysical views about space and time.

10. Quoted in Nicholas Pastore, *Selective History of Theories of Visual Perception, 1650–1950* (Oxford: Oxford University Press, 1971), p. 68.

11. See Richard J. Herrnstein and Edwin G. Boring, *A Source Book in the History of Psychology* (Cambridge, Mass.: Harvard University Press, 1968), pp. 113–17.

12. Cited in Pastore, op. cit., p. 414.

13. G. W. Leibniz, *New Essays on Human Understanding*, abridged ed.,

translated and edited by Peter Remnant and Jonathan Bennett (Cambridge: Cambridge University Press, 1982), p. 138.

14. See Pastore, op. cit., the relevant selections in Herrnstein and Boring, op. cit., and T. E. Jessop, *A Bibliography of George Berkeley* (The Hague: Martinus Nijhoff, 1973), Introduction.

15. Arthur Warda, *Immanuel Kants Bucher* (Berlin: Verlag von Martin Breslaner, 1922), p. 46.

16. The situation is somewhat cloudy because Jessop never saw the translation he lists. The early editions of *Alciphron* all had the *Essay on Vision* as an appendix. In 1734 a French translation was made, which included the *Essay*. According to Jessop, a German translation was made from the English and the French. Further, as Geoffrey Keynes points out in *A Bibliography of George Berkeley* (Oxford: Oxford University Press, 1976), Jessop does not tell us where to find any copies of this edition. The question of Kant's knowledge of Berkeley's writings has often been raised. For a recent discussion, see G. J. Mattey, "Kant's Conception of Berkeley's Idealism," *Kant-Studien 74* (1983): 161–75.

17. According to Hamann, Tetens book lay open on Kant's desk as he wrote the *Critique*. See Jürgen Bona Meyer, op. cit., p. 56.

18. Leipzig, 1777, republished by the Kantgesellschaft (Verlag, 1913). Page references are to the later edition.

19. Ibid., Introduction, p. 36.

20. Ibid., pp. 42ff.

21. Ibid., p. 194. Cf. also p. 271.

22. Ibid., pp. 42–43ff.

23. *Kants Erkenntnispsychologie, Kant-Studien Ergängungshefte 101* (1971), pp. 1–176, pp. 90–91. Satura offers a useful discussion of the history of these sources and the controversies surrounding them, pp. 4–24.

24. Gregor, op. cit., p. 49, (AA VII:173).

25. See "Hume's Absence" section.

26. In *Kant: Selected Pre-Critical Writings and Correspondence with Beck*, edited by G. B. Kerford and D. E. Walford (New York: Barnes and Noble, 1968), p. 55 (AA II:392–93).

27. Ibid. (AA II:393).

28. The *Dissertation* account is somewhat confusing, because he describes "sensations" both as the effects of objects on the sensory organs *and* as the matter of sensory representations.

29. For further discussion of Kant's use of the term "intuition" see Chapter 3, "Representing Objects."

30. Kant makes this point explicitly in his anthropology lectures; see Gregor, op. cit., p. 35 (AA VII:156–57).

31. Kerford and Walford, op. cit., p. 55 (AA II:393).

32. Henry E. Allison, *The Kant–Eberhard Controversy*, op. cit., pp. 135–36 (AA VIII:221–23).

33. Kerford and Walford, op. cit., pp. 73–74 (AA II:906).

34. See Chapter 1. "Transcendental Psychology."

35. I will not discuss the third and fourth arguments of the Metaphysical Exposition where this distinction is crucial, because I do not think the transcendental psychology of spatial perception is particularly prominent in those passages. The problem of distinguishing between and relating conception and perception will be prominent in Chapter 6.

36. *Reflexion* 3958 (AA XVII:366).

37. Compare Kerford and Walford, op. cit., p. 68, but see AA II:402. I am grateful to my former colleague Jasper Hopkins for retranslating this passage for me. Hopkins pointed out that while the standard translations use a technical term like "abstracted" or "derived," Kant's Latin expression *"hauriri"* is nontechnical. (It would be used in such ordinary contexts as drawing water out of a well.)

38. See Vaihinger, op. cit., pp. 71–88. Robert Pippin's interesting discussion of forms, op. cit., does not investigate the theory of spatial perception, because he accepts the common view that Kant just assumes that sensation involves "formless material," p. 56.

39. Vaihinger, op. cit., p. 180.

40. Kemp Smith actually refers the reader to B207 (op. cit., p. 86), but he must mean B208. Here I offer what I take to be fairly standard readings of Kant's terms "intensive" and "extensive." In providing these glosses I do not try to resolve any serious questions about Kant's putative distinction between the two types of magnitude. My point is that Vaihinger and his followers have inverted the logic of Kant's reasoning at A166/B208, whatever meanings are assigned to "intensive" and "extensive."

41. See Pastore, op. cit., pp. 6–10.

42. My analysis places great weight on our inability to sense the *third* dimension. Henry Allison has objected to me that Kant does not stress the three-dimensional character of space and that many of his examples of geometrical properties (e.g., at most one straight line through two points) are drawn from planar geometry. Although this is true, I do not believe the examples undercut my interpretation. Kant refers often enough to the "space [not planes] of the geometers" and to its three-dimensional character [e.g., B41, *Prolegomena*, op. cit., pp. 28–29 (AA IV:284–85), and *Dissertation*, op. cit., p. 60]. Further, the standard mathematical view was that geometry describes space and that planar geometry abstracts from full three-dimensional space. Presumably Kant expected his readers to understand his position against this background. I am also grateful to Lorne Falkenstein, who sent me a paper critical of my original discussion of these issues in "Discovering the Forms of Intuition," op. cit. Like Allison, Falkenstein objects to the weight I place on the third dimension. I hope the present discussion clarifies my original, excessively cryptic presentation.

43. *The Works of George Berkeley Bishop of Cloyne*, vol. I, edited by A. A. Luce and T. E. Jessop (London and Edinburgh: Nelson, 1967), pp. 186–89.

44. The view that touch informs vision about extent and distance has enjoyed widespread popularity at different times. Recent work suggests that it is, however, false. In a survey of the literature, Eleanor Gibson and Elizabeth Spelke

draw the following conclusions: "There does, thus, seem to be a primitive eye–arm coordination in the newborn that is adapted to the three-dimensional layout of objects *well before grasping and manipulation occur*" (p. 7, my emphasis). "There was little active manipulation before 24 weeks. . . . Even the youngest age group differentiated the object from its picture, however . . . "(p. 8). See Gibson and Spelke, "The Development of Perception," in John H. Flavell and Ellen M. Markman, eds., *Cognitive Development* (*Handbook of Child Psychology*, vol. 3, Paul H. Mussen, general ed. (New York: Wiley, 1983), pp. 1–76).

45. Remnant and Bennett, op. cit., p. 137. In this discussion, I do not consider Kant's well-known philosophical objections to Berkeley's theory of space. From the perspective of his own system, Kant chastises Berkeley for being a transcendental realist about space and for not recognizing its *a priori* character, among other complaints. At this point in the Transcendental Aesthetic, however, Kant is in no position to argue from the truth of his own system to the shortcomings of Berkeley's. He must first find reasonably uncontroversial premises to establish his own theory. Margaret Wilson offers an informative discussion of some of Kant's philosophical objections to Berkeley in "Kant and 'The *Dogmatic* Idealism of Berkeley,' " *Journal of the History of Philosophy* (1971): 459–75.

46. Leibniz describes retinal images as "paintings (as it were) that he forms at the back of his eyes." Remnant and Bennett, op. cit., p. 138.

47. Ibid., p. 137, Leibniz's emphasis.

48. See, for example, Remnant and Bennett, op. cit., p. xiii.

49. AA. XVIII:69.

50. Satura reads Kant as claiming that the third dimension is registered by touch (op. cit., p. 90). The crucial evidence is the following passage about bodily form from the *Anthropology*:

[Touch] . . . by touching the surface of a solid body we can find out what shape it has. . . . Without this sense organ we should be unable to form any concept at all of the shape of a body. So the other two senses of this first class must be referred originally to its perceptions, if they are to provide experiential knowledge [Gregor, op. cit., pp. 33–34 (AA VII:155)].

Satura's reading of this passage is quite plausible. Further, the passage suggests that Kant might reject Leibniz's claims about paralyzed individuals learning geometry that I present him as accepting in the text. This is a difficult exegetical puzzle. Although Satura's gloss is plausible if the passage is read in isolation, it is flatly inconsistent with Kant's claims about space and form in the *Dissertation* and the *Critique*. Whatever reason one gives for Kant's denial that our perceptual information about extent and form derives from the senses, there is no question that he does deny this. Faced with contradiction, the natural assumption would be that the major works offer a more precise account of Kant's considered views.

The reading that yields contradiction is not forced on us, however. Kant does not say that touch yields sensations [*Empfindungen*] or *sensa* of space or form, although he has this precise vocabulary available; what he claims is that touch involves *perception* [*Wahrnehmung*] of form and is necessary for the concept of bodily form. It is not surprising that Kant would hold this view, since most of his predecessors, Leibniz included (see Remnant and Bennett, op. cit., pp. 77, 122–24), believed that touch was important to empirical knowledge and that it had a special role in our acquiring the idea of solidity.

51. Kant has a well-known argument that there is only one space, thc fourth metaphysical exposition in A (third in B): We can represent to ourselves only one space. However, I do not see how the considerations he raises there, that spaces are limitations of space, provide any argument that different sense could not furnish different, incommensurable spaces.

52. Luce and Jessop, op. cit., vol. I, pp. 187–88.

53. See note 35.

54. See Allison's discussion of this issue in *Kant's Transcendental Idenlism*, op. cit., pp. 82–86.

55. It is sometimes argued that Berkeley and perhaps other Empiricists held that sensations were completely aspatial. If this interpretation is accepted, then Kant would have an easier but less interesting argument against them. See Gary Hatfield and William Epstein, "The Sensory Core and the Medieval Foundations of Early Modern Perceptual Theories," *ISIS 70* (1979): 363–84.

56. AA II:402. See note 37.

57. Gottfried Wilhelm Leibniz, *Philosophical Papers and Letters*, edited by Leroy E. Loemker (Amsterdam: D. Reidel, 1976), pp. 703–704. Kant may also have been thinking of Christian Wolff's closely related view. For an account of Wolff's position and its differences from Leibniz's, see Beck, *Early German Philosophy* (Cambridge, Mass.: Harvard University Press, 1969), pp. 268–70.

58. Kant may also be noting that Leibniz's own position in the correspondence with Clarke suggests that our representation of space involves *a priori*$_o$ elements. Leibniz claims that we perceive objects in various positions relative to one another. We then abstract from the objects and think of the positions themselves, filling in the currently unoccupied places in the perception, to reach the intellectual idea of space as a system of positions for actual and possible objects. Thus, Leibniz seems committed to the view that the creative subject is responsible for elements in our representation of space. So Kant's point may also be that it is inconsistent for Leibniz to characterize [the representation of] space as a product of the creative activity of the subject and then to claim to have shown that it depends on actual objects encountered in perception.

I do not wish to downplay the difficulties in interpreting Leibniz, but I think my interpretation of the fifth letter to Clarke is fairly widely held. See John Earman, "Was Leibniz a Relationist?" in *Midwest Studies*, vol. IV, Peter French, Ted Uehling, and Howard Wettstein, eds. (Minneapolis: University of Minnesota Press, 1979); Martial Gueroult, "Space, Point, and Void in Leibniz's Philosophy," *Leibniz: Critical and Interpretive Essays*, edited by Michael Hooker (Minneapolis: University of Minnesota Press, 1982); Robert McRae, *Leibniz:*

Perception, Apperception and Thought (Toronto: University of Toronto Press, 1976); Jill Buroker, *Space and Incongruence* (Amsterdam: D. Reidel, 1981).

59. Guyer, op. cit., p. 357ff. Guyer presents a number of telling citations from the *Reflexionen* and from student lecture notes (*Metaphysik Mongrovius*, vol. 29 of AA). Let me give just one example:

That synthetic *a priori* propositions are possible only through the subjective form of sensibility, consequently that their objects can be represented only as appearances, is to be recognized from the fact that they are accompanied with necessity, but not from concepts by means of analysis... [R6355, 18:681, Guyer's translation, p. 358].

This passage shows that Kant believes the subjectivity of space to be crucial to the possibility of *a priori* knowledge [of Geometry]. It does not imply that he denies the importance of other considerations, however. Neither does it emulate Berkeley's dramatic gesture of offering to stake his case for immaterialism on the inability to imagine an unperceived tree. None of the passages Guyer cites implies that Kant rests his whole case on Geometry. The issue is difficult, because here I am only arguing from the absence of evidence. In the text I offer positive reasons for believing that other considerations stand behind the theory of space.

I discuss Guyer's views on Geometry further in Chapter 5, note 63. Hatfield, op. cit., also lays great emphasis on the importance of Geometry in Kant's theory of spatial perception.

60. "The Historical and Conceptual Relations between Kant's Metaphysics of Space and Philosophy of Geometry," *Journal of the History of Philosophy 11* (1973): 483–512. See especially pp. 485–87, 497–500.

61. See Chapter 1, "Transcendental Psychology," for the meaning of *a priori*$_L$.

62. "Kant's Theory of Geometry," *Philosophical Review 94* (1985): 455–506.

63. Kerford and Walford, op. cit., pp. 69–70, 71 (AA II:402–403, 404).

64. "Infinity and Kant's Conception of the 'Possibility of Experience,' " *Philosophical Review 73* (1964): 182–97; reprinted in *Kant*, edited by Robert Paul Wolff (Garden City, N.Y.: Anchor Books, 1967), pp. 37–52. I later criticize Parson's interpretation of these matters in the *Critique*. I should note, however, that many of Kant's remarks about Geometry and the form of outer perception in the *Dissertation* accord very well with Parsons's reading. See especially the passages cited in the previous note.

65. Besides Parsons's own critique, see James Hopkins, "Visual Geometry," *Philosophical Review 82* (1973): 3–34, especially p. 4, and Kitcher, "Kant and the Foundations of Mathematics," op. cit., pp. 31ff.

66. See above, "Kant's Empirical Assumptions."

67. See Earman, op. cit.

68. The case may be different for the *Dissertation*. See notes 63 and 64.

69. Pippin, op. cit., draws a similar conclusion, pp. 84–87.

70. Herrnstein and Boring, op. cit., pp. 125–31. The discovery of binocular vision was sometimes used to support nativism in perception, which was often taken to be Kant's position. See Hatfield's discussion, op. cit., p. 273.

71. See David Marr's discussion of this problem in *Vision* (San Francisco: W. H. Freeman, 1978), pp. 111–59.

72. Below I consider a theory that is an explicit defense of Kant's view. I think the work of Marr and his associates at MIT was strongly Kantian in spirit. Marr hypothesized that general facts about the structure of the world to be ✓ perceived are built into the perceptual system. See my "Marr's Computational Theory of Vision," *Philosophy of Science 55* (1988): 1–24.

73. (Princeton, N.J.: Princeton University Press, 1947).

74. "The Geometry of the Visibles," *Nous 8* (1974): 87–117.

75. Barbara Landau, Henry Gleitman, and Elizabeth Spelke, "Spatial Knowledge and Geometric Representation in Child Blind from Birth," *Science 213* (1981): 1275–78.

76. B. White, F. Saunders, L. Scadden, P. Bach-y-Rita, and P. Collins, "Seeing with the Skin," *Perception and Psychophysics 7* (1970): 23–27.

77. See Chapter 6, "Kant's Long Argument."

78. *The Hippocampus as a Cognitive Map* (Oxford: Oxford University Press, 1978).

79. As I understand O'Keefe and Nadel's description, a set of spatial transformation rules is a set of rules that so defines a space that any point in that space can be expressed as a function of any other point.

80. Israel Leiblich and Michael Arbib, "Multiple Representations of Space Underlying Behavior," *Behavioral and Brain Sciences 5* (1982): 627–59.

81. Thomas Kuhn, *The Structure of Scientific Revolutions*, 2nd ed. (Chicago: University of Chicago Press, 1970), Chapter 10.

Chapter 3

1. Robert Paul Wolff, op. cit., is a notable exception to this generalization.

2. See Kemp Smith's discussion of this issue in his *Commentary*, op. cit., pp. xix–xxv.

3. Bennett, *Kant's Analytic*, op. cit., p. 100.

4. Guyer, op. cit., Part II.

5. Op. cit., p. 171. Allison goes on to suggest things are not quite as bad as they seem, because Kant is able to establish a number of "analytic" claims (pp. 171–72). As I argue in Chapter 1, however, Kant does not conceive of the theses established by his transcendental method as analytic.

6. See Chapter 6, "Kant's Long Argument" and "¶ 26 as Completing the Argument of the Metaphysical Deduction."

7. The view that Kant's arguments are analytic, even if not obviously so, may be encouraged by a quick reading of the opening sentence of the A Deduction: "It is entirely contradictory and impossible that a concept should originate *a priori* and relate to an object, unless it is either contained in the concept of possible experience, or else consists in elements of a possible experience"

(A95, my translation). Those who offer analytic interpretations assume that the first option is the more relevant; but it is clear from Kant's explicit discussion in the Methodology that his transcendental method employs the second. See Chapter 1, "Transcendental Psychology."

8. See Beiser's account of the "Garve–Feder" review, which is often thought to have been a spur to Kant's recasting of the chapter for the second edition. Op. cit., pp. 172–77.

9. This reading is elaborated in Karl Ameriks, "Kant's Transcendental Deduction as a Regressive Argument," *Kant-Studien 69* (1978): 273–87.

10. See Chapter 1, "Kant Against 'Psychology.' "

11. For an account of the difference between epistemic analyses and analyses of empirical capacities, see Chapter 1, " Transcendental Psychology."

12. "Mental state" is another possibility for the generic term. As Henry Allison pointed out to me, however, this would include volitions, and pleasure and pain, which are not dealt with until the later Critiques. Although "cognitive state" is somewhat clumsy, it is true to the spirit of transcendental psychology in being a dummy name for a state that performs a role in cognition, but whose nature we do not understand.

13. Ak IX:91.

14. Although the passage in the *Logic* and other passages (see A19/B34, B208, A320/B376-77) make it clear that Kant does not believe that all *Vorstellungen* represent, in the *Critique* he says: "All representations have, as representations, their objects, and can themselves in turn become objects of other representations" (A108). I do not believe that this indicates substantive confusion, but it does require terminological clarification. Still such remarks are misleading. So, for example, Robert Howell (op. cit.) asserts that Kant believed that all representations are representational.

15. Typically, when Leibniz discusses perceptions, he is content to note that we must acknowledge their existence and their alleged properties, because the soul presents us with clear examples. See, for example, *Monadology* 14–17 in Loemker, op. cit., p. 644.

16. Remnant and Bennet, op. cit., p. 114. See also Max Dessoir, *Geschichte der Neueren Deutschen Psychologie* (Amsterdam: E. J. Bonset, 1964), *Zweite Auflage*, p. 39.

17. Tetens, op. cit., p. 8.

18. *Monadology* 16, in Loemker, op. cit., p. 644.

19. Dessoir, op. cit., p. 69; see also Blackwell, op. cit., pp. 344–47.

20. "Kant's Sensationism," *Synthèse 47* (1981): 229–55. It is possible that sensationism was also part of the background to Kant's discussion of space. As George notes, Condillac claims that the eye cannot grasp even simple shapes directly (See *Condillac's Treatise on the Sensations*, translated by Geraldine Carr (Los Angeles: University of Southern California Press 1930), p. 68. Condillac goes on to discuss the problem of how sight learns distance from touch, and the results of the Cheselden case (pp. 59–60). So his discussion takes place against the general background I present in Chapter 2. Kant might have been especially

influenced by this discussion of the issue, but I know of no reason to think so. I discuss this passage again in note 23 of Chapter 6.

21. See for example, Tetens, op. cit., p. 264.

22. Manfred Kuehn argues for the influence of Reid and other Scottish philosophers on German philosophy in *Scottish Common Sense in Germany, 1768–1800: A Contribution to the History of the Critical Philosophy*, (Montreal: McGill-Queen's University Press, 1987). I discuss Reid's views further in Chapter 6.

23. In Chapter 6, "Differences Between the Editions," I suggest that parts of the A Deduction may have been shaped by Reid's view that perception involves a concept of the object. However, I disagree with George's assessment that Kant always took perception to involve concepts. At least in the B Deduction, he avoided this substantive and controversial assumption. (See Chapter 6,) "¶ 26 in the B Deduction."

24. George, op. cit., pp. 236, 244. Although I agree with much of George's argument for the influence of Condillac, I do not understand his suggestion that Kant does not think of the mind as actually gathering up the elements in cognitive states and putting them altogether (p. 236). Presumably this is exactly what Kant means when he says that the synthesis of apprehension must run through and hold together the multiple contents of cognitive states (A99; see also A77/B103 and A120a).

25. Warda, op. cit., p. 50.

26. *Inquiry*, op. cit., p. 62. Compare *Treatise*, op. cit., pp. 98ff.

27. *Inquiry*, op. cit., p. 63.

28. Ibid. pp. 62–63.

29. Ibid., p. 67.

30. Among other sources, Kant was aware of many of the *Treatise*'s discussion through James Beattie's lengthy citations in *Essay on the Nature and Immutability of Truth, vol. IV, Beattie's Works*, (Philadelphia: Hopkins and Earle, 1809).

31. Treatise, op. cit., pp. 197–218.

32. Ibid., p. 218.

33. George, op. cit., p. 231. See also Blackwell's discussion on pp. 344–46.

34. *Reflexion 695* (AA XV:308–9). This passage was drawn to my attention by George's discussion and I amend his translation (op. cit., p. 232). See also F. E. England, *Kant's Conception of God* (with translation of the *Nova Dilucidatio*) (New York: Humanities Press, 1968), pp. 246–47.

35. For a classic discussion, see William Porterfield, *A Treatise on the Eye and the Manner and Phenomena of Vision*, vol. III (Edinburgh: G. Hamilton and J. Balfour, 1759), pp. 221, 336. Porterfield's work was cited by Reid in the *Inquiry*, which as noted earlier, was widely known in Germany. This assumption is still standard in work in perception. See David Marr's discussion of zero-crossings in *Vision*, op. cit., pp. 67–74.

36. See, for example, Remnant and Bennett, op. cit., pp. 53–58; *Treatise*, op. cit., p. 252.

37. Dessoir notes that this theory had been conclusively overthrown by the time Kant was writing (op. cit., p. 400).

38. Op. cit., p. 26 (AA IV:282).

39. J. J. Gibson, *The Senses Considered as Perceptual Systems* (Boston: Houghton Mifflin, 1966), p. 5. For Gibson's general position see also J. J. Gibson, *The Ecological Approach to Visual Perception* (Boston Houghton Mifflin, 1979).

40. For example, Marr, op. cit., pp. 29–30.

41. R. P. Wolff is also an exception to this generalization. I discuss his position in the section "Robert Paul Wolff on Rules of Synthesis." After completing this chapter, I became aware of Hansgeorg Hoppe's book-length study of synthesis, *Synthesis Bei Kant* (Berlin: Walter de Gruyter, 1983). Unlike most contemporary philosophers, Hoppe tries to deal with synthesis by considering its relation to some psychological claims, specifically Piaget's work. Both Ralph C. S. Walker and Paul Guyer have written about synthesis. However, they do not explore Kant's account of synthesis—what it really asserts and whether it is reasonable—but simply read the doctrine of *a priori* synthesis as the doctrine that the mind imposes various properties on the objects of knowledge. (See Guyer's "Kant on Apperception and *A Priori* Synthesis," *American Philosophical Quarterly 17* (1980): 205–12, and Ralph C. S. Walker, "Synthesis and Transcendental Idealism," *Kant-Studien 76* (1985): 14–27.)

Robert Howell (op. cit.) also discusses synthesis but never considers it as a psychological doctrine. Following Hintikka's analysis of intuitions as analogues of singular demonstratives, he describes synthesis as a means of cross-possible-world identification (p. 214). Henry Allison's depsychologized version of synthesis is more typical. Allison starts by suggesting that Kant's views about synthesis do not in any way rest on contemporary assumptions about what the inputs to our minds are like. I do not see how this can be so. Here and in our later discussion it is obvious that Kant's remarks only make sense if we see them as rooted in various contemporary assumptions about the data of sense. (Certainly they presuppose the falsity of the *simulacra* theory.) Allison transforms Kant's psychological doctrine into an acceptable logical form. "[Synthesis is a] logical act. . . . The consciousness of this act, that is, the consciousness of synthesis is therefore, the consciousness of the form of thinking" (op. cit., p. 144). This strategy is vulnerable to Walsh's objection to Paton: How can something merely logical be an act?

42. In the Paralogisms chapter, he maintains that arguments about the necessary capacities for knowledge are incapable of yielding such information. See Chapter 7, "Understanding the First Paralogism."

43. Although I describe the representation as "stable," I should reiterate that Kant says nothing about the *nature* of representations. So, for example, these representations need not endure for appreciable amounts of time, or be located in any one place in the mind or brain. In fact, there is nothing in Kant's doctrine that would rule out the sort of ephemeral, distributed representations recently suggested by work in Parallel Distributed Processing (or Connectionism as it is

also known). See James L. McClelland and David E. Rumelhardt, *Parallel Distributed Processing* (Cambridge, Mass.: MIT Press, 1986).

44. Kemp Smith's translation blunts this point somewhat. Kant's original German is "... Regel ..., *welche die Reproduction des Mannigfaltigen a priori nothwendig und einen Begriff, in welchem dieses sich vereinigt, möglich macht.*" Kemp Smith renders this: "a rule ... as makes the reproduction of the manifold *a priori* necessary and renders possible a concept in which it is united." That is, he takes the scope of "*macht*" to include both clauses, but leaves out the *möglich*, when rendering the clause about reproduction. Although Kant's compound modalities are very hard to render, I think this is an error.

45. By not mentioning representations explicitly, Kant seems to suggest that the mind produces the regularity in the contents of mental states that is necessary for the law of association to work. Were he to claim that the mind creates its own content, he would go against all the principles on which his theories of cognition and transcendental idealism are based.

46. Tetens observes that since the time of Locke the so-called law of association has been regarded as a fundamental law in psychology. Like Kant, he thinks that it is inadequate, because it merely involves the reproduction of past sequences and not the production of new representations (op. cit., vol. I, pp. 108ff).

47. Tetens, op. cit., p. 266.

48. I discuss this issue further in Chapter 6.

49. R. P. Wolff, op. cit., pp. 125ff.

50. Ibid., p. 131.

51. *The Groundwork of the Metaphysics of Morals*, translated by Lewis White Beck (Indianapolis: Bobbs-Merrill, 1959), p. 29.

52. This confusion was probably fostered by Christian Wolff's view that we observe all that transpires in our our minds. See Chapter 1, "Kant Against 'Psychology.' "

53. I discuss this passage further in Chapter 4, "Judgments."

54. O'Neill, op. cit.

55. Ibid., p. 158.

56. Anne Treisman, "Features and Objects in Visual Processing," *Scientific American 225* (November 1986): 114B–25.

57. See A. M. Treisman and H. Schmidt, "Illusory Conjunctions in the Perception of Objects," *Cognitive Psychology 14* (1982): 107–41; and A. M. Treisman and G. A. Gelade, "A Feature Integration Theory of Attention," *Cognitive Psychology 12* (1980): 97–136.

58. Patricia Churchland made this observation in conversation.

59. Immanuel Kant, *Metaphysical Foundations of Natural Science*, op. cit., pp. 13–14.

60. Paton suggests that A. G. Baumgarten and G. H. Meier were Kant's specific targets (Paton, op. cit., vol. I, p. 522n).

61. Tetens, op. cit., vol. 1, p. 361.

62. Locke, op. cit., vol. II, p. 362.

63. Condillac, essay, pp. 74–75.
64. Ibid, vol. 1, p. 365.
65. The topic of this passage is badly obscured by Kemp Smith's rendering of *Erkenntnisse* as "modes of knowledge" here.
66. I present a more detailed account of this argument in Chapter 6, "Kant's Long Argument."
67. See, for example, Bennett, op. cit., Chapter 6.
68. The only exception would be syntactic relations that were grounded in our ways of processing information derived from sensory encounters with objects.

Chapter 4

1. Rorty asked this question during his Kant seminar at Princeton in the fall of 1970, which I attended. While he meant it ironically, I thought it was an interesting question.
2. For example, see Roger Scruton, *Kant* (Oxford: Oxford University Press, 1982), p. 32, and T. E. Wilkerson, *Kant's Critique of Pure Reason* (Oxford: Oxford University Press, 1976), p. 49.
3. This seems to be the case for Wilkerson, loc. cit.
4. It will be clear in the discussion of the Deduction chapter here and in the discussion of the Paralogisms in Chapter 7 that Kant's objection to the *cogito* is not only that it cannot sustain claims about the soul's simplicity or immortality. Kant's critique cuts to the heart of the *cogito*. Like Hume and unlike Descartes, Kant does not believe that we can introspect a self.
5. This reading has been so popular that I will not try to list all its adherents. Strawson certainly holds it and it is presupposed by Jonathan Bennett and Paul Guyer. Both have argued that Kant is simply wrong in believing that consciousness requires self-consciousness, so the central tenet of the deduction must be abandoned. See Bennett, op. cit., p. 105, and Guyer, "Kant on Apperception," op. cit. In an earlier paper ("Kant's Real Self," in Wood, op. cit.) I tried to figure out why Kant held this view. I now believe that he does not offer any good arguments in favor of this position because he does not hold it.
6. Strawson, op. cit., p. 98.
7. Wilkerson, op. cit., p. 52.
8. Ralph C. S. Walker, *Kant* (London: Routledge and Kegan Paul, 1978), p. 80.
9. Scruton, op. cit., p. 32.
10. In the *Bounds of Sense*, op. cit., Strawson also suggests that there is an argument about intuitions and concepts—about seeming and being—that is required for self-ascription (see pp. 100–101). This point has not been as popular among subsequent interpreters, however.
11. Ibid., p. 104.
12. See Chapter 1, "In Defense of Transcendental Psychology."

13. In criticizing Strawson's reconstruction on interpretive grounds, I may be thought to be missing the point: A reconstruction is not meant to be an interpretation. The problem with this move is that, as will be clear in the text, Strawson often defends his reading as if it were meant as an interpretation and it is often taken to be an interpretation. Thus, I think it is reasonable and necessary to criticize it as an interpretation. For an opposing view, see Christopher Janaway, "History of Philosophy: The Analytic Ideal I," in *Proceedings of the Aristotelian Society Supplement LXVII* (1988): 169–89.

14. For example, he uses *gehören* at A116 and A117a, at B132 he uses *gehören, angehören*, and *gehörig*. At B134, he again uses *gehören*.

15. See Prolegomena, op. cit., pp. 36–40. See also B69–70, and the note to Bxl.

16. See his "Self-Ascription and Objectivity," *Philosophia: Philosophical Quarterly of Israel 10* (1981): 189–98.

17. See Chapter 5, "The Problem of Self-Consciousness." S. C. Patten also denies that apperception is primarily about self-ascription in "Kant's *Cogito*," in *Kant-Studien 66* (1975): 331–41. Richard Aguila registers some doubts about the importance of self-ascription in *Matter in Mind* (Bloomington: Indiana University Press, 1989).

18. Wilkerson, op. cit., p. 52.

19. Allison, *Kant's Transcendental Idealism*, op. cit., p. 144.

20. Hector-Neri Castaneda has pursued a project that is sometimes described as a formal study of the "I." I think it is more clearly described as an account of the peculiarities of indexical reference. See, for example, "He: A Study in the Logic of Self-Consciousness," *Ratio 8* (1966).

21. "Formal" is sometimes contrasted with "empirical." Since empirical apperception is understood as a doctrine in empirical psychology, this contrast is also ultimately grounded in the contrast between "formal" and "psychological."

22. Among the commentators that hold this view are Strawson, op. cit.; Bennett, *Kant's Analytic*, op. cit.; Henrich, *Identität und Objektivität: Eine Untersuchung über Kants transzendentale Deduktion* (Heidelberg: C. Winter); Wolff, op. cit.; and Guyer, op. cit. Allison, op. cit., is a rare exception.

23. I explain this dependency more fully in "Synthesis and Apperception" and "Arguing for the Synthetic Unity of Apperception."

24. *Treatise*, op. cit., Part IV, Chapter 2.

25. See Chapter 6, "How the Argument Fails."

26. As I argue in Chapter 7, "Leibniz and the Simplicity of the Soul," the Second Paralogism appears to be a critique of Leibniz's argument for the simplicity of the soul. See Margaret Wilson's "Leibniz and Materialism," *Canadian Journal of Philosophy 3* (1974): 495–513.

27. April 1776, as printed in *Beattie Works,* op. cit., *Essays*, vol. I. See Kemp Smith's prefatory comments about the importance of this discovery in his *Commentary*, op. cit., pp. xxviiiff.

28. Ibid., p. 207. See also the note, p. 207.

29. Robert Paul Wolff, "Kant's Debt to Hume via Beattie," *Journal of the*

History of Ideas 21 (1960): 117–23. I read Wolff's paper after discovering Kemp Smith's error myself. Oddly, his recognition that Kant was aware of Hume's devastating critique of Descartes' view of the self did not seen to affect his reading of the Deduction. He offers four different reconstructions of the Deduction argument (on pp. 116, 119, 132, 161) and each one begins with a premise that all my representations are bound up in a unity—a premise that begs the question against Hume.

30. I checked the sixth edition against the second, and the only difference is that "Hume" is used in the second and "our author" in the sixth. The citations that follow are from the sixth edition.

31. Kuehn, op. cit., pp. 92–93, 92–93n.

32. Tetens, op. cit., pp. 392–94. As noted earlier, Kant read Tetens' book with care (Chapter 2, note A). The citation is from p. 393. Lewis White Beck's discussion in *Early German Philosophy* drew my attention to this book (Cambridge, Mass.: Harvard University Press, 1969), p. 419. (However, his references for Tetens' discussion of Hume on p. 419n are incorrect.)

33. Beattie, op. cit. These excerpts appear on pp. 79, 249–50. The excerpted passages appear on pp. 251, 252, and 253 of L. A. Selby-Bigge's edition of the *Treatise*, op. cit.

34. See *Treatise*, op. cit., pp. 261, 633ff.

35. *Inquiry*, op. cit., p. 64.

36. *Treatise*, op. cit., p. 636.

37. Ibid., p. 634.

38. There is one sentence in the *Inquiry* that seems to contradict this interpretation. Hume appears to analyze the causal relation in terms of existential dependence:

> we may define a cause to be *an object followed by another, and where all the objects, similar to the first, are followed by objects similar to the second.* Or, in other words, *where, if the first object had not been, the second never had existed* [*Inquiry*, op. cit., p. 87].

If causal relations connect the states of one mind and involve existential dependence, then my account must be rejected. I do not think that this passage can be taken at face value, however. Either Hume did not take "in other words" to imply material equivalence, or he did not understand that the two analyses flanking this phrase are not materially equivalent, or somehow he intended the second analysis to be a notational variant of the first. Since the first two options make Hume either sloppy or obtuse, the third is preferable. I think that he intended the first statement to present the constant conjunction analysis and that he intended the disputed statement to be understood not subjunctively, but as a summation of past experience that reinforces the constant conjunction analysis: we say "cause" where we have never encountered a case where, if the first object had not been present, the second object had been present.

39. *Treatise*, op. cit., p. 635. I have changed Hume's archaic spelling.

40. Barry Stroud (*Hume* (London: Routledge and Kegan Paul, 1977),

pp. 131–40) notes that the text is ambiguous between two possible c.... Hume believes either that he cannot explain some actual tie that binds the states of one mind together, or that he cannot explain what leads us to *think* that perceptions are connected in individual selves. While the text allows either, the systematic considerations I raise in the text show that the former hypothesis is correct. Although I disagree with Stroud's ultimate position, my discussion is indebted to his. See also Don Garrett's interesting analysis in "Hume's Self-Doubts About Personal Identity," *Philosophical Review XCV* (1981): 337–58.

41. My treatment of this issue is somewhat different here than in "Kant on Self-Identity," *Philosophical Review XCI* (1982): 41–72. In the paper I assumed that Hume's explanations of mental activity themselves implied the need for existential dependence among cognitive states. Here my claim is only that his account requires the soundness of reference to individual selves.

42. *Inquiry*, op. cit., p. 44.

43. At A121, Kant claims that without a productive imagination cognitive states would only be reproduced as they came together, and this would produce only *"regellosse haufen derselben"* [lawless heaps of them]. Kemp Smith's translation of "accidental collocations" is misleadingly genteel.

44. Chapter 1, "Transcendental Psychology."

45. Allison, op. cit., p. 140. I should note, however, that his discussion of this whole passage differs somewhat from mine.

46. See the discussion of these various senses of *"a priori"* in Chapter 1, "Transcendental Psychology."

47. Robert Pippin, "Kant on the Spontaneity of Mind," *Canadian Journal of Philosophy 17* (1987): 449–76, 459. Specifically, Pippin objects that the process of synthesis could yield a further state, which I claim to be a representation of an object, even though the subject does not "take" a presented object as m, for example (p. 468). Since I read Kant as claiming that what it is for a subject to represent something in a certain way, either in perception or by concepts, to "take" it in a certain way, is to construct a representation of it through acts of synthesis, I don't see how there can be a resulting state without a "taking."

48. I return to this issue briefly in Chapter 5.

49. See Richards, op. cit., p. 237, note 10, and Blackwell, op. cit., p. 340.

50. Loemker, op. cit., pp. 637, 638, 645–46.

51. Ibid., p. 638.

52. Gregor, op. cit., p. 9 (AA VII:127).

53. Pippin, op. cit., p. 460.

54. Pippin suggests that to remember or assert it must be possible to be aware that that one is asserting or remembering. I assume that this means that one could consciously attend to the state and recognize what it is. Although this seems plausible, I do not agree with his further claims that engaging in such tasks requires one to be aware of one's entire mental history. As he notes, this is a rather controversial issue and requires more defense than he offers.

55. See the discussion in Chapter 3, "Representing Objects."

56. Gregor, op. cit., p. 16 (AA VII:135).

57. In light of this retraction, and others (e.g., B134), it is puzzling that Dieter Henrich makes A108 (which asserts that we observe acts of synthesis, and that it is only because we observe such acts that we know the identity of the self) as the foundation of his analysis of the deduction. See Henrich, op. cit., pp. 81ff.

58. Richard Aquila offers the following objection to my functionalist reading of Kant:

"functionalism appears to get things backward. This is because, for Kant, causes and effects, at least insofar as they are possible objects of knowledge, are essentially governed by systems of causal laws. So according to the functionalist approach, the very idea of conceptual content would have to presuppose the idea of a system of causal laws. . . . But in Kant's own thinking, the very *idea* that a system of laws naturally obtains seem to be derivative from the idea of a being who is capable of representing determinate sorts of objects" [*Matter in Mind: A Study of Kant's Transcendental Deduction* (Bloomington: Indiana University Press, 1989), p. 31].

My claim is not that the idea of content presupposes the idea of a system of causal laws. I take Kant to be offering a substantive claim that cognitive states cannot have content in the absence of synthetic connections. As I note in the text, these discussions of synthesis do not presuppose the strong notion of "cause" defended in the Second Analogy. Indeed Kant uses a wealth of synonyms—produce, bring forth, generate—to avoid hanging anything on the expression "cause." In "Kant's Functionalism," op. cit., Ralf Meerbote supports a functionalist reading of many of Kant's discussions.

59. See Chapter 3, "Associationism."

60. Tetens, *Philosophische Versuche*, vol. I, first two passages, p. 17, third, p. 20.

61. See Dennett, op. cit., p. 122.

62. See Chapter 3, "Representing Objects."

63. Remnant and Bennett, op. cit., p. 54.

64. Gregor, op. cit., p. 16 (AA VII:135).

65. Remnant and Bennett, op. cit., pp. 53–59.

66. This is Kant's estimation. Leibniz thought that all perceptions had some effect on all subsequent perceptions. Ibid., p. 114. Given the myriad of *petites perceptions*, however, this view seems somewhat farfetched.

67. *Kant Philosophical Correspondence 1759–1799*, edited and translated by Arnulf Zweig (Chicago: University of Chicago Press, 1967), pp. 153–54 (AA XI:52).

Chapter 5

1. This appears to be one occurrence of "*a priori*" where it indicates temporal priority. See the discussion of Kant's more standard uses in Chapter 1, "Transcendental Psychology."

2. An important exception to this trend has been Wilfrid Sellars. He dis-

cussed Kant's views in "this I or he or it (the thing) which thinks," op. cit., and in "Metaphysics and the Concept of a Person," op. cit.

3. At least this assumption was not obvious to me. See "Kant on Self-identity," op. cit., pp. 54ff and "Kant's Real Self," op. cit., pp. 117–18.

4. Here I do not mean to suggest that Hume was the thoroughgoing skeptic he is often made out to be, but only that he is a skeptic about personal identity.

5. Henry E. Allison ("Kant's Refutation of Materialism," *The Monist* 72 (1989): 190–208), Robert B. Pippin "Kant on the Spontaneity of Mind," op. cit.), and Richard Aquila (op. cit., p. 32) all object that earlier versions of my account of apperception do not do justice to the link between apperception and spontaneity. I considered Aquila's basic objection to my functionalist reading in note 58 of Chapter 4.

As Allison observes (p. 192), Kant links spontaneity and apperception quite strongly, when he claims that the cognitive state with content "I think" is an act of spontaneity, and, as such, cannot be regarded as belonging to the senses (B132). At the very beginning of the B Deduction, however, Kant explains that combination is an act of spontaneity, and so does not belong to the senses, but to the understanding (B130). In characterizing the unity of apperception as the outcome of acts of synthesis (or combination), I present it as involving spontaneity. The real disagreement is about the kind of spontaneity. I take it to be a "relative spontaneity," whereas both Allison and Pippin think it is absolute.

There is a decisive objection to interpreting apperception in terms of absolute spontaneity, however. If the doctrine of apperception, or synthesis, implied absolute spontaneity, then Kant would have a proof of transcendental freedom in the First Critique, something he manifestly does not believe that he has. Although he might have been tempted by this sort of move at various times, his position in the *Critique* is clear. The *Critique* allows for the possibility of freedom by establishing the phenomenal–noumenal distinction (Bxxvi). Pippin sees the problem and offers a reply: "Proving that reason must be assumed spontaneous in one context [the epistemic context], does not prove that in other contexts... it must be spontaneous too" (p. 473). This rebuttal is too weak, however. Absolute freedom in thinking does not entail absolute freedom in acting, but it would be a giant step in the right direction. If the universal sway of determinism is once breached, then the plausibility of other exceptions would increase dramatically, as Kant would fully appreciate.

6. See *Content and Consciousness* (London: Routledge and Kegan Paul, 1969), pp. 93–96.

7. See Chapter 7, "Understanding the First Paralogism."

8. See Chapter 5 of Perry's dissertation, *Identity* (Ann Arbor, Mich.: University Microfilms) and the Introduction to his anthology, *Personal Identity* (Los Angeles: University of California Press, 1975), pp. 7–12.

9. In a well-known article, Williams argued that this would occur if two people had good claims to remember all the events of Guy Fawkes life. See Williams, "Personal Identity and Individuation," *Proceedings of the Aristotelian Society LVII* (1956–57).

10. See *Essay*, op. cit., p. 454.

11. As noted in Chapter 2, Kant probably read this work in 1769. For two interesting discussions of many issues in this debate that I do not touch on, see Edwin Curley, "Leibniz and Locke on Personal Identity," in Michael Hooker, ed., *Leibniz: Critical and Interpretive Essays* (Minneapolis: University of Minnesota Press, 1982), pp. 302–26), and Nicholas Jolley, *Leibniz and Locke: A Study of the "New Essays on Human Understanding"* (Oxford: Clarendon Press 1984), Chapter 7.

12. Remnant and Bennett, op. cit., p. 114.

13. See Chapter 3, "The Law of Association."

14. As Kant introduces the relation of synthesis, it covers any case where elements of earlier states are comprehended in a later state. Thus, memory would also be an example of a synthetic connection between states, since the contents of the later depend of those of the earlier state. So would the law of association. By contrast *transcendental* syntheses are those syntheses governed by *nonassociative* rules that are necessary for knowledge. Is the unity of apperception produced by syntheses or only by transcendental syntheses? This distinction collapses for Kant, because he makes the substantive assumption that the categories are the only possible rules for combining elements of cognitive states. Since I not think that his arguments warrant this assumption, I believe that the sound part of the doctrine of apperception is that apperception is produced by the synthetic connections yielded by syntheses necessary for knowledge. I am grateful to Henry Allison for drawing my attention to this possible source of confusion.

15. "Discourse on Metaphysics," para. 34. Loemker, op. cit., p. 325.

16. This is clear in the following citations from the *Essay*: "...person... stands for a thinking, intelligent being, that has reason and reflection, and can consider itself as itself, the same thinking thing, in different times and places; which it does only by that consciousness which is inseparable from thinking..." "... for since consciousness always accompanies thinking, and it is that which makes everyone to be what he calls self, and thereby distinguishes himself from all other thinking things, in this alone consists personal identity, i.e., the sameness of a rational being: and as far as this consciousness can be extended backwards to an past action or thought, so far reaches the identity of the person...," op. cit., pp. 448–49.

17. See "Discourse on Metaphysics," para. 34, in Loemker, op. cit., p. 325; Jolley, op. cit., pp. 134–35; and Robert McRae, *Leibniz: Perception, Apperception, and Thought* (Toronto: University of Toronto Press, 1976), pp. 44–45.

18. See Margaret Wilson, "Leibniz, Self-Consciousness, and Immortality: In the Paris Notes and After," *Archiv für Geschichte der Philosophie*, Sonderheft 58 (1976): 335–52.

19. See Remnant and Bennett, op. cit., pp. 236–37 and 114 and the discussions of Jolley and McRae cited in note 17.

20. Tetens, op. cit., for example, pp. 194–98.

21. For example, at A104 and B134.

Notes

22. I discuss this trend at greater length in "Kant's Patchy Epistemology," op. cit.

23. Kant makes some remarks about children becoming self-conscious in the *Anthropology* (op. cit., pp. 9–10; AA VII:127–28), but nothing of philosophical interest. In the second edition of the Paralogisms chapter, he notes that during life others can use the body to ascribe experiences to a continuing person (B415).

24. In his introduction to John Perry, ed., *Personal Identity* (Los Angeles: University of California Press, 1975), see pp. 11–12.

25. Although he has been a major figure in this debate, I do not discuss the views of Bernard Williams in the text. One reason is that his most important contribution—the argument that mental continuity criteria must be rejected because they conflict with the law of the transitivity of identity—has been refuted, as noted in "The Issue" section. Williams has offered other arguments, but these turn on what people would say or feel about various situations. As I suggest in the text, this does not seem to me a very fruitful approach. I have offered specific criticisms of Williams's more recent views in "Being Selfish About Your Future," *Philosophical Studies 32* (1977): 425–31.

26. See H. P. Grice, "Personal Identity," reprinted in John Perry, ed., op. cit., pp. 73–95; Anthony Quinton, "The Soul," also reprinted in Perry; Terence Penelhum, "Personal Identity, Memory, and Survival," *Journal of Philosophy* (1959); Sydney Shoemaker, *Self-Knowledge and Self-Identity*, (Ithaca: Cornell University Press, 1963) and "Persons and Their Pasts," *American Philosophical Quarterly* (October, 1970); John Perry, "Can the Self Divide?" *Journal of Philosophy* (September, 1972): 463–88; and David Lewis, "Survival and Identity," in Amelie Rorty, ed., *The Identities of Persons* (Los Angeles: University of California Press, 1969), pp. 17–40.

27. Shoemaker, op. cit., pp. 22–35.

28. As noted in Chapter 4, synthetic connection is a stronger relation than causation, if causation is not held to entail existential dependence. I do not think this difference is significant, since few people would maintain a Humean analysis of causation.

29. For example, David Lewis, op. cit. See also the discussion of Parfit in "Parfit's Denial of Personal Identity."

30. One reason to think that there is very little similarity of belief is that small children appear to use quite different concepts from adults. See Susan Carey, *Conceptual Change in Childhood* (Cambridge, Mass.: MIT Press 1985).

31. Perry, *Personal Identity*, op. cit., p. 7.

32. Curley notes that Locke was not concerned with the proper usage of the expression "same person" either, despite the tendency to read his discussion in the light of contemporary linguistic philosophy. Curley, op. cit., pp. 310–314.

33. I defend this point at greater length in "Natural Kinds and Unnatural Persons," *Philosophy 54* (1979): 541–47. David Wiggins expresses a view very like the one I defend in the text, although he casts it in terms of the "concept" 'person'. See "Locke, Butler, and the Stream of Consciousness: And Men as a Natural Kind," in Rorty, ed., op. cit., pp. 139–73.

34. Both Perry and Wiggins make this point. See Perry, "The Importance of Being Identical," in Rorty, ed., op. cit., pp. 67–90, and Wiggins, op. cit.

35. See *Sameness and Substance* (Cambridge, Mass.: Harvard University Press, 1980), pp. 163ff.

36. In "Locke, Butler, and the Stream of Consciousness: And Men as a Natural Kind," op. cit., p. 158.

37. "Personal Identity," *Philosophical Review 80* (January 1971): 3–27; "Later Selves and Moral Principles," in A. Montefiore, ed., *Philosophy and Personal Relations* (London: Routledge and Kegan Paul, 1973); and *Reasons and Persons* (Oxford: Clarendon Press, 1984).

38. See *Reasons and Persons*, op. cit., p. 206.

39. Ibid., Chapter 15.

40. See Curley's useful discussion of this matter, op. cit., pp. 318–19.

41. I should note that this criterion does not tell us whether what we think of as continuing minds, namely, continuing human beings, actually are continuing minds. It simply states the facts that are relevant.

42. Parfit suggests briefly that a position like Kant's might undermine his critique of absolutism. However, he reads Kant through Strawson's eyes, and so believes that the issue concerns the necessity of self-ascription of mental states for knowledge. He says that he is unsure how to respond to this type of abstract argument. Ibid., p. 225. Since I do not think this position is Kant's, I do not consider it in the text.

43. Christine Korsgaard argues that Parfit's claim that identity does not matter can be undermined by looking at Kant's theory of agency. See "Personal Identity and the Unity of Agency: A Kantian Response to Parfit," *Philosophy and Public Affairs* (in press).

44. See A363–64n and B415–18n and Chapter 7.

45. See Chapter 4, "Intuitions."

46. This does not violate the condition noted in "Refining the Account of Synthetic Connection," that synthetic progenitors cannot contribute to the contents of a product state through an additional outer sensation.

47. See " Leibniz Versus Locke" section.

48. In the note to the Third Paralogism where he raises the possibility of a series of substances, Kant describes the situation in terms of one substance communicating its motion to later ones (A363–64a). So he may think of a "trace" as some sort of permanent motion induced in a material or immaterial medium by cognitive states.

49. For a discussion of this view, see Alan Baddeley, *Working Memory* (Oxford: Clarendon Press, 1986), pp. 19–29.

50. See Jerry A. Fodor, *The Modularity of Mind* (Cambridge, Mass.: MIT Press, 1983); David Marr, op. cit.; Zenon Pylyshyn, "Cognition and Computation: Issues in the Foundations of Cognitive Science," *Behavioral and Brain Sciences 3* (1978): 111–32; and Michael Posner, *Chronometric Explorations of Mind* (Hillsdale, N.J.: Erlbaum, 1978).

51. See Pylyshyn, op. cit.

52. Fodor, op. cit., Part 4.

53. See Chapter 1, "In Defense of Transcendental Psychology."

54. Although this is sometimes put in terms of a two-self theory, Kant's view is better understood as claiming two perspectives on the self. This point is made forcefully by, among others, Erich Adickes in *Kants Lehre von der Doppelten Affektion unseres Ich as Schlüssel zu seiner Erkenntnistheorie* (Tübingen, 1929), p. 3, and Karl Ameriks, op. cit., p. 266.

55. Sellars suggests something very like this at the end of his Presidential Address (". . . the I, He, or It . . . ," op. cit.).

56. See Strawson, op. cit., pp. 235–39, 247–49.

57. Ibid, p. 249. Strawson casts this point in terms of noumenal objects appearing to the noumenal self. Do they appear in time or out of time? Since the I of apperception must be phenomenal, I recast his point in terms of the synthetic processes themselves.

58. Strawson, op. cit., p. 249.

59. The obvious way to avoid the inconsistency is to claim that the doctrine that time is phenomenally real and transcendentally ideal does not amount to a denial that time is real. I believe that the inconsistency is hopeless, because I do not see how this strategy can produce a doctrine that is both coherent and Kantian.

60. See Strawson, op. cit., pp. 15, 20–22, 32, 38–42, 247–50.

61. The principal evidence for this claim is Kant's paper on "Regions of Space." He notes first that the endeavors of philosophers to settle the question of whether space can exist independently of all matter have been "futile." He then observes that the one attempt to settle this issue by an *a posteriori* proof (Leonhard Euler's *Refléxions sur l'espace et le temps*) also ended in failure. Kant goes on to present his own *a posteriori* proof, the argument from incongruent counterparts. He is not very sanguine about his own results, however, and notes that there are many difficulties with this concept, if we really try to understand it. See Handyside, op. cit., pp. 20–21, 29.

62. This point was recognized in Trendelenberg's famous objection about the neglected alternative. Since space and time might be *both* forms of intuition and independently real, it is not sufficient to argue from the fact that they are forms to the fact that they are not real. See Kemp Smith's discussion in his *Commentary*, op. cit., pp. 113–14.

63. In his recent book (op. cit., pp. 354ff), Paul Guyer argues that this conclusion does follow. He regards the argument for space and time as forms of intuition as ruling out the possibility that they are real. According to Guyer, this is Kant's reasoning. We have *a priori* knowledge of space (i.e., geometry). This is possible because space is the form of intuition. *But if something can be known *a priori*, then it cannot be a real determination of things. Therefore, space and time are not real. The crucial claim is the one I have starred. As Guyer recognizes, his argument goes through only if what we know *a priori* has a certain logical form. Specifically, if what we know is not:

(A) □ If we are to perceive an object, then it *is* spatial and Euclidean.

but:

(B) If we perceive an object, then □ it is spatial and Euclidean.

What (A) means is that in any possible world in which we perceive something, that thing is spatial; conversely, (B) means that if we perceive something (in the actual world), then in all possible worlds that thing is spatial. In the standard terminology, (B) asserts a *de re* modality. Although I disagree with other assumptions of Guyer's analysis (see later), the simplest way to put my objection is that *de re* modalities do not fit naturally into Kant's philosophy. For Kant, something is necessary (and universal) if it is true of all those worlds of which we can have experience, constituted as we are. Unlike Leibniz, Kant does not operate with an absolute notion of necessity. (See Philip Kitcher, "Kant on the Foundations of Mathematics," op. cit.) So for Kant, Guyer's second interpretation (B) should really be: If we perceive an object, then, in all those worlds in which we can have experience, it is spatial and Euclidean. This is not quite the same as (A), since there might be objects in the actual world which we do not happen to perceive in other possible worlds, even though we can experience objects in those world constituted as we are. Still this difference does not seem significant, since we could experience the object.

Guyer's analysis also presupposes that geometry is the central concern of the Aesthetic. This difference is far-reaching. While I recognize that Kant was concerned with the epistemic status of geometry, I take the driving force behind the ideality doctrine to be the scientific and metaphysical grounds I note in the text. See Chapter 2, "What the Transcendental Aesthetic Is About" and "The Transcendental Exposition" for further discussion. Despite this fundamental disagreement, I do agree with Guyer on one important point—Kant did not simply neglect the possibility that space and time might be both real and something else; he was antecedently convinced that they could not be real.

64. Strawson raises a crisply formulated attack on transcendental idealism and transcendental psychology. However, there is also a common, but vaguer worry about coherence that might be provoked by my suggestion that the doctrine of apperception be regarded as phenomenal. According to transcendental idealism, the world appears to us as it does partly because of the ways in which our senses and higher faculties are constituted. Apperception concerns our higher faculties. So, if it is a phenomenal doctrine, then it provides an account of how our faculties influence the way we think that is itself influenced by the way we think. (In another context, the objection continues by noting that it cannot be a noumenal doctrine.) Although this seems circular, it is intrinsically no more problematic than writing an English grammar in grammatical English.

Chapter 6

1. See Chapter 3, "Representing Objects" and "Making Judgment About Objects."

2. I discuss how this type of argument is supposed to establish a special role for the categories further in "Universal Applicability and Objective Validity."

3. See Chapter 3, "Representations and Concepts."

4. Kant vacillates somewhat in the passage. Perhaps without the categories we could have intuitions without thought [*gedankenlose Anschauung*], but in this circumstance we would lose all reference to objects. Since intuitions are supposed to have reference to objects (see Chapter 3, "The Problem"), he seems to be groping in the passage.

5. See Chapter 3, "The Synthesis of Intuitions."

6. Interestingly, Paton thought that it was a reasonable interpretation of the text to see Kant as concerned with what it is for different states to be states of one self. He rejected this reading only because he believed that taking self-identity to consist in the interrelation of cognitive states destroys knowledge, because it does not permit the unity of the subject. Op. cit., vol. I, p. 406.

7. As Kant notes, even though General Logic is general, it does not create the contents of any cognitive states but only relates contents that have already been created (A56/B80).

8. Despite the parenthetical aside, Kant clearly does not equate objective validity with truth. As he says, there is no criterion of truth, and only a fool looks for one (A58–59/B82–84). His point is that we cannot have true cognitions, without having cognitions. Certain conditions are required for cognition, however, and those conditions are objectively valid.

9. William Porterfield, op. cit., vol. III, p. 329.

10. (Leipzig, 1787–1796), 6 vols, cited in Hatfield, op. cit. See Hatfield for a fuller discussion of the standard view.

11. Gregor, op. cit., p. 35 (AA VII:156–57).

12. Thomas Reid, *An Inquiry into the Human Mind,* edited by Timothy Duggan (Chicago: The University of Chicago Press, 1970), for example, p. 236.

13. Kuehn cites Eberhard's views, op. cit., p. 106. Among psychologists, versions of this position have been held by Helmholtz, Jerome Bruner, and Richard Gregory. Among recent philosophers, D. M. Armstrong and George Pitcher have both proposed belief theories of perception.

14. *Essay*, op. cit., p. 191.

15. Etienne Bonnot de Condillac, *An Essay on the Origin of Human Knowledge* (1758), a facsimile reproduction of the translation of Thomas Nugent, with a introduction by Robert G. Weyant (Gainesville, Fl.: Scholars' Facsimiles & Reprints, 1971), p. 27. (I have updated the spelling.)

16. See Chapter 3, "Representations and Concepts."

17. Paul Guyer makes A99 central to his interpretation of the argument of the deduction. See Guyer, op. cit., pp. 89, 109, 121–22, 148, 151, 157, 171, 178, 207, 211, 255, 256, 289, 299, 301, 302, 347, 456. However, he never considers that this passage is intended as preparation for the discussion at A119–20.

18. See Reid, op. cit., pp. 46–47; Condillac, op. cit., p. 67; Tetens, op. cit., for example, pp. 263ff.

19. Gregor, op. cit., p. 19 (AA VII:138).

20. These notes were from metaphysics lectures given some time between 1773 and 1785, but probably closer to the latter end of the period. They were

er the title, *Immanuel Kants Vorlesungen über die Metaphysik*, ölitz in 1821. For a discussion of the history of these notes and , see Satura, op. cit., pp. 7–20.

_ _. ~ited in Satura, op. cit., pp. 114–15, my translation.

22. Satura cites a letter in which Kant worries that even capable students select what to write down and what to omit and so do not present a very accurate picture. Op. cit., p. 5.

23. Kant's position here is very close to Condillac's. In explaining how we are able to attain the idea of an extended thing, Condillac writes:

[The eye] cannot grasp the whole of the simplest shape until it has analyzed it, that is to say until it has noticed successively all its parts. It must make a judgment on each individual part, and another judgment on the whole of them together. It must say: here is one side, bounded by three sides, and from it results this triangle.

Condillac, op. cit., p. 68. Kant may also have derived some support for this view from his reading of Burke. In *A Philosophical Enquiry into the Origin of Our Ideas of the Sublime and the Beautiful* (Oxford: Basil Blackwell, reprinted 1967), Edmund Burke raises the possibility that:

there is but one point of any object painted on the eye in such a manner as to be perceived at once; but by moving the eye, we gather up with great celerity, the several parts of the object, so as to form one uniform piece (p. 137).

Rolf George's article (op. cit.) led me to these interesting discussions in Condillac and Burke.

24. For a recent summary of musical perception, see Diana Deutsch, "Auditory Pattern Recognition," in K. R. Boff, L. Kaufman, and J. P Thomas, eds., *Handbook of Perception and Human Performance*, vol. II (New York: Wiley, 1986), Chapter 32. Jay Rosenberg discusses this issue in *The Thinking Self* (Philadelphia: Temple University Press, 1986), pp. 226, 236.

25. See Chapter 3, "Representations and Concepts."

26. In *Kant's Analytic*, op. cit., Jonathan Bennett dismisses the idea of providing an account of concept application as a fool's errand. This view was probably inspired by the antipsychological direction set in philosophy of mind by Ryle and the later Wittgenstein, and I doubt that Bennett still holds it. There can be silly accounts of concept application that lead to infinite regress, but there is nothing wrong with the project and nothing wrong with Kant's view. A regress threatens only if the proposal is that we consciously apply concepts by consciously applying others. On Kant's view, however, these syntheses are carried out unconsciously, by the imagination, a "blind but indispensable function of the soul." For further discussion see Chapter 8. In the text I am deliberately noncommittal about how we represent concepts—by list of features, prototypes, or whatever.

27. In ¶ 24, Kant describes the *figurative* synthesis of the imagination. This

synthesis applies to sensory representations but is directed by the categories of the understanding. This discussion seems to anticipate the results of ¶ 26, which will be described later. Roughly, it anticipates Kant's argument that the functions which enable us to perceive spaces and times are identical with the syntheses associated with the categories. The idea that figurative syntheses are directed by the categories suggests that the imagination is subordinate to the understanding. On the other hand, a coordination model seems to be presupposed in a discussion of following the thread of conversation in the *Anthropology*, op. cit., p. 52 (AA VII:177):

> Whether in silent thought or in conversation, there must always be a theme on which the manifold is strung, so that understanding too must be operative in it. In such a case the play of imagination still follows the laws of sensibility, which provides the material, and this is associated without consciousness of the rule but still in keeping with it. So the association is carried out *in conformity* with understanding, though it is not derived *from the understanding*.

28. "The Proof-Structure of Kant's Transcendental Deduction," *Review of Metaphysics 22* (1969): 640–59.

29. Gregor, op. cit., p. 16 (AA VII:135).

30. In his most formal account of the relations among the faculties, Kant claims that "perception" is the genus for "intuition" and "concept" (A320/B376–77). Yet elsewhere he describes "perceptions" as "representations accompanied by sensation" (B147), which would mean that concepts were accompanied by sensation. Although the terminology is somewhat fluid, I think he intends "intuition" to cover both perceptions and intuitions that we do not notice but have theoretical reasons for assuming.

31. "Apprehension" was changed to "apperception" in the 4th edition.

32. Although this is a minimal sense of "perceive," it is somewhat more restrictive than Kant's claim that the categories apply to "anything that can be presented to our senses" (B160). Still, I take the opening claim to provide only a rough idea of what Kant has in mind. He must intend the argument to be about objects we perceive; otherwise there would be no point in considering the synthesis of apprehension required for perception.

33. Is the mention of geometrical proof meant to establish that we have intuitions of spaces and times, or merely to illustrate the fact? Some, Allison, for example (op. cit., pp. 97–98), have taken the focus of this section to be a special intuition involved in mathematical proof. That interpretation is inconsistent with two points in Kant's discussion, however. He illustrates the abstract point of the section with examples of perceiving a house and the freezing of water. In conclusion, he refers to "everything that is represented as determined in space and time" (B161). Both these points indicate that Kant's topic is not the perception of pure intuitions, but of particular spaces and times. Further, this reading appears to be inconsistent with the passage at B137 just cited.

34. I am grateful to Henry Allison for pointing out that even though it is not

a Critical doctrine, the distinction between judgments of experience and judgments of perception provides some confirmation of my account of what is going on in B ¶ 26.

35. Op. cit., p. 41. I change the singular "perception" to "perceptions," since Kant uses the plural (AA IV:298).

36. See Chapter 1, "Transcendental Psychology," where I consider the differences between Kant's position and simple nativism.

37. In *Kant's Analytic*, Bennett suggests that the way to understand Kant's claim that the categories apply to all experience is that at least one category applies to every experience (or cognition). Op. cit., pp. 76–83.

38. See Chapter 3, "The 'One-Step' Deduction."

39. See the passage to which note 7 is appended.

40. See the discussion of indirect synthetic connection in Chapter 5, "Is It Too Strong?"

41. I am grateful to Philip Kitcher for several helpful discussions about this issue.

42. Even David Marr, who offers a "bottom-up" account of perception has concepts involved in the final stages of perception. See, *Vision*, op. cit., Chapter 5.

43. See "The Centrality of ¶ 26."

44. Henrich, op. cit., p. 646.

45. Ibid., p. 652.

46. See Allison, *Kant's Transcendental Idealism* op. cit., pp. 160–72.

47. Ibid; see especially the discussions on pp. 162, 166.

48. Ibid., pp. 170–71.

49. Ibid., p. 167–70.

50. Walsh, op. cit., p. 70.

51. Guyer, *Kant and Knowledge*, op. cit., pp. 208, 215.

52. DeVleeschauwer, op. cit., p. 82.

53. Guyer, op. cit., pp. 237–49.

54. I should note that this argument shows only that it is necessary to use a concept of causation that includes necessity. In the Second Analogy, Kant does not consider either the degree of universality involved in causal laws or the sources from which they derive whatever degree of nomic necessity they possess. These issues are not taken up until the Dialectic and the *Critique of Judgment*.

55. Guyer, op. cit., p. 258. Allison tries to avoid this difficulty by suggesting that it is not particular causal rules, but the schema of causality itself that enables us to determine temporal position (*Kant's Transcendental Idealism*, op. cit., pp. 229–32). The problem with this suggestion is that ordering states of affairs in time must be a matter of ordering *particular* states of affairs. How could the schema of causality help in this project? Seemingly, we can only order particular states of affairs by appealing to particular causal laws. The laws need not be ultimate, in the sense that they correctly and exhaustively capture the causal structure of the world. They could be quite crude.

56. Loc. cit.

57. It is not clear that the argument Guyer reconstructs from the Refutation is sound. He assumes that there are no laws governing cognitive states (op. cit., p. 307) However, Kant may not have been committed to this view (see Chapter 1, "Kant Against 'Psychology'"). Further, even if Kant believed it, it is almost certainly false. In Chapter 4, "Strawson and the 'Self-Ascription' Reading," I offered further reasons for denying the Refutation of Idealism a central role in interpreting the deduction of the categories.

58. Although Locke, Hume, and Reid discuss the perception of time, they never see this problem. See Locke, op. cit., vol. I, pp. 238–46; Hume, *Treatise*, op. cit., pp. 34–35; and *Thomas Reid's Essays on the Intellectual Powers of Man*, edited and abridged by A. D. Woozley, (London: Macmillan, 1941), pp. 206–12.

59. William Harper discusses motor detectors in a recent paper on the Second Analogy. However, he sees them as offering evidence in favor of Kant's position. I disagree, because, like Guyer, I believe that the basic thrust of Kant's argument is that information about our states themselves cannot determine order. That is, the subjective order of our states tells us nothing about the order of states of affairs. I do not see how this can be squared with motor detectors. They detect motion precisely by picking up on the sequence of our inner states. See "Kant's Empirical Realism and the Difference Between Subjective and Objective Succession," in William Harper and Ralf Meerbote, eds., *Kant on Causality, Freedom, and Objectivity* (Minneapolis: University of Minnesota Press, 1984), pp. 108–37.

60. J. A. Fodor, T. G. Bever, and M. F. Garrett, *The Psychology of Language* (New York: McGraw-Hill, 1974), pp. 249–54.

61. Arthur Melnick, *Kant's Analogies of Experience* (Chicago: University of Chicago Press, 1973), p. 84.

62. Probably the best-known early discussion of this phenomenon is William James. See, for example, *Psychology: The Briefer Course* (New York: Harper Torchbooks, 1961), pp. 147–48 (originally published in 1892).

Chapter 7

1. Richards, op. cit., p. 229.

2. Margaret Wilson argues that Leibniz as well as Descartes is a target of Kant's criticisms in "Leibniz and Materialism," op. cit.

3. See Richards, op. cit., and Blackwell, op. cit., for more detailed discussion.

4. Sellars discusses this chapter in two papers, "Metaphysics and the Concept of a Person," op. cit., and "... this I or he or it (the thing) which thinks," op. cit. I am happy to acknowledge my indebtedness to these papers, particularly for the suggestion that the Paralogisms chapter extends the discussion of the self in the Transcendental Deduction. Although Sellars makes this suggestion, he does not try to develop it, so his own account of the Paralogisms chapter is

not really illuminated by his understanding of the connection between these two texts. I discuss several aspects of his accounts in notes 10 and 20.

5. Jonathan Bennett devotes a paper, "The Simplicity of the Soul," *Journal of Philosophy LXIV* (Oct. 26, 1967): 648–60, and three chapters of *Kant's Dialectic* (Cambridge, 1974) to the Paralogisms, but I do not think that he is able to unravel this part of the *Critique* with his usual dexterity. I raise several objections to Bennett's analysis in notes 11 and 29. I also discuss Jay Rosenberg's analysis in note 10 and touch on Strawson's brief account of the Paralogisms in *The Bounds of Sense* (Methuen, 1966) in note 28. Karl Ameriks has offered a book-length study of the Paralogisms, *Kant's Theory of Mind: An Analysis of the Paralogisms of Pure Reason* (Oxford: Clarendon Press, 1982). This offers some interesting discussions but is very much rooted in the antipsychological tradition I oppose. I discuss one part of Ameriks' analysis in note 42.

6. I could simply follow Kemp Smith in translating "*Vorstellung*" as "representation" here. Although this would be somewhat less cumbersome, I think it is helpful to stress the ambiguity of *Vorstellung* in Kant's philosophy, even though in this context it is quite clear that he means to indicate the contents of a cognitive state. In the B edition, he characterizes the thinking self as that which is "thought" as the subject (B410–11).

7. See Chapter 1, "Transcendental Psychology."

8. See Loemker, op. cit., p. 307.

9. Kemp Smith places the "I's" in quotation marks, even though this is not indicated in the German. I remove the quotation marks here and throughout, because they amount to an interpretive addition, by implying that Kant intends to talk about the representation or symbol "I" rather than about I's.

10. In his Presidential Address " . . . this I or he or it (the thing) which thinks . . . ," op. cit., Wilfrid Sellars argues that the central and common mistake of all the Paralogisms is the attempt to infer properties of I's from properties of the representation "I." This interpretation is also suggested by Kemp Smith, op. cit., pp. 457–58. Jay Rosenberg offers a recent version of the Sellarsian interpretation in " 'I Think': Some Reflections on Kant's Paralogisms," op. cit. As will be clear below, I think that *part* of Kant's diagnosis of the errors of the Paralogisms involves illicit inferences from properties of representations to properties of things. But I am not convinced that this is the key to the Paralogisms for two reasons. First, in Rosenberg's version, for example, he thinks that Kant is scouting the following modal fallacy:

X is $\Box$ represented as phi.
Whatever is phi is $\Box$ psi.
X is $\Box$ psi.

The problem with this analysis is that it is not clear that Kant would accept the first claim. Although there may be necessary properties of certain kinds of representations, I do not think he believes that any real thing is *necessarily* represented in a particular way. I base this on his interesting discussion of the impossibility of proving the law of contradiction in the *Nova Dilucidatio*. There he claims that we cannot prove the law through symbols, because we presuppose it in deciding to use symbols. (See F. E. England, *Kant's Conception of God* (New York: Humanities Press, 1968), p. 217.) I take the general moral to be that our decision to employ a certain representation must be based on considerations of its suitability to an object. Thus, whether a certain representation should be used of an object depends on contingent facts about the properties of the object. The second objection is related to the first. If this interpretation is to work, it still needs to provide an account of why Kant believes that the representation "I" will have certain properties, and, even more fundamentally, why he believes that we need to use this representation at all. My own analysis concentrates on answering this two questions.

11. *Kant's Dialectic*, op. cit., p. 75. Bennett thinks that the interesting part of the minor premise comes in the final clause, "this representation of myself cannot be employed as predicate of any other thing." By Bennett's lights, this clause means that the term "I" is "irreducibly substantival;" further, Kant endorses this part of the "Rationalist" position because he has grasped the genuine insights of the "Cartesian basis." Both these interpretive notions, the "irreducibly substantival" and the "Cartesian basis," are elusive, but I think Bennett has something like the following in mind. The "Cartesian basis" is the position of methodological solipsism, that is, the view that when contemplating the body of knowledge we have, we (or I) must recognize that all the knowledge we (or I) have is founded upon knowledge or our own mental states. According to Bennett, Kant grasped the essential correctness of the Cartesian basis and thus asserted that "I" is "irreducibly substantival," meaning that any complete and accurate description of the world must include a referential use of this term. Kant's point against the Rational Psychologists is that they construe the fact that I and my mental states play a special epistemological role, so that I am something like an epistemological substratum, to mean that I am a special sort of substance. I resist Bennett's interpretation of the First Paralogism, because I do not think that Kant accepts the Cartesian basis.

12. Bennett notes this point in *Kant's Dialectic*, op. cit., p. 74, but dismisses it as unimportant.

13. There is one piece of the minor premise that I have not tackled. Why does Kant describe the I as the "absolute" subject of judgments? One possibility is that "absolute" is simply a synonym for "necessary." A more likely explanation is that this usage is an another attempt to connect the Paralogism to the general discussion of the "transcendental ideas," where he talks about the "absolute (unconditional) unity of the thinking subject" (A334/B391). Laying stress on this piece of the Paralogism suggests that it is a criticism of the Monadology. Leibniz was certainly a main target in Kant's opening description of the errors to be exposed in the Dialectic. In the text of the First Paralogism, however, there is no elaboration of this type of metaphysical error.

14. Loemker, op. cit., p. 646.

15. E. S. Haldane and G. R. T. Ross, translators, *The Philosophical Works of Descartes*, vol. I, (Cambridge: Cambridge University Press, 1972), p. 196.

16. See Blackwell, op. cit., p. 340.

17. "*etwas von ihm zu kennen, oder zu wissen.*" Kemp Smith renders this phrase "without knowing anything of it either by direct acquaintance or otherwise," p. 337. I do not find this translation very satisfactory because "direct acquaintance" is a twentieth-century term of art and because nothing in the translation captures the force of "wissen."

18. This position may seem inconsistent with the premise of contemporary cognitive science that psychology, neurophysiology, and so forth, can mutually inform each other. Kant's point is that an abstract analysis of the faculties required for a particular cognitive task cannot *by itself* determine the constitution of the faculty that performs the task. Contemporary cognitive scientists would agree. Psychology can still inform neurophysiology (and vice vera), however, because given a functional decomposition of a task *and* further information about what kinds of mechanisms could perform the tasks, and what kinds of mechanisms are available in the brain, we can move from abstract functional description to claims about particular mechanisms.

19. See A230–41/B300 and the *Logic*, op. cit., pp. 144–46 (AA IX:143–145). As I note in Chapter 8, Kant did not believe that any but arbitrary concepts could be defined.

20. Ibid., p. 144.

21. In " . . . this I or he or it (the thing) which thinks . . . ," Sellars characterizes one of the great insights of the chapter as Kant's recognition that thinking is a "functional concept." Unfortunately, he does not address the question of how Kant came to this view and I think his suggestion that Kant simply recognized that mental terms like "thought" are functional is implausible. See para. 21. My contention is that Kant's own attempts to characterize the necessary properties of a thinking self led him to this recognition.

22. B422–23a. See Blackwell's discussion of Wolff's version, op. cit., p. 341.

23. I discuss the problems this passage raises for Transcendental Idealism in Chapter 5, "Too Many Selves."

24. Zeno Vendler, *The Matter of Minds* (Oxford: Clarendon Press, 1984), pp. 110–11.

25. Thomas Nagel, *The View from Nowhere* (New York: Oxford University Press, 1986), p. 33.

26. Ibid., p. 40.

27. See Locke, op. cit., p. 448; Remnant and Bennett, op. cit., pp. 236ff; and Loemker, op. cit., p. 325, "Discourse on Metaphysics," para. 34.

28. In the absence of this interpretive handle, even gifted readers of Kant have had difficulty making any sense of this section of the *Critique*. So, for example, in a his brief account of the Paralogisms, Strawson credits Kant with the insight that we need *physical* criteria for reidentifying persons. While he regards this as the overall message of the chapter, presumably it should be most sharply etched in the Third Paralogism where the explicit topic is self-identity. There is no mention of physical criteria for reidentification in these passages, however. Strawson rests his interpretation on one slender text, namely, Kant's remark that during life the permanence of the soul is evident, "since the thinking

being (as man) is itself likewise an object of outer sense" (B415). Earlier Kant had noted that *in common parlance* we speak of *man* as thinking (A359–60). I take Kant's point at B415 to be that for ordinary purposes of reidentification we do not need Rational Psychology to inform us about the continuity of thinking beings. Rational Psychology is supposed to offer us philosophical proof that souls *must* continue to exist even after death (B415). Putting this point in Strawson's own preferred idiom, I take Kant's observation to be simply that during life bodily continuity is the usual way to determine continuity of the self, not that bodily continuity is "criterial evidence" for self-identity. Also see the discussion of Bennett in the next note.

29. Bennett has trouble with these passages, because he cannot explain why Kant believes that from my own point of view I *must* attribute identity and permanence to myself. He takes the minor premise to assert that when a person is conscious of, that is, remembers, a past mental state, he automatically attributes that state to himself. According to Bennett, Kant's great insight, which precisely anticipates an important argument given by Sydney Shoemaker in "Persons and their Pasts," (*American Philosophical Quarterly*, October, 1970) is that this attribution is too hasty because for all the person knows "he" may have "branched" since the remembered event, so that his apparent memory is only a "quasi-memory." The case for this interpretation rests on Bennett's reading of the outside observer passage. Allegedly, Kant appeals to the outside observer to demonstrate the point about quasi-memory. An outside observer might have seen the individual branch and so realize that the inference from a quasi-memory to identity is false. (I give a different account of this passage in the text.) But this interpretation has serious problems. There is not a single reference to memory or its potential fallibility in the entire chapter. And, as Bennett admits, he has no idea why Kant believes that a subject must attribute identity to himself at different times (*Kant's Dialectic*, op. cit., pp. 93–102).

30. See Chapter 2, "The Isolation Argument," and Chapter 4, "Transcendental Synthesis." In this section of Chapter 4 I note that Kant's argument for the *a priori*$_o$ status of apperception is insufficient.

31. On this point I agree with the interpretation offered by R. I. G. Hughes in "Kant's Third Paralogism," *Kant-Studien 74* (1983): 405–11. I note some disagreements in the text and in note 32.

32. R. I. G. Hughes criticizes this interpretation (which I offered originally in "Kant's Paralogisms," *Philosophical Review XCI* (1982): 515–47) on the grounds he can find no warrant in the text for the claim that this is the problem with the outside observer: there will be times when he does not or cannot attribute a mental state to me (Ibid., see his note 5). I take the warrant to be the following: "For just as the time in which the observer sets me is not the time of my own but of his sensibility, so the identity which is necessarily bound up with my consciousness is not therefore bound up with his, that is, with the consciousness which contains the outer intuition of my subject" (A363). Here I take Kant to be stressing that the time in which the observer sets me is the time of *his* sensibility. But his sensibility will obviously include many states that have nothing to do with me and my states. So Kant concludes that the identity

that must be present in all moments in which I am conscious will not be a feature of his consciousness. Further, the outside observer is intended as a contrast with my own case. And the peculiar feature of our own cases, that Kant repeats four times between pages A363 and A365, is that since time is the form of inner sense, at all times of which I am conscious, I am conscious of a state that I must attribute to myself.

33. Ibid., p. 406.
34. Wilson, "Leibniz and Materialism," op. cit.
35. See AA XX:308. This passage was drawn to my attention by Allison's paper "Kant's Refutation of Materialism," op. cit.
36. Loemker, op. cit., p. 644, "Monadology," para. 17.
37. She bases this interpolation on a number of passages. See the references cited in "Leibniz and Materialism," op. cit., pp. 506–508.
38. This direction of argument is suggested by the passages she cites from "A New System of the Nature and Communication of Substances" and from the "Correspondence with Arnauld" (Loemker, op. cit., p. 456, 339).
39. This is the argument that is repeated in *On the Progress of Metaphysics* (AA XX:308).
40. Wilson, "Leibniz and Materialism," op. cit., p. 509.
41. Ibid., p. 513.
42. I believe that this is all that Kant means at B420 (and in the discussion of this issue in *On the Progress of Metaphysics*) when he claims that this argument shows the falsity of materialism. Both Karl Ameriks, op. cit., Chapter 2, and Henry Allison ("Kant's Refutation of Materialism," op. cit.) fasten on these texts to suggest that Kant believes that he can argue against materialism. That is true only in a very limited sense. Materialism has no ready explanation for the needed synthetic connection. Kant recognizes fully in the Second Paralogism, especially in the note about to be discussed, that this is equally true of immaterialism, however.
43. John Searle, "Minds, Brains, and Programs," reprinted in John Haugeland, ed., *Mind Design* (Cambridge, Mass.: Bradford/MIT Press, 1981), pp. 282–306, 299.
44. While Searle's discussion is a blatant example of the Rational Psychologist's fallacy, Ned Block also falls into this error, despite his efforts to be cautious. In "Troubles with Functionalism" (in C. Wade Savage, ed., *Minnesota Studies in the Philosophy of Science*, vol. IX (Minneapolis: University of Minnesota Press, 1978), he offers the following argument. A homunculi-headed robot does not seem able to have qualitative states. Since we do not know how a brain can have qualitative states, one might think that the same doubt arises in this case. But we know that brains do have qualitative states, so in this case our empirical knowledge allows us to overcome the doubt. Again, the fallacy is the same. Since we do not know what ordinary or remarkable properties of brains enable them to have qualitative states, we cannot argue that other systems cannot have them, and that only brains can, until we know how brains can have such states. *Pace* Block it is not enough to know that brains can have qualitative states. (See pp. 293–94.)

Chapter 8

1. Logic, op. cit., p. 13 (AA IX:11).
2. Op. cit., pp. 7–8 (AA IV:471).
3. So, for example, Kant notes that " . . . the empirical unity of apperception, upon which we are not here dwelling, and *and which besides is merely derived from the former under given conditions* in concreto, has only subjective validity" (B140, my emphasis). Further, he regards his analyses as providing the basis for all the activities of the understanding: "The first pure knowledge of understanding, then, *upon which all the rest of its employment is based . . .*" (B137, my emphasis).
4. Rosch's original paper was "On the Internal Structure of Perceptual and Semantic Categories," in T. E. Moore, ed., *Cognitive Development and the Acquisition of Language* (New York: Academic Press, 1973). For a standard overview of the subsequent literature (to 1981), see Edward E. Smith and Douglas L. Medin, *Categories and Concepts* (Cambridge, Mass.: Harvard University Press, 1981).
5. See, for example, Susan Carey, *Conceptual Change in Childhood* (Cambridge, Mass.: MIT Press, 1985); Frank Keil, *Concepts, Kinds, and Cognitive Development* (Cambridge Mass.: MIT Press, 1989); and Ellen Markman, *Categorization and Naming in Children* (Cambridge, Mass.: MIT Press, 1989).
6. Smith and Medin, op. cit., p. 1, introduce this useful terminology.
7. Here I use "concept" to indicate both a classification and the mental representation that enables individuals to use a classification. Although this usage is somewhat awkward, I think this ambiguity is present in both the philosophical and the psychological literature.
8. Ludwig Wittgenstein, *The Philosophical Investigations*, translated by G. E. M. Anscombe (Oxford: Blackwell), 1953, pp. 31ff.
9. Smith and Medin, op. cit. p. 182.
10. Ibid. See the discussion of Frank Keil's work, pp. 175–79.
11. Here I am relying on Douglas Medin's later discussion in "Concepts and Conceptual Structure," *American Psychologist* 44 (1989) 1469–81.
12. Ibid., pp. 7–9.
13. Smith and Medin, op. cit., p. 182.
14. T. P. McNamara and R. J. Sternberg, "Mental Models of Word Meaning," *Journal of Verbal Learning and Verbal Behavior* 22 (1983): 449–74.
15. See Chapter 6, "Concept Application."
16. Similar proposals have recently been developed and have met with some success. So, for example, the "motor theory" of phone perception claims that we classify acoustic signals as different phones on the basis of considerations about how we as speakers, would articulate the sounds. We would classify a range of acoustic signals as "ba's," for instance, not on the basis of their intrinsic acoustic similarity, but on the basis of whether all of the sounds could be produced by the same articulatory movements. (Cited in Sally P. Springer and and Georg Deutsch, *Left Brain, Right Brain* (San Francisco: W. H. Freeman, 1981), pp. 201–202).

17. I am grateful to Margery Lucas for drawing this point to my attention when I presented parts of this chapter at Wellesley College in April of 1989.

18. *Logic*, op. cit., p. 142 (AA IX:141–42). See also A727–28/B755–56.

19. See, e.g., ibid., p. 97 (AA IX:92–93).

20. As will be clear later, Kant has further requirements for empirically adequate concepts beyond the Empiricist criterion of generation by sensory contact with objects.

21. The only exception I am aware of is Jerry Fodor in *The Language of Thought* (New York: Thomas Y. Crowell, 1975).

22. I borrow the example from Daniel Dennett, "Intentional Systems," in *Brainstorms*, op. cit., p. 17.

23. W. V. Quine, *Ontological Relativity and Other Essays* (New York: Columbia University Press, 1969), pp. 114–39.

24. Ibid., p. 123.

25. Ibid., p. 128.

26. Quine notes that his account of how children are able to learn "yellow"— namely, through having quality spaces like those of adults—cannot be extended to more complicated terms. But he does not offer any further psychological mechanisms to underlie these more sophisticated conceptual acquistions. Ibid., pp. 123–24.

27. Ibid., p. 128.

28. Keil offers the label and his criticisms in *Concepts, Kinds, and Cognitive Development*, op. cit. Quine's position is also criticized by Gregory L. Murphy and Douglas L. Medin, in "The Role of Theories in Conceptual Coherence," *Psychological Review*, 92 (July, 1985): 289–316.

29. Susan A. Gelman and Ellen M. Markman, "Young Children's Inductions from Natural Kinds: The Role of Categories and Appearances," *Child Development*, 58 (1987): 1532–41.

30. It is possible that even younger children just rely on appearances, but it is not clear how this could be tested.

31. Susan Carey, op. cit.

32. Frank Keil, op. cit.

33. Carey's view is inconsistent with this position. Her central point is that the theories underlying children's uses of concepts are *different* from adult theories.

34. Medin, op. cit., p. 1476.

35. See F. C. Keil, "On the Development of Biologically Specific Beliefs: The Case of Inheritance," forthcoming in *Cognitive Development*, and Elizabeth Spelke, "On the origins of physical knowledge," in L. Weiskrantz (ed.), *Thought without Language* (New York: Oxford University Press, 1988), pp. 168–83.

36. Murphy and Medin, op. cit., passim.

37. Medin, op. cit., p. 1479.

38. Loc. cit., p. 1477.

39. See especially Gelman and Markman, op. cit., and John H. Holland, Keith J. Holyoak, Richard E. Nisbett, and Paul R. Thagard, *Induction* (Cambridge, Mass.: MIT Press, 1986).

40. See Fodor's discussion of this paradigm in "On The Present Status of the Innateness Controversy," in *Representations*, op. cit., pp. 257–316, esp. 266–268.

41. See Dreyfus's discussion of Patrick Winston's concept learning program in Hubert L. Dreyfus, *What Computers Can't Do* (New York: Harper & Row, 1979), pp. 21ff.

42. *First Introduction to the Critique of Judgment*, translated by James Haden (Indianapolis: Bobbs-Merrill, 1965), p. 10, note 3 (AA XX:206).

43. See Chapter 3, "The Synthesis of Intuitions."

44. C. G. Hempel, "Aspects of Scientific Explanation," in *Aspects of Scientific Explanation and Other Essays* (New York: The Free Press, 1965), p. 374.

45. Allison, op. cit., Part 1, Chapter 2, passim.

46. Logic, op. cit., p. 104 (AA IX:98).

47. Ibid., pp. 64–65 (AA IX:59).

48. Ibid., p. 66 (AA IX:60).

49. Ibid., p. 64 (AA IX:58).

50. Ibid., p. 65 (AA IX:59).

51. Ibid., p. 67 (AA IX:61).

52. Several passages in this discussion strongly imply a different reading:

> Necessary characteristics, finally, are those which must always be found in the matter conceived [Ibid., p. 66 (AA IX:60)].

***

> To the logical essence belongs nothing but the cognition of all predicates in respect of which an object is determined by its concept. . . . And into this we can easily have insight . . . we do not have to search out data for this in nature; we only need to direct our reflection to those characteristics which as essential elements (*constitutiva, rationes*) originally constitute its basic concept [Ibid., p. 67 (AA IX:61)].

Contrary to the general interpretation I have been offering, these passages suggest that Kant held something like a necessary and sufficient conditions view of concepts. However, the natural reading of these remarks not only is inconsistent with my interpretation but also is flatly inconsistent with Kant's position on defining empirical concepts in the *Critique*:

> an *empirical* concept cannot be defined at all, but only *made explicit*. For since we find in it only a few characteristics of a certain species of sensible object, it is never certain that we are not using the word, in denoting one and the same object, sometimes so as to stand for more, and sometimes so as to stand for fewer characteristics. . . . We make use of certain characteristics only so long as they are adequate for the purpose of making distinctions; *new observations remove some properties and add others; and thus the limits of the concept are never assured* [A727–28/B755–56, my emphasis].

There are two ways to reconcile these views. Perhaps the discussion in the *Logic* is not meant to apply to empirical concepts. Although this is possible, nothing in the text indicates that this is not a perfectly general discussion of concepts. The second, and I believe better, strategy is to assume that the *Logic*'s discussion is about how logic, by invoking principles of coordination and subordination, can capture the [current] mental representation of a concept. Since this section is about the logical perfection of cognition, the first part of the interpretation seems justified. I would justify the second—the appeal to a *current* mental representation—on two grounds. Within the passage, Kant claims that finding the logical essence is very easy. We look not at nature, but to our own representation. Second, there is no inconsistency in holding that empirical concepts cannot be fixed and that at any time, on the basis of previous experience, some characteristics are regarded as necessary for everything in the extension of the concept.

53. *First Introduction to the Critique of Judgment*, op. cit., p. 20n (AA XX:216).

54. *Metaphysical Foundations of Natural Science*, op. cit., pp. 40–49 (AA IV:496–503).

55. Although not, of course, a fact about our mental powers in themselves (A648/B676).

56. Some experiments by D. Billman suggest that we acquire groups of interrelated rules (or correlations) more easily than single correlations. See the discussion of Billman's work in Holland et al., op. cit., pp. 200ff.

57. Barbara Landau, Linda B. Smith, and Susan S. Jones, "The Importance of Shape in Early Lexical Learning," *Cognitive Development* 3 (1988): 299–321.

58. I owe this point to Jean Mandler.

59. Murphy and Medin, op. cit., pp. 297–98.

60. Keil made this point in a presentation at a Sloan conference on theories and concepts in children, held at Stanford University on January 7–8, 1989.

61. See note 53.

62. Perhaps I am misinterpreting Medin's appeal to essences. I take an essence to be the set of properties that make an individual, or a kind, the individual or kind that it is. As such, once the essence has been determined, there is nothing more to be said about these items. In particular, there is no sense in trying to fathom deeper similarities that they might share with other objects. That is why a commitment to essences blocks a wider system of inferences. This may be an overly technical reading of something Medin intends in a much looser sense. If the "essentialist" heuristic is just meant to indicate that we prefer concepts where deeper attributes explain more superficial similarities, however, then it would be reasonable to view it as one of the heuristics serving the systematizing demands of reason. Medin offers a further discussion of this issue in Medin, D. L., and Ortony, A., "Psychological Essentialism," in S. Bosiniadow and A. Ortony, eds., *Similarity and Analogical Reasoning* (New York: Cambridge University Press, 1989), pp. 179–95.

63. I am happy to record my indebtedness to the participants in the Sloan conference on theories and concepts in children at Stanford on January 7–8, 1989, which was organized by Ellen Markman. The papers and discussions stimulated many of the ideas of this chapter.

BIBLIOGRAPHY

Adickes, Erich. *Kants Lehre von der Doppelten Affektion unseres Ich as Schlüssel zu seiner Erkenntnistheorie.* Tübingen, 1929.

Allison, Henry E. "Kant's Refutation of Materialism," *The Monist* 72 (1989), 190–208.

Allison, Henry E. *Kant's Transcendental Idealism: An Interpretation and Defense.* New Haven: Yale University Press, 1983.

Allison, Henry E. *The Kant–Eberhard Controversy.* Baltimore: The Johns Hopkins University Press, 1973.

Ameriks, Karl. "Kant's Transcendental Deduction as a Regressive Argument," *Kant-Studien* 69 (1978), 273–87.

Ameriks, Karl. *Kant's Theory of Mind: An Analysis of the Paralogisms of Pure Reason.* Oxford: Clarendon Press, 1982.

Angell, R. B. "The Geometry of the Visibles," *Nous* 8 (1974), 87–117.

Aquila, Richard. *Matter in Mind: A Study of Kant's Transcendental Deduction.* Bloomington: Indiana University Press, 1989.

Arnauld, Antoine. *The Art of Thinking.* James Dickoff and Patricia James (trans.). Indianapolis: Bobbs–Merrill, 1964.

Baddeley, Alan. *Working Memory.* Oxford: Clarendon Press, 1986.

Beattie, James. "*Essay on the Nature of Immutability of Truth*," in *Beattie's Works.* Philadelphia: Hopkins and Earle, 1809.

Beck, Lewis W. *Early German Philosophy.* Cambridge, Mass.: Harvard University Press, 1969.

Beiser, Frederick. *The Fate of Reason.* Cambridge, Mass.: Harvard University Press, 1987.

Bennett, Jonathan. "The Simplicity of the Soul," *Journal of Philosophy* LXIV 20 (Oct. 26, 1967), 648–60.

Bennett, Jonathan. *Kant's Analytic.* Cambridge: Cambridge University Press, 1966.

Bennett, Jonathan. *Kant's Dialectic.* Cambridge: Cambridge University Press, 1974.

Berkeley, George. *The Works of George Berkeley Bishop of Cloyne.* A. A. Luce and T. E. Jessop (eds.). London and Edinburgh: Nelson, 1967.

Blackwell, Richard J. "Christian Wolff's Doctrine of the Soul," *Journal of the History of Ideas* XXII (1961), 339–54.

Block, Ned. "Troubles with Functionalism," in C. Wade Savage (ed.), *Minnesota Studies in the Philosophy of Science*, vol. IX. Minneapolis: University of Minnesota Press, 1978.

Bona Meyer, Jürgen. *Kant's Psychologie*. Berlin: Wilhelm Hertz, 1870.

Brett, George Sidney. *Brett's History of Psychology*. R. S. Peters (ed.). London: George Allen and Unwin, 1962.

Brueckner, Anthony L. "Transcendental Arguments I," *Nous* 17 (1983), 551-75.

Brueckner, Anthony L. "Transcendental Arguments II" *Nous* 18 (1984), 197-225.

Burke, E. *A Philosophical Enquiry into the Origin of Our Ideas of the Sublime and the Beautiful*. Oxford: Basil Blackwell, 1967.

Buroker, Jill. *Space and Incongruence*. Amsterdam: D. Reidel, 1981.

Carey, Susan. *Conceptual Change in Childhood*. Cambridge, Mass.: MIT Press, 1985.

Castaneda, Hector-Neri. "He: A Study in the Logic of Self-Consciousness," *Ratio* 8 (1966).

Condillac, E. B. *An Essay on the Origin of Human Knowledge*. A facsimile reproduction of the translation of Thomas Nugent, with an introduction by Robert G. Weyant. Gainesville, Fla.: Scholars' Facsimiles & Reprints, 1971.

Condillac, E. B. *Condillac's Treatise on the Sensations*. Geraldine Carr (trans.). Los Angeles: University of Southern California, 1930.

Cummins, Robert. "Functional Analysis," *Journal of Philosophy* 72 (1975), 741-60.

Curley, E. "Leibniz and Locke on Personal Identity," in M. Hooker (ed.), *Leibniz: Critical and Interpretive Essays*. Minneapolis: University of Minnesota Press, 1982, 302-26.

Davidson, Donald. "Mental Events," in *Essays on Actions and Events*. Oxford: Clarendon Press, 1980, 207-25.

De Vleeschauwer, H. J. *La Deduction Transcendentale dans l'Oeuvre de Kant*. Paris: Le Hague, 1934-1937.

Dennett, Daniel. "Artificial Intelligence as Philosophy and as Psychology," in *Brainstorms*. Cambridge, Mass.: Bradford Books, 1978, 109-26.

Dennett, Daniel. "A Cure for the Common Code," in *Brainstorms*. Cambridge, Mass.: Bradford Books, 1978, 90-108.

Dennett, Daniel. *Content and Consciousness*. London: Routledge and Kegan Paul, 1969.

Descartes, Rene. *The Philosophical Works of Descartes*. E. S. Haldane and G. R. T. Ross (trans.). Cambridge: Cambridge University Press, 1972.

Dessoir, Max. *Geschichte de Neueren Deutschen Psychologie*. Amsterdam: E. J. Bonset, 1964.

Deutsch, D. "Auditory Pattern Recognition," in K. R. Boff, L. Kaufman, and J. P. Thomas (eds.), *Handbook of Perception and Human Performance*, vol. II. New York: Wiley, 1986.

Dreyfus, Hubert L. *What Computers Can't Do*. New York: Harper, 1979.

Dummett, Michael. *Frege: Philosophy of Language*. New York: Harper & Row, 1973.

Earman, John. "Was Leibniz a Relationist?" *Midwest Studies*, vol. IV. Minneapolis, Minn.: University of Minnesota Press, 1979, 263–76.

England, F. E. *Kant's Conception of God* (with a translation of the *Nova Dilucidatio*). New York: Humanities Press, 1968, 246–47.

Fauconnier, Giles. *Mental Spaces*. Cambridge, Mass.: MIT Press, 1985.

Fodor, J. A. "On The Present Status of the Innateness Controversy," in *Representations*. Cambridge, Mass.: MIT Press, 1981, 257–316.

Fodor, J. A. *The Language of Thought*. Cambridge, Mass.: Bradford Books, 1975.

Fodor, J. A. *The Modularity of Mind*. Cambridge, Mass.: MIT Press, 1983.

Fodor, J. A., Bever, T. G., and Garrett, M. F. *The Psychology of Language*. New York: McGraw-Hill, 1974.

Frege, G. *The Foundations of Arithmetic*. J. L. Austin (trans.). Oxford: Basil Blackwell, 1968.

Friedman, Michael. "Kant's Theory of Geometry," *Philosophical Review* 94 (1985), 455–506.

Garrett, Don. "Hume's Self-Doubts About Personal Identity," *Philosophical Review*, xc (1981), 337–58.

Gelman, Susan A., and Markman, Ellen M. "Young Children's Inductions from Natural Kinds: The Role of Categories and Appearances," *Child Development* 58 (1987), 1532–41.

George, Rolf. "Kant's Sensationism," *Synthese* 47 (1981), 229–55.

Gibson, J. J. *The Ecological Approach to Visual Perception*. Boston: Houghton Mifflin, 1979.

Gibson, J. J. *The Senses Considered as Perceptual Systems*. Boston: Houghton Mifflin, 1966.

Gibson, E., and Spelke, E. "The Development of Perception," in John H. Flavell and Ellen M. Markman (eds.), *Cognitive Development*, Volume III of *Handbook of Child Psychology* (Paul H. Mussen, general ed.). New York: John Wiley & Sons, 1983, 1–76.

Goldman, Alvin I. *Epistemology and Cognition*. Cambridge, Mass.: Harvard University Press, 1986.

Grice, H. P. "Personal Identity," reprinted in John Perry (ed.), *Personal Identity*. Los Angeles: University of California Press, 1975, pp. 73–95.

Gueroult, Martial. "Space, Point, and Void in Leibniz's Philosophy," in Michael Hooker (ed.), *Leibniz, Critical and Interpretive Essays*. Minneapolis: University of Minnesota Press, 1982.

Guyer, Paul. "Kant on Apperception and *A Priori* Synthesis," *American Philosophical Quarterly* 17 (1980), 205–12.

Guyer, Paul. *Kant and the Claims of Knowledge*. New York: Cambridge University Press, 1987.

Handyside, John. *Kant's Inaugural Dissertation and Early Writings on Space.* La Salle, Ill.: Open Court, 1929.

Harman, Gilbert. "Quine on Meaning and Existence I," *Review of Metaphysics* XXI (1967), 124–51.

Harper, W. "Kant's Empirical Realism and the Difference Between Subjective and Objective Succession," in W. Harper and R. Meerbote (eds.), *Kant on Causality, Freedom, and Objectivity.* Minneapolis: University of Minnesota Press, 1984, 108–37.

Hatfield, Gary, and Epstein, William. "The Sensory Core and the Medieval Foundations of Early Modern Perceptual Theories," *ISIS* 70 (1979), 363–84.

Hatfield, Gary. *The Natural and Normative: Theories of Perception from Kant to Helmholtz.* Cambridge, Mass.: MIT Press, in press.

Hempel, Carl G. "Implications of Carnap's Work for the Philosophy of Science," in Paul Arthur Schlipp (ed.), *The Philosophy of Rudolf Carnap.* La Salle, Ill.: Open Court, 1963, 685–709.

Henrich, D. "The Proof-Structure of Kant's Transcendental Deduction," *Review of Metaphysics* 22 (1969), 640–59.

Henrich, Dieter. *Identität und Objektivität: Eine Untersuchung über Kants Transzendentale Deduktion.* Heidelberg: C. Winter, 1976.

Herrnstein, Richard J., and Boring, Edwin G. *A Source Book in the History of Psychology.* Cambridge, Mass.: Harvard University Press, 1968.

Hintikka, Jaakko. "On Kant's Notion of Intuition (*Anschauung*)," in T. Penelhum and J. MacIntosh (eds.), *The First Critique: Reflections on Kant's Critique of Pure Reason.* Belmont, Ca.: Wadsworth, 1969, 38–53.

Holland, John H., Holyoak, Keith J., Nisbett, Richard E., and Thagard, Paul R. *Induction.* Cambridge, Mass.: MIT Press, 1986.

Hopkins, James. "Visual Geometry," *Philosophical Review* 82 (1973), 3–34.

Hoppe, Hansgeorg, *Synthesis Bei Kant.* Berlin: Walter de Gruyter, 1983.

Howell, Robert. "Intuition, Synthesis, and Individuation in the *Critique of Pure Reason*," *Nous* XX (1973), 207–32.

Hughes, R. I. G. "Kant's Third Paralogism," *Kant Studien* 74 (1983), 405–11.

Hume, David. *Inquiry Concerning Human Understanding.* Eric Steinberg (ed.). Indianapolis: Hackett, 1981.

Hume, David. *A Treatise of Human Nature*, L. A. Selby–Bigge (ed.). Oxford: Oxford University Press, 1962.

Humphrey, Ted. "The Historical and Conceptual Relations Between Kant's Metaphysics of Space and Philosophy of Geometry," *Journal of the History of Philosophy* 11 (1973), 483–512.

Husserl, Edmund. *Logical Investigations*, vol. I. J. N. Findlay (trans.). New York: Humanities Press, 1970.

James, W. *Psychology: The Briefer Course.* New York: Harper Torchbooks, 1961.

Janaway, Christopher. "History of Philosophy: The Analytic Ideal I," *Proceedings of the Aristotelian Society Supplement*, LXVII (1988), 169–89.

Jessop, T. E. *A Bibliography of George Berkeley.* The Hague: Martinus Nijhoff, 1973.

Jolley, Nicholas. *Leibniz and Locke: A Study of the "New Essays on Human Understanding."* Oxford: Clarendon Press, 1984.

Kant, I. *Anthropology from a Pragmatic Point of View.* Mary Gregor (ed. and trans.). The Hague: Martinus Nijhoff, 1974.

Kant, I. *First Introduction to the Critique of Judgment.* James Haden (trans.). New York: Bobbs-Merrill, 1965.

Kant, I. *Kant's Critique of Pure Reason,* Norman Kemp Smith (trans.). New York: St. Martin's, 1968.

Kant, I. *Kant: Philosophical Correspondence 1759–99.* Arnulf Zweig (ed. and trans.). Chicago: University of Chicago Press, 1967.

Kant, I. *Kant: Selected Pre-Critical Writings and Correspondence with Beck.* G. B. Kerford and D. E. Walford (eds.). New York: Barnes and Noble, 1968.

Kant, I. *Kants gesammelte Schriften. Akademie* edition, edited by the *Koniglichen Preussischen Akademie der Wissenschaften,* 29 volumes. Berlin and Leipzig: Walter de Gruyter and predecessors, 1902–.

Kant, I. *Logic.* R. S. Hartman and W. Schwarz (trans.). New York: Bobbs-Merrill, 1974.

Kant, I. *Prolegomena to Any Future Metaphysics That Will Be Able to Come Forward as Science.* James Ellington (trans.). Indianapolis: Hackett Publishing Company, 1977.

Kant, I. *The Groundwork of the Metaphysics of Morals.* Lewis White Beck (trans.). New York: Bobbs-Merrill, 1959.

Kant, I. *The Metaphysical Foundations of Natural Science.* J. Ellington (trans.). New York: Bobbs-Merrill, 1970.

Keil, F. C. "On the Development of Biologically Specific Beliefs: The Case of Inheritance," *Cognitive Development* (in press).

Keil, F. C. *Concepts, Kinds, and Cognitive Development* Cambridge, Mass.: MIT Press, 1989.

Kemp Smith, Norman. *A Commentary to Kant's "Critique of Pure Reason."* New York: Humanities Press, 1962.

Keynes, Geoffrey. *A Bibliography of George Berkeley.* Oxford: Oxford University Press, 1976.

Kitcher, Patricia. "Being Selfish About Your Future," *Philosophical Studies* 32 (1977), 425–31.

Kitcher, Patricia. "Discovering the Forms of Intuition," *Philosophical Review* XCVI (1987), 205–48.

Kitcher, Patricia. "Kant on Self-Identity," *Philosophical Review* XCI (1982), 41–72.

Kitcher, Patricia. "Kant's Paralogisms," *Philosophical Review* XCI (1982), 515–47.

Kitcher, Patricia. "Kant's Patchy Epistemology," *Pacific Philosophical Quarterly* XX (1987), 306–16.

Kitcher, Patricia. "Kant's Real Self," in Allen W. Wood (ed.), *Self and Nature in Kant's Philosophy*. Ithaca, N.Y.: Cornell University Press, 1984, 113–47.

Kitcher, Patricia. "Natural Kinds and Unnatural Persons," *Philosophy* 54 (1979), 541–47.

Kitcher, Philip. "How Kant Almost Wrote 'Two Dogmas of Empiricism' (and Why He Didn't)," in J. N. Mohanty and Robert W. Shahan (eds.), *Essays on Kant's Critique of Pure Reason*. Norman: University of Oklahoma Press, 1982, 217–49.

Kitcher, Philip. "Kant and the Foundations of Mathematics," *Philosophical Review* 84 (1975), 23–50.

Kitcher, Philip. "Kant's Philosophy of Science," in Allen W. Wood (ed.), *Self and Nature in Kant's Philosophy*. Ithaca, N.Y.: Cornell University Press, 1984, 185–215.

Korsgaard, Christine. "Personal Identity and the Unity of Agency: A Kantian Response to Parfit," *Philosophy and Public Affairs* (in press).

Kuehn, Manfred. *Scottish Common Sense in Germany, 1768–1800: A Contribution to the History of the Critical Philosophy*. Montreal: McGill-Queen's University Press, 1987.

Kuhn, Thomas. *The Structure of Scientific Revolutions*, Second Edition. Chicago: University of Chicago Press, 1970.

Landau, B., Gleitman, H., and Spelke, E. "Spatial Knowledge and Geometric Representation in a Child Blind from Birth," *Science* 213 (1981), 1275–78.

Landau, B., Smith, L. B., and Jones, S. S. "The Importance of Shape in Early Lexical Learning," *Cognitive Development* 3 (1988) 299–321.

Leary, David E. "Immanuel Kant and the Development of Modern Psychology," in William R. Woodward and Mitchell G. Ash (eds.), *The Problematic Science: Psychology in Nineteenth Century Thought*. New York: Praeger, 1982, 17–42.

Leary, David E. "The Philosophical Development of the Conception of Psychology in Germany, 1780–1850," *Journal of the History of the Behavioral Sciences* XIV (1978), 113–21.

Leary, David E. "The Psychology of Jakob Friedrich Fries (1773–1843): Its Context, Nature, and Historical Significance," *Storia e Critica della Psicologia* III (1982), 217–48.

Leiblich, I., and Arbib, M. "Multiple Representations of Space Underlying Behavior," *Behavioral and Brain Sciences* 5 (1982), 627–59.

Leibniz, Gottfried Wilhelm. *New Essays on Human Understanding*, Abridged Edition. Peter Remnant and Jonathan Bennett (trans. and eds.). Cambridge: Cambridge University Press, 1982.

Leibniz, Gottfried Wilhelm. *Philosophical Papers and Letters*. Leroy E. Loemker (ed.). Amsterdam: D. Reidel, 1976.

Lewis, David. "Survival and Identity," in A. Rorty (ed.), *The Identities of Persons*. Los Angeles: University of California Press, 1969, 17–40.

Locke, John. *An Essay Concerning Human Understanding*, 2 vols. A. C. Fraser (ed.). New York: Dover, 1959.

Luneberg, R. K. *Mathematical Analysis of Binocular Vision*. Princeton, N.J.: Princeton University Press, 1947.

Markman, Ellen. *Categorization and Naming in Children*. Cambridge, Mass.: MIT Press, 1989.

Marr, David. *Vision*. San Francisco: Freeman, 1982.

Martindale, Colin. "Can We Construct Kantian Mental Machines?" *Journal of Mind and Behavior* 8 (1987), 261–68.

Mattey, G. J. "Kant's Conception of Berkeley's Idealism," *Kant-Studien* 74 (1983), 161–75.

McClelland, James L., and Rumelhardt, David E. *Parallel Distributed Processing*. Cambridge, Mass.: MIT Press, 1986.

McNamara, T. P., and Sternberg, R. J. "Mental Models of Word Meaning," *Journal of Verbal Learning and Verbal Behavior* 22 (1983), 449–74.

McRae, Robert. *Leibniz: Perception, Apperception and Thought*. Toronto: University of Toronto Press, 1976.

Medin, Douglas. "Concepts and Conceptual Structure," *American Psychologist* 44 (1989) 1469–81.

Meerbote, Ralf. "Kant's Functionalism," in J. C. Smith (ed.), *Historical Foundations of Cognitive Science*. Dordrecht, Holland: Reidel, 1989.

Melnick, A. *Kant's Analogies of Experience*. Chicago: University of Chicago Press, 1973.

Murphy, G. L., and Medin, D. L. "The Role of Theories in Conceptual Coherence," *Psychological Review* 92 (1985), 289–316.

Nagel, Thomas. *The View from Nowhere*. New York: Oxford University Press, 1986.

Newell, Allen, and Simon, Herbert. *Human Problem Solving*. Englewood Cliffs, N.J.: Prentice-Hall, 1972.

O'Keefe, John, and Nadel, Lynn. *The Hippocampus as a Cognitive Map*. Oxford: Oxford University Press, 1978.

O'Neil, Onora. "Transcendental Synthesis and Developmental Psychology," *Kant-Studien* 75 (1984), 149–67.

Parfit, D. *Reasons and Persons*. Oxford: Clarendon Press, 1984.

Parfit, D., "Later Selves and Moral Principles," in A. Montefiore (ed.), *Philosophy and Personal Relations*. London: Routledge and Kegan Paul, 1973.

Parfit, D., "Personal Identity," *Philosophical Review* 80 (1971), 3–27.

Parsons, Charles. "Infinity and Kant's Conception of the 'Possibility of Experience'," *Philosophical Review* 73 (1964), 182–97.

Pastore, Nicholas. *Selective History of Theories of Visual Perception, 1650–1950*. Oxford: Oxford University Press, 1971.

Paton, H. J. *Kant's Metaphysics of Experience*, vols. I and II. New York: Humanities Press, 1965.

Patten, S. C. "Kant's *Cogito*," Kant-Studien 66 (1975), 331–41.

Penelhum, Terence. "Personal Identity, Memory, and Survival," *Journal of Philosophy* XX (1959), 882–903.

Pereboom, Derk. "Kant's Notion of the *A Priori* and the Transcendental," ms.

Perry, J. "Can the Self Divide?" *Journal of Philosophy* XX (1972), 463–88.

Perry, J. "The Importance of Being Identical," in A. Rorty (ed.), *The Identities of Persons*. Los Angeles: University of California Press, 1969, 67–90.

Perry, John. *Identity*. Ann Arbor, Mich.: University Microfilms, 19 (Doctoral Dissertation).

Perry, John. *Personal Identity*. Los Angeles: University of California Press, 1975.

Pippin, Robert. "Kant on the Spontaneity of Mind," *Canadian Journal of Philosophy* 17 (1987), 449–76.

Pippin, Robert. *Kant's Theory of Form*. New Haven, Conn.: Yale University Press, 1982.

Porterfield, William. *A Treatise on the Eye and the Manner and Phenomena of Vision*. Edinburgh: G. Hamilton and J. Balfour, 1759.

Posner, Michael. *Chronometric Explorations of Mind*. Hillsdale, N.J.: Erlbaum, 1978.

Pylyshyn, Zenon. "Cognition and Computation: Issues in the Foundations of Cognitive Science," *Behavioral and Brain Sciences* 3 (1978), 111–32.

Quine, W. V. "Carnap on Logical Truth," in *The Ways of Paradox*. New York: Random House, 1966.

Quine, W. V. "Truth by Convention," in *The Ways of Paradox*. New York: Random House, 1966, 77–106.

Quine, W. V. "Two Dogmas of Empiricism," in *From a Logical Point of View*. New York: Harper, 1961, 20–46.

Quine, W. V. *Ontological Relativity and Other Essays*. New York: Columbia University Press, 1969.

Quine, W. V. *Word and Object*. Cambridge, Mass.: MIT Press, 1960.

Quinton, A. "The Soul," in John Perry (ed.), *Personal Identity*. Los Angeles: University of California Press, 1975.

Reid, T. *An Inquiry into the Human Mind*. T. Duggan (ed.). Chicago: University of Chicago Press, 1970.

Reid, T. *Essays on the Intellectual Powers of Man*, Abridged Edition. A. D. Woozley (ed.). London: Macmillan, 1941.

Richards, Robert J. "Christian Wolff's Prolegomena to Empirical and Rational Psychology: Translation and Commentary," *Proceedings of the American Philosophical Society* 124 (1980), 227–39.

Ricketts, Thomas G. "Rationality, Translation, and Epistemology Naturalized," *Journal of Philosophy* 79 (1982), 117–36.

Rorty, Richard, "Verificationism and Transcendentaal Arguments," *Nous* 5 (1971), 1–14.

Rorty, Richard. *Philosophy and the Mirror of Nature*. Princeton, N.J.: Princeton University Press, 1979.

Rosch, Eleanor. "On the Internal Structure of Perceptual and Semantic Categories," in T. E. Moore (ed.), *Cognitive Development and the Acquisition of Language*. New York: Academic Press, 1973.

Rosenberg, J. " 'I Think': Some Reflections on Kant's Paralogisms," ms.

Rosenberg, J. *The Thinking Self*. Philadelphia: Temple University Press, 1986.

Rostenreich, Nathan. "Self-Ascription and Objectivity," *Philosophia: Philosophical Quarterly of Israel* 10 (1981), 189–98.

Russell, Bertrand. *The Philosophy of Leibniz*, 2nd Edition. London: Allen and Unwin, 1937.

Ryle, Gilbert. *The Concept of Mind*. New York: Barnes and Noble, 1949.

Satura, Vladimir. "Kant's *Erkenntnispsychologie,*" *Kant-Studien* XX (1971), 1–176.

Scruton, Roger. *Kant*. Oxford: Oxford University Press, 1982.

Searle, John. "Minds, Brains,and Programs," *Behavioral and Brain Sciences 3* (1980), 417–424. (Reprinted in John Haugeland (ed.), *Mind Design*. Cambridge, Mass.: MIT Press, 1981.)

Sellars, Wilfrid. " . . . this I or he or it (the thing) which thinks," Presidential Address to the Eastern Division of the APA, 1970.

Sellars, Wilfrid. "Metaphysics and the Concept of a Person," in Karel Lambert (ed.), *The Logical Way of Doing Things*. New Haven, Conn.: Yale University Press, 1969, 219–32.

Shoemaker, Sydney. "Persons and Their Pasts," *American Philosophical Quarterly* XX (1970), pp. 269–85.

Shoemaker, Sydney. *Self-Knowledge and Self-Identity*. Ithaca, N.Y.: Cornell University Press, 1963.

Sluga, Hans. *Gottlob Frege*. Boston: Routledge & Kegan Paul, 1980.

Smith, E. E., and Medin, D. L. *Categories and Concepts*. Cambridge, Mass.: Harvard University Press, 1981.

Spelke, Elizabeth. "On the Origins of Physical Knowledge," in L. Weiskrantz (ed.), *Thought Without Language*. New York: Oxford, University Press, 1988, 168–83.

Springer, S. P., and Deutsch, G. *Left Brain, Right Brain*. San Francisco: W. H. Freeman, 1981.

Strawson, Peter F. *The Bounds of Sense*. London: Methuen, 1966.

Strawson, Peter F., and Grice, H. P. "In Defense of a Dogma," *Philosophical Review* LXV (1956), 141–58.

Stroud, Barry. "Transcendental Arguments," *Journal of Philosophy* 65 (1968), 241–56.

Stroud, Barry. *Hume*. London: Routledge and Kegan Paul, 1977.

Tetens, Johan Nicholas. *Philosophische Versuche über die menschliche Natur und ihre Entwicklung*, 2 vols. Leibzig: M. G. Weidmans Erben und Reich, 1777. (Reprinted by the *Kantgesellschaft Verlag*, 1911.)

Thomson, J. J. "Private Languages," *American Philosophical Quarterly* 1 (1964), 20–31.

Thomson, M. "Singular Terms and Intuitions in Kant's Epistemology," *Review of Metaphysics* 26 (1972), 314–43.

Treisman, A. M., and Gelade, G. A. "A Feature Integration Theory of Attention," *Cognitive Psychology* 12 (1980), 97–136.

Treisman, A. M., Schmidt, H. "Illusory Conjunctions in the Perception of Objects," *Cognitive Psychology* 14 (1982), 107–41.

Vaihinger, H. *Commentar zu Kants Kritik der reinen Vernunft*, vol. II. New York: Garland Publishing Company, 1970.

Vendler, Zeno. *The Matter of Minds*. Oxford: Clarendon Press, 1984.

Walker, Ralph C. S. *Kant*. London: Routledge and Kegan Paul, 1978.

Walker, Ralph C. S. "Synthesis and Transcendental Idealism," *Kant-Studien* 76 (1985), 14–27.

Walsh, W. H. "Philosophy and Psychology in Kant's Critique," *Kant-Studien* 56 (1966), 186–98.

Warda, A. *Immanuel Kants Bucher*. Berlin: Verlag von Martin Breslaner, 1922.

Watson, J. B. "Psychology as the Behaviorist Views It," reprinted in R. J. Herrnstein and E. G. Boring (eds.), *A Source Book in the History of Psychology*. Cambridge, Mass.: Harvard University Press, 1965, 513–14.

White, B., Saunders, F., Scadden, L., Bach-Y-Rita, P., and Collins, P., "Seeing with the Skin," *Perception and Psychophysics* 7 (1970), 23–27.

Wiggins, David. "Locke, Butler and the Stream of Consciousness: And Men as a Natural Kind," in A. Rorty (ed.), *The Identities of Persons*. Los Angeles: University of California Press, 1969, 139–73.

Wiggins, David. *Sameness and Substance*. Cambridge, Mass.: Harvard University Press, 1980.

Wilkerson, T. E. *Kant's Critique of Pure Reason*. Oxford: Oxford University Press, 1976.

Williams, Bernard. "Personal Identity and Individuation," *Proceedings of the Aristotelian Society* LVII (1956), 302–26.

Wilson, Margaret. "Kant and 'The Dogmatic Idealism of Berkeley,'" *Journal of the History of Philosophy* xii (1971), 459–75.

Wilson, Margaret. "Kant and the Refutations of Subjectivism," in L. W. Beck (ed.), *Kant's Theory of Knowledge*. Dordrecht: Reidel, 1974, 208–17.

Wilson, Margaret. "Leibniz and Materialism," *Canadian Journal of Philosophy* lll (1974), 495–513.

Wilson, Margaret. "Leibniz, Self-Consciousness, and Immortality: In the Paris Notes and After," *Archiv für Geschichte der Philosophie*, Sonderhelf 58 (1976), 335–52.

Wittgenstein, Ludwig. *The Philosophical Investigations*. G. E. Anscombe (trans.).

Wolff, R. P. "Kant's Debt to Hume Via Beattie," *Journal of the History of Ideas* 21 (1960), 117–23.

Wolff, R. P. *Kant's Theory of Mental Activity*. Cambridge, Mass.: Harvard University Press, 1963.

Wolff, R. P. (ed.). *Kant*. Garden City, N.Y.: Anchor Books, 1967.

Yolton, J. W. *Perceptual Acquaintance from Descartes to Reid*. Minneapolis: University of Minnesota Press, 1984.

Young, J. M. "Kant's View of Imagination," *Kant-Studien* 79 (1988), 140–64.

Index of Cited Passages

This index includes the passages quoted or cited from Kant. The location of the citation precedes the semicolon; the location in this book follows it. Citations from the *Critique of Pure Reason* are located by the standard A and B numbers. Other citations are located by the volume and page numbers of the *Akademie* edition.

Critique of Pure Reason

Aviii; 11
Axii; 13, 62
Axv; 16, 23
Axvi; 65
Axvii; 14, 224
A6/B10ff; 27
A11–12/B25; 14
A19/B33; 113, 237 *n.* 3, 244 *n.* 14
A19–20/B32–34; 36
A19–20/B34; 68
A20/B34; 36, 37
A20/B35; 39
A20–21/B35; 40
A21/B35; 30
A21/B36; 36
A22/B36; 39
A22/B37; 43, 44
A23/B38; 46
A24/B39; 48, 51
A26/B42; 39
A26–27/B42–44; 19, 39, 51
A29; 37, 39
A31–32/B47; 171
A36–37/B53–54; 141
A39/B56; 141

A40/B57; 48
A44/B61–62; 15
A50/B74; 13
A51/B75; 111
A53/B77; 26, 206
A54–55/B78–79; 11–12, 26, 206, 206, 269 *n.* 3
A55–56/B80–81; 13, 14, 234 *n.* 63, 259 *n.* 7
A56–57/B80–81; 25
A57/B82; 94
A58–59/B82–84; 259 *n.* 8
A68/B93; 74, 112
A69/B94; 88
A77/B103; 74, 103, 118, 245 *n.* 24
A77–79/B103–4; 83, 209
A79/B105; 159
A84/B116; 210
A86/B118–19; 12, 15
A86–87/B119; 15
A88/B121, B144; 173
A90/B122; 142–43
A90/B123; 144, 155
A95; 243 *n.* 7
A96; 73

A97; 90
A98–99; 134
A99; 85–86, 149, 152, 201, 245 n. 24, 259
	n. 17
A100; 78, 79
A102; 201
A103; 83, 107, 110, 153, 201
A103–4; 209
A104; 254 n. 21
A104–5; 66, 71–74, 76, 77, 79, 94, 143,
	247 n. 44
A106; 81, 209
A107; 100, 101, 102, 107, 187, 188
A108; 107, 126, 201, 244 n. 14, 252 n. 57
A109; 73, 82
A111; 143, 167
A112; 134
A113; 201
A116; 93, 108–9, 113, 119, 134, 135, 188,
	249 n. 14
A116–18; 118
A117a; 108, 113, 186, 249 n. 14
A118; 104, 119, 122
A119–20; 149, 259 n. 17
A120; 81, 113, 151, 152
A120a; 151, 152, 158, 245 n. 24
A120–21; 158
A121; 70, 79, 251 n. 43
A122; 93, 145, 167, 188
A123; 134
A123–24; 201
A125; 145–46
A128; 170
A133/B172; 209
A133–34; 122
A140/B179–80; 153
A141/B180; 209
A143/B183; 195
A165/B206; 44, 54
A166/B208; 40, 239 n. 40
A179/B222; 102
A192/B237; 176
A193/B238; 176, 177
A195/B240; 176
A224/B271; 151
A230–31/B300; 266 n. 19
A241/B300; 185
A241–42; 184
A242–43/B300–301; 184, 188

A248/B305; 184
A296/B352–53; 184
A298/B355; 185
A299/B355; 224
A301–2/B358; 219
A303/B359ff; 90
A320/B376; 66
A320/B376–77; 244 n. 14, 261 n. 30
A334/B391; 265 n. 13
A339/B397; 185
A340/B398; 190
A346/B404; 190
A348; 184, 187
A349; 184, 185, 186, 188, 195
A350; 94, 100, 182, 185–86, 187, 188, 190
A351; 198
A352; 200
A353; 202
A354; 185, 201
A354–55; 199, 201
A355; 189, 192, 200
A356; 185, 199, 201–2
A359–60; 267 n. 28
A361; 195
A361–62; 195
A362; 195, 196
A362–64a; 124, 185, 196–98, 256 n. 44,
	48, 267 n. 32
A364; 196
A365; 185, 192, 197, 268 n. 32
A381; 100, 187
A381–82; 189, 194
A398; 191
A399; 191
A400; 182
A402; 183–84, 188
A403–4; 190
A643/B670; 225
A645/B673; 224
A647/B675; 224, 228–29
A648/B676; 272 n. 55
A649/B677; 223
A649/B677ff; 223
A651/B679; 225
A652/B680; 219, 221
A713/B741; 17
A727–28/B755–56; 270 n. 19, 271 n. 52
A736–37/B764–65; 24
A783/B810; 17

A783/B811; 14–15, 17
A848/B876; 11

Bx1; 94, 249 *n.* 15
Bxviii; 228
Bxxvi; 253 *n.* 5
Bxxvii–xxix; 139
B2–3; 16
B3–4; 15
B39; 171
B40; 50
B41; 51, 239 *n.* 42
B69–70; 249 *n.* 15
B128–29; 89, 188
B130; 158, 209, 253 *n.* 5
B131; 92
B131a; 201
B131–32; 188
B132; 76, 93, 107, 113, 127, 135, 145, 201, 249 *n.* 14, 253 *n.* 5
B132–34; 109, 119
B133; 122, 126, 127, 134, 209
B133–34; 100, 187
B134; 72, 104, 107–8, 119, 249 *n.* 14, 252 *n.* 57, 254 *n.* 21
B134a; 186
B135; 104, 119, 186
B137; 82, 86, 201, 261 *n.* 33
B137–38; 157
B138; 175
B139; 82
B139–40; 94
B140; 206
B141; 87
B142; 87, 88
B143; 89, 143

B144–45; 170
B147; 261 *n.* 30
B149; 185
B151; 151
B151–52; 171
B152; 11, 160
B153; 106
B157, 192
B157a; 193
B157–58a; 192
B159; 122
B159–160; 155
B160; 147, 156, 157, 160, 162, 163, 261 *n.* 32
B160a; 157–58, 162, 163
B160–61; 161
B161; 147, 163, 164, 261 *n.* 33
B161a; 162
B162; 156, 162
B167; 170
B208; 244 *n.* 14
B234; 177
B288; 185
B407; 186
B409; 191, 199
B410–11; 184, 264 *n.* 6
B411; 183–84, 190
B411a; 184, 190, 192
B413; 100, 187
B415; 255 *n.* 23, 267 *n.* 28
B415–18*n*; 256 *n.* 44
B418a; 202
B420; 268 *n.* 42
B421–22; 188
B422–23a; 139, 192, 193

*Gedanken von der wahren Shätzung der Lebendigen Kräfte
(Thoughts on the True Estimation of Living Forces)*

AA I:24–25; 31

AA I:139–40; 31

*De Mundi Sensibilis atque Intelligibilis Forma et Principiis
(Inaugural Dissertation)*

AA II:392–93; 35
AA II:393; 36, 38
AA II:402; 40, 47, 239 *n.* 37

AA II:402–3; 52
AA II:404; 52
AA II:906; 38

Prolegomena zu einer jeden künftigen Metaphysik
(Prolegomena to Any Future Metaphysics)

AA IV:282; 71
AA IV:298; 159

AA IV:471; 11, 206
AA IV:496–503; 223–24

Kritik der Practischen Vernuft
(Critique of Practical Reason)

AA V:47; 20

Der Streit der Fakultäten
(The Conflict of the Faculties)

AA VII:34; 113–14

Anthropologie in pragmatischer Hinsicht
(Anthropology from a Pragmatic Point of View)

AA VII:121; 11
AA VII:127; 107
AA VII:127–28; 255 *n.* 23
AA VII:135; 109, 156
AA VII:138; 150

AA VII:140–41; 12
AA VII:155; 240 *n.* 50
AA VII:156–57; 36, 148
AA VII:177; 261 *n.* 27

Über eine Entdeckung
(On a Discovery)

AA VIII:173; 35
AA VIII:221–23; 15–16, 38

Logik
(Logic)

AA IX:10; 13
AA IX:11; 206
AA IX:33; 13
AA IX:58; 221–22
AA IX:59; 221, 222
AA IX:60; 221, 271 *n.* 52
AA IX:61; 222, 271 *n.* 52

AA IX:91; 66
AA IX:92; 13
AA IX:92–93; 270 *n.* 19
AA IX:94; 13
AA IX:98; 221
AA IX:141–42; 209, 210

Kant's Briefwechsel
(Correspondence)

AA XI:52; 114

Kants handscriftlicher Nachlass
(Fragments)

AA XII:370; 27
AA XV:308–9; 70
AA XVII:366; 40
AA XVIII:69; 42

AA XVIII:681; 242 *n.* 59
AA XX:206; 218
AA XX:216; 223
AA XX:308; 268 *n.* 35, 268 *n.* 39

General Index

Adickes, Erich, 61, 257 *n*.54
Allison, Henry, 4, 62, 94, 105, 169, 170–71, 221, 239 *n*.44, 244 *n*.12, 253 *n*.5, 254 *n*.14, 257 *n*.54, 261–62 *n*.34, 262 *n*.55, 268 *n*.42
Ameriks, Karl, 244 *n*.9, 257 *n*.54, 268 *n*.42
Amphiboly, 15
Analogies of Experience, 101–2, 168, 174–75
Analytic of Concepts, 29, 61
Analyticity, 13, 25–27, 34, 54, 160, 166
  and apperception, 166
  and Berkeley, 34
  and cognitive science, 212
  and intuition, 160
  and logic, 13
  and perception, 54
  and psychology, 25–26
Angell, R. B., 56
Anthropology, 6, 11, 12, 107, 113, 148, 150, 154
Antinomies, 140
Apperception, 12, 21, 91–92, 106–7, 127, 133, 137, 139–42, 183, 186, 197, 200–201
  and the categories, 144, 166–67
  unity of, 96, 104–5, 108–9, 113, 115, 117–23, 133, 136, 138, 144–46, 164, 190, 193
Apprehension, 148–49, 151, 156

Apriority, 15–19
  a priori$_K$, 16–17
  a priori$_L$, 15
  a priori$_O$, 15–16
  vs. innate, 37–38
Aquila, Richard, 249 *n*.17, 252 *n*.58, 253 *n*.5
Arnauld, Antoine, 234 *n*.57
Austin, J. L., 8–9
Axioms of Intuition, 54

Bach-Y-Rita, Paul, 57
Barrow, Isaac, 33
Beattie, James, 98, 100–01
  Essay on Truth, 99
Beck, L. W., 241 *n*.57
Behaviorism, 10
Beiser, Frederick, 232 *n*.13, 16, 233 *n*.28, 244 *n*.8
Beltrami, Eugenio, 7
Bennett, Jonathan, 4, 61, 186, 264 *n*.5, 265 *n*.11, 12, 267 *n*.29
Berkeley, Bishop George, 33–35, 44, 47, 93, 179, 240 *n*.45
  on representation, 68
  Theory of Vision, 33, 41
Bever, T. G., 179
Billman, D., 272 *n*.56
Binding problem, 84–86
Blackwell, Richard J., 266 *n*.22
Block, Ned, 268 *n*.44

Bona Meyer, Jurgen, 6–7
Brentano, Franz, 66
Brueckner, Anthony L., 236 *n*.87
Bruner, Jerome, 169
Buffon, Georges-Louis Leclerc, Comte
    de, 34
Buroker, Jill, 241–42 *n*.58

Carey, Susan, 215, 255 *n*.30, 270 *n*.33
Carnap, Rudolph, 8
Carroll, Lewis, 131
Castaneda, Hector-Neri, 249 *n*.20
Categories, 89, 105, 127, 142, 146, 162–
    64, 166, 171–73, 184
    and apperception, 167
    and cognition, 164
    and experience, 172
    and intuition, 155, 171
    and judgments, 144
    and knowledge, 143
    and perception, 157
    and synthesis, 143
    and understanding, 173
Categorization, 226–28
Causality, 176–77, 262 *n*.54, 55
Cheselden, William, 33, 34
Churchland, Patricia, 85, 247 *n*.58
Clue to the Discovery of All Pure Con-
    cepts of the Understanding. *See*
    Metaphysical Deduction
Cognition, 107, 115, 137–38, 141, 146–47,
    163, 178–79, 184, 190–91, 193, 213,
    218, 221, 228
    a priori origins, 15
    a priori sources, 18
    features of, 19
    universal features of, 24, 25
Cognitive science, 28, 205–6, 212, 218,
    266 *n*.18
Cognitive states, 117–19, 123, 129, 134,
    136, 144, 151, 187, 195, 196, 200, 244
    n.12
Concept, 66, 82, 213, 216, 217, 227, 229,
    269 *n*.7, 271–72 *n*.52
    a priori, 15
    acquisition, 214–25, 218
    classification, 214
    and consciousness, 212
    empirical, 210–13, 221, 224–25, 229

and essence, 222
Locke on, 12
necessary and sufficient conditions,
    206–7, 209–10, 213, 222
origin of, 15
and prototype, 208
relations among, 221
as rules, 82 ff., 209
schemata, 109–10, 190, 153–54
of the self, 194
spatiotemporal, 159–64, 168
structure of, 221, 228
and synthesis, 80
system of, 225–26
and understanding, 22
unity of, 224, 225
Condillac, Etienne Bonnot de, 34, 68, 81,
    87, 148–50, 248 *n*.63, 260 *n*.23
Consciousness, 5, 107–9, 112–13, 115,
    122, 126–27
    personal identity, 196
    unity of, 166, 188–89, 195, 200–201
Content, 10–11, 113, 201
Cummins, Robert, 235 *n*.72
Curley, Edwin, 254 *n*.11, 255 *n*.32, 256
    n.40

D'Alembert, Jean Le Rond, 34
Davidson, Donald, 233 *n*.33
Deduction, 64, 65
    of the categories, 61, 62, 93, 96, 100,
        122, 138, 140, 142, 144–47, 149, 155,
        158, 163, 170, 172
    of consciousness of the self, 100
    and judgment, 165
    and synthesis, 164
    and transcendental psychology, 63–65
Dennett, Daniel, 112, 122, 235 *n*.72, 270
    n.22
Descartes, Rene, 29, 32–33, 126, 127,
    181, 187, 189, 197
    Cogito, 91–92, 95, 127
    common sense, 151
    on consciousness, 5
    La Dioptrique, 32–33
    natural geometry, 33, 35
DeVleeschauwer, H.-J., 174
Dialectic, 184–85
Diderot, Denis, 34

Dreyfus, Hubert L., 271 *n*.41
Dummett, Michael, 233 *n*.38

Earman, John, 241 *n*.58, 262 *n*.67
Eberhard, Johann August, 15, 27, 38, 148
Empirical Psychology, 12
Empiricism, 20
  and judgment, 87–88
  Kant's view of, 79–80
  and representations, 67–68, 69–70, 77–79
  and spatial perception, 46–47
Epistemology, and psychology, 8
Eschenbach, Johann Christian, 34
Essentialism, 272 *n*.62
Experience, 6, 17
  and the *a priori*, 18
  and cognition, 22
  and skepticism, 28
  and transcendental psychology, 23

Falkenstein, Lorne, 239 *n*.42
Feder, Johann Georg Heinrich, 40
Fichte, J. G., 27
First Introduction to the Critique of Judgment, 223
Fischer, Kuno, 6
Fodor, J. A., 137, 179, 218, 270 *n*.21
Form
  as process, 36, 37, 44, 50–51, 52, 157–58, 160
  as product, 36, 37
  pure, 37–40
Forms of intuition, 7, 31, 39, 55, 60, 140–41, 158, 168
  pure, 56
  pure process, 49, 52, 160
  pure product, 37, 43, 44–45
  space and time, 162–63, 165, 173
  space as, 47, 50
Frege, Gottlob, 7–9
Freud, Sigmund, 137
Friedman, Michael, 51, 54
Fries, Jakob Friedrich, 5, 7, 8, 22–23
Functionalism, 111–12, 252 *n*.58

Garrett, Don, 251 *n*.40
Garrett, Merrill, 179, 263 *n*.60
Gehler, Johann, 148–49

Gelman, Susan, 214–15, 226, 270 *n*.39
Geometry, 49, 242 *n*.59, 257–58 *n*.63
  natural, 33
  theories of, 7
Geometry [Euclidean], 50–54, 56
  and synthetic *a priori*, 50
George, Rolf, 68, 81, 244 *n*.20, 245 *n*.23, 24, 33, 34, 260 *n*.23
Gibson, J. J., 72, 246 *n*.39
Goldman, Alvin, 8, 9, 233 *n*.42
Gregory, Richard, 169
Grice, H. P., 128
Gueroult, Martial, 241 *n*.58
Guyer, Paul, 4, 49, 62, 174, 234 *n*.65, 235 *n*.70, 242 *n*.59, 246 *n*.41, 257–58 *n*.63, 259 *n*.17, 263 *n*.57
  on the Second Analogy, 174–78

Hamann, Johann Georg, 232 *n*.14
Harper, W., 263 *n*.59
Hartley, David, 34
Hatfield, Gary, 13, 231 *n*.13, 232 *n*.20, 25, 234 *n*.57, 235 *n*.75, 241 *n*.55, 242 *n*.70
Helmholtz, Hermann von, 7, 169
Hempel, Carl Gustav, 220
Henrich, Dieter, 4, 155–56, 169–71, 249 *n*.22, 252 *n*.57
Herbart, Johann Friedrich, 8, 9, 40
Herz, Marcus, 114
Hintikka, Jaakko, 31, 237 *n*.3
Hopkins, James, 232 *n*.25, 242 *n*.65
Hopkins, Jasper, 239 *n*.37
Hoppe, Hansgeorg, 246 *n*.41
Howell, Robert, 237 *n*.4, 244 *n*.14, 246 *n*.41
Hughes, R. I. G., 197, 267 *n*.31, 32
Hume, David, 20, 63, 95–96, 97, 99, 103, 107–9, 113, 121, 124, 176, 178, 194, 250–51 *n*.38–41
  on beliefs in objects, 69–70
  on causation, 98, 101, 175–77
  on distinct existences, 100–02
  on experience, 34
  law of association, 69–70, 77–79
  on mental unity, 50, 95
  on perception, 150
  on personal identity, 97–99, 100–102, 128, 138

on representation, 69
Humphrey, Ted, 50, 242 *n*.60
Husserl, Edmund, 8, 19

Ideal of Reason, 217–28
Ideality thesis, 140–41
Identity of the self. *See* Personal identity
Imagination, 22, 151, 153–54
    and perception, 153
    and schemata, 154
    and synthesis, 81, 83
Inaugural Dissertation, 34, 35, 40, 42, 43, 47, 50
    on sensory representations, 38
    on spatial perception, 35, 52
Inference, 219–20, 223, 228
Innate, 15, 37–38
Introspection, 6, 10, 11, 12
Intuition, 36, 37, 38, 52–54, 66, 73, 104, 109–12, 113–15, 141, 164–65, 170–71, 183, 190, 201–2. *See also* Forms of intuition
    and the categories, 158, 171
    construction of, 160
    objects of, 164
    outer, 31, 48, 49, 54, 55, 158
    of the self, 191, 199, 203
    as sensory representation, 36
    and space, 32, 45
    and space and time, 157
    synthesis of, 145

James, William, 200
Janaway, Christopher, 249 *n*.13
Jessop, T. E., 34, 238 *n*.16
Jolley, Nicholas, 254 *n*.11, 17, 19
Jones, Susan, 226–27
Judgment, 20, 86, 89–90, 110–11, 113, 115, 145, 159, 164–65, 170, 186–88, 190–91, 217–18
    analytic, 27
    and the categories, 144
    and law of association, 87
    and reason, 20
    and representation, 88
    and synthesis, 165–66
    temporal, 179

Keil, Frank, 214–15, 228, 270 *n*.28, 35
Kemp Smith, Norman, 4, 21, 29, 30–31, 40, 42, 48, 61, 66, 75, 93, 97–98, 100, 118
Kitcher, Philip, 233 *n*.38, 41, 234 *n*.64, 235 *n*.67, 69, 236 *n*.83, 242 *n*.65, 267 *n*.11
Knowledge, 13, 36, 66, 143, 217, 220–21
    a priori, 15–18, 23, 51
    and experience, 16
    and faculties, 19
    and philosophy, 65
    requirements of, 26
    of self, 194, 195
    sources of, 121
    of space, 25
    transcendental, 15, 25
Korsgaard, Christine, 256 *n*.43
Kowaleski, A., 34
Kuehn, Manfred, 245 *n*.22, 259 *n*.13
Kuhn, Thomas, 60

Landau, Barbara, 226–27
Law of association, 69, 77–80, 81, 89, 103, 152
Leary, David, 232 *n*.13
Leibniz, Gottfried Wilhelm, 35, 43–44, 45, 48–49, 53, 55, 57, 120, 126, 127, 138, 181, 185, 189, 191–92, 197, 241 *n*.58
    apperception, 106–7
    judgments, 218
    on materialism, 198–99
    mental traces, 135–36
    monads, 204
    on perception, 67, 149
    personal identity, 33–34, 124–25
    petite perceptions, 113–14, 134, 156
    on representation, 70, 71
    on spatial perception, 33–34, 42
    unity of representation, 75
Lewis, David, 128, 255 *n*.26, 29
Linnaeus, Carolus, 223
Locke, John, 12, 32, 120, 123–27, 132, 138, 164, 197, 235 *n*.66
    common sense, 151
    on concepts, 18–19
    on judgment, 87

on perception, 99, 149
person, definition, 195
on personal identity, 128
on representation, 68, 71
Logic, 8, 94, 233 *n*.39
  in The Anthropology, 13
  and cognitive faculties, 23
  Frege on, 7
  and judgment, 87
  and psychologism, 9, 27
  and psychology, 8, 11
  Quine on, 27
  and understanding, 206
Logic, 66, 206, 210, 221
Lossius, J. C., 98
Lucas, Margery, 270 *n*.17
Luneberg, R. K., 56

McNamara, T. P., 208
McRae, Robert, 241 *n*.58
Malebranche, Nicolas, 33, 68
Markman, Ellen, 214–15, 226, 270 *n*.39
Marr, David, 243 *n*.72, 245 *n*.35, 262 *n*.42
Materialism, 268 *n*.42
Mattey, G. J., 238 *n*.16
Medin, Douglas, 208, 216, 226, 228
Meerbote, Ralf, 231 *n*.5
Melnick, Arthur, 179–80
Memory, 14, 124–25, 126
Mental representations. *See*
  Representation
Mental states, 66
  comental, 134–35, 136
  Leibniz on, 67
  traces of, 135–36
  unity of, 203
Mental unity, 98–102, 117–21, 123, 126–
  27, 128, 129, 130, 133
  cognitive criterion of, 129, 131–32, 133–
  35, 136
Metaphysical Deduction, 62, 63, 89, 143–
  45, 173
Metaphysical Exposition, 45
Metaphysical Foundations of Natural Sci-
  ence, 11, 86, 206, 223
Methodology, 24, 51, 54, 210
Modularity, 137
Molyneux, William, 8, 32, 34, 41, 42

Monads, 67
Murphy, G. L., 228

Nadel, Lynn, 58
Nagel, Thomas, 182, 194
Nativism, 7, 37–38
Nature, Order of, 219, 221
Necessary and sufficient conditions, 211–
  12
Necessity, 23–24
Newell, Allen, 25
Newton, Isaac, 35, 48, 53, 55, 224
Noumenal, 139–40, 219

O'Keefe, John, 58
O'Neill, Onora, 83–84, 231 *n*.5, 247 *n*.54,
  55

Paralogisms, 25, 75, 100, 122, 126, 181–
  83, 185–88, 190–91, 192–96, 197, 198,
  199–203
Parfit, Derek, 128, 131–33
Parsons, Charles, 53, 54
Paton, H. J., 4, 61, 247 *n*.60, 259 *n*.6
Patten, S. C., 249 *n*.17
Penelhum, Terrence, 128
Perception, 36, 113, 146, 149, 156, 160,
  163, 165, 166, 175, 179, 186, 241 *n*.50
  and cognition, 147
  construction of, 168
  depth, 55
  and Euclidean space, 7
  and images, 150
  J. J. Gibson on, 72
  of objects, 58
  objects of, 152
  and representation, 151
  and sensibility, 22
  of space and time, 157
  and synthesis, 154
  synthesis of, 158
  of the third dimension, 32–33
  of time, 175
  unity of, 161, 171
  visual, 147–48, 151
Pereboom, Derk, 236 *n*.85
Perry, John, 123, 128, 129–30, 253 *n*.8

Personal identity, 122, 127–28, 124–25, 128, 131–33, 138, 195, 197
Petite perceptions. *See* Leibniz, Gottfried Wilhelm
Phenomenal, 139–40, 219
Pippen, Robert, 105–6, 107, 234 *n.*57, 239 *n.*38, 242 *n.*69, 251 *n.*47, 53, 54, 253 *n.*5
Plato, 137
Pölitz, K. H. L., 150–51, 259–60 *n.*20
Porterfield, William, 147–48, 245 *n.*35
Prauss, Gerold, 4
Principle of sufficient reason, 233 *n.*39
Principles, 62, 63, 64, 142, 144, 146, 162, 170, 172–73, 174
Prolegomena, 35, 38, 49, 71, 93
Psychologism, 4, 7, 8
definition of, 9
Pylyshyn, Zenon, 137, 256 *n.*51

Quine, W. V., 27, 214–15, 226, 229, 236 *n.*82
Quinton, Anthony, 128

Rational Psychology, 11, 12, 14, 181–83, 186, 188–89, 198, 200, 203, 205
Reagan, Ronald, 46
Reason, 51, 221, 223, 224–25, 228–29
faculty of, 19–20
practical, 20
and systematicity, 225
Reflexionen, 70
Refutation of Idealism, 92, 93, 94, 178
Regulative Use of the Ideas of Reason, 217, 221
Reid, Thomas, 34, 98, 164, 169
distinction between sensation and perception, 68, 148
on perception, 150
Reinhold, Karl Leonhard, 5, 6, 7, 9, 22–23, 25
Representation, 65, 70, 71, 90, 108–9, 112, 113, 115, 149, 154, 191, 217, 244 *n.*14
apriority of, 79–80
and concept, 82
conceptual and sensory, 40
and form, 36
and imagination, 81

and judgment, 88
and law of association, 77–79
Leibniz on, 67
Lockeans on, 67–68
object of, 70
of objects, 80, 143
and perception, 158
processes of, 84–85
pure, 37
Reinhold on, 5
of space and time, 158, 170
spatial, 42–44, 46–48, 55, 56, 57, 58
and synthesis, 74
unit of, 76
unity of, 72–73, 82, 88
Richards, Robert J., 181
Riemann, Georg Friedrich Bernhard, 7
Rorty, Richard, 91, 248 *n.*1
Rosch, Eleanor, 206–7
Rosenberg, Jay, 260 *n.*24, 264 *n.*10
Rostenreich, Nathan, 94
Russell, Bertrand, 8

Satura, Vladimir, 34, 238 *n.*23, 240 *n.*50, 259–60 *n.*20–22
Schultz, J. G., 27
Science, 222–24, 225
and empirical psychology, 11
Scruton, Roger, 92, 248 *n.*2, 248 *n.*9
Searle, John, 182, 203
Second Analogy, 64, 92, 103, 146, 174, 175–80
Self-ascription, 92–94, 126–27
Self-knowledge. *See* Knowledge
Self-observation, 6, 7
Sellars, Wilfrid, 182, 235 *n.*77, 252 *n.*2, 257 *n.*55, 263–64 *n.*4, 264 *n.*10, 266 *n.*21
Sensa, 36, 38, 40
Sensation, 36, 57, 148
and reference, 70
Sensationism, 68
Sense impression, 57
Sensibility, 22, 151, 161
theory of, 50–52, 54
Shoemaker, Sydney, 128, 255 *n.*26, 27
Simon, Herbert, 25
Simulacra theory, 71
Skepticism, 20, 121–22

Sluga, Hans, 233 *n.*30, 32, 37
Smith, Linda, 208, 226–27
Smith, Robert, 34
Solidity, 223–24
Soul, 191, 202
  identity of, 196
  and psychology, 12
  simplicity of, 199–200, 202
  and thought, 197–98
Space, 257 *n.*61
  theories of, 7
Spatial perception, 7, 33, 34, 40–46, 48–52, 54–60
  transcendental psychology of, 31–32
Spelke, Elizabeth, 239 *n.*44, 243 *n.*75
Spontaneity, 122, 253 *n.*5
Starke, F. C., 34–35
Sternberg, R. J., 208
Strawson, P. F., 3, 4, 9, 21, 23, 62, 92–93, 236 *n.*82, 249 *n.*13, 266 *n.*28
  on transcendental idealism, 140
Stroud, Barry, 236 *n.*88, 250–51 *n.*40
Substance, 185
Synthesis, 73, 76–77, 82, 88, 90, 102–3, 104, 105, 108, 109–12, 115, 120–21, 124, 136, 137, 143, 146, 147, 153, 158, 165, 200–202, 210, 246 *n.*41, 254 *n.*14
  of apperception, 155
  of apprehension, 151–52, 155, 158, 171
  and concepts, 80, 159, 160, 161–64
  definition of, 74–75
  figurative, 260–61 *n.*27
  and intuitions, 160
  and perception, 158, 161–63, 168–69, 175
  and representation, 74, 82–83
  of Reproduction in Imagination, 77–78
  rule governed, 82, 84
  synthetic connection, 117–22, 125, 126, 127, 129, 134, 141
  and time, 85–86
  and unity, 96
  and unity of apperception, 144–45
Synthetic *a priori*, 17

Tetens, Johann Nicolas, 67, 81, 87, 98, 105, 112, 126, 135, 148, 238 *n.*17, 247 *n.*46, 61

on perception, 149–50
on spatial perception, 34
Third Paralogism, 123, 126
Thomson, J. J., 236 *n.*88
Thomson, Manley, 237 *n.*3
Thoughts on the True Estimation of Living Forces, 31
Time, 185, 267–68 *n.*32
  as the form of inner sense, 195–96
  perception of, 175
Transcendental, definition of, 184, 190
Transcendental Aesthetic, 25, 29, 30–31, 35, 44, 45, 50, 54, 62–63, 140, 142, 146, 170, 170–71, 196, 203
Transcendental Deduction, 12, 103, 104, 108–110, 115, 138, 159, 182, 186–87, 190, 196, 200, 205
Transcendental Exposition, 45, 50–54
Transcendental idealism, 21, 28, 49, 63, 140–41, 258 *n.*64
Transcendental Logic, 13, 23
Transcendental psychology, 3–5, 11, 14, 19, 21, 23–26, 28, 64–65
  definition of, 21, 22
  and empiricism, 22, 44
  and philosophy, 10
  and spatial perception, 44
  Strawson on, 23
  and twentieth-century psychology, 10
Treisman, Anne, 85, 247 *n.*56, 57

Understanding, 13, 22, 154, 158
  and logic, 8, 12, 206
  unity of, 94, 152

Vaihinger, Hans, 30, 40, 42, 61
Vendler, Zeno, 182, 194
Vision. *See* Perception
Voltaire, 34

Walker, Ralph C. S., 92, 236 *n.*87, 246 *n.*41
Walsh, W. H., 4, 10, 232 *n.*12, 233 *n.*44, 246 *n.*41
Watson, J. B., 10
Wheatstone, Charles, 55, 56
Wiggins, David, 128, 131, 255 *n.*33
Wilkerson, T. E., 92, 94, 248 *n.*2, 3, 7
Williams, Bernard, 123, 253 *n.*9, 255 *n.*25

Wilson, Margaret, 181, 188, 200, 236
    n.89, 240 *n*.45, 249 *n*.26, 254 *n*.18,
    263 *n*.2
Wittgenstein, Ludwig, 8, 207
Wolff, Christian, 12, 67, 181, 186, 189,

192, 247 *n*.52, 266 *n*.22
Wolff, Robert Paul, 9, 14
    on synthesis, 82–83

Young, J. M., 231 *n*.5